Transnational Torture

Transnational Torture

*Law, Violence, and State Power in
the United States and India*

Jinee Lokaneeta

NEW YORK UNIVERSITY PRESS
New York and London

NEW YORK UNIVERSITY PRESS
New York and London
www.nyupress.org

First published in paperback in 2014

Library of Congress Cataloging-in-Publication Data
Lokaneeta, Jinee.
Transnational torture : law, violence, and state power in the United States and India /
Jinee Lokaneeta.
p. cm. Includes bibliographical references and index.
ISBN 978-0-8147-5279-1 (cl : alk. paper) — ISBN 978-1-4798-1695-8 (pb : alk. paper)
1. Torture—United States. 2. Torture—India. I. Title.
K5410.T6L65   2011
345.025—dc23   2011017407

Parts of chapter 2 were previously published as "Torture Debates in the Post-9/11 United
States: Law, Violence, and Governmentality," *Theory and Event* 13 (2010): 1. Parts of chapter
3 were previously published as "A Rose by Another Name: Definitions, Sanitized Terms, and
Imagery of Torture in 24," *Law, Culture, and Humanities* 6 (2010): 2, 1-29. Parts of chapter
4 were previously published as "Torture in Postcolonial India: Struggle within the Jurisprudence," *Rights, Citizenship, and Torture: Perspectives on Evil, Law, and the State,* Welat
Zeydanlıoğlu and John T. Parry (eds.) (Oxford: Inter-Disciplinary Press, 2009).

Contents

Acknowledgments

As fragments of ideas, thoughts, and arguments congeal into a book, the collective nature of the work becomes realized. I thank my mentors—Judith Grant, Howard Gillman, and Marita Sturken—for their contributions in molding this work over the years. I am grateful to Judith for readily responding to my distress calls when needed and for constantly cheering me on, to Marita for her consistent face-to-face mentorship that has fortunately continued in New York City, and Professor Gillman for his advice and the proud congratulatory notes he sends me even on my slightest achievements.

The nudging for the book came from Timothy Kaufman-Osborn in his uniquely persuasive tone at a time when "post-Ph.D.–new assistant professor blues" were most intense. I am grateful to Tim-KO for encouraging me at that very crucial stage to begin work on this book, and his intellectual influence and mentorship have been truly formative and delightful. A constant figure of inspiration and encouragement has also been Austin Sarat, who from the very first time I met him has been instrumental in reminding me, both through his own work and through conversations, of the importance of studying law's violence (regardless of how many disciplines continue to marginalize it). I trace my decision to study torture to two other formative influences in India. First, I was impacted by the civil liberties and democratic rights activists in whose shadow I grew up: my father, Manoranjan Mohanty, and the incredible People's Union for Democratic Rights (PUDR) group in Delhi that he was a part of, which consisted of Subba Rao, Sudesh Vaid, Uma and Anand Chakravarti, and the Hyderabad group, including K. Balagopal, G. Haragopal, and K. G. Kannabiran. The second influence was that of the feminist activists and academics with whom I worked on sexual violence in Delhi University: Pratiksha Baxi, Janaki Abraham, and Suman Bisht (in the Gender Study Group); Uma Chakravarti, Madhvi Zutshi, and N. Jacob (in the Forum against Sexual Harassment); and Shahana Bhattacharya and Saumyajit Bhattacharya (in Parivartan) in close proximity to Sahelis: Ranjana, Sadhna, Lata, and Laxmi.

Several individuals have generously given me comments over the years: Timothy Kaufman-Osborn, Upendra Baxi, Anand Chakravarti, Uma Chakravarti, John Parry, Austin Sarat, Manoranjan Mohanty, Marita Sturken, Judith Grant, Usha Ramanathan, Paul Passavant, Pratiksha Baxi, Ruchi Chaturvedi, Susan Burgess, Richard Leo, Nasser Hussain, Jonathan Simon, Michael Musheno, the anonymous reviewers in journals that both accepted and rejected my articles, and the anonymous reviewers for the book, who helped give the work the much-needed final push. I am grateful to all of them for engaging with my work and for challenging me. Thanks also to Janelle Wong for continuing to be a major source of support through the book-writing process and to University of Southern California professors Jeb Barnes and Ann Crigler for their encouragement.

My research trip in India in 2003-2004 was made memorable thanks to the amazing set of friends who sustained me then and continue to do so whenever I go to India—friends who make you laugh and spoil you; with whom you share dreams, fears, and visions; and, above all, who provide you with that life-sustaining energy: Pratiksha Baxi, Kishore Jha, Janaki Abraham, Suman Bisht, Nivedita Menon, Aditya Nigam, Shahana Bhattacharya, Alok Dash, Amit Bhattacharya, Amiti Sen, Rinku Pegu, Mukul Manglik, Subhash Gatade, Anjali Sinha, Ritu Mishra, Yogendra Tyagi, Ujjwal Singh, Shomu, Tarun Bharatiya, Avinash Jha, and many others. One is equally lucky to have friends abroad who are constant pillars of support, sustenance, and togetherness: Archana Agarwal, Art Auerbach, Zoe Corwin, Charles Lee, Stephanie Nawyn, Sangha Padhy, and Linda Veazey (friends from graduate school); Savita Patel, Ashok Prasad, Ramaa Vasudevan, Madhvi Zutshi, N. Jacob, Abha Sur, and Julia Kramer (transnational friends) and Ritu, Anubha, and Prita (from high school). Many thanks to my friends Jayeeta Sharma (Jo) and Daniel Bender (Dan), who have painstakingly guided me through confusing moments.

Life in New York City has been made infinitely richer by my friends in South Asia Solidarity Initiative (SASI), who patiently heard stories of why the current project lingered on, and have helped create this meaningful and inspirational political and personal community: Ruchi Chaturvedi, Rupal Oza, and Ash Rao (a delightful journey of friendship from Delhi University to New York City), Sangeeta Kamath, Saadia Toor, Murli Natrajan, Biju Mathew, Prachi Patankar, Vidya Kalaramadam, Ali Mir, Bhavani Raman, Varuni Bhatia, Toy, Svati Shah, and Ahilan Kadirgamar.

Thanks to my brother, Berkeley Sanjay, and sister-in-law, Brinda Vasisht, for being the bedrocks of all my endeavors, and to my adorable nieces,

Adya and Raeva, who continue to be the constant joys and marvels of our lives. Thanks also to my extended family—Rabi and Sudha Sahoo, my in-laws Rangnath Mishra and Chandrakali Devi (and the Bihar family for their warmth, effort, and amazing food each time), G. K. and Bulbul Das, Itishree Sahoo, Kalyani Mohanty, Biswajit Mohanty, Babita Verma, Meeta, and Rickie Patnaik for their love and support. Thanks to Rabi Sahoo (Mousa), whose indomitable spirit, energy, and idealism constantly inspire me, and to Mark Juergensmeyer (Uncle), whose prolific and committed writing I greatly admire.

Thanks to some individuals who have traversed my life in multiple ways: Nivedita Menon and Aditya Nigam, whose syncretic combining of friendship, academics, and activism is a remarkable model of inspiration. Thanks to Uma and Anand Chakravarti for engaging with my work despite the distance and for challenging me intellectually and politically as only comradely mentors can. Thanks to Upendra Baxi, for being a constant feature of my life in different ways, always provocative, and forever a mine of ideas and inspiration. Thanks to Pratiksha Baxi; your being, your vision, your work, your lifelong friendship, and our intersecting lives keep me thriving.

I feel a special gratitude to my students at Drew University, particularly to the students in the torture seminar, for letting me try out my ideas and helping this work evolve, and to Catherine Costigan, Hannah Ogden, and Leandra Graziano for their research assistance. I am thankful to my colleagues at Drew, from Pat McGuinn, who generously shared his prospectus, to Phil Mundo, who followed and encouraged the book process every step of the way, to Deb Liebowitz, Andrea Talentino, Hans Morsink, Joe Romance, and Catherine Keyser, who readily heard the woes of writing, commented on my presentations, and cheered me on. Special thanks go to Andrea, Tom, and Lucien for the lovely Christmas dinners and to Deb for her comaraderie. I am particularly grateful to Carlos Yordon, who (along with Tiffany and Sophia) has been an incredible friend and who read the manuscript in its entirety (alongside making excellent birthday flans) despite his unrelenting schedule. Thanks also to former dean Paolo Cucchi, Dean Jonathan Levin, and Associate Dean Wendy Kolmar for their support, especially to Wendy for being a constant source of encouragement from the time she first became my "faculty buddy." Other Drew colleagues, Marc Boglioli, Maliha Safri, Richard Greenwald, (Late) Paul Wice, and Jeremy Varon made Drew a fun place to be. I am grateful to President Weisbuch for being personally excited about the book and for institutionally creating opportunities for junior faculty. And of course I am grateful to Lydia Feldman from our department for her unwavering support in so many different ways: from listening (without flinching once!) to being there for me through these years.

The junior sabbatical that I spent as a visiting scholar at the Center for the Study of Law and Society (CSLS), Berkeley, the release time grant, and the research grants from Drew really made the book possible. Many thanks to the executive director of CSLS, Rosann Greenspan, for arranging appointments with a host of scholars, and to Director Calvin Morill and Lauren Edelman at the CSLS for their support. During the last year of writing, intense discussions with scholars such as Paul Kahn and Carol Greenhouse and colleagues like Doran Larson, Bill Rose, and Mathew Anderson at the five-week NEH seminar on Rule of Law: Legal Studies and the Liberal Arts in Maine in Summer 2009; time spent with Francoise Briegel, Shalini Gera, Daniel Margolies, Anu Mandavilli, Kurt Parli, and Balaji Narasimhan in Berkeley in fall 2009; and conversations with Ruchi Chaturvedi, Anuj Bhuwania, and the South Asia Reading Group in spring 2010 were crucial in broadening the scope of the book and in the process gave me another set of great friends.

Librarians at Drew University, University of Southern California, the Indian Law Institute, the Police Library, the National Human Rights Commission, and the Law Faculty Library in Delhi University were crucial to the research process. I also thank my editors at NYU Press, Deborah Gershenowitz, Despina Papazoglou Gimbel, and Gabrielle Begue, for their unwavering enthusiasm for the project and for patiently guiding me through the process.

Finally, this book is dedicated to three people: my parents, Bidyut and Manoranjan Mohanty, and my husband, Sangay Mishra. It is mostly because of my parents and the democratic spirit they infused into our household that I strive to live a life of my choice. They have created a vision of living life to its fullest with humor, patience, generosity, and sincere commitment, and as a proud daughter I dedicate this book to them.

This book is also dedicated to Sangay, my companion in life, politics, and friendship, for believing in me and, in addition to reading and listening to endless versions of half-baked ideas, for being the unrelenting voice in my head telling me to keep going and helping me do it more systematically than I would have done otherwise. He has been there every step of the way, intellectually, politically, and emotionally, during all the ups and downs, never wavering once.

Introduction: Do the Ghosts of
Leviathan Linger On?

Law, Violence, and Torture in Liberal Democracies

The 2009 Oscar hit was a British/Indian film titled *Slumdog Millionaire* about a boy from a Mumbai slum who manages to win twenty million rupees in a game show, thereby enacting a true "rag to riches" story.[1] Less talked about is the framing of this incredibly popular film, which provides an insightful comment on the discourse on torture in contemporary India. In the very first scene of the film, one observes a constable beating up the boy while the senior police official calmly watches, both assuming that the boy has been winning the game show by cheating. Interestingly enough, news reports mention that initially the senior official was seen as torturing the boy, but the Indian government asked the film producers to change the role of the torturer in the film. As *New York Times* reporter Somini Sengupta explains,

> On one occasion, Mr. Colson [the producer of the film] recalled, the Indian authorities took umbrage at a scene in the script in which a suspect is tortured by a police commissioner during interrogation. The Indian authorities told Mr. Colson to take out the police commissioner. No police officer above the rank of inspector should be shown administering torture, they said. The makers of "Slumdog Millionaire" obeyed.[2]

Here, it is striking that instead of asking for scenes of torture to be removed entirely as being improbable, indeed impermissible in a liberal democracy, the Indian government appears to have been more specific in its request that no senior police officer be represented in an act of torture. In this moment, the film simultaneously captures the routineness of torture in the Indian criminal justice system even while complying with the govern-

1

ment's request not to subvert the state's recent interventions, which rely on a "clean" image of its senior officials.[3]

Another key moment in 2009 was the public disagreement of the former U.S. vice president Dick Cheney with President Obama just as the latter was announcing the plans to close down the prison at Guantánamo Bay and espousing an unequivocal rejection of torture. When asked whether the interrogation techniques used against "high-value detainees," including waterboarding, were authorized by him, Cheney said,

> I was aware of the program, certainly, and involved in helping get the process cleared, as the agency in effect came in and wanted to know what they could and couldn't do. . . . And they talked to me, as well as others, to explain what they wanted to do. And I supported it. . . . It's been a remarkably successful effort, and I think the results speak for themselves.[4]

Cheney publicly admitted his support for waterboarding, widely considered a form of torture, despite statements against torture by the administration he represented. Thus, in 2009, in both these liberal democracies, India and the United States, despite the long history of laws against torture, justifications of this violence crept directly or indirectly into popular and legal/political discourses.

This study focuses on the legal and political discourses on torture in India and the United States to theorize the relationship among law, violence, and state power in liberal democracies. In liberal legal and political theory, one of the foundational principles is that law in modern societies is primarily based on certain norms/rules and principles. In legal theory, H. L. A. Hart and Ronald Dworkin assert that law based on coercion, as upheld by John Austin and Thomas Hobbes, has been largely replaced in modern societies by law based on rules and principles.[5] Hence, there is an assumption by political and legal theorists that violence occupies a secondary place in the legal process. This assumption in legal and political theory has been successfully challenged by critical theorists such as Robert Cover, Austin Sarat, and Timothy Kaufman-Osborn, who, using the example of the death penalty, point to law's continued dependence on violence in modern societies.[6]

With regard to torture in particular, Michel Foucault has argued that torturous spectacles used in ancient regimes to represent the sovereign's (state) power have been largely replaced by disciplinary and surveillance mechanisms in modern societies.[7] This has meant that the state relies less on force and more on discipline. In contrast, theorists such as Darius Rejali argue that instead of disciplinary institutions replacing torture, as Foucault suggests, torture actually becomes a part and parcel of those disciplinary institutions.[8] He thus rightly argues that torture is not simply a feature of premodern society but also a key aspect of modern society.[9] Further, Talal Asad points out that the existence of modern torture has a practical logic since it is "integral to the maintenance of the nation state's sovereignty" in policing and upholding national security.[10]

Following this tradition of analyzing the role of violence in liberal democracies, specifically torture, I examine the jurisprudence of interrogations in the United States and India to examine how their legal discourses address the question of torture. In this study I argue that even before recent debates on the use of torture in the "war on terror," the legal discourses were much more ambivalent about the infliction of excess pain and suffering than most political and legal theorists have acknowledged.[11] Rather than viewing the recent policies on interrogation as anomalous or exceptional, I argue that efforts to accommodate excess violence are long-standing features of interrogations in both the democracies.

Torture in Democracies: A Liberal Paradox

Images of U.S. soldiers engaging in torture at the Abu Ghraib prison in Iraq in 2004 brought the debate on torture back to the forefront of legal and political discourse both in the United States and worldwide. Official U.S. memos authorizing "harsh interrogation techniques," such as waterboarding, and the military tribunals under the Military Commissions Act of 2006 debating the admissibility of coercion-based evidence, confirmed that these images were not mere aberrations. These images and memos resulted in a proclamation by both the critics and the defenders of these policies that the post-9/11 United States had witnessed a return of the unthinkable: torture. This articulation is premised on the assumption that in liberal democracies, instances of torture are considered either features of the past or, at worst, aberrations that occur rarely. As the 1999 *U.S. Report on Torture* to the Committee against Torture states, "Torture does not occur in the United States except in aberrational situations and never as a matter of policy."[12] Similarly, in India, the late Indian prime minister Rajiv Gandhi stated in January 1988, "We don't torture anybody. I can be very categorical about that. Wherever we have had complaints of torture we've had it checked and we've not found it to be true."[13] The assertions continue despite the documentation of acts of torture in both these democracies.

In this section, I explore why torture appears as a paradox for liberal democracies both theoretically and historically. One of the self-defining features of liberal democracies is the absence of torture or indeed any "unnecessary" state violence. This appears both in the political rhetoric (noted earlier) and in liberal theory. Thus, Michael Ignatieff, in his discussion of the United States as a liberal democracy, refers to it as "a constitutional order that sets limits to any government's use of force."[14] Of course, liberal democracies are characterized not just by their relationship to violence. As Steven Lukes notes,

> Democracy, definable in different ways, is on almost every account a system with mechanisms that hold its officials responsive and responsible to the people's wills or preferences. A liberal democracy will have a further feature: it will hold its officials responsible for respecting the principles of liberal equality: for not violating their citizens' rights and *respecting their dignity*.[15]

Thus, there are a number of other features that characterize liberal democracies, such as the rule of law, representational government, state accountability through a system of checks and balances, separation of powers, and protection of individual rights and liberties, including a respect for human dignity. All these features have one thing in common: they are conceptually and ostensibly based on consent.

After all, as one of the foremost theorists of classical liberalism, John Locke, put it, "For 'tis not every compact that puts an end to the state of nature between men, but only this one of *agreeing together mutually* to enter into one community, and make one body politic."[16] Locke goes on to explain, "all men are naturally in that state [of nature], and remain so, till by their *own consents* they make themselves members of some politic society."[17] Thus, John Locke emphasized the importance of consent in the formation of the government.

Of course, the liberal state, while being based on consent, continues to be closely related to violence, as noted in Max Weber's famous statement that "legal coercion by violence is the monopoly of the state."[18] As Weber explains,

> Sociologically, the question of whether or not guaranteed law exists in such a situation depends on the availability of an *organized coercive apparatus* for the nonviolent exercise of legal coercion. This apparatus must also possess such power that there is in fact a significant probability that the norm will be respected because of the possibility of recourse to such legal coercion.[19]

Weber does recognize the significance of norms in the regulation of society, but he asserts that respect for these norms exists only because they can be backed by legal coercion. Thus, the functioning of the state is closely related to the concrete possibility of legal coercion. Liberal theorists, while accepting the role of violence, however, specify that the state does not govern primarily through violence and that any violence it employs is actually constrained. As Ignatieff puts it,

> [L]iberal states seek both to create a free space for democratic deliberation and to set *strict limits to the coercive and compulsory powers of government.* This is the double sense in which democracies stand against violence: positively, they seek to create free institutions where public policy is decided freely, rather than by fear and coercion; negatively, they seek to reduce, to a minimum, the coercion and violence necessary to the maintenance of order among free peoples.[20]

For Ignatieff, the liberal state both ensures the freedom for people to deliberate and also subjects them only to the minimal violence required to maintain law and order in society. Indeed, the liberal state not only views coercion as a necessary "evil"; it also requires that much introspection take place before the administration of pain and suffering. As Ignatieff notes, "Only in liberal societies have people believed that the pain and suffering involved in depriving people of their liberty must make us think twice about imposing this constraint even on those who justly deserve it."[21] Thus, coercion, violence, pain, and suffering are subject to scrutiny and kept to a minimum, according to Ignatieff's framework of a liberal state and democracy.

Therefore, despite Weber's blatant assertion about the state's monopoly on violence, it is undisputed that the liberal state exhibits an attempt to constrain the violence. Whether the limits to violence are put in place for the purpose of masking its real nature, gaining legitimacy, or displaying a developed respect for human dignity, it is this feature of liberal democracy that makes torture and excess violence a particularly paradoxical proposition.[22]

Indeed, if one traces the standard narrative of the history of Western torture, one discerns a similar assumption that the decline of torture is associated with the emergence of the Enlightenment era and a "civilized" modern society.[23] As Jeremy Waldron articulates it, "torture is certainly seen by most jurists—or has been seen by most jurists until very recently—as inherently alien to our legal heritage."[24] Historically, in Europe, apart from the Greeks and the Romans, the use of torture due to the influence of Roman canonical law began in the twelfth century and was institutionalized as a practice.[25] Subsequently, a demand for reform in the eighteenth century by Enlightenment philosophers such as Cesare Beccaria and Voltaire, who focused on the human body and human dignity, led to the removal of many "barbaric" forms of punishment (penal torture) and interrogation (judicial torture).[26] In many narratives on the history of Western torture, the eighteenth and nineteenth centuries were considered to be the period when torture was abolished in almost all countries of Europe, and this phase was seen as marking the emergence of modernity.

There are of course variations on this standard narrative of Western torture. In a fascinating book, *Inventing Human Rights*, Lynn Hunt traces the process by which human rights became self-evident in the eighteenth century, particularly in the American Declaration of Independence in 1776 and the French Revolution in 1789. Hunt explains that during this time, "New kinds of reading (and viewing and listening) created new individual experiences (empathy), which in turn made possible new social and political concepts (human rights)."[27] More specifically, in the context of torture, Hunt notes that the decline of torture was integrally connected to the ways in which notions of empathy and autonomy emerged in Europe at this time. However, these changes did not occur just because "judges gave up on it or because Enlightenment writers eventually opposed it." Rather, she suggests, "Torture ended because the traditional framework of pain and personhood fell apart, to be replaced, bit by bit, by a new framework, in which individuals owned their bodies, had rights to their separateness and to bodily inviolability, and recognized in other people the same passions, sentiments, and sympathies as in themselves."[28]

Karl Shoemaker also locates the transformation of punishment from painful to painless methods in terms of a change in the understanding of pain from medieval to modern times. In modern times, he notes, there emerged an aversion to pain and a desire to control it.[29] Lisa Silverman maps this change within the medical profession, which evolved from treating the root cause of a problem through surgery to treating the pain associated with the problem and getting rid of it.[30] Thus, scholars point to a consensus among the abolitionists of torture in Europe in the eighteenth century that pain had to decline and torture had to be seen as primarily a negative tool to be used in extremely rare cases.[31]

These scholars complicate the standard narrative on the decline of torture to the extent that they link that decline to transformations in larger social processes, such that the contribution of the abolitionists must be seen merely as moral justification of the reforms rather than as their primary cause. However, these studies continue to fit neatly into the Enlightenment narrative of the decline of torture from medieval to modern times. In the process, they fail to explain why the revival of torture in the twentieth century could take place in many of the same European countries despite the progress against pain. In addition to the colonial powers, England and France (which used torture even prior to the twentieth century), Nazi Germany, Stalinist Russia, Italy, and Spain also used forms of torture in their regimes.[32] The so-called revival of torture also questioned the dominant explanation that it was the moral and humane considerations in modern societies that led to the decline of torture in the first place.

In contrast to the "fairy tale" (as Langbein terms it) of abolition of torture as a story of progress in modern societies, Edward Peters and John Langbein point to other reasons why the use of torture declined.[33] Langbein notes that it was mainly two juridical forces that led to the rejection of torture in Europe: first, the development of "new criminal sanctions"; and second, a "revolution in the law of proof" in the seventeenth century.[34] Thus, in addition to death and disfigurement as punishments, there was now a range of alternatives, including the disciplinary institutions such as prisons and correctional facilities. The laws of evidence also began to be based on more circumstantial and physical evidence because of the rise of new technologies. Therefore, torture was no longer seen as an unavoidable part of the legal criminal procedure. The disappearance of the "legal and technical underpinnings of torture" allowed torture to be the target of "logical, moral, and social criticisms."[35] Indeed, Lisa Silverman suggests that even Beccaria recognized the limitations of torture as a mechanism for gaining the truth.[36] In other words, a change in the requirements of the legal system also allowed torture to become less important in Europe in the eighteenth century. Ironically enough, although Enlightenment philosophers campaigned against torture both as contradictory to the rights and will of the citizen (humanistic reasons) and as inefficient (pragmatics), their contributions continue to be highlighted primarily in terms of a moral condemnation of torture.

Darius Rejali and Edward Peters point out that consequently, torture continues to be considered primarily in "moral and sentimental terms," thereby limiting the debate on torture and especially moving the discussion away from the pragmatics of the phenomenon.[37] Addressing the pragmatics of torture in modern democracies is of course not intended to remove the moral aspects of the issue but, rather, is meant to allow for better recognition of the significance of both morality and pragmatics, historically and in modern times.[38]

The "fairy tale" of abolition of torture is significant also because it allows for the association of torture with different stages of society. Torture is associated not only with either the ancient or medieval regimes, as noted earlier, but also with the "other," generally non-Western societies, which continue to be considered more "primitive" and "barbaric." Conversely, the focus on torture as a feature of the "other" suggests that it is inherently absent in more modern, "civilized," democratic (often Western) societies. Waldron notes that even as early as 1911, the Encyclopedia Britannica noted that "the whole subject [of torture] is now one of only historical interest as far as Europe is concerned," thereby absolving the entire continent of the "sin" of torture.[39]

This notion of the impermissibility of torture as an indicator of modern, civilized societies makes an appearance each time practices of torture appear. In fact, immediately after September 11, 2001, when FBI officials appeared on talk shows and gave statements in the newspapers about the possibility of using torture, one FBI agent who had been involved in the 9/11 investigation was quoted as saying, "'We are known for humanitarian treatment, so basically we are stuck.'"[40] Legal scholar Edward Greer rightly characterizes this inherent belief in the absence of torture in the following way: "In the hegemonic legal ideology of the United States, torturing people is taboo."[41] Thus, the United States cannot appear to be condoning an "uncivilized" and "medieval" practice such as torture. Echoing a similar sentiment, in *D. K. Basu v. State of West Bengal*, the Indian Supreme Court stated the following:

> The word torture today has become synonymous with the *darker side of human civilization. . . .* It is a calculated assault on human dignity and *whenever human dignity is wounded, civilisation takes a step backward—[the] flag of humanity must on each such occasion fly half-mast.*[42]

Thus, theoretically, rhetorically, and historically, the standard narratives on the history of torture have created a discourse of impermissibility of torture in modern liberal democracies and indeed deemphasized the role of violence in the very functioning of the state and law. In such a framework, any reappearance of torture in image or in policy is considered an exception, and it is this assumption that I unravel in the course of this study.

Debates on Law and Violence in Legal and Political Theory

In *Discipline and Punish: The Birth of a Prison*, Michel Foucault describes the transformation in the nature of power from the use of torture that marked the body of the condemned to a power based on control through discipline in modern society.[43] Foucault notes that one of the major changes in eighteenth- and nineteenth-century Europe is the "disappearance of torture as a public spectacle," as had been the case in the execution of Damiens.[44] In the classical age, according to Foucault, the sovereign's body and power were directly threatened by any criminal act and had to be avenged by reasserting the difference—"dissymmetry of relations"—between the criminal and the sovereign power. The point was not so much deterrence by example but was rather an "exercise in terror." The torture inherent in that kind of punishment highlighted the enormity of the crime (called "atrocity") and functioned by means of an "excess."[45] The excessive aspect of the power is best illustrated in an example in which a corpse is cut into pieces.[46]

Foucault did concede that even in modern times, suffering was considered desirable for the condemned due to the wrongs committed by him or her and, thus, there was always a certain amount of physical pain involved in punishment. Foucault writes, "There remains, therefore, a trace of 'torture' in the modern mechanisms of criminal justice—a trace that has not been entirely overcome, but which is enveloped, increasingly, by the noncorporal nature of the penal system."[47] However, this trace of torture, according to Foucault, is a far cry from the fifteenth to the eighteenth centuries, when every penalty included some amount of torture or *supplice* that involved a certain amount of "horrible" pain.

Despite acknowledging the continuation of some amount of pain in modern societies, for the most part Foucault emphasizes an emergence of "micro systems of power" that transformed individuals from free, independent subjects to disciplined ones. In the course of this transformation in the system of social control, there is no longer "recourse, in principle at least, to excess, force or violence. It is a power that seems all the less 'corporal' in that it is more subtly 'physical.'"[48] The "economy of power" thus required that disciplinary practices take over from the use of excess violence. In his famous essay on governmentality (which I explore in chapter 2), Foucault further introduced the notion of an art of government as a form of social control that actually channelizes the productive power of individuals, and once again deemphasizes the role of "excess" violence. In contrast, in my work, I argue that even while "excess" of the kind that Foucault noted in the era of Damiens may no longer be compatible with liberal democracies, the current debates on torture point to the possibility of accommodation of other forms of "excess violence."[49] In order to further understand the nature of the excess violence accommodated, one has to briefly revisit the debates on the relationship between law and violence that led to the deemphasis on the role of violence in law in mainstream liberal legal and political theory.

As noted earlier, the debate within legal and political theory centered on whether law is primarily based on coercion or on rules and principles. John Austin, for instance, argued that law is based on the "sovereign's" coercive commands. Austin writes that "law is a command which obliges a person or persons to a *course* of conduct."[50] The command is backed by "*might*: the power of affecting others with evil or pain."[51] Both H. L. A. Hart and Ronald Dworkin critique Austin's idea of a sovereign by questioning how one could define a single sovereign in the present legal system. Hart and Dworkin further point out that Austin's definition fails to account for the difference between the orders of the sovereign and those of an outlaw since he defines "obligation as subjection to the threat of force."[52] Notwithstanding the critique of the limited definition, Austin's attempt to link law to violence is a crucial one that is not addressed by the positivistic Hartian notion of rules or by Dworkin's principles.

Indeed, within liberal theory, the relationship between law and violence exists at several levels. First, law emerges because there is the danger of violence becoming the dominant feature in society. Thomas Hobbes, for instance, points out that it is due to the fear of the "state of nature" becoming a "state of war" that "men" decide to give themselves to the Leviathan.[53] They agree to give up their rights to the "brute beast" in order to preserve the one basic right they want for themselves: namely, the right to self-preservation. Hobbes writes,

> This done, the Multitude so united in One person, is called a COMMON-WEALTH in latine CIVITAS. This is the Generation of that great LEVIA-THAN, or rather (to speak more reverently) of that *Mortall God*, to which wee owe under the *Immortall God*, our peace and defence. For by this Authoritie, given him by every particular man in the Common-Wealth, *he hath the use of so much Power and Strength conferred on him, that by terror thereof, he is inabled to (con) forme the wills of them all,* to Peace at home, and mutuall ayd against their enemies abroad.[54]

The fear of anarchy and an imagined state of war is the source of social order. As Austin Sarat and Thomas Kearns point out, "what brings us to law, and holds us, is fear—not just fear of law but fear of life without law."[55] Or, as a prominent legal theorist, lawyer, and human rights activist, K. G. Kannabiran, writes, "None of us seem [sic] to feel free without restraint."[56] Hence, the need to check anarchy of any kind leads to the emergence of law, which is necessarily backed by violence.

Second, since law originates in order to check violence, it cannot legitimize itself only on the basis of violence. This is the basis of the criticism of Hobbes and Austin by subsequent theorists. According to Hart and Dworkin, what is missing in the narratives of Hobbes and Austin is the link between law, norms, and justice, and the importance of consent. Hart adds a normative component to the rules by emphasizing the distinction between "being obliged" and "being obligated." The latter may be followed because of a normativity, which goes beyond just being coerced to obey. Hence, what distinguishes the gunman from the legally sanctioned officer for Hart is that the latter has authority, which is not based on just sheer force.[57] Dworkin notes that while for Austin the basis of legitimacy lay in "their [sovereigns'] monopoly of power," for Hart, it lay in the "constitutional standards," which were accepted by the community as the "rule of recognition."[58] Instead of relying on the coercive sanctions of the sovereign, as Austin suggests, law comes to be based on certain rules, norms, and principles that create obligations for individuals.

As a result, law then becomes focused on legal interpretation—the process rather than the force. For Dworkin, law is neither the "will" of the judges nor the "power to back it up with force" nor "chiseled rules"—it is about legal interpretation based on the principles of justice. Here "law and philosophy tend to merge."[59] As Sarat and Kearns point out, the need to have normative principles in legal theory required the "forgetting of violence."[60] Recovering the link between law and justice is an extremely important project, which explains Hart's and Dworkin's preoccupation with dissociating themselves from Austin and Hobbes.

Austin Sarat explains that law's relationship to violence—violence as the basis of "founding the legal order," "law as regulator of force" and, finally, violence as "a means through which law acts"—is constantly denied.[61] One could, of course, argue that while the violence involved in the founding of the legal order is generally recognized, the emphasis is on the emergence of an alternative basis for law thereafter, whether the basis is rules or principles. The overall assumption is that the modern legal systems have moved away from their reliance on force. Here, I give two examples of the way this denial of the significance of violence in law appears as a dominant frame of reference. In the context of the torture debate, one observes the influence of this approach in Jeremy Waldron's essay on legal archetypes, an archetype being defined "as a rule which has significance not just in and of itself, but also as the embodiment of a pervasive principle."[62] Waldron notes,

> The rule against torture is archetypal of a certain policy having to do with the relation between law and force, and the force with which law rules. The prohibition on torture is expressive of an important underlying policy of the law, which we might try to capture in the following way: Law is not brutal in its operation. Law is not savage. Law does not rule through abject fear and terror, or by breaking the will of those whom it confronts. *If law is forceful or coercive, it gets its way by nonbrutal methods which respect rather than mutilate the dignity and agency of those who are its subjects.*[63]

Since Waldron's intervention is intended to provide a reference point for post-9/11 torture debates in the United States that attempted to push against the prohibition of torture, he focuses on a complete separation between law and brutality. However, in the process, he fails to specify the actual nature of the relationship between law and violence, indeed overemphasizing the role of respect for the dignity and agency of subjects in law.

Another example of understanding the relationship between law and violence is Phillippe Nonet and Philip Selznick's effort to explain the transition of law and society from "repressive law" (where the coercion is "extensive" and "weakly restrained") to "autonomous law" (where coercion is "controlled by legal constraints").[64] From there Nonet and Selznick see a move towards a "responsive law," wherein the coercive aspects of law are replaced by a "positive search for alternatives, e.g., incentives and self-sustaining systems of obligations."[65] While the basis of legitimacy in the repressive legal regime is coercion, force, and violence, especially of the direct kind, one observes an emergence of the legitimacy of law as no longer based on coercion or force but rather on the autonomous rule of law. The basis of law's legitimacy, thus, moves from force to rules and consent based on reason. If this is the case, then what is the role of violence? This theory of the legitimacy of law suggests that violence plays a more secondary role and is the result of the action of agents, who are only instruments, enforcing the results of bureaucratic judicial decision making.[66] The question for the critics of "norm-" and "consensus-building" notions of law, such as Robert Cover, is whether the legal interpretation by the judges is completely divorced from violence.

Cover, in his seminal essay "Violence and the Word," pointed toward this integral connection between legal interpretation and *physical* violence.[67] Cover's contribution was that he looked at the role of the very judges seen as providing justice as being involved in violence. One of his most famous statements is, "Legal interpretation takes place in a field of pain and death."[68] A judge may interpret a text in such a way that it has a violent impact on the victims—the victim may lose his or her freedom, property, children, and life as a result of the judgment. Yet there continues to be an emphasis on the commonality of meaning that law seeks to create through its association with justice. Cover's focus on violence aims not at rejecting the interpretive enterprise but at reminding the judges of the responsibility of legal interpretation. "It reminds us that the interpretative commitments of officials are realized, indeed, in the flesh."[69] This is to emphasize that the legal act is not a "mental and spiritual act" but one with physical implications that have been denied in mainstream legal theory.

Cover not only analyzed the violent impact of legal interpretation but also focused attention on how force used by law always appears to be legitimate by virtue of it being "law's violence." As Sarat explains, "What this claim to legitimacy implies, in this minimal answer, is that law's violence is rational, controlled, and purposive, that law makes force the servant of the word."[70] This contentious relationship between law and violence is best illustrated in some of the significant works on the death penalty in the United States by Sarat and Kaufman-Osborn. These theorists focus on the role played by judges in ensuring that law's violence appears to be controlled and justified. At the same time, judges themselves have to appear to be removed from the violence that occurs at the level of enforcement. Timothy Kaufman-Osborn's work on the death penalty, for instance, powerfully points to the apparent distancing of the act of execution from the courtroom where the death penalty is pronounced, and he illustrates how "words" and "deeds" are in fact integrally related.[71] The judge not only announces the execution but also has to ensure a "structure of cooperation" in order for his or her sentence to be carried out by the state apparatus. In order to ensure compliance, the judge even has to justify the use of violence as necessary.

Furthermore, law's violence has to appear controlled. Austin Sarat points to the change in the methods of execution as an example of the way law's violence always has to project itself as humane, in contrast to the illegal violence of nonstate actors, in order to legitimize itself.[72] Here law in general plays an important role in legitimizing state violence by delegitimizing the violence used by the nonstate actors. Upendra Baxi explains this point further:

The legal system draws the crucial distinction between prescribed and proscribed threat or uses of force. Apart from reasonable use of force in self-defence by subjects of the legal order, the legal system, always and everywhere, *seeks to delegitimise and criminalize violence by actors other than those authorized to use violence (normally, the agents of the State—the police, the para-military forces and the armed forces)* and provides a normative language which camouflages the core coercion underlying the law.[73]

Thus, the need to deny its reliance on violence and simultaneously justify the use of some controlled violence for maintaining order creates a constant source of tension for law. It is this tension that law has with violence that I further explore in this project on torture in liberal democracies in the context of India and the United States.

Illustrations of Liberal Democracies: India and the United States

This project studies the jurisprudence of interrogations in the United States and India. I focus on the United States since some of the most significant public debates on torture in democracies have come up in the post-9/11 U.S. context. I take the case of India as my second illustration because focusing on a non-Western liberal democracy such as India squarely challenges the imaginary of liberal democracies as primarily Western. The study also draws from the tradition of recent comparative law scholarship that compares the legal systems in both these countries due to certain historical and contemporary similarities.[74] Both India and the United States have a common law history emerging from their colonial interaction with the British legal system. In addition, both countries have strong and independent supreme courts that have powers of judicial review and have played a key role in the development of civil liberties, especially in the context of torture and interrogations. Further, U.S. constitutional principles have had an impact on the Indian Constitution, there have been regular dialogues between the judges and other legal actors in the two countries, and in many cases the Indian Supreme Court has made a direct reference to American jurisprudence.[75] In fact, this has led influential legal scholars to debate whether Indian jurisprudence is completely determined by Anglo American jurisprudence.[76]

To address this question, Upendra Baxi's differentiation among the three kinds of continuities between the BILS (British Indian legal system) and the ILS (Indian legal system) is useful.[77] First, Baxi argues, the ILS has deliberately adopted some of the features of the BILS as a result of a reflective process of engagement, a good example being the embracing of an adversarial legal system. Second, the continuities are reflected in the many unchanged laws that remain on the books as the result of "sheer inertia." Third, Baxi identifies certain continuities as "colonial" because they reflect a conscious preservation of the "status quo" by the Indian governing elites. Indeed, some of the copying of Anglo American features by the ILS comes close to what Baxi provocatively calls "juristic dependencia."[78] This phenomenon is especially observed in the Indian system's high reliance on Anglo American law for legislative and judicial initiatives, such that "the ILS became a subordinate, almost a vassal legal system, thereby only occasionally serving the needs of Indian society."[79]

True enough, in a number of Indian cases on the issue of interrogation, one finds Indian judges especially prone to quote U.S. justices and cases as precedents. Nonetheless, a close study of these cases suggests that sometimes Indian judges are conscious of the hegemonic influences, but they continue to refer to Western jurisprudence for very specific reasons such as the origins of many modern laws in the colonial period.[80] In other instances, the Indian justices borrowed certain principles from Western jurisprudence because they believed in the existence of some universal humanist principles. As Justice Iyer writes in the context of the Satpathy case inspired by the Miranda decision,

> India is Indian, not alien, and jurisprudence is neither eternal nor universal but moulded by the national genius, life's realities, culture and ethos of each country. Even so, humanist jurists will agree that in this indivisible human planet certain values, though divergently expressed, have cosmic status, spreading out with the march of civilization in space and time. To understand ourselves, we must listen to voices from afar, without forsaking our identity.[81]

As the above quotation indicates, the Indian justices believed that some humanist values could serve as guiding principles in decision making as long as there is a self-reflexive struggle to ensure the compatibility of the principles to the specific cultural and national context.

Thus, while there are formal continuities with and an extensive reliance on the Anglo American legal systems, there is no easy answer to the question whether this can be termed "juristic dependencia." As Baxi himself points out, juristic dependencia is not an unproblematic concept, particularly because it does not look at the "demarcating line between 'copycatism' and cross cultural diffusion."[82] In addition, more importantly, calling a system "colonial," Baxi notes, prevents an analysis of the ILS on its own terms. Thus, in this study, I focus on the ways in which the jurisprudence of interrogation in both the Indian and the U.S. supreme courts speak to each other (directly or indirectly) and, more significantly, on how the courts in these two liberal democracies conceptualize law and excess violence.

While there has been some focus on the impact of the U.S. legal system on different legal institutions and practices around the world, there has been little study of the innovations and perspectives emerging from Indian jurisprudence that provide insights regarding the debates in the United States. For example, the concept of "custodial violence," developed by the Indian Supreme Court to deal with torture and deaths in custody, provides a useful tool for analyzing the struggle of the United States with excess violence in similar contexts. Finally, I situate this project in a moment when legal scholars and the media have directly linked up the debates in India and the United States in the context of the "global war on terror," prompting the need for new legislation in both the countries.[83]

Although there appear to be several points of similarity between the two countries in terms of the jurisprudence of interrogations, I am conscious of the problems involved in comparing legal systems in very diverse social contexts. The particular political, economic, cultural, social, and historical contexts give different meanings to similar legal terms and institutions, and postcolonial theory has rightly pointed to the dangers of hegemonic universal definitions. Talal Asad, for example, points to this danger in the context of torture.[84] Asad criticizes the Universal Declaration of Human Rights for assuming certain definitions of torture and cruel, inhuman, or degrading treatment and punishment as universal when they may have actually emerged from a European liberal understanding of what is "human" and "inhuman." Asad notes that while certain violent practices that are technologically advanced, such as war, are seen as acceptable, other "traditional" forms of violence are automatically considered more barbaric.[85]

The attempt in this study is, thus, not to compare India and the United States in terms of their similarities and differences. The study uses the empirical analysis of their very particular jurisprudence of interrogations, primarily at the Supreme Court level, to make some generalizations about liberal democracies' struggle with torture and excess violence. The limitations of these generalizations are accepted at the outset, but the attempt is to get to some "structural" patterns of understanding torture in liberal democracies. Here I use as the basis of my project David Garland's justification for focusing on two distinct countries—the United Kingdom and the United States—

for his book *The Culture of Control*. Garland writes, "such an analysis allows me to get at structural patterns that are not otherwise available to inspection."[86] In that sense, this project examines the relationship among law, violence, and state power in liberal democracies, focusing on torture, with India and the United States as particular illustrations. As a researcher interested in postcolonial and cultural studies, I have tried to be conscious of the particular distinctions and to analyze the jurisprudence in each of these countries on their own terms. Yet the impulse to compare and make some general observations does make it a constantly challenging task. In the next section, I put forth my own theoretical argument on torture in liberal democracies, but first it may be useful to identify some of the significant ways in which the torture debate has been approached in recent times.

Contours of the Torture Debate

There are three primary ways in which the torture debates have developed, particularly in the post-9/11 context but also more broadly in the context of "terrorism." I discuss each of them before putting forward my own framework of analysis. First, I discuss what I call the "should we?" debates, or the philosophical and ethical debate on the use of torture that predates the 9/11 context but has been revisited more centrally in current times. Second, I analyze a framework that suggests that torture is an exception in contemporary liberal democracies. Finally, I focus on those studies that connect law to violence and put forward my own approach of analyzing torture as a manifestation of law's struggle with excess violence.

The "Should We?" Approach to Torture

Around the seventh season of the U.S. television show *24*, Jack Bauer (played by Kiefer Sutherland, who was nominated for a Golden Globe award for being the "cop who saves the country 24 hours a day") was subject to a Senate investigation for his use of torture in an episode aptly titled "Redemption."[87] Ironically enough, the Senate hearing had to be stopped, since Jack Bauer was subpoenaed by the FBI and the hero of *24* once more was asked to save his country from a terrorist rebel group from Africa and their supporters within the United States. Torture once again constantly appeared in the series, though, interestingly, at this point used by precisely the same FBI agents who had previously condemned Bauer for using the illegal techniques. We see FBI agent Renee Walker, who started off being completely dismissive of Bauer's tactics, gradually allowing him to use torture and even becoming the torturer herself in a desperate situation of necessity despite her boss's reminder that torture is illegal. Once again, Jack Bauer demonstrated to the world that *he* was not a cold-blooded torturer. Rather, he only used "whatever it takes" in situations where nothing else works and American lives are in danger. That the "converted" torturing agent in *24* is from the FBI is striking because many FBI personnel have been extremely critical of the CIA and OGA (other government agencies) for using torture in the post-9/11 U.S. "war on terror."[88] Thus, in popular culture, the dilemma emerging from what has been termed "the ticking bomb scenario" has often reappeared and been easily resolved by turning to torture. The show *24* has been particularly influential in creating a justificatory discourse in the post-9/11 context (as I discuss in chapter 3). But the "should we?" debate has been the subject of much more philosophical agonizing than one ever sees in popular culture, and I illustrate the framework of that debate in this section.

Just as there had been an assumption that torture as a practice no longer/never exists in a democracy, even the philosophical and ethical debates on torture had been considered a subject of the past. As Jean Elshtain notes in her essay "Reflection on the Problem of 'Dirty Hands,'" she had never imagined herself writing on the subject of torture in the context of the United States. She writes,

> Before the watershed event of September 11, 2001, I had not reflected critically on the theme of torture. I was one of those who listed it in the category of *"never."* It did not seem to me possible that the United States would face some of the dilemmas favored by moral theorists in their *hypothetical musings* on whether torture could ever be morally permitted. Too, reprehensible regimes tortured. End of question. Not so, as it turns out.[89]

Here, Elshtain articulates the emergence of a new paradigm of thinking about torture in terms of a complete break from all earlier times, almost seeming to assume that these debates on torture were taking place for the very first time. Here it is important to note that debates on the justification of torture had not been observed as openly prior to the 9/11 moment. However, the fact that philosophical "musings" had predated this moment, and not just musings about "reprehensible regimes," suggests that theorists and philosophers have always recognized the existence of these questions in all societies, democratic or authoritarian.

One of the dominant positions in the "should we?" debate is represented by those for whom torture is never permissible under any circumstances, such as Ariel Dorfman.[90] The UN Convention against Torture's nonderogable prohibition of torture also personifies this sentiment.[91] The primary emphasis is on the a priori commitment to human dignity and the assertion that torture cannot be allowed under any circumstances, not just because it is violence against the body, the mind, and the imagination but also because it destroys the entire normative world of the tortured. Dorfman articulates this position in the post-9/11 context, referring to the horrors of the past, recalling equally the history of torture in Chile and that of the Nazis in Germany: "I can only pray that humanity will have the courage to say no, no to torture, . . . under any circumstance whatsoever, . . . no matter who the enemy, what the accusation, what sort of fear we harbor; . . . no matter what kind of threat is posed to our safety; no to torture anytime, anywhere; no to torturing anyone; no to torture."[92] In some ways, Slavoj Žižek's insistence on not even contemplating the question of torture signifies a position similar to Dorfman's— that some things are beyond conversation or contemplation. As Lukes puts it, quoting Žižek, "'essays . . . which do not advocate torture outright, [but] simply introduce it as a legitimate topic of debate, are even more dangerous than an explicit endorsement of torture,' for we thereby legitimize torture and this 'changes the background of ideological presuppositions and opinions much more radically than its outright advocacy.'"[93] However, this position representing a moral condemnation of torture in a sense fails to acknowledge the legal and political pragmatics of torture and the discussions therein (as noted earlier).[94] As Baxi notes in another context, "absolutist stances lead to complacency: to regard torture as self-evidently bad prevents us from meeting the arguments of those to whom, for weal or woe, it is not so *manifestly* bad."[95] Thus, even though an "absolute right against torture" is an important normative framework for this book, the working premise is that an absence of discussion on torture may not acknowledge the complexities and challenges of the current debate.

The opposing position to the absolutist prohibition is represented by those scholars who have philosophically and pragmatically addressed the question of torture. Even though many of them reject torture normatively, they do concede that it can be used in some rare instances. However, they disagree on two things: whether those rare circumstances ever really exist; and whether torture could ever be institutionalized. Henry Shue, in his classic essay of 1978, compares torture to killing in war and wonders whether accepting the latter (complete destruction) requires acceptance of torture (only partial destruction).⁹⁶ However, Shue concludes that torture cannot be compared with killing in a "just war" because unlike in a declared war, torture takes place in a context of complete submission of a defenseless person. Shue also notes that it is not as if giving the information in interrogational torture can provide escape to the defenseless due to the difficulties of distinguishing between the "innocent bystander, ready collaborator or a dedicated enemy."⁹⁷ However, even Shue in the 1978 essay agreed that torture could be used in a "ticking bomb scenario," his version being "a hidden nuclear device to explode in the heart of Paris."⁹⁸ In such a case, for Shue, torture is permissible and indeed necessary since absence of action in this situation would be irresponsible due to the large number of lives that are endangered. It is this particular example (in various forms) that has been used by many theorists and philosophers to argue that torture can be justified in certain rare circumstances that most also concede never actually occur.

The acceptance (even if rarely) of this "ticking bomb" scenario raises the question whether one can actually institutionalize torture or in effect remove the absolute legal prohibitions on torture. In recent years, Alan Dershowitz has suggested that since there are certain situations that have always warranted the use of force against terrorists, there should be an attempt to legalize the effort and ensure the accountability of the officers using torture. His proposal was the use of torture warrants that would be handed out by judges only if they were convinced that the person might have some information.⁹⁹ In terms of interrogation methods, he suggests the use of nonlethal methods such as a truth serum. He claims that for a judge to allow such an injection would be similar to a judge allowing involuntary withdrawal of blood from a defendant and asks why, if the latter process is not seen as attacking a person's dignity, the former should be. As he puts it, "Certainly there can be no constitutional distinction between an injection that removes a liquid and one that injects a liquid."¹⁰⁰ For Dershowitz, instituting torture warrants is a way to "reduce the use of torture to the smallest amount and degree possible, while creating public accountability for its rare use."¹⁰¹

However, Dershowitz's idea about institutionalizing torture has possibly been the most controversial one, and even those theorists who agonize about the possibility of using torture in the rarest of cases draw the line on this proposal. Apart from Shue's cautionary statement that "hard case[s] make bad law" and "artificial case[s] make bad ethics,"¹⁰² Elaine Scarry argues that the rare instance should not lead to any dilution of the absolute safeguards against torture. Scarry holds this position because she believes that the "ticking bomb scenario" is never actually realized in practice since it assumes a level of knowledge about the situation that is almost impossible for anyone to have. As Scarry puts it, "it assumed a population that is (against robust evidence) omniscient."[103] She also argues that if such a situation were ever to occur, it should be left to the person in charge to make the decision about torture and then that person should be willing to explain the act to a jury of peers.[104] Scarry here comes close to Michael Walzer's framework of dealing with what he terms "the problem of dirty hands."[105] While acknowledging more readily than Shue that there are situations in which a politician has to dirty his or her hands, including the need to authorize torture to save lives, Walzer also rejects the idea that such an action taken by a "moral politician" (with however heavy a heart) to save lives can be excused. Neither is it adequate for the politician to suffer only internally. Rather, taking his cue from Albert Camus' *Just Assassins*, Walzer argues that the politician who dirties his hands also has to be ready to pay for it by "doing penance or accepting punishment."[106] Thus, in contrast to Dershowtiz, most of the other theorists/philosophers are against institutionalizing torture in any form.

Indeed, in light of the recent arguments that an exception for torture should be made (sometimes using his earlier essay), Henry Shue in a more recent article actually rejects his previous position. As Shue puts it, "To try to leave a constrained loophole for the competent 'conscientious offender' is in fact to leave an expanding loophole for a bureaucracy of routinized torture, as I misguidedly did in the 1978 article."[107] Shue not only explains that the hypothetical is utterly unrealistic because it is so "idealized" and "abstract" as to become "superior to reality," but he also very persuasively points out that there is a basic flaw in an argument that allows for exceptional instances of torture based on the ticking-bomb scenario. He explains that in order for a person to be an effective torturer in exceptional instances, he or she needs to be trained over time. As Shue writes,

> Torture is not for amateurs—successful torturers need to be real "pros," and no one becomes a "pro" overnight. At a minimum, one must practice—perhaps do research, be mentored by the still more experienced. In short, torture needs a bureaucracy, with apprentices and experts, of the kind that torture in fact always has. Torquemada was not an independent consultant. Torture is an institution.[108]

Thus, Shue notes that even in terms of its practicality, it is not possible to have a "moderate position on torture."

Dershowitz, however, gets more support from another set of scholars who intervene in this torture debate through a more pragmatic attempt to balance liberty and security while deemphasizing the normative implications of using torture. In this liberty versus security debate, some scholars and activists continue to reject the need for any special laws, while others propose an explicit suspension of laws.[109] However, I focus on the third strand, which advocates the enactment of new laws by accommodating expansion of state powers during emergencies, especially concerning torture and detention.

Embodying this third impulse is Bruce Ackerman's proposal of an Emergency Constitution that involves the short-term mass detention of suspects for up to forty-five days on the basis of "reasonable suspicion" before the normal criminal process sets in.[110] Ackerman argues that terrorism is neither a war nor similar to a criminal activity, but rather represents a challenge to the "effective sovereignty" of the state that "destabilize[s] a foundational relationship between ordinary citizens and the modern state."[111] In order to recover the effective sovereignty of the state so that it can resume its normal functioning, a framework must be applied that Ackerman calls the "reassurance interest," which requires the state to reassure its citizenry in two primary ways: symbolic and functional. For him, symbolically, actions such as proclamation of an emergency will reassure the public that the state is prepared for a second attack, and, functionally, such a proclamation would mean preempting the second strike by taking certain extraordinary steps, such as short-term mass detention.[112]

Overall, Ackerman perhaps makes the most "reasonable" case for detention. He gives an analogy of a medical quarantine to show other contexts where the demands of public safety require a segment of the population to be cordoned off. In order to contain the president, Ackerman suggests the introduction of a "supermajoritarian escalator" that would allow the Congress to control the executive by forcing the otherwise unrestrained president to ensure a greater majority within Congress each time he wanted to extend the emergency. Ackerman also insists that the state should take all responsibility for these detention camps and ensure that compensation be given to those who turn out to be innocent. He puts the role of maintaining the integrity of the Emergency Constitution in the hand of the judges, especially in ascertaining whether the situation does indeed constitute an emergency.

David Cole, in response, opposes Ackerman's proposal rigorously: "Putting innocent people who pose no danger behind bars to reassure a panicked public is normatively unacceptable, no matter what 'supermajoritarian escalator' has been put in place, and no matter how much we 'compensate' them after the fact."[113] While accepting that preventive detention could be used in some instances, Cole objects to the removal of two basic protections in this proposal: suspicion and judicial review. Cole also critiques the overemphasis on the supermajoritarian escalator, stating that the indefinite aspect of the detention is not the only problem in this framework. Rather, Cole rightly points out, the problem in past detentions was that "[t]housands of people who posed no danger were nonetheless rounded up, not based on objective, individualized suspicion, but often based in significant part on their perceived racial, ethnic, religious, or political identities."[114] Ackerman, of course, rejects any possibility of using torture but in the process fails to recognize the close relationship between detention and torture in many instances. For other scholars, the balancing of liberty and security does not actually stop at detentions and requires the accommodation of torture as well.

Adrian Vermuele and Eric Posner suggest that coercive interrogations (that within their framework overlap with torture and CIDT (cruel, inhuman, and degrading treatment) to some extent) "should be legalized and subjected to regulatory oversight."[115] Their proposal has to be understood within the framework of two theses. The first of these they term the "tradeoff thesis," namely, that "during emergencies, when new threats appear, the balance shifts; government should and will reduce civil liberties in order to enhance security." The second thesis is the "deference thesis," which is that "the executive branch, not Congress or the judicial branch, should make the tradeoff between security and liberty."[116] They do acknowledge that coercive interrogation is a "grave evil." However, they equate it to other grave evils that are allowed to exist in a liberal democracy, such as use of deadly force in law enforcement or in the context of war, stating that these actions by themselves are not rendered impermissible but rather are regulated by law.

In a similar vein, Richard Posner, in his book *Not a Suicide Pact: The Constitution in a Time of National Emergency,* writes that while the constitutional limitations of "brutal interrogation," such as the "shock the conscience" test emerging from the Rochin case, are drawn for law enforcement purposes, similar limits may not be applicable if the purpose of the interrogation is to gain intelligence, especially if that intelligence is used to "ward off a great evil." As he puts it, "Many consciences will not be shocked at the use of torture when it will ward off a great evil and no other method would work quickly enough to be effective."[117] At another point, acknowledging that torture may not always be effective, Posner notes, "But this is just to identify another cost of torture—the many false positives that it produces. It is not to say that there never are net benefits."[118]

Here the authors reject the notion that there is something special about coercive interrogation or torture that prevents democracies from using these practices.[119] As Richard Posner puts it, "the importance of revulsion as a factor in morality and law cannot be denied, but it should not be allowed to occlude consideration of instrumental considerations."[120] Underlying these proposals for balancing security and liberty is the doctrine of "necessity" propounded to gain valuable information in the war on terror. These authors insist that the necessity doctrine is compatible with the U.S. Constitution and a liberal democracy, something completely rejected by scholars such as Thomas Crocker. One of the primary reasons Crocker rejects this particular balancing of liberty with security is that the very balance used in this context is skewed in favor of security. As Crocker puts it,

> Recall that the image of balance imbedded in Justitia is that there is a single issue to be resolved, and the goddess must weigh the relative merits of arguments for each opposing side of that issue. The presumption is that there really are two robust sides to weigh. Balancing, in the hands of the apologists, has only one side—national security.[121]

The tradeoff, he suggests in contrast to the apologists, is made between the constitutional culture and institutional framework adopted by liberal democracies, on the one hand, and the challenges confronted by them during emergencies, on the other. As he puts it, "liberal democracies have committed to acting within certain broad constitutional constraints that respect human dignity and promote liberty, even if in so doing achieving some policy objectives is made more difficult. What liberal democracies really trade off is the easy resort to torture from the more difficult path of intelligence gathering free from such excuse."[122] Thus, Crocker rejects this favoring of security over liberty as incompatible with the constitutional culture of a liberal democracy.

Even though there is an obvious difference between the absolutist position against torture and the position in favor of using torture (however rarely) and institutionalizing it, the focus in this debate remains on the normative question of whether torture should or should not be used in liberal democracies. As noted earlier, the absolutist position leaves little space for addressing the legal and political pragmatics of torture. For our purpose, absolutist stances also tend to strengthen the assumption that torture is impermissible and to foreclose any in-depth analysis of this violence despite its presence in liberal democracies. In that sense, those analyzing the pragmatics of torture focus attention on the slipperiness of definitions and the significance of contexts and have to be squarely countered at those levels as well. Apart from the normative debate on torture, scholars in recent times have also studied the ways in which torture appears or reappears in a democracy. Central to that framework is the idea of torture as an exception.

Torture as an Exceptional Act

A number of scholars in both India and the United States have argued that the policies introduced in the "war on terror" constitute a "state of exception," a state in which laws applicable under ordinary times are suspended. In this context, Giorgio Agamben's work has been especially influential in conceptualizing state policies.[123] Agamben has argued that the post-9/11 context of the United States not only represents a state of exception but also reflects a process of an exception becoming a rule.[124] He considers the "unclassifiable and unnameable" status of the detainees in Guantánamo to be the perfect example of "bare life"—that is, a life reduced to being "subhuman," in a state of exception.[125] Within Agamben's framework, one could argue that torture only *now* has become a part of governing in a liberal democracy. Invoking an image similar to Agamben's, Amy Kaplan states that "Guantánamo would become the story of our future, our world where this 'floating colony will become the norm rather than the anomaly.'"[126] Similarly, Judith Butler put forward the concept of the "new war prison" to characterize the post-9/11 context.[127] This language of the state of exception is also reflected in the statements of U.S. government officials while characterizing the post-9/11 context. As President Bush stated in his memo in February 2002, the post-9/11 era is a "[n]ew paradigm" . . . that "requires a new thinking in the law of war."[128] Similarly, Judge Gonzales wrote in January 2002, "In my judgment, this *new paradigm* renders *obsolete* Geneva's strict limitations on questioning of enemy prisoners and renders *quaint* some of its provisions."[129] Thus, the language of "exception," "new paradigm," or "legal black hole" has gained currency in recent times, suggesting that the post-9/11 policies on torture and interrogation were the result of the suspension of preexisting laws.

Agamben bases his ideas regarding the state of exception on Carl Schmitt's conception that the "Sovereign is he who decides on the Exception."[130] The sovereign is the one who decides on all important aspects of the emergency. The sovereign declares the emergency, decides when to declare it, and makes all the decisions in relation to that time. For Agamben, it is not just totalitarian systems that deal with the problem of the state of exception. Rather, the state of exception is increasingly becoming more visible as a technique of government even in democracies. Within his framework, Guantánamo was a lawless exception where the sovereign (commander-in-chief) made a decision to suspend existing laws regarding detention and interrogation for the detainees. One could even add that since for Foucault, historically, the inscription of violence on the bodies of subjects was an integral part of the sovereign's power, the reemergence of torture inflicted on the bodies of enemy combatants as a direct result of the U.S. executive's orders is an indication of the reemergence of the all-powerful sovereign.

This framework of a state of exception in which all preexisting laws seem to be inapplicable is also the theoretical basis for the critique developed by human rights groups and scholars. For instance, Joseph Margulies, who has been a leading lawyer for the detainees at Guantánamo, explains that the very conceptualization of this space by the United States was that of a "lawless"[131] prison or a "prison beyond the law,"[132] thus representing abuse of power by the president. Explaining this dominant reading of Guantánamo, Fleur Johns notes, "By expressly disavowing the entitlement of detainees to certain due process guarantees enshrined in international law and US constitutional law, the US executive has, it is said, sought to create an abomination: a 'legal no man's land'; a place 'beyond the rule of law.'"[133] Thus, in popular conceptions, in national and international human rights critiques, and in the administration's own thinking, the dominant framework of analysis for Guantánamo has been that of the exception.[134]

In the context of India, even though analyses and critiques of the long history of extraordinary legislations regarding antiterrorism have always existed, more recently these policies have been explicitly conceptualized as "exceptional." As Ujjwal Singh writes, "central to extraordinary laws is the idea of 'exception,' since extraordinary laws are manifestations of situations, which are not ordinary or 'normal,' but 'emergent' and 'temporal.'"[135] Similarly, Mayur Suresh, in his analysis of extraordinary laws, emphasizes that in the context of India, "Exceptional and emergency laws have not been created by sovereign prerogative or by lawless acts of the state, but instead have been duly enacted by parliament, and have even received the stamp of approval from the Supreme Court."[136] While discussing the case of S. A. R. Geelani, a university professor who was picked up as a suspect in the December 13, 2001, attack on the Indian Parliament, Ananya Vajpayi used Agamben's formulation of "bare life" in the following way: "Consider this startling fact: S. A. R Geelani is the *homo sacer* of the Indian state, which seeks to bolster its fragile sovereignty by *sequestering this man, chosen at random, from every discourse of law,* justice, politics or religion, and killing him, plain and simple, *because it can.*"[137]

For Agamben, of course, the *homo sacer* is closely linked to the notion of the state of exception.[138] Thus, even in the context of India, scholars have used Agamben's framework to view as exceptional the extraordinary laws and the people impacted by them, thus reiterating Peter Fitzpatrick's point on the subject: "It has to be a puzzle how Giorgio Agamben's evocation of 'an obscure figure of archaic Roman law' has assumed such a purchase on recent political and philosophical thought."[139]

Agamben in his own work does acknowledge the close relationship between the routine and the exception and the blurriness of deciding whether the exception is inside or outside of law, and many Indian and U.S. scholars using his work also recognize this to some extent. However, for our purposes, there are two notable points in this discussion. First, the language of exception as a complete break from the routine has become such a dominant frame of analysis that it has almost assumed a life of its own such that the complexities in the formulations of these authors are lost. Consequently, the exception framework appears to reassert the understanding that extraordinary laws are "temporal" and "bounded" events that are completely distinct from the routine. Second, even when scholars analyze the relationship between the routine and the exception, their focus is more on how the exception stays beyond its stipulated time/region/people and consequently transforms the routine. In contrast, in this study, I focus on how the tensions in the routine context help in constituting the exception in democracies. Furthermore, for the torture debates, the exception framework suggests a return of torture or excess violence only in this new, extraordinary phase, thereby assuming that the routine discourse had ensured the impermissibility of excess violence. In the process, the exception framework obfuscates the fact that the violence, claimed by the state to be unnecessary, is a constantly negotiated category not only in exceptional contexts but also in routine times.

Connecting Law to Violence in Modern Societies

In my study, as noted earlier, I draw upon those critical theorists who focus on the close relationship between law and violence. However, I depart from their work in two significant ways. First, theorists such as Robert Cover argue that violence is an ontological part of law. I, however, agree with Jonathan Simon's critique of Cover, which is that by considering violence as an ontological part of law, Cover fails to look at the manifestations of violence in specific communities.[140] In addition, while Cover recognizes the relationship of law to violence, he gives a very "ahistorical" picture of this relationship—it becomes "essentialized," and the changing role of the various state actors in the different phases of history is not understood in a dynamic way.[141] Thus, while accepting that some coercion is inherent to law (as discussed in chapter 1), I argue that the relationship between law and excess violence is a constantly negotiated one and impacts different communities disparately. In that sense, I am somewhat sympathetic to Jeremy Waldron's critique of Sarat and Kearns, which is that they appear to ignore the distinctions between the different kinds of violence when, using Cover's work, they point to the inherent relation between law and violence. As Waldron puts it,

> Those, like Sarat and Kearns, who maintain dogmatically that law is always violent and that the most important feature about it is that it works its will in "a field of pain and death," . . . will be unimpressed by the distinctions I am making. For them, law's complicity with torture in the cases I have discussed is just business as usual.[142]

However, unlike Waldron, I also find Sarat and Kearns's framework extremely useful because there is a deliberate attempt in their work to foreground the significance of violence in law, which tends to be less important for others.

Second, both Kaufman-Osborn and Sarat seem to accept the Foucauldian assumption that excess violence is no longer used in law, at least in the context of the death penalty, such that execution by lethal injection can be analyzed theoretically as a "painless," "rationalized" procedure.[143] However, the change in the form of execution or torture may not necessarily lead to the complete disappearance of excess pain and suffering in liberal democracies.[144] As I explain in the next section, in both the democracies I study I illustrate that despite the claims made by liberal democracies, law is not able to contain excess violence entirely.

Connecting law to violence can be attempted in many ways, so it is important to clarify what I am not focusing on. In my study I focus on the jurisprudence of interrogations in the United States and India. Thus, I emphasize how the violence is connected to the law itself and not separate from it.[145] In other words, I do not just restrict my attention to the practices of torture at the sites of enforcement but rather find the connections between the enforcement and the legal decision making.

International institutions such as the United Nations and human rights groups such as Amnesty International are known for their path-breaking contributions on torture. Since their first major report on torture in 1975, Amnesty has emphasized that torture is a worldwide phenomenon and has continued to highlight the issue.[146] Over the decades, the group has focused on information about the torturers and their sponsor institutions, the socio-economic, legal, and political factors affecting torture, and the impact of torture on the victims.[147] Their reports also suggest that torture is linked to discrimination against women, children, and sexual minorities since they are often the targets.[148] Impunity on the part of the state is also identified by the Amnesty reports as a problem in the eradication of torture.

Over the decades, efforts by human rights groups and individuals have contributed to several initiatives by the United Nations, which puts pressure on its member countries to prohibit torture in their own contexts. Some of the prominent initiatives in this area are the UN Declaration on Protection from Torture in 1975, the UN Convention against Torture in 1984, which came into force in 1987, the Committee against Torture (CAT), the Special Rapporteur on Torture, and several regional treaties.[149] The UN and human rights organizations have contributed significantly toward highlighting the issue of torture and attempts to deal with it. However, my project is distinct from their framework because these initiatives are primarily concerned with the sites of violence or the sites of enforcement, and do not focus as much on the jurisprudence or official legal and political discourse, especially in the context of liberal democracies. In such initiatives, as Sarat and Kearns note, "Force and coercion are disconnected from law."[150] In liberal democracies, often the formal laws and legal safeguards against torture appear to have strong foundations. Only a careful examination of the legal discourse in relation to the practices of torture in these democracies allows for an analysis of the possible gaps therein, and that is the focus of my study.

Another way to connect law to violence would be to analyze the reasons underlying the persistence of torture in liberal democracies. Darius Rejali, in his monumental study, *Torture and Democracy,* notes that there are three different reasons for the continued persistence of torture in democracies that he explains through the following models: the national security model, the juridical model, and the civic discipline model. As Rejali explains, "In the National Security model . . . officers practice torture as part of a proactive strategy to combat an enemy in an emergency . . . [to gain] information."[151] The second model for the persistence of torture in democracy is the juridical model, in which the emphasis in the legal system itself is on confessions.[152] The third model for Rejali is the civic discipline model, in which certain sections of society end up bearing torture as a marker of their status in society, whether it be the marginalized sections in India and the United States or the immigrant sections in France or Italy.[153]

Rejali notes that more than one model can apply in one case and indeed strikingly writes that "in the study of torture, hell is in the details."[154] But the difficulty emerging from this classification is that different countries get associated with one particular model more than the other. For example, in his discussion of the juridical model, Rejali focuses on Japan as a perfect example of a reliance on confessions. This framework suggests that other countries may not rely on confessions as much. In contrast, in both the United States and India, there is an overreliance on confessions, as has been pointed out by Peter Brooks and Ujjwal Singh (and as discussed in chapters 1 and 5). Similarly, while each of Rejali's models focuses on the "political enemy," the "criminal," and the "marginal citizen," respectively, in countries such as India, the conflations and overlapping among the three categories of people make the persistence of torture even more complex (as discussed in chapter 5).

More recently, John T. Parry, in a fascinating book, points to the role that torture and violence play in society. As Parry puts it,

> My point is that torture sits on a continuum of violent state practices, where the use of these forms of violence by modern states as a *way of regulating populations* is far more significant than whether "torture" is the particular form of violence used. Indeed, one could say that violence or the threat of violence against any political subject is a basic aspect of governance.[155]

In this study, however, I focus less on why torture persists in liberal democracies than on understanding how torture (which I consider to be a form of excess violence) continues to exist in liberal democracies. In other words, I study the ways in which the legal discourse itself addresses the question of torture to illustrate the ways in which law's relationship with excess violence gets constantly negotiated.

Theorizing Torture in Liberal Democracies

Torture has been defined in many different ways over the years, such that there is difficulty in identifying one standard definition of torture. One of the more well-known definitions of torture is, of course, propounded by the UN Convention against Torture and Other Cruel, Inhuman, or Degrading Treatment or Punishment, which defines torture as any act by which severe pain or suffering, whether physical or mental, is intentionally inflicted on a person for such purposes as obtaining from him or a third person information or a confession, punishing him for an act he or a third person has committed or is suspected of having committed, or intimidating or coercing him or a third person, or for any reason based on discrimination of any kind, when such pain or suffering is inflicted by or at the instigation of or with the consent or acquiescence of a public official or other person acting in an official capacity. It does not include pain or suffering arising only from, inherent in or incidental to lawful sanctions.[156]

The UN definition of torture is a culmination of intense discussions and deliberations and is definitely a point of reference for both international and national discussions on torture.[157] However, in this study, I do not adopt the UN definition of torture as the only point of reference by which to study the jurisprudence of interrogations in liberal democracies, for two reasons. First, both the countries that I am focusing on—India and the United States—have a very different relationship with the UN Convention. India has signed the Convention against Torture but has not ratified it, while the United States has both signed and ratified the treaty but with reservations, the implications and interpretations of which are discussed in chapter 2. Second, and more significantly, neither of the two countries has adopted the UN Convention's definition of torture as the sole official definition in regards to its jurisprudence on interrogations, either historically or in contemporary times.

Thus, in the context of these two democracies, I focus on the legal discourses emerging from the constitutional, statutory, and/or judicial safeguards against the use of torture in interrogations. The starting point of my study is the claim by liberal democracies that torture is completely impermissible in a democracy—a claim made long before the UN initiatives. In the absence of a standard definition of torture, I focus on the gradual development of these safeguards in these two democracies and analyze whether the jurisprudence has unequivocally prohibited the acts of torture.[158]

Although I focus on interrogations in this study, torture is obviously not an issue only in this context. Rather, as the UN Convention's definition indicates, torture has been used in the context of punishment, discrimination, or intimidation, sometimes being used for more than one purpose. More broadly, torture can also be understood as a form of violence that "destroys the capacity to communicate," as Robert Cover and Elaine Scarry point out, or as a form of "complete domination," as John Parry argues.[159] I focus on interrogations because, as discussed earlier, historically torture has been integrally related to confessions and the extraction of evidence and information within the legal system. And ironically, in the case of both India and the United States, one of the contexts in which the debates on torture have reemerged is the interrogation of "terrorists" in the "war on terror," although the use of torture is, by no means, restricted to that site alone.

The main argument of my study is that the recent debates on torture have to be analyzed as a manifestation of the liberal state's inability to contain excess violence. Regardless of whether there is a consensus that these acts of excess violence constitute torture in all instances, I argue that it is in fact the contentious definition of torture that allows the legal and political discourse to ignore, accommodate, or justify torture in some instances. In the study, I primarily use the term "excess violence" in my attempts to understand the debates on torture. "Excess violence" is a term I reclaim from Foucaldian literature and define as a constantly negotiated category that exists on a continuum of acts ranging from coercion to torture. Here the category of excess violence is conceptually distinct from coercion inherent in state action and the "necessary pain" allowed by the state. The latter is captured well in Jeremy Waldron's reference to the coercion inherent in penalties and confinement. However, for Waldron, the inherent coercion in law suggests the importance of the prohibition of torture as a legal archetype. As he puts it,

> So when I say that the prohibition on torture is an archetype of our determination to draw a line between law and savagery or brutality, I am not looking piously to some paradise of force-free law, but rather to the well-understood idea that law can be forceful without compromising the dignity of those whom it constrains and punishes.[160]

However, what this kind of formulation does is to create a binary between torture on one hand and inherent coercion on the other, not recognizing both that there is a continuum between the two that is not explored in the process and that these are constantly negotiated categories—historically and empirically. While the difficulties in defining "inherent coercion" and "necessary pain" are significant for debates on law and violence, this study primarily focuses on the "excess pain and suffering" that the liberal states themselves claim to be "unnecessary" and yet, my study shows, continues to be allowed. The category of excess violence is used precisely to capture the constant difficulty of defining and distinguishing among different forms of state violence: torture, cruel, inhuman, degrading, humiliating treatment, and coercion. The larger theoretical argument that I develop in the study (in chapter 2 as an illustration and in the conclusion more broadly) is that the Foucaldian analysis of state power has to be reconceptualized to acknowledge the role of excess violence as a feature of governmentality in contemporary liberal democracies.

In chapter 1, I analyze U.S. legal discourses by historically tracing the constitutional mechanisms that constitute protections against torture and note the ambiguities regarding excess violence expressed in routine discourses, particularly in situations of necessity. In chapter 2, I focus on the legal discourse on torture in the post-9/11 United States to analyze whether policies on interrogation and torture constitute a "state of exception" or represent a continuity in state policies. The main argument is to point to the continuities between the routine and the exception, and to suggest different modes through which the liberal state struggles to accommodate excess violence such as by the creation of the juridico-medical apparatus.

In chapter 3, I explore how the popular imagery of torture, such as in the U.S. TV show 24, both informs the legal and political discourse on torture and is reconstituted by it. The significance of analyzing the popular imagery of torture is that it establishes legitimacy for narrow legal definitions of torture. Further, the official and popular discourses create space for apparently less severe forms of violence through the use of sanitized terms and comparison with routine activities. In chapter 4, I analyze the dominant explanations for the persistence of torture in India and in addition explore how the jurisprudence of interrogations in postcolonial India addresses the issue of torture and point to law's continuing struggle to contain excess violence. In chapter 5, I focus on two major legal regimes that represent the extraordinary legislations on interrogations and confessions in contemporary India, namely, the Terrorism and Disruptive Activities (Prevention) Act (TADA) and the Prevention of Terrorism Act (POTA). In the chapter, I point to the ways in which the ambivalence in the jurisprudence of interrogations regarding torture and excess violence expressed in the routine discourse plays a constitutive role in the formation of exceptional laws. Finally, I conclude with some theoretical formulations on law, violence, and state power emerging from the transnational debates on torture.

1

Law's Struggle with Violence

Ambivalence in the "Routine" Jurisprudence of Interrogations in the United States

> It is sufficient to say that in pertinent respects the transcript reads more like pages torn from some medieval account, than a record made within the confines of a modern civilization which aspires to an enlightened constitutional government.
>
> —*Brown v. Mississippi* (1936)[1]

In the post-9/11 context, when a debate ensued in the media about whether torture could be used against suspected terrorists in the United States, even the debate itself was characterized as a radical break from previous eras. When Jonathan Alter wrote immediately after the 9/11 attacks that "in this autumn of anger, even a liberal can find his thoughts turning to torture," the responses to his article reflected the prevailing sentiment against torture.[2] Readers wrote passionately that contemplating torture is similar to "going back into the middle ages," is "traitorous to the ideals that keep America on the high moral ground," and "negates the values on which our civilization was founded."[3]

The debate itself seemed a radical break from previous eras because torture was considered impermissible in the United States. As noted earlier, in the reigning discourse, prohibition of torture represents a defining feature of a "civilized" liberal democracy. Most of all, the existence of torture becomes the point of distinction between democratic and nondemocratic systems. Since torture continues in a more blatant manner in many nondemocracies, its persistence also strengthens the claims that democracies do not allow this form of violence.[4] In addition to the rhetoric against torture, there are actual formal provisions applicable to torture that back this claim in democracies. However, a close reading of the legal and political discourse regarding torture in one such democracy, namely, the United States, indicates a more complex story.

34

In this chapter, I analyze the U.S. legal discourse on torture by historically tracing the mechanisms in the Constitution that serve as protections from torture: the due process clause (Fourteenth and Fifth Amendments), the prohibition against cruel and unusual punishment (Eighth Amendment), and the guarantee of the right against self-incrimination (Fifth Amendment). Given the focus on interrogations in this study, I focus on the jurisprudence concerning the Fifth and the Fourteenth Amendments of the U.S. Constitution.[5]

A study of the jurisprudence of interrogations suggests that while the political rhetoric and formal law unequivocally claim that torture is impermissible in the United States, this protection from torture is fraught with challenges. Specifically, what the formal discourse conceals in its claim of freedom from torture is the gradual nature of this negotiation and the continuing struggle of the jurisprudence with excess violence. The chapter concludes by asserting that while extreme forms of torture, primarily physical torture (Brown model), are unequivocally prohibited by the legal discourse, there is ambiguity regarding several other forms of excess violence that exist at the borders of legality and illegality. While there may not be unanimity about the characterization of some of these forms of violence as torture, I argue that it is in fact the lack of clarity on the nature of violence prohibited by the legal discourse that makes it significant for debates on torture. The chapter illustrates a continuing accommodation of excess violence by the U.S. jurisprudence that is particularly visible in situations of necessity. Thus, the chapter points to a central problem in liberal democracies, namely, the law's continuing struggle with excess violence, not just in extraordinary times but also in routine contexts.

A Chronology of "Progress" against Torture

In this section, I briefly present what I term the chronology of "progress" against torture by discussing how the Supreme Court has addressed the issue of torture and excess violence in interrogations. In the United States, there have been predominantly three regimes of constitutional protections that are relevant to our study of torture in interrogations—the voluntariness doctrine related to the Fifth Amendment right against self-incrimination (Bram model), voluntariness related to the due process clause of the Fourteenth Amendment (Brown model), and the Miranda regime related to the Fifth Amendment (Miranda model).

The first major case that connected the Fifth Amendment prohibition of compulsion to incriminate oneself in trials with the concern for voluntariness in confessions during interrogations was *Bram v. United States* (1897). The Fifth Amendment of the United States Constitution states that "[n]o person . . . shall be compelled in any criminal case to be a witness against himself," and Bram extended this right in trials to interrogations.[6] Bram, a U.S. sailor, was taken into custody for questioning related to a crime committed on an overseas American vessel and made some self-incriminating statements. The Supreme Court, however, noted that the circumstances under which the admission was made by Bram rendered it involuntary. The Court pointed out that the accused considered himself a prisoner of the police at Halifax, had no access to a U.S. counsel, and was ignorant of his status vis-à-vis U.S. or local law. Bram was asked to come in for an interview and subsequently ordered to strip by a foreign detective and, thereafter, interrogated. The Court stated that these conditions constituted "compulsion or inducement." The admission could not be considered free and voluntary under the circumstances because Bram may have spoken due to fear of hurting himself by keeping quiet or due to a hope of benefiting by speaking. Using the Fifth Amendment in the case, the Supreme Court wrote,

> The human mind under the pressure of calamity, is easily seduced; and is liable, in the alarm of danger, to acknowledge indiscriminately a falsehood or a truth, as different agitations may prevail. A confession, therefore, whether made upon an official examination or in discourse with private persons, which is obtained from a defendant, either by flattery of hope, or by the impressions of fear, *however slightly the emotions may be implanted*, is not admissible evidence; for the law will not suffer a prisoner to be made the deluded instrument of his own conviction.[7]

Thus, in Bram, the Court emphasized that complete voluntariness in confessions excludes even the slightest pressure of hope or fear. The previous concern in involuntary confessions had been unreliability of information, but now, focus on the circumstances of interrogation was an important principle to be upheld and served as a protection against compulsion, coercion, and violence of any kind.[8]

After Bram, the Fifth Amendment did not really become the standard for determining the admissibility of confessions for all cases. This is primarily the case because the Fifth Amendment was not applicable to the states until 1964, and it was the Fourteenth Amendment due process clause that was initially applied to state confessions.[9] The issue of torture has, thus, been considered primarily in the context of the voluntariness doctrine related to the due process clause of the Fourteenth Amendment.

It is the *Brown v. Mississippi* case in 1936 that epitomizes the U.S. protections against torture. Indeed, it is the single most frequently cited case on torture and confessions in the pre-9/11 constitutional law case books, exemplifying the significance of the case for U.S. jurisprudence on interrogations.[10] This case arose in the context of southern treatment of African Americans in the era of Jim Crow. The case involved the indictments of three black men accused of murdering a white man, and the question for the Court was whether convictions of the defendants primarily based on confessions "extorted by brutality and violence" were consistent with the due process of law mandated by the Fourteenth Amendment. This was only one in a series of cases against African Americans charged with interracial crimes, particularly rape and murder, who were subjected to the worst kind of police abuse to gain confessions.[11] In the case, the defendants claimed that the confessions were false and had been obtained by physical torture unaddressed by the trial court and admitted despite objections from the counsel.

In the case, one of the defendants was hanged on a tree and whipped again and again on two different days by a deputy accompanied by a mob until he agreed to make the confession. The two other defendants were whipped with leather straps after being stripped by the deputy sheriff and forced to confess in great detail as prompted by the deputy sheriff, jailors, and a mob. The Supreme Court was shocked at the facts of the case and stated that due process required the state to ensure that the action did not "offend some principle of justice so rooted in the traditions and conscience of [our] people as to be ranked as fundamental."[12] One of the important principles suggested by the Court as a result was that "the rack and torture chamber may not be substituted for the witness stand" and that all state actions had to follow the "fundamental principles of liberty and justice."[13] The Supreme Court, thus, found the state action in the case not only unacceptable but revolting and completely rejected the confessions derived from physical torture.

Despite the landmark nature of this decision jurisprudentially, according to Michael Klarman, the impact of Brown is difficult to assess due to lack of information on the exact amount of physical coercion used in the South. However, he suggests that given the blatantly racist attitude of the sheriff during the trial and the infrequency of cases of torture reaching the courts, the practice of beating blacks to extort confessions may have actually continued long after the Brown case.[14]

Subsequent cases, such as *Ashcraft v. Tennessee* (1944), extended the protections against involuntary confessions as a result of physical torture to persistent and prolonged questioning, though the latter cases were mostly divided decisions. For instance, in Ashcraft, the case involved the conviction of a husband in his wife's murder as an accessory before the fact. He was questioned for thirty-six hours incommunicado without sleep or rest, and the Supreme Court decided that this interrogation was "so inherently coercive that its very existence is irreconcilable with the possession of mental freedom by a lone suspect against whom its full coercive force [was] brought to bear."[15] However, even in this case, the dissent did state that questioning for thirty-six hours did not necessarily lead to inadmissibility of evidence despite the coerciveness.[16] According to most scholars, in this phase, while there seemed to be a consensus about the Brown case, there was rarely unanimity about the due process violations in cases in which the interrogation fell short of physical torture and brutality.[17] The Court, however, did develop the voluntariness doctrine, in which the emphasis was not only on the unworthiness of the admissions but also on an attempt to ensure that the confessions were a result of "rational intellect and free will" and not an "overborne will."[18] The inconsistent results of the voluntariness doctrine, however, could not stand the scrutiny of the Court's own endeavor to deal with coerced confessions, and there was a gradual move by the Court towards the Miranda model.[19]

One of the major protections under the Fifth Amendment, as a result, has been the translation of the privilege against self-incrimination into safeguards known as the Miranda rights. In *Miranda v. Arizona* (1966), the Court stated that a person has to be rendered explicit warnings before being subjected to custodial questioning.[20] The main question in Miranda was whether statements acquired from the suspects during custodial interrogation could be introduced as evidence in a trial in the absence of procedural safeguards protecting the Fifth Amendment. The case involved four individual defendants in four different cases who had been subjected to interrogation without adequate safeguards, including a right to counsel.[21] The Court decided that neither exculpatory nor inculpatory statements made during custodial interrogation were admissible if certain procedural safeguards regarding the privilege against self-incrimination were not ensured. The Court followed the logic of Bram that the Fifth Amendment privilege essentially represents the right not to incriminate oneself, emerging historically from the reactions against the star chamber oath in seventeenth-century England and transported to the United States as a person's right to "remain silent unless he chooses to speak in the unfettered exercise of his own will."[22] The Court notes that just as a "'noble principle often transcends its origins," so the privilege has come rightfully to be recognized in part as an individual's substantive right, a "right to a private enclave where he may lead a private life. That right is the hallmark of our democracy."[23] In order to convict a person, the Court noted, law enforcement had to get evidence against a suspect through "its own independent labors, rather than by the cruel, simple expedient of compelling it from his own mouth."[24] The emphasis on the right to a private enclave where individual integrity was protected emerged clearly in the Miranda discussions despite the divided nature of the decision. As a result, after Miranda, the Court considered the Fifth Amendment applicable to the protection of individuals from compelled confessions not only during trials but also during custodial interrogations by law enforcement officials.

Thus, the story of legal protections against torture and, indeed, excess violence of any kind appears to have moved smoothly and chronologically from Bram to Brown to the Miranda warnings, the latter suggesting that violence could no longer even be an issue in interrogations. In the process, there appeared to be little focus on how law actually interacted with violence jurisprudentially. Each of the significant cases on interrogations in its own way stood in as final answers on law's relationship to violence despite never specifying the exact nature of violence. Questions such as the following were often left unanswered. What do these protections against torture actually represent? What is the violence that the jurisprudence allows and disallows? What are the parameters of pain and suffering permitted in interrogations?

In this sense, other arenas of law's struggle with violence have developed very distinctly from the jurisprudence of interrogations. The jurisprudence emerging from the Eighth Amendment protection against cruel and unusual punishment and, in particular, the death penalty debates has a completely different history. There has been an extremely public jurisprudential debate on the amount of pain that can be inflicted in state killing. The methods of execution have changed accordingly from hanging to electric chair to lethal injection.[25] But more significantly, the courts have often engaged in determining the amount of necessary pain and suffering that could accompany state killing and have clarified that the execution has to avoid "wanton" and "unnecessary" pain. As Justice Stewart stated in *Gregg v. Georgia* (1976),[26]

When a form of punishment in the abstract . . . is under consideration, the inquiry into "excessiveness" has two aspects. First, the punishment must not involve the unnecessary and wanton infliction of pain. . . . Second, the punishment must not be grossly out of proportion to the severity of the crime.[27]

As recently as 2008, the Court looked into whether lethal injection, the most humane form of execution to date, constitutes cruel and unusual punishment, examining whether the current drug protocol necessarily causes pain to the convicted.[28] The difficulty in determining the precise meaning and scope of terms such as "wanton" and "unnecessary" pain has led to fascinating debates among both the justices and critical theorists—the latter pointing to the irresolvable tensions within the jurisprudence.[29] However, the fact remains that this history has allowed the jurisprudence on the Eighth Amendment to address issues of pain and suffering—physical and mental— in the sphere of state killing.

In contrast, there is an absence of such agonizing over the exact meanings of violence in the routine jurisprudence of interrogations. This raises a question whether the lack of clarity on excess violence in interrogations is a function of the status of torture in liberal legal systems. Since torture is assumed to be absent in a democracy, it is never fully theorized. When torture does appear, the conflation of "physical torture" with "torture" makes the nonphysical forms of torture and excess violence even less the focus of discussion. Thus, the dominant narrative about the jurisprudence of interrogations seems to be the gradual but complete eradication of violence in interrogations but is actually an obfuscation of the law's struggle with violence historically and in contemporary times. Yet, the formal protections against torture allow a politics of denial to emerge in U.S. society when acts of torture do become a matter of debate in public discourse.

Countering the Politics of Denial: Wickersham Commission Report

> We would never allow something like that to happen, so it could not have happened.
>
> —Stanley Cohen, 2001[30]

One of the vexing issues in the post-9/11 context was the consistent denial by President Bush and other U.S. officials that torture was ever authorized for the "war on terror." With the photographs, memos, reports, and testimonies of torture from Guantánamo Bay in Cuba, Abu Ghraib prison in Iraq, the prison at Bagram in Afghanistan, and numerous other "dark" sites, it is extremely difficult for U.S. officials to really claim that they did not authorize torture. But here I move away, for the moment, from the facticity of the claim to explore the importance of the politics of denial, which by no means is a new phenomenon. States, whether totalitarian or democratic, rarely proclaim that they torture, but the latter are more careful about maintaining the legitimacy of their institutions and their legal prohibitions against torture.[31] Thus, it is not surprising that there are strong denials in democracies when allegations of torture occur. The nature of denials in the post-9/11 context remains the backdrop of this discussion, but here I wish to point to the recurrent cycles of denial that exist in a democracy. Specifically, I explore a narrative of denial in the context of a government commission report—the Wickersham Commission Report—instituted precisely to look into the prevalence of the third degree in the 1930s United States. The politics of denial that the Wickersham Commission Report encounters and effectively challenges reflects the strength of the notion of the impermissibility of torture in liberal democracies, which stems from the presence of legal safeguards despite the ongoing practices of torture.

In 1931, a National Commission on Law Observance and Enforcement headed by George W. Wickersham was set up that brought out fourteen reports, and one of them was a report on the third degree, called *Report on Lawlessness in Law Enforcement,* written by Zechariah Chafee Jr., Walter H. Pollack, and Carl S. Stern (referred to hereafter as the Wickersham Commission Report).[32] According to the Wickersham Commission Report, despite the well-established legal stipulations against the use of torture in the United States, torture, or the third degree, continued to be an issue of concern.[33] The Wickersham Commission Report noted that between 1920 and 1930, there were sixty-seven cases in the appellate courts where there was no doubt about the use of the third degree for confessions and thirty-nine cases with some doubt or inconsistencies. The report also stated that this was only a "small proportion" of actual instances of the third degree, since many cases never reached the courts or were "weeded out" of the case load even before they came up for appeal. The report's study of fifteen U.S. cities also showed prevalent use of the third degree. The Wickersham Commission concluded that despite the difficulties in collecting data due to the secrecy involved in the use of the third degree, there was no doubt about a widespread existence of the third degree in the United States.[34] In the report, "third degree" meant "the employment of methods which inflict suffering, physical or mental, upon a person in order to obtain information about a crime."[35] The definition of "third degree" thus included both mental and physical suffering, and the term "severe" was not specifically used as a prefix to these forms of suffering, in contrast to the contemporary definitions of torture such as those of the UN Convention and the U.S. Federal Torture Statute.[36] Forms of the third degree ranged from physical brutality such as whipping and beating with fists to forms of mental (and other) violence that included "softening-up" methods such as sleep and food deprivation during illegal detention and protracted questioning.

According to Edward Peters, the specificity of this kind of torture has to be situated in the history of the origin of the police force. Policing is where the third degree took place in the United States, as opposed to "judicial torture" in Europe.[37] Peters suggests that the independent functioning of the police allowed them to use the third degree, or torture, in their functioning to fulfill their role as the defenders of law and order. It was mainly after the Wickersham Commission Report that the police became associated with the judiciary and the Constitution.[38] Prior to that, the admittance of confessions in judicial trials, particularly in the lower courts, as recorded by the Wickersham Commission Report, indicates that the judiciary was also not totally against the use of the third degree at the time.

Apart from the startling conclusions about the pervasiveness of torture in the United States, another noticeable fact about the Wickersham Report was the presence of a debate on whether torture even exists in a democracy. There were several police officials who asserted that the third degree was an act of the past and that if torture took place at all, it was not a regular pattern. This denial of the persistence of torture even at a time when a government commission on the third degree was instituted is extremely suggestive of the tension between the use of torture and its denial by the dominant political and legal discourse of a democratic society concerned to reiterate its liberal credentials.

Stanley Cohen, in his fascinating work, *States of Denial*, discusses three different kinds of classic official denials in the context of torture and other atrocities: literal denial (no torture), interpretive denial (something happened but not torture), and implicatory denial (it happened but was necessary).[39] In this section, I employ Cohen's categories to illustrate the different kinds of denial apparent in the 1920s and 1930s United States. Cohen writes that the more repressive and authoritarian regimes find it easier to literally deny that anything happened at all. This is the case because of an absence of "internal counterclaims" within their societies due to tight state control over the media and little outside scrutiny. But even democratic states sometimes adopt a policy of literal denial because of their formal adherence to the official declaration of human rights.[40] Indeed, a close examination of the writings of the police officials in the early 1900s reflects several instances of literal denial by them about the use of the third degree.

The Wickersham Commission Report notes that in the International Association of Chiefs of Police (IACP) annual meeting in 1910, the president of the association asserted that the concerns of the police had shifted to probation and detention homes and the more "humane treatment of offenders" and claimed that this shift clearly indicated that torture was no longer used. The IACP even attempted to set up a committee to "refute" the findings of the commission.[41] Even though the Wickersham Commission showed that the third degree was present throughout the country, the chiefs' denial was interesting because it was predicated on the presence of formal safeguards regarding their roles. Further, if torture did not actually exist, someone created the narrative and here many of the chiefs pointed to the media, especially yellow journalism, as the creators of the torture narrative, the exaggerated reports, and the sensationalized notions about the third degree.[42] This defense was clearly accepted even by the famous jurist John Henry Wigmore, who wrote, "There is probably much popular misunderstanding on this subject [how often violence is used by police officers to get confessions], due largely to the exploitation of a few instances by the reckless press and the doctrinaire critics of government."[43] Apart from the critics and the media, the police also found the defense lawyers to be equally implicated in this act. As Matheson, a captain of detectives in 1929, explained in an article, "In plain English, all this anti-third-degree nonsense is to prevent the introduction of rebuttal testimony in criminal cases."[44]

The denials by the police chiefs were both literal and interpretive. Cohen explains interpretive denial as an assertion that "what is happening is really something else." In other words, there is some acknowledgment that something happened, but what happened is not understood as torture. Cohen writes, "The harm is cognitively reframed and then reallocated to a different, less pejorative class of event."[45] According to Cohen, usually the legal and commonsense meaning of the term is interpretively denied in four ways: through euphemism, legalism, isolation, and denial of responsibility. The latter two can be best illustrated by the U.S. police chiefs' attempt in the 1900s to explain the occasional use of the third degree by aberrant individuals (isolation) while denying their own role in authorizing the actions (denial of responsibility). These two strategies have reappeared in the "few bad apples" theory and in the denial of responsibility by U.S. officials regarding the Abu Ghraib prison in 2004. Euphemism is best exemplified by the language of "enhanced interrogation techniques" being used in post-9/11 Guantánamo to deny the narratives of torture. Legalism, or the use of law to negate the presence of an act, also contributes toward a denial. As Cohen brilliantly puts it, "Then comes the magical syllogism: torture is strictly forbidden in our country; we have ratified the Convention Against Torture; therefore what we are doing cannot be torture."[46] In President Bush's assertions that "we don't torture people in America. And people who make that claim just don't know anything about our country"[47] is as much a moral claim as it is a claim based on legalism.

Cohen's categories of interpretive denial do explain the post-9/11 state denials as well as the actions of the chiefs of police in the 1930s, which forsake responsibility for the "isolated" incidents of torture by pointing to the presence of legal safeguards. However, in the case of these police chiefs, an interesting linguistic puzzle also emerges; here the police do not need to use a euphemism as a strategy of denial. This is the case because the pejorative term that is being denied is not "torture" but the popular notion of the third degree. As Richard Leo notes, "The term 'third degree' connotes, in American folklore, extreme interrogation."[48] The origin of the term "third degree," even according to the Wickersham Commission Report, is usually explained in the following way: arrest as the first degree, confinement as the second degree, and interrogation as the third degree. The report, of course, considers an act to be third degree only if it was accompanied by "mental or physical suffering." However, the origin of this term itself does not imply the infliction of pain and suffering that became commonly associated with the popular notion of this term. Thus, in contrast to the meaning of torture linked to suffering, Bingham (a police official) could claim that the media merely exaggerated or created the meaning of this term. "The third degree is neither more nor less than a severe cross-examination—not under oath—and in no respect worse than many of those grilling cross-examinations to which witnesses, on oath, are subjected by lawyers in open court—to which no objection has yet been raised."[49] Thus, the police claim to be the victims in this narrative of exaggeration by the media or the critics. Instead of denying the presence of the third degree itself, here the attempt was to indignantly reclaim the original meaning of the term from its exaggerated popular notions. The narrative for the police was that they were just questioning or interrogating or using the third degree, which is a necessary part of their jobs, thereby creating a separation between a necessary act and its unnecessary vilification. Thus, the interpretive denial appears in an additional way beyond Cohen's categories of euphemism in terms of reclaiming what I call the "original meaning" of the term. Here the linguistic distinction between the horror always associated with the very term "torture" and the third degree linked "originally" to mere questioning becomes another source of denial.

Sometimes, the police chiefs also found a way to justify whatever they were ostensibly not doing, thereby utilizing the implicatory denial based on necessity that Cohen points to. As Bingham explains,

> Let us face the facts honestly and fearlessly. Society, in a thousand years, has learned that it must protect itself *by force*. The police are the guardians of civilization and of progress. They are and must be an instrument of force, not of philanthropy or polite persuasion; and they must be backed up by society at its peril.[50]

Even though Bingham does not explain what the nature of the force would be, he does emphasize the importance of using force to protect society. Thus, in addition to emphasizing the original meaning—mere questioning—which no one could deny was a legitimate activity, the police attached questioning to coercion as necessarily following it. This emphasis on coercion as accompanying the legitimate activity of interrogation without complete clarification of the nature of the coercion is a core issue of the interrogation debate that continues even in the Miranda regime to be discussed shortly.

What is the significance of this politics of denial that appears and reappears in liberal democracies? I suggest that the politics of denial, encountered even by a commission meant to investigate the third degree, reflects the notion of impermissibility of torture that exists in democracies by virtue of the presence of formal legal safeguards and the chronology of "progress" represented by landmark decisions.

The politics of denial was, of course, squarely countered by the Wickersham Commission Report primarily because there were other reports and studies quoted by the 1931 report that indicated the prevalence of both physical and mental kinds of third degree.[51] Indeed, the fact of the third degree was so well known in the 1920s and 1930s that one could invoke Michael Taussig's notion of the "public secret" to characterize this phenomenon. The information about the act is shared yet repressed such that it "*is generally known, but cannot be articulated.*"[52] The Wickersham Report is radical precisely because it attempts to document and expose the public secret. As Leo notes, "Before publication of the Wickersham Commission Report in 1931, the police largely succeeded in keeping the third degree from becoming a major public scandal."[53] The Wickersham Commission Report boldly exposed the third degree but ended up with very mild recommendations. In fact, Samuel Walker criticizes the report for this, suggesting that perhaps the nature of the report was so critical that the recommendations actually reflected a compromise.[54] Welsh White also writes that the report's "unequivocal" "condemnation" of the third degree was not accompanied by any recommendation for "sweeping changes."[55] Taussig asserts that a public secret is a truth waiting to be revealed. However, the lack of conclusions and recommendations for reform suggests that the nature of the revelations was so threatening that the practices of the third degree were returned to the status of the "public secret." Even though the Wickersham Commission went a long way in exposing the pervasiveness of the third degree, the lack of strong recommendations meant that the inquiry itself ended up standing in for any major impact of the act. Furthermore, over time, the report became a symbol of primarily addressing the physical third degree, even though the report itself adopted a broader definition of the third degree.

The politics of denial that appeared in the early 1900s came from the police, whether in the Wickersham Commission Report or in legal and police journals. But even the judiciary did not directly address torture till 1936. This was the case despite the fact that several reports, including the Wickersham Commission Report, highlighted not just the practice of the third degree in the United States but also the fact that judicial decisions accepted some of the evidence attained through the third degree. In the 1931 report, the number of reversals in the appellate courts due to the use of third-degree confessions was forty-five out of sixty-seven (and one with doubtful third degree) cases.[56] Thus, even in the cases where there seemed to be no doubt about the third degree, the cases were not necessarily reversed. Gradually, when the Court did start intervening, sometimes it struggled in terms of its motivation for intervention: to prevent violence and unreliable confessions, or to preserve its own legitimacy as a normative institution.

Court as a Normative Institution

Martin Shapiro, in his classic work on courts, *Court: A Comparative and Political Analysis*, points to the existential concern of the courts—the quest for legitimacy.[57] He writes, "A substantial portion of the total behavior of courts in all societies can be analyzed in terms of attempts to prevent the triad from breaking down into two against one."[58] Shapiro argues that every function of the court, whether it be conflict resolution, social control, or policy making, points to the basic instability of the triad due to the potential for partiality toward a particular individual or regime. Shapiro concludes, "Thus, while the triadic mode of conflict resolution is nearly universal, courts remain problematical in the sense that considerable tension invariably exists between their fundamental claims to legitimacy and their actual operations."[59]

Yet, in law and political science, the centrality of the courts cannot be questioned precisely because of their perceived independence and neutrality from all other institutions, namely, the political branches that nominated the justices (say at the U.S. Supreme Court level) and the popular democratic pressures in society. Whether that makes the courts less political, less attitudinal, or less strategic is a matter of intense debate in political science and empirical legal studies, but nonetheless, almost all these streams accept a strong assumption about the independence of the courts as an institution that the justices insist on and that these scholars seek to either uphold or question.[60] The courts' obsession with legitimacy then occasionally also mediates the jurisprudence, including that of interrogations, in specific but influential ways.

Here, I recall a moment in legal history when the significance of maintaining the legitimacy of the courts became a greater motivation for a judge than the need to outlaw violence in any form. In the *Brown v. Mississippi* case in 1936, one of the most powerful denunciations of torture is found in the state court's dissenting opinion by Judge Griffith that is quoted by the U.S. Supreme Court. The dissenting opinion recounts the horrors of torture in this case, noting that "the pincers, the rack, the hose, the third degree or their equivalent, are still in use."[61] He takes a strong position against these methods, which are reminiscent of the star chambers and inquisitions, and states that "it [the trial] was never anything but a fictitious continuation of the mob which originally instituted and engaged in the admitted tortures." But in addition, he also adds the following.

It may be that in a rarely occasional case which arouses the flaming indignation of a whole community, as was the case here, we shall continue yet for a long time to have outbreaks of the mob or resorts to its methods. But, if mobs and mob methods must be, it would be better tha[t] their existence and their methods shall be kept wholly separate from the courts; that there shall be no blending of the devices of the mob and of the proceedings of the courts; *that what the mob has so nearly completed let them finish;* and that no court shall by adoption *give legitimacy* to any of the works of the mob, nor cover by the frills and furbelows of a pretended legal trial the body of that which in fact is the product of the mob, and then, by closing the eyes to actualities, complacently adjudicate that the law of the land has been observed and preserved.[62]

A judge strongly against the tortures of the past still makes a distinction between the mob completing the process and the court legitimizing it. Here the irony is even more apparent because he is the main dissenting voice in the state court's opinion, strongly voicing his protest against the torture. Yet even he cannot restrain himself from expressing that the basic issue for him is the court's representation of itself rather than the protection of the human dignity of an individual. Does, at that moment, representation overtake the concern for the individual and the values that form the basis of the institution? More significantly, has the image of the courts as being the bearer of the values of a liberal society become more important than the protection from torture itself? The court as a bearer of liberal values of independence, impartiality, and rules providing its legitimacy cannot be seen as engaged in violence, precisely the violence that the mobs are engaged in. After all, that is what differentiates the mobs from the legal actor. Yet the Griffin opinion of the state court refuses to take responsibility for addressing the brutal violence per se, choosing instead to emphasize the court's own legitimacy.

In Brown, the Supreme Court did overturn the state court's decision and certainly did not make this distinction between intervening for the sake of its own legitimacy and addressing the violence. Thus, is the dissenting opinion just an anomaly? In the contemporary post-9/11 context, to remind oneself of the dissenting opinion is to note that the current Supreme Court has not addressed the question of torture squarely and has not taken up any case of torture directly. The question is whether a discussion of torture by a highly divided Court today would delegitimize the Court as a normative institution. As narratives of physical and mental torture abound in the legal and political discourse, what explains the silence of the Court? Are courts once again showing concern with their own legitimacy by not taking the risk of entering this highly fraught arena of torture in democracies? In the process, what does the court's silence mean, especially if the courts alone have been the repositories of truth about torture in the past? Even in the Wickersham Commission Report, written at a time when torture or the third degree was routinely used in the criminal justice system, as substantiated by the victims of torture and indeed sometimes admitted by the police, the final form of authentication still lay with the judicial decisions. As the Wickersham Commission Report says, "The most trustworthy account of individual instances of third-degree practices appears in the reported judicial decisions. When appellate courts declare that such practices have been employed, we have the highest form of authentication."[63] The silence of the courts in the debates on torture and excess violence in the U.S. contemporary context is explored in detail in the next chapter. Yet there was a time in the history of the jurisprudence of interrogations when the Court was willing to explain its theorization of violence to some extent (beyond the Brown case) in the context of interrogations, and this brings us to the story of Miranda—its innovations and its limits.

Miranda and Violence: Theorizations and Silences

The Supreme Court's opinion in Miranda is a story of the Court's acknowledgment of the continued struggle of law with excess violence. The majority opinion in Miranda readily admits the Court's previous inability to deal with excess violence in interrogations and sets forward its theorization on violence in custodial contexts. But at the same time, the story of Miranda is also a testament to its incompleteness and to the silences and tensions it contains.

The Miranda opinion explains law's struggle with violence by distinguishing among three different forms of violence: physical, mental, and inherently coercive. First, the Court notes the continuing cases of police brutality even in the 1960s. The Court quotes the Wickersham Commission Report on the third degree in the 1930s as well as the 1961 Commission on Civil Rights, which stated that the police continued to resort to physical force to get confessions. Here the emphasis of the Court appears to be on physical brutality or physical torture despite the fact that the Wickersham Commission Report represented a broader understanding of the third degree.

Second, the Miranda opinion noted a persistent use of psychological coercion against suspects during interrogation. It is, of course, significant that despite mentioning the continued use of physical forms of violence, the Court goes on to state,

> The modern practice of in-custody interrogation is more psychologically than physically oriented. As we have stated before, "since *Chambers v. Florida*, this court has recognized that coercion can be mental as well as physical, and that the blood of the accused is not the only hallmark of an unconstitutional inquisition."[64]

The Court's suggestion that physical force is no longer important is of course belied by its own reference to the continuing reports of police brutality, which remains an issue even today, as reflected in the Chicago police cases.[65] At the same time, as noted earlier, this formulation reaffirms the notion of the impermissibility of torture by emphasizing that at least the more obvious forms of torture have declined, thereby equating torture mainly with extreme physical violence. Here again, we see the chronology of progress setting in to minimize the significance of those forms of violence that continue or remain unaddressed. Within this framework, mental violence is merely a lesser form of excess violence that needs to be addressed gradually. Yet the question is whether mental violence is addressed squarely by the Miranda court.

In the opinion, the Miranda Court actually progressed to making the third form of violence more prominent: the inherently coercive nature of interrogation. The Court recognizes that since interrogation takes place in private, there is no way of actually knowing the practices used in the interrogation rooms. The Court, therefore, relies on the texts and manuals used by the police and other interrogators to determine the nature of the practices.[66] The opinion emphasizes the incommunicado nature of the interrogations conducted "in a police – dominated atmosphere."[67] After a discussion of the manuals that advocate the use of trickery, persistence, role playing, and secrecy in the conduct of the questioning, the Court concluded that the interrogation process was inherently coercive. Thus, the Court writes, "Even without employing brutality, 'the third degree' or the specific stratagems described above, the very fact of custodial interrogation exacts a heavy toll on individual liberty and trades on the weakness of individuals."[68] While emphasizing the inherently coercive nature of interrogation, the Court writes,

> The potentiality for compulsion is forcefully apparent, for example, in *Miranda*, where the indigent Mexican defendant was a seriously disturbed individual with pronounced sexual fantasies, and in Stewart, in which the defendant was an indigent Los Angeles Negro who had dropped out of school in the sixth grade. To be sure, the records do not evince overt physical coercion or patent psychological ploys. The fact remains that in none of these cases did the officers undertake to afford appropriate safeguards at the outset of the interrogation to ensure that the statements were truly the product of free choice.[69]

Miranda, thus, took a big step forward in explaining the three different kinds of violence but was mostly concerned with the inherently coercive nature of interrogations. Further, the Court allowed for the waiver (which allowed the interrogation process to continue once the warnings were given) to govern interrogations despite acknowledging the coerciveness of the context itself. In the process, as far as the nature of violence is concerned, there was little clarity about the forms of violence that were allowed or disallowed short of physical brutality—the latter being self-explanatory due to its physical visibility (see chapter 3).

Thus, there was little progress from previous jurisprudence in this regard. Prior to Miranda, the jurisprudence had similarly struggled with the consistency of the "totality of circumstances test" to determine voluntariness in interrogation, though the focus was on the reliability of the confessions. As Yale Kamisar notes, "'in 99 cases out of 100,' a confession's voluntariness would be determined on the basis of whether the "interrogation methods employed . . . create[d] a substantial risk that a person subjected to them will falsely confess—whether or not this person did."[70]

In that period, however, there was less clarity on the permissibility of specific methods of interrogation. For instance, Welsh White points out that since thirty-six hours of continued interrogation was disallowed in the Ashcraft case, that suggested an objective standard set by the Court.[71] However, Joseph Grano, in his reading of Ashcraft, suggests that there was both an objective assessment (adequate pressure) and a subjective understanding of whether these circumstances compelled him to confess.[72] Thus, the pre-Miranda "totality of circumstances" test was inconsistent and could be subject to various interpretations and, in particular, reflected an inability to decide whether the particular methods themselves were coercive or not.

Consequently, there was also little clarification on the nature of psychological or mental violence. For instance, if one takes the case of *Chambers v. Florida*, which is mentioned by the Miranda majority, as disallowing psychological coercion, even there the Court's attempt to clarify the nature of violence is limited. The Court notes,[73]

> For five days petitioners were subjected to interrogations culminating in Saturday's (May 20th) all night examination. . . . The very circumstances surrounding their confinement and their questioning without any formal charges having been brought, were such as to fill petitioners with *terror and frightful misgivings*.[74]

In deciding the case, however, the emphasis of the Court was on the totality of circumstances and the impact of the act on the will of the suspects and not so much on explaining the scope of the mental violence. Indeed, for the Court, both Brown and Chambers are unacceptable because of the compulsion they create. In Chambers, the Court explains,

Just as our decision in *Brown v. Mississippi* was based upon the fact that the confessions were the result of compulsion, so in the present case, the admitted practices were such as to justify the statement that "The undisputed facts showed that compulsion was applied."[75]

Even though the Court in Chambers does start off by making a distinction between physical ill treatment and mental, in the final analysis, they both represent forms of compulsion. Thus, the Court loses another opportunity to explain distinctions between physical and mental violence. Therefore, while cases such as Chambers and Ashcraft have been taken as examples of mental forms of coercion being disallowed by the Court, it is important to note the emphasis on the totality of circumstance in determining the outcome of a case, rather than a conceptualization of some forms of interrogation being coercive or violent because of their impact on the suspect. Similarly, while Miranda starts off by trying to distinguish among physical, mental, and inherently coercive forms of violence, it also stops short of fully explaining the nature of violence permitted in interrogations.

Just as the Miranda majority fails to clarify the extent of the violence allowed, the dissenting justices in the case, especially Justice Harlan, muddied the waters even more by arguing that the Miranda majority was completely disallowing the use of pressure in interrogations and indeed rejecting any confessions altogether. In contrast, according to Justice Harlan, due process was the standard for determining the admissibility of confessions, and "the outcome was a continuing re-evaluation on the facts of each case of *how much* pressure on the suspect was permissible."[76] For Harlan, what the Constitution proscribes is not any pressure but *undue pressure.*[77] In fact, according to Justice Harlan, in the majority opinion's disallowing of pressure, "The aim in short is toward 'voluntariness' in a utopian sense, or to view it from a different angle, voluntariness with a vengeance."[78] Therefore, he argues that the constitutional protections could be ensured even if some pressure is allowed. It is important to note that the focus of both the Miranda majority and the dissents has been on the inherently coercive nature of the interrogations—the former assuming that the warnings would be adequate to overcome the effects of the coercion, the dissents wanting to hold onto that coercion as necessary for the interrogations.

But neither the majority nor the dissent specifies the nature of coercion. What lies between physical brutality and inherently coercive treatment? Even Justice Harlan had accepted in the past that "apart from direct physical coercion . . . no single default or fixed combination of them guaranteed exclusion and synopses of the cases will serve little use because the overall gauge has been steadily changing, usually in the direction of restricting admissibility."[79] Given the post-9/11 debates on what constitutes torture or excess violence, the lack of discussion of some of the actual methods disallowed and the parameters of the violence permitted during interrogations remains a major limitation in the Miranda decision despite the progress made in terms of theorization. The continuity among the three different forms of violence, from stratagems to mental coercion to physical coercion, is completely ignored by the Miranda Court.

It was primarily to deal with the uncertainty in the pre-Miranda jurisprudence that the Miranda protections emerged. As Welsh White writes, "the court itself began to look for per se rules that would alleviate the inherent problems with determining the legitimacy of police interrogation practices on a case-by-case basis."[80] The Court certainly achieved that with the Miranda rules. However, one could argue that it did so in a way that bypassed one of the key issues that plagued the pre-Miranda jurisprudence: the nature of violence allowed or disallowed by law. In sum, the story of violence that Miranda tells fails to go beyond the pre-Miranda jurisprudence, which had assumed the prohibition of physical torture and the few specific methods of mental coercion designated within the totality-of-circumstances test as the prohibition of all excess violence. Furthermore, even while the Miranda majority did not specify the nature of coercion, it did serve as a relegitimizing factor establishing that coercion is once and for all not allowed in the United States. Just as the presence of formal safeguards, landmark decisions, and radical reports leads to denials of torture and excess violence even when they are not fully effective, in the post-Miranda jurisprudence, the presence of warnings and waivers almost ends the discussion on violence within interrogations.

How the Silence on Violence Continues: Troubling Confessions,[81] Gatehouses and Mansions,[82] and Jurisprudence

Miranda did find one solution to the problem of violence by focusing on safeguards right at the moment of interrogation, but the actual methods of interrogation prohibited and allowed and the nature of the violence remain unclear. The post-Miranda jurisprudence and legal scholarship have similarly moved further and further away from the question of violence in interrogations. Instead they have focused on the efficacy and constitutionality of the safeguards, which have implications for the question of violence but do not address it centrally. One strand of Miranda scholarship represented by Joseph Grano and Paul Cassell has highlighted the adverse effect of Miranda on law enforcement, especially in terms of decreasing the number of confessions.[83] These scholars also challenged the constitutionality of the Miranda warnings, advocating a return to the pre-Miranda totality-of-circumstances test. The second strand of scholars has studied whether Miranda warnings have actually been effective in protecting criminal defendants from confessing falsely. Here scholars such as Welsh White, Yale Kamisar, Richard Leo, and others reject the argument put forth by the critics of Miranda that the warnings have led to a decline in confessions. Rather, they argue that the Miranda warnings have not even been able to stop false confessions.[84]

Given the highly divided nature of the Miranda decision and the major backlash against it, the legal and political community expected the Miranda case to be overruled by the Supreme Court in subsequent years.[85] However, in the 2000 Dickerson case, when the constitutionality of Miranda was challenged, surprising a number of Miranda supporters and opponents alike, Chief Justice Rehnquist refused to overturn Miranda and stated the following:

> We hold that Miranda, being a constitutional decision of this Court, may not be in effect overruled by an Act of Congress, and we decline to overrule Miranda ourselves. We therefore hold that Miranda and its progeny in this court govern the admissibility of statements made during custodial interrogation in both state and federal courts.[86]

Here the Court rejected an act of Congress (18 USC § 3501) that clearly wanted to reinstate the pre-Miranda "totality of circumstances" test.[87] Instead, the Supreme Court held that the Miranda warnings were applicable to the states because the Miranda decision was a constitutional rule and not a supervisory one and the warnings were such an integral part of the national and legal culture that there was little justification for change.[88]

The Dickerson opinion has only further intensified the discussion on the efficacy of Miranda safeguards in stopping false confessions. Yale Kamisar, for instance, recalls that it is often forgotten that the Miranda decision was a compromise by the Court with the more radical position taken by the ACLU that only the "actual presence of a lawyer" would counter the compulsion inherent in interrogation and that simply informing a person of his or her rights would not accomplish this aim.[89] Further, Kamisar writes,

Over three decades, Miranda had acquired a number of exceptions that significantly weakened it (or, as critics of Miranda might put it, made the doctrine more workable). It seems clear that Chief Justice Rehnquist was talking about how the cases carving out exceptions to Miranda had reduced its adverse impact on police activity when he noted that "our subsequent cases have reduced the impact of the Miranda rule on legitimate law enforcement."[90]

Kamisar points out that despite the hostility of the Rehnquist Court to Miranda, there seemed to be a pragmatic recognition by the then–chief justice that living with the present form of Miranda, with its exceptions, may be better than overruling the decision controlling in about sixty cases.[91] Even police officials and prosecutors had accepted Miranda in its present form, as noted by George C. Thomas III, who points out that in habeas corpus claims in 1993, these law enforcement officials filed amicus briefs in favor of keeping the Miranda rights.[92] Thomas suggests that part of the reason may have been their ability to adjust to the requirements of the system even while getting the incriminatory statements from the suspects. As Thomas puts it, "And so it goes with police interrogation. Rules come and rules go and police who need incriminating statements get them most of the time." In fact, if there are waivers, judges do not scrutinize the confessions closely to independently ensure their voluntariness.[93] Thus, in both the pre- and post-Dickerson contexts, scholars have continued to debate the efficacy of these safeguards or lack of them.

Apart from the debates on constitutionality and the efficacy of safeguards, there have also been detailed studies of interrogations by Richard Leo, Welsh White, and others that have direct relevance for our discussion on the continued struggle of law with violence. Leo, for instance, argues that deception, trickery, and other methods of manipulation and control continue to be major methods of interrogation.[94] Similarly, Welsh White explains, "Except for prohibiting extreme tactics, such as violence or threats of violence, the post-Miranda constitutional limitations impose virtually no limit on police interrogation practices." The powerful critique set forth by these scholars is that the use of these "pernicious" methods leads to false confessions.[95] Indeed, the criterion suggested by White for assessing the reliability of methods of interrogation is whether or not they lead to false or untrustworthy statements. As White explains, "If there is sufficient likelihood that the government's employment of a particular technique will produce false or untrustworthy statements, then that interrogation technique should be improper."[96] However, even these powerful and detailed studies of interrogations are more focused on the stratagems that contribute to the inherently coercive aspects of the interrogation that the safeguards failed to counter. In the process, these critics of Miranda do not focus on the unaddressed issue of the scope of violence in interrogations and the continuum of violence that lies between inherently coercive interrogations and physical violence.

This is not to say that the critique of these interrogation methods is not important because ultimately the coercive methods "compel" the suspects to speak and often lead to false confessions. This strengthens Peter Brooks's point that there exists a culture of reliance on confessions by law enforcement in the contemporary U.S. system. Brooks writes, "And the law still today—as in medieval times—tends to accept confession as the 'queen of proofs.'"[97] In his classic work, aptly termed *Troubling Confessions*, Brooks makes the argument that the reliance on confessions by the legal system in the contemporary United States is troubling precisely because the act of confession may be derived from an urge to confess that may have little to do with guilt in the legal sense. He points to the growth of confessions in almost all spheres of life—in therapy, in church, and on television—which suggests a lack of trustworthiness of these admissions as far as the legal system is concerned. This is the case because a person may be confessing due to multiple impulses. As Brooks puts it, "the motives of confessing are often far from determinate: confessions activate inextricable layers of shame, guilt, contempt, self-loathing, attempted propitiation, and expiation."[98] This desire to confess, of course, becomes even more prominent in an interrogation room under circumstances of coercion or compulsion.

Yet Brooks is not concerned with the violence during interrogations per se. Rather, for him, the centrality of confessions in the legal system reflects one of the most paradoxical features of a liberal system: the emergence of the Fifth Amendment right against self-incrimination as a way to protect human dignity and privacy while allowing for interrogation methods that undermine precisely this right As Brooks explains,

> The law itself, in its principles and its exercise, seems to be pulling in two different directions. The effort to produce the confessional truth would seem, in very many cases, to produce as the very condition of its production a state of abjection that undercuts the very claim of voluntariness on which the definition of truth reposes, and, beyond that, the very notion of human agency that the law must promote in order to do its judging.[99]

Thus, for Brooks it is not surprising that false confessions continue because that is how the system is set up. In a recent study on interrogations, Richard Leo explains that the reason why American police interrogation is "strategically manipulative and deceptive" is a "fundamental contradiction." He writes, "On the one hand, police need incriminating statements and admissions to solve many crimes, especially serious ones; on the other hand, there is almost never a good reason for suspects to provide them."[100] The culture of confessions underwrote the desire of the Miranda dissents and the Miranda critics to hold onto confessions at all costs by claiming either that they are reliable and/or that confessions allow for the emergence of a "good conscience."[101] While Brooks acknowledges the Supreme Court's attempts to clarify notions of voluntariness, he also suggests that the Court does not resolve the question completely precisely because the legal system above all needs confessions. Brooks writes,

> But to ask the law to recognize the Dostoevskian nature of the situation might be to disable it entirely. Better, we may say, to live with a fiction in which the Supreme Court debates voluntariness in high-flown abstractions while the police continue to obtain confessions by almost any means, short of physical torture.[102]

Here Brooks comes close to acknowledging that short of physical brutality, anything is allowed, but ultimately he is concerned with an inherent contradiction in this situation between a need for confessions and its effect on voluntariness. Here then I make a distinction between the inherent coercion that even the law acknowledges and accepts and the excess violence that law does not acknowledge. To some extent, the courts have accepted what Brooks talks about—that the inherently coercive aspect can only be minimized, not entirely removed. To recall the Miranda decision one more time, Chief Justice Warren notes,

> It is obvious that such an interrogation environment is created for no purpose other than to subjugate the individual to the will of his examiner. This atmosphere carries its own badge of intimidation. To be sure, this is not physical intimidation, but it is equally destructive of human dignity. The current practice of incommunicado interrogation is at odds with one of our Nation's most cherished principles—that the individual may not be compelled to incriminate himself. Unless adequate protective devices are employed to dispel the compulsion inherent in custodial surroundings, no statement obtained from the defendant can truly be the product of his free choice.[103]

Even Chief Justice Warren concedes that safeguards are created to minimize the impact of coercion, not remove it entirely. Similarly, another dissent in Miranda—Justice White's— appears to agree with Brooks when he writes, "Although in the Court's view in-custody interrogation is inherently coercive, the Court says that the spontaneous product of the coercion of arrest and detention is still to be deemed voluntary."[104] Unlike Brooks and Chief Justice Warren, of course, Justice White simply rejects the notion that there is any inherent pressure involved in interrogation.

But what I refer to is the unacknowledged violence, the lack of clarity on what is allowed and disallowed in interrogations, particularly with regard to the mental coercion and/or the psychological torture that lie between physical brutality and illegal trickery and deception. In that sense, what Brooks finds useful to acknowledge in the context of confessions can be assumed to be true in the case of violence as well. "We seem, as a system of justice and perhaps as a society, to have concluded for now that we can live with the ambiguities of confession. They're too useful to give up."[105] Similarly, the ambiguities and silences regarding violence in the law are something to live with.

Even as I critique the silences in law, I am reminded of Marianne Constable's argument about finding justice within the silences in law, especially in the Miranda warnings. But Constable's recent attempt to read Miranda rights as exhibiting a possibility of justice suffers from a similar malaise in ignoring the lack of discussion on violence. In her fascinating book, Constable points to the performative aspect of the speech act, namely, the Miranda warnings, as cautioning the suspect of the dangers to come in the formal legal process.

> Responding to the extraordinary circumstances in which the accused finds him—or herself, the *Miranda* warning is an invitation or opening to justice. . . . The warning initiated a transformation of circumstances that do not seem compatible with the conventions of proper speech. Upon felicitous warning, an accused is given to understand that his or her statements have different import at interrogation and at trial than they otherwise would.[106]

Constable acknowledges that in order for the speech act to represent a possibility of justice, the warning has to be delivered in good faith, which often does not exist empirically, but her understanding still points to the potential of justice that is often overlooked in the reading of the Miranda warnings. To an extent, the critics of Miranda who empirically show the inefficacy of the warnings do overlook the significance of the speech act itself since they focus more on the scope of the constitutional safeguards and what follows after the act of warning.[107] But what Constable does not acknowledge is that just as the scholars she criticizes do not look at the speech act, so she, like the others, does not recognize that the warning also simultaneously hides the silence about the violence that the Court is unwilling to define. Here the criticism is not just of Miranda warnings and waivers that have replaced due process claims against coercion, or the coercion that necessarily accompanies interrogation, but the law's silence about the violence it does not address.

Thus, a focus on the efficacy of the safeguards, an inherent contradiction between interrogations and voluntariness, and the continuing false confessions have been the arena of conversations in the routine discourse on interrogations. In contrast, I point to the limits of the Miranda regime in explaining the parameters of permissible and impermissible violence. While Miranda did introduce the warnings as protection against some violence in interrogations, it started representing the ultimate protection against any form of excess violence.[108] In that sense, the Miranda warning, which suggests the protection of a right against the three forms of violence that the majority was concerned about, becomes the very guise under which the law gets away with not explaining its exact relationship to violence. This is the case because while it does explain its relationship with excessive physical violence and the inherently coercive nature of interrogations, it does not clarify the range in between.

One could argue that the silence in law about the nature of violence allowed or disallowed does not indicate acceptance of excess violence. Indeed, if the jurisprudence and legal scholars have indicated that it is primarily the efficacy of the safeguards in disallowing false confessions that is at issue today, why is this silence on the nature of violence significant? This chapter makes two assertions: first, that this ongoing struggle with excess violence needs to be made visible precisely because it challenges the notion of impermissibility of torture and excess violence even at the level of jurisprudence; and second, that the ambivalent status of violence in law becomes significant in the jurisprudence of interrogations in situations of necessity in both routine and extraordinary times.

Violence and Necessity in the Routine Discourse

In the jurisprudence on interrogations, another significant theme for our discussion on law and violence is the discourse on necessity. The necessity discourse has two aspects: do certain situations require the use of violence beyond what is normally allowed, or does the characterization of an act as unacceptable violence depend on the necessity of the act? While the necessity discourse has gained particular significance in the domestic terrorism cases, for instance in the 2010 case of Faisal Shahzad, Times Square attempted bombing suspect, it is important to note that this has always been an underlying theme in the routine jurisprudence on interrogations.[109] In some instances, the Court has indirectly referred to the logic of "necessity" by asserting the absence of it in a case. In *Haynes v. Washington* (1963), for instance, where the suspect, Haynes, was kept incommunicado for sixteen hours and despite requests was not allowed to meet his wife or attorney until he confessed, the Court did reverse the conviction.[110] However, the Supreme Court also pointed out that

> [t]here is no reasonable or rational basis for claiming that the oppressive and unfair methods utilized were in any way *essential to the detection or solution of the crime or to the protection of the public.* The claim, so often made in the context of coerced confession cases, that the devices employed by the authorities were requisite to solution of the crime and successful prosecution of the guilty party cannot here be made.[111]

Here the Court did not specify the situations in which "oppressive and unfair methods" may be essential, but the logic of necessity did make a brief appearance.

Necessity in relation to public safety is more squarely addressed in *New York v. Quarles* (1984), which is also being invoked in the Shahzad case.[112] This case concerned the applicability of Miranda warnings in a situation where the police questioned a suspect for attempted rape about the location of a gun before giving him the Miranda warnings.[113] In this case, Chief Justice Rehnquist introduced a public safety exception to the Miranda warnings. He wrote, "We conclude that the need for answers to questions in a situation posing a threat to the public safety outweighs the need for a prophylactic rule protecting the Fifth Amendment's privilege against self-incrimination."[114] Further, the majority felt that this minor exception to Miranda would not be difficult for the police to use because

> [i]n each case it will be circumscribed by the exigency which justifies it. We think police officers can and will *distinguish almost instinctively* between questions necessary to secure their own safety or the safety of the public and questions designed solely to elicit testimonial evidence from a suspect.[115]

The trust in the ability of the police to distinguish between necessary and unnecessary questioning is surprising given the history of coercion and torture in interrogations and other contexts. The public safety exception was, thus, criticized by the dissent, particularly Justice Marshall, as moving away from the clarity of Miranda. The dissenting justice stated that there would always be a difference of opinion about the volatility of a situation, as evident in the different interpretations of the situation by the various courts in the Quarles case itself.

In addition, Justice Marshall wrote,

> That the application of the "public safety" exception in this case entailed coercion is no happenstance. The majority's ratio decidendi is that interrogating suspects about matters of public safety *will* be coercive. In its *cost-benefit analysis*, the Court's strongest argument in favor of a "public safety" exception to Miranda is that the police would be better able to protect the public's safety if they were not always required to give suspects their Miranda warnings. . . . The "public safety" exception is efficacious precisely because it permits police officers to coerce criminal defendants into making involuntary statements.[116]

There was no explicit use of physical and mental violence in this case, but *New York v. Quarles* seemed to admit coercive interrogations in the context of public safety.

Justice Marshall also noted that the irony of the case was that public safety in any case was protected without abridgement of the Fifth Amendment. He wrote,

> *If a bomb is about to explode or the public is otherwise imminently imperiled*, the police are free to interrogate suspects without advising them of their constitutional rights. Such unconsented questioning may take place not only when police officers act on instinct but also when higher faculties lead them to believe that advising a suspect of his constitutional rights might decrease the likelihood that the suspect would reveal life-saving information. If trickery is necessary to protect the public, then the police may trick a suspect into confessing. While the Fourteenth Amendment sets limits on such behavior, nothing in the Fifth Amendment or our decision in *Miranda v. Arizona* proscribes this sort of emergency questioning. All the Fifth Amendment forbids is the introduction of coerced statements at trial.[117]

Here Justice Marshall unwittingly brings up one of the most vexing issues of the torture debate: the ticking-bomb scenario. Marshall not only creates a discourse on emergency questioning in the case but also addresses the classic dilemma for theorists—utilitarians and nonutilitarians alike—about what is permitted when the public is in danger.[118] And he goes on to suggest that in such a situation, the safeguards can be bypassed. Hence, the very dissenting judge who proscribes the creation of a public safety exception due to its encouragement of coercive behavior also agrees that there are certain circumstances that allow the bypassing of safeguards. While undoubtedly he does not allow for the use of just any kind of behavior, the question is, what defines the limit? He reiterates the Fourteenth Amendment (due process clause) as the deciding test, but as stated earlier, there has always been a very unclear notion of what is prohibited by the totality-of-circumstances test short of physical brutality.

The main question is, once a public safety exception is created or, even worse, if there is an unwritten rule that methods bypassing the safeguards can be used, has a slippery slope been set up? As Thomas Crocker points out in the context of the Fourth Amendment jurisprudence, exceptions have slowly transformed the meaning of privacy, especially when considered in the context of the "war on terror," resulting in practices such as random searches on subways. Crocker notes, "We move by accretive creep from a point of specific 'special need' to a general 'special need.' . . . As necessity becomes normal in some defined sphere, altered practices give rise to changed constitutional culture."[119] In Fifth Amendment jurisprudence, if one were to add the hitherto ignored fact that there is a lack of clarity on the methods allowed, short of physical brutality, what would these statements about bypassing safeguards come to mean? Do they mean that the public-safety exception or the bypassing of safeguards would allow for mental coercion or psychological pressure to be used? If yes, what sets the limits for these methods? Is the difference between the majority and the dissenting justices in the *New York v. Quarles* case mainly that the latter do not want coercion to be institutionalized but do not object to the use of coercion per se? The silence regarding the violence allowed and disallowed in interrogations never has more significance than in situations where necessity becomes a factor in determining the permissibility of an act.

In lower courts, of course, even physical violence has occasionally been accepted when used in the context of necessity. In the *Leon v. Wainwright* case,[120] the police officers were trying to find the location of a kidnapped suspect, and when Leon, the kidnapper, refused to reveal the information, "'he was set upon by several of the officers . . . they threatened and physically abused him by twisting his arm behind his back and choking him until he revealed where Louis [Gachelin] was being held.'"[121] Later, Leon was taken to the police station and questioned by another set of detectives, and he confessed this time, after being informed of his Miranda rights. The Court of Appeals for the Eleventh Circuit came to the conclusion that the "totality of circumstances" test suggested that the second confession was a voluntary one because there was a break between the two events.

The court explained,

> We do not by our decision sanction the use of force and coercion by police officers. Yet this case does not represent the typical case of *unjustified force*. We did not have an act of brutal law enforcement agents trying to obtain a confession in total disregard of the law. This was instead a group of concerned officers *acting in a reasonable manner* to obtain information they needed *in order to* protect another individual from bodily harm or death. This record provides overwhelming evidence to support the conclusion that appellant understood his rights, had a clear and free mind not dominated by the earlier physical abuse and voluntarily made his confession to the police.[122]

Here the nature of physical force is not as brutal as, for instance, in Brown, and the nature of the justification is not as blatant as provided by the racist sheriff in the 1930s. Yet, one can clearly observe an attempt to justify the violence on the basis of exigent circumstances. If necessity due to public safety or immediate danger to a person can lead to bypassing of Miranda, it also leads to the justification of pressure or coercion and even physical violence in other instances.

It is the *Chavez v. Martinez* case in 2003 that most clearly explicates the Supreme Court's most current discourse on necessity.[123] The case involved a civil claim under 42 U.S.C. § 1983 by Martinez against law enforcement officials for using "excessive force, and subjecting him to a coercive interrogation while he was receiving medical care."[124] Martinez was shot by the police several times in the course of a struggle during a narcotics investigation. As the appeals court describes it, "One bullet struck Martinez in the face, damaging his optic nerve and rendering him blind. Another bullet fractured a vertebra, paralyzing his legs. Three more bullets tore through his leg around the knee joint. The officers then handcuffed Martinez."[125] The supervisor, Chavez, accompanied Martinez to the hospital and started a taped interview in the trauma room without giving him the Miranda warnings. Chavez questioned Martinez even while the medical personnel were working on him; though he did leave the room at the request of medical personnel, he subsequently returned to resume tape-recorded questioning. Martinez did not respond to the questions, claiming that he was in extreme pain and stating that he was going to die and should be left alone for treatment. Twice Martinez explicitly stated that he did not want to be questioned anymore. In response to Martinez's case, Chavez claimed qualified immunity and the Supreme Court agreed.

First, the Supreme Court asserted that there was no violation of the Fifth Amendment because there was no prosecution in this case against Martinez and his statements were not used to incriminate him in a criminal trial. The Court clarified that this was not to say that "torture or abuse" was allowed by the Constitution but that it was controlled by the due process clause rather than the Fifth Amendment.[126] Thus, despite the fact that the Miranda decision focused on different forms of violence in its opinion and suggested safeguards to protect the defendants from these forms, the Court brought the discussion back to the Fourteenth Amendment due process clause, making a rigid separation between the Fifth Amendment right against self-incrimination and the Fourteenth Amendment due process clause.

Second, regarding the Fourteenth Amendment, even though the question was sent back on remand, one opinion of the court, written by Justice Thomas (and joined by Justice Scalia and Chief Justice Rehnquist), did suggest that Chavez did not violate due process rights because he did not find Chavez's behavior to be "egregious" or "conscience shocking."[127] The opinion specified, "As we noted in Lewis, the official conduct 'most likely to rise to the conscience-shocking level,' was the 'conduct intended to injure in some way unjustifiable by any government interest.'"[128] In this case, the justices found that Chavez did not delay the treatment or interfere in it or increase the injuries. In addition, there was also *an identifiable government interest* in finding out what had happened that would have been lost if Martinez had died. Further, the opinion asserted that "unwanted police questioning" is not such a "fundamental" right that it cannot be abridged absent a "compelling state interest."[129] The Chavez case, therefore, introduced a new category regarding the definition of violence in a very explicit way. As John Parry explains, the Chavez Court linked the constitutionality of coercive interrogations with the question of necessity of information.[130] The severity of an act was connected to whether the act was necessary or not.

Chavez v. Martinez was a case in 2003. The Court here comes closest to explaining its understanding of excess violence in interrogations during times of necessity. Police questioning a suspect without Miranda rights when he was paralyzed and writhing in pain, giving him the impression that his treatment might stop if he did not cooperate, was no longer considered coercion, let alone torture. The justification was that it was not "shocking." In contrast, this police behavior is characterized by both dissenting judges and some scholars as torture.

Justice Stevens in his dissent wrote,

> As a matter of fact, the interrogation of respondent was the functional equivalent of an attempt to obtain an involuntary confession from a prisoner by *torturous* methods. As a matter of law, that type of *brutal police* conduct constitutes an immediate deprivation of the prisoner's constitutionally protected interest in liberty.[131]

Similarly, Justice Kennedy rejected the separation between the Fifth and Fourteenth Amendments, claiming that the case represented a violation of both: "A constitutional right is traduced the moment torture or its close equivalents are brought to bear. Constitutional protection for a tortured suspect is not held in abeyance until some later criminal proceeding takes place."[132] Scholar Jerome Skolnick also points out that the persistent questioning by Chavez when Martinez was writhing in pain did amount to torture.[133] However, for some justices on the Court, the characterization of this act as torture is linked to whether it is conducted in the name of an identifiable government interest.

The plurality here not only opened the way for theoretically claiming the possibility of bypassing constitutional safeguards, as was the case in *New York v. Quarles,* but also made necessity an important factor in determining whether the violence was excessive. The thinking of the Court in this context becomes a little more apparent in the oral argument when Justice Scalia asked Martinez's lawyer whether there was a necessity exception that could be used to justify beating up someone with a rubber hose. Justice Scalia said, "So let's assume somebody is . . . you think he's going to blow up the World Trade Center. I suppose if . . . if we have this necessity . . . this necessity exception, you . . . you could beat him with a rubber hose."[134] Martinez's lawyer answered, "I would hope not, Your Honor." Justice Scalia went on to say, "Oh, it's necessary . . ." Although the discussion eventually moved away from the hypothetical terrorist situation, which even the lawyer agreed was a more difficult one (and Scalia did not clearly articulate his position), the exchange between the lawyer and Justice Scalia indicated the possibility of accepting a necessity exception in such an instance.[135] Here the use of the example of beating a person with a rubber hose is important because it is precisely a form of violence that does not leave marks on the body and thereby is not typically defined as "physical torture."

In the same oral argument, Justice Ginsburg also asked the lawyer whether coercion would be allowed if a child was kidnapped and had a life-threatening condition that needed immediate medication.[136] The lawyer initially struggled with the answer, alluding to some of the arguments made against the ticking-bomb scenario—such as the difficulty in confirming whether the person actually knew something or was in fact the right person. Justice Scalia, however, intervened to say, "They know this is the guy that . . . that buried the child, or deprived the child of medication or whatever. It's not a hard question at all."[137] With justices from both sides of the ideological spectrum exploring the possibility of a necessity exception, the lawyer eventually agreed that perhaps some "degree of coercion" might be "permissible."[138]

The "degree of coercion" permissible during interrogations, which has never been adequately specified in the jurisprudence, becomes even more troublesome when linked to situations of necessity. Instead of specifying the degree of violence available during interrogation, some of the Supreme Court justices suggest that necessity be a factor in determining constitutionality, although one could argue that discussions on the use of rubber hoses and prolonged interrogations of a person in pain do reflect glimpses of what the justices may be contemplating. Connecting the severity of an act with necessity and actually discussing a necessity exception could be considered a recent development, even a manifestation of the post-9/11 period, given the explicit mention of torture in the dissenting opinions and Scalia's reference to the World Trade Center in the oral arguments. Indeed, Jerome Skolnick argues that the Chavez case in 2003, while it was a case of torture, was an atypical one and, thus, he concludes that the issue in interrogations is primarily an issue of bypassing Miranda or using deception and trickery.[139] In contrast, as illustrated in this section, one can argue that the connection between necessity and the acceptability of violence has been an ongoing theme in the jurisprudence of interrogations.

Thus, it is unsurprising that when Faisal Shahzad was arrested in May 2010 in relation to the attempted Times Square bombing case, the FBI under the law-abiding Obama government turned to the necessity discourse and the public safety exception developed by the U.S. Supreme Court.[140] Since

Shahzad was a U.S. citizen, he was entitled to Miranda rights, but the FBI used the public safety exception to question him and only then proceeded to Mirandize him. The fact that Shahzad actually waived the Miranda rights and continued to talk suggests that there may be an unnecessary fear about Mirandizing people. But more significantly, the implications of the public safety exception are made more explicit in this context. In law, there is silence about what violence is permitted and what violence is prohibited (short of physical torture), and necessity is allowed to determine the severity of the act. These features collectively illustrate the ongoing tensions in law regarding violence in interrogations.

"Being Helplessly Civilized Leaves Us at the Mercy of the Beast"

Post-9/11 Discourses on Torture in
the United States

The hooded Iraqi man standing on a box with his outstretched arms tied to electric wires, the goggled and muffled prisoners at Guantánamo, and the former U.S. army reservist Lynndie England smilingly pointing to the naked Iraqi detainees are just some of the iconic images that have shocked the world in recent years.[1] Yet much before these pictures were released in 2004, there were comments by U.S. state officials about the need for unprecedented actions in the post-9/11 context. For instance, Cofer Black, the CIA's former counterterrorism chief, in his testimony before the U.S. Congress, said in 2002, "There was a before-9/11 and an after-9/11. After 9/11, the gloves came off."[2] Similarly, former vice president Dick Cheney proclaimed right after 9/11, "defeating terrorists meant that we also have to work . . . sort of the dark side. . . . A lot of what needs to be done here will have to be done quietly, without any discussion,"[3] thereby earning his nickname of Darth Vader.[4] President George W. Bush, while denying the use of torture by the United States, simultaneously made comments such as, "I will never relent in defending America—whatever it takes."[5] These comments collectively reflected an exceptional rhetoric that emerged right after 9/11, their meanings becoming more visible only in the 2004 Abu Ghraib pictures.

In this chapter, I analyze the post-9/11 debates on torture in the United States concerning Guantánamo Bay, Cuba. I examine the theorizations by scholars that Guantánamo constituted a state of exception or a space without legal and political rights.[6] In particular, I ask whether the state-of-exception argument adequately captures the torture debate in the context of Guantánamo (and by extension Abu Ghraib). While Guantánamo has certainly not been the only site of the torture debates, especially given the extraordinary rendition program under which detainees were transferred to countries that torture, or to secret CIA prisons, here I focus on Guantánamo as a primary site of the torture debates in part because of the symbolic and normative significance of this space for the post-9/11 debates.

In the chapter, I suggest that in contrast to the state-of-exception argument, a more useful framework for understanding the torture debate is to analyze the tension between law and violence in liberal democracies. This tension is most apparent in the withdrawal of the so-called torture memo by the United States.[7] The liberal state's need to distinguish its own "humane" violence from "inhumane" violence forces the state to find ways of "taming" the violence both literally (by withdrawing the memo) and rhetorically. Rhetorically, the state first attempts to deny the very existence of torture and subsequently characterizes the acts of violence as "not torture" rather than torture.[8] The reason why it is able to do so is that the extent of violence permitted and prohibited is by definition ambiguous.

The withdrawal of the torture memo, of course, does not indicate that the state stops using excess violence. The state allows law to accommodate the possibility of using violence as long as it does not reach the threshold of its own definition of torture. Thus, the introduction of aggressive methods against particular subjects at Guantánamo is a manifestation of a constant negotiation of the state and law with violence. Even the Supreme Court's nonintervention in the post-9/11 torture debate is emblematic of the ambiguous status of excess violence in liberal democracies. The broader implication of law's constant struggle with violence is that it is necessary to reconceptualize state power by rethinking Foucault's notion of governmentality. I suggest that excess violence should be considered not merely as a remnant of past spectacular torture but rather more centrally as a part and parcel of the art of government. Here I illustrate the use of medical personnel in developing interrogation techniques as just one instance of the way excess violence functions within the art of government through the formation of what Foucault has termed the juridico-medical complex.

Undoing the Exception

As indicated in the introduction, post-9/11 policies in the United States have been primarily analyzed as representing a "state of exception" or a "legal black hole" where no legal or political rights exist. To recall one of the most influential conceptions in this regard: Giorgio Agamben has argued that the "unclassifiable and unnameable" status of the detainees in Guantánamo provides the perfect example of "bare life," which is a life reduced to a subhuman level, in a state of exception.[9] Similarly, Judith Butler characterizes the treatment of the detainees in the "Guantánamo Limbo" in the following way: "They are outside the law, outside the framework of countries at war imagined by the law, and so outside the protocols governing civilized conduct."[10] In contrast to this conceptualization of the post-9/11 policies on detention and interrogation as an exception, a closer analysis of the memos suggests that Guantánamo exhibits not a suspension of laws per se but a more selective albeit aggressive engagement with the laws.

Here Nasser Hussain's analysis of memos that focus on detention and lack of rights for detainees is useful. As Hussain puts it, Guantánamo is more of a "legal loophole" than a "legal black hole."[11] He notes, "It is empirically the case that what one witnesses in contemporary emergency is a proliferation of new laws and regulations passed in an ad hoc or tactical manner, administrative procedures, and the use of older laws and cases tweaked and transformed for newer purposes."[12] Hussain describes the proliferation of laws and detailed analysis in these memos as exhibiting a form of "hyperlegality."[13] Similarly, Fleur Johns points out, "Far from a space of 'utter lawlessness' . . . one finds in Guantánamo Bay a space filled to the brim with expertise, procedure, scrutiny and analysis."[14] Indeed, even though these authors do not focus on the torture memo in their analysis, I illustrate that the latter also represents a form of "hyperlegality" that involves a more aggressive use of gaps within the preexisting laws on torture. Thus, the torture memo could be termed as an instance of "aggressive hyperlegality" where the hyperlegality is meant specifically to narrow the protections possible under the laws. Further, even conceptually, the meaning of emergency or exception is belied by the recent policies. As Hussain writes,

> That is, traditionally an emergency or exception, at least as an ideal type, [is] operated by suspending regular law and utilizing a range of maneuvers that were both temporary and specific in order to confront a given situation. Today most emergency laws are neither temporary nor categorically distinct from a larger set of state practices.[15]

Thus, both in terms of the traditional notion of exception as a more bounded concept—temporary and specific—and in terms of the aggressive use of gaps within actual laws against torture and indefinite detention, the state-of-exception framework appears inadequate. Further, I contend that the state-of-exception argument does not explain three particular aspects of the torture debate. First, it does not explain why the liberal state withdrew the so-called torture memo (which narrowed the protections against torture) despite insisting on the validity of its arguments. Second, as noted earlier, it does not acknowledge that the state memos do not represent complete lawlessness but rather exhibit an aggressive use of preexisting gaps within the laws. Third, it does not address the continuities in the practices of torture in the pre- and post-9/11 period, which are crucial to explaining the significance of violence in the art of government. The analysis of the post-9/11 memos as aggressive hyperlegality thus becomes particularly crucial at this time because, as I illustrate, even when some of the so-called exceptional policies are withdrawn, the preexisting tensions in law toward excess violence still continue to function as a continuously negotiated part of governmentality.

Contextualizing the Torture Debate

The post-9/11 torture saga in the United States became explicitly visible only in 2004. In that year the infamous abuses in the Abu Ghraib prison, Iraq, emerged in the public arena in the CBS show *Sixty Minutes* when the show aired the pictures of Iraqis being tortured and abused by U.S. personnel. Even though immediately after 9/11 there had been numerous allegations of torture of detainees at Guantánamo Bay, Cuba, it was the shocking pictures of torture that confirmed the presence of these practices at Abu Ghraib and, later, in Guantánamo. These abuses ranged from acts of physical torture, such as beating, jumping on the back and legs, sexual assault, kicking to the point of bleeding and, often, becoming unconscious to forms of mental torture, for example, being stripped naked, forced to wear women's underwear (up to fifty-one days as the sole article of clothing), frightened through the use of phobias, put on leashes, hooded, deprived of food, sexually humiliated, and denied religious requirements.[16]

The pictures were soon followed by the leak of a number of formerly classified official U.S. memos. These memos, written in the 2001-2003 period, seemed to suggest that the acts of torture were not "aberrations" but rather were part of an authorized policy for Guantánamo (if not for Iraq). If one looked at the methods authorized by the state for Guantánamo at one point or another, they were sleep deprivation, stress positions, isolation up to thirty days, use of phobias such as fear of dogs, removal of clothes, environmental manipulation, and mild, noninjurious physical contact such as grabbing and poking in the chest with the finger as well as light pushing.[17] Thus, there appeared to be a clear relationship between many of the methods authorized in the leaked memos and the acts at Abu Ghraib. The state responded by first trying to delink the discussions in the memos about the use of aggressive methods in Guantánamo Bay from torture in Iraq.[18] Yet that strategy did not work, because the logic of the memos was apparent in both the review of methods authorized in Guantánamo Bay and in the pictures of torture in Iraq. The second major step in 2004 was the withdrawal of the most egregious of these memos, the Bybee memo (which I discuss below), and the replacement of this by the Levin memo. I use this example of withdrawal of the memo both as symbolizing the limitations of the state-of-exception analysis and for strengthening an alternative framework for analyzing the torture debate: namely, the continuing struggle of law with excess violence.

The Liberal State and the Act of Withdrawal: Why Was the Bybee/Yoo Memo Withdrawn?

As noted in the last chapter, states rarely admit their reliance on torture, but a liberal state in particular has to distance itself from torture precisely because the absence of these acts represents the success of the "progressive narrative" that Paul Kahn refers to.[19] Thus, when there emerged in 2004 memos linking acts of torture to actual policy discussions, and authorizing documents, a moment of crisis was potentially created. The anxiety was reflected in the multiple strategies employed by the United States, which initially denied the existence of torture and then, when it proved impossible to sustain that denial, denied authorship of policies related to these acts especially in Iraq.

Despite these classic strategies of official denial that the United States invoked, a particularly crisis-generating memo in the post-9/11 period was the August 2002 memo signed by the then–assistant attorney general, Department of Justice, Jay S. Bybee (now widely believed to have been authored by another state official, John Yoo, and henceforth referred to as the Bybee/Yoo memo). This memo has been considered an exceptional document because of its attempt to narrow protections against torture, thereby threatening to challenge one of the basic premises of a liberal democracy: that democracies do not condone torture under any circumstances.[20] A close examination of the Bybee/Yoo memo illustrates the ways in which it transgressed the delicate balance that a liberal state seeks to maintain between relying on legal violence and transforming itself into the "brutal other." The Bybee/Yoo memo attempted to maintain the balance by indulging in what

I term an aggressive hyperlegality and yet had to be withdrawn precisely because of its inability to do so.

Many scholars suggest that the Bybee/Yoo memo was primarily written for the CIA and, therefore, may not be directly relevant for understanding the torture debate at Guantánamo because of its status as a U.S. naval base.[21] However, I focus here on the Bybee/Yoo memo because the memo remains both symbolically and conceptually one of the most controversial and significant moments of the torture debate. This is the case primarily because it was one of the first memos to emerge after the Abu Ghraib pictures were leaked and soon became a symbol of the exceptional policies of the administration, since it was read as authorizing torture. The memo became so controversial that it was publicly withdrawn and replaced by a new memo—an action unprecedented as far as the other memos and documents were concerned. Further, the Bybee/Yoo memo is pertinent because even its arguments regarding the scope of the commander-in-chief powers and the definition of torture are reiterated in many different memos and documents of the post-9/11 context. Indeed, some of the same arguments that form the foundation of the Bybee/Yoo memo were echoed in another John Yoo memo, written in March 2003 (that surfaced in 2008), this time explaining how protections against torture were limited in relation to the military as well.[22] As the author of the two memos, John Yoo, told *Esquire* in 2008, "The basic substance of the memo released yesterday [2008] and the one released in 2004 is the same."[23] Therefore, Yoo himself notes the similarities in his interpretation of laws regarding the CIA and the military interrogators for a certain period. Further, the memos and documents that emerged in 2009 concerning the high-value detainees (defined as high-ranking al Qaeda and affiliate members, with knowledge of imminent threat and potentially threatening to the United States if released) echo some of the core arguments.[24] Thus, even though the continued emergence of new memos explains specific parts of the puzzle regarding different sites and actors, the Bybee/Yoo memo retains particular significance in understanding the torture debate.

The Bybee/Yoo memo follows the same framework as the other formerly classified memos in the 2001-2002 period regarding the nonapplicability of U.S. and international laws to the detainees at Guantánamo. The 2002 John Yoo memo on detention claimed that the Geneva Conventions were not applicable to the detainees at Guantánamo Bay because of the unique nature of the conflict and thereby made the Federal Torture Statute (based on the UN Convention on Torture) the focus of attention.[25] This is the case because the Federal Torture Statute (1994) characterized any attempt or act of torture by U.S. state officials outside the United States as a criminal offense.[26]

Two of the more controversial suggestions of the Bybee/Yoo memo were that the executive as commander-in-chief could unilaterally introduce aggressive methods of interrogation beyond the ones permissible under the Federal Torture Statute, and certain excuses or justifications could be provided for methods that violate this statute. The Bybee/Yoo memo emphasized the unprecedented nature of the terrorist attacks and suggested that even if cases regarding the aggressive methods of interrogation authorized by the president come up for prosecution under the Federal Torture Statute, the courts should not entertain these cases since that would challenge the president's authority.[27] In fact, the memo suggests that even the application of the congressional statute against torture could be considered unconstitutional if the commander-in-chief authorized certain methods as necessary for the war. The Bybee/Yoo memo also stated that if some officials did violate the statute, "standard criminal law defenses of necessity and self-defense" may be used to bypass criminal prosecutions.[28] The conditions for evoking the necessity and self-defense arguments were by definition fulfilled by the context of terrorism.

Since the Bybee/Yoo memo did not directly address why the military would not be bound by the several other laws that could apply to the use of torture, the 2003 Yoo memo illustrates that the Bybee/Yoo logic could simply be extended to almost all the other laws. In other words, the commander-in-chief could override any laws if the methods prohibited under them were considered necessary for the war. Just for example, the Yoo memo notes the following regarding the federal criminal laws that prohibit assault, maiming, and torture: "if they were misconstrued to apply to the interrogation of enemy combatants," they "would conflict with the Constitution's grant of the Commander in Chief power solely to the President."[29]

These memos, ironically enough, identify the source of the president's inherent authority as the U.S. Constitution. On the basis of the "text, structure and history of the Constitution,"[30] Yoo places in the executive the entire responsibility of declaring war, conducting war, and protecting the security of the nation. His positions differ little in his academic writings, particularly regarding the president's commander-in-chief powers. As David Shultz writes, "To read *The Powers of War and Peace* is to read the ideological latticework upon which the Bush Administration's grasp for presidential power is constructed."[31] Sure enough, in his book, Yoo writes, "If we assume that the foreign affairs power is an executive one, Article II effectively grants to the president any unenumerated foreign affairs powers not given elsewhere to the other branches."[32] Once Yoo establishes that the executive does have control over foreign affairs, including the conduct of war, it is not difficult for him to conclude that "in wartime, it is for the President alone to decide what methods to use to best prevail against the enemy."[33]

For Yoo, the position is further strengthened by the post-9/11 actions of the Congress and the past decisions of the Supreme Court. Yoo, for instance, points to the Supreme Court's acceptance in the past (reiterated to some extent by the Thomas opinion in Hamdi)[34] that the president had the power to decide the exact nature of the operations within the context of the war.[35] Yoo also notes that by passing the Authorization of Military Force (AUMF) resolution in 2001, the Congress designated the president as the authority responsible for conducting the war against al Qaeda (and the Taliban).[36] War operations, according to Yoo, included not only killing and capturing the enemies in the battlefield but also detaining and interrogating them. Indeed, by describing the nonstate (almost invisible) nature of the multinational terrorist group al Qaeda, Yoo creates a powerful defense for detention and for gaining "information [as] . . . perhaps the most critical weapon for defeating al Qaeda."[37]

Yoo's theoretical justifications of the president's powers have been subject to much criticism by constitutional law scholars and human rights activists.[38] However, even while recognizing that Yoo's arguments provided an unprecedented ideological justification for the increased powers of the executive after 9/11, it is significant that these arguments were essentially based on a particularly aggressive reading of the existing U.S. Constitution that did not require a formal suspension of the laws.

Of course, even while the memos suggested that the commander-in-chief powers regarding interrogations cannot be challenged in times of war, especially by congressional statutes, the Bybee/Yoo memo writers also needed to make sure that in case this interpretation were not accepted, the definition of torture within existing statutes was narrowly interpreted. As further evidence of aggressive hyperlegality, the Bybee/Yoo memo circumscribed the scope of the main statute on torture, namely, the Federal Torture Statute, by suggesting a very narrow way of defining torture as involving the most egregious physical acts.[39] Here the significance of the memos on detention that declared the nonapplicability of the Geneva Conventions to the detainees (thereby removing the prohibitions under the Uniform Code of Military Justice and the War Crimes Act for the military) becomes especially visible. The main hurdle to the introduction of harsh interrogation techniques then becomes the Federal Torture Statute.[40]

The Federal Torture Statute (Section 2340A) defines torture as an "act committed by a person acting under the color of law specifically intended to inflict severe physical or mental pain or suffering (other than pain or suffering incidental to lawful sanctions) upon another person within his custody or physical control."[41] It is important to note here that the United States had introduced certain reservations during the ratification of the UN Convention against Torture that were reflected in the Federal Torture Statute.[42] But as another indication of its aggressive hyperlegality, the Bybee/Yoo memo used these reservations to vigorously restrict the scope of the U.S. torture statute, especially with regard to defining terms such as "severity" and "specific intent." For instance, one of the major differences between the U.S. statute and the UN convention was that in the UN convention there was little clarity about "intent," whereas the United States wanted to emphasize "specific intent" rather than "general intent" as far as the act of torture was concerned.[43] The Bybee/Yoo memo went a step further to ensure that "specific intent" was extremely narrowly defined "as the intent to accomplish the precise criminal act that one is [was] later charged with."[44] In this case, "severe pain and suffering" had to be the precise purpose of the act for it to be culpable, thereby rendering mere knowledge of pain resulting from the actions as inadequate for establishing culpability, making it almost impossible to prove specific intent.

Further, in the absence of an accepted definition of "severity" in the legal discourse, the memo specified a certain understanding of severity based on discussions in certain health statutes. The Bybee/Yoo memo states, "These statutes suggest that 'severe pain,' as used in Section 2340, must rise to a similarly high level—the level that would ordinarily be associated with a sufficiently *serious physical condition or injury such as death, organ failure, or serious impairment of body functions*—in order to constitute torture."[45] Here the lack of clarity in discussions within Congress on the precise meaning of the term "severe" led to the memo focusing on other statutes regarding health benefits to shed light on what constituted severity. Thus, a particularly narrow legal regime seemed to have been created by the Bybee/Yoo memo, wherein the protections against torture were limited to the most egregious physical pain. A narrow way of defining torture made it difficult to consider a number of controversial methods of interrogation authorized and visible at Guantánamo and Abu Ghraib as torture, and if by chance they were challenged under the torture statute, the methods could be defended as having being authorized by the commander-in-chief.

Unsurprisingly, the Bybee/Yoo memo has been the subject of much criticism. The memo has been criticized from a more normative point of view as being a "disgrace" for the United States.[46] Some others have considered this memo as exemplifying the role of "right-wing radicals" under the Bush administration.[47] Thus, both these formulations see this memo as an exceptional moment in the U.S. context. A very powerful critique of the memo has been written by David Luban, who not only looks at the fallacies in the legal arguments used by the Bybee/Yoo memo but also suggests that the memo represents an explicit creation of a "liberal ideology of torture."[48] This liberal ideology of torture is a peculiarly liberal phenomenon that ironically emerges from a rejection of four other aims of torture, namely, cruelty, punishment, judicial torture, and terrorizing people, each of which is, according to Luban, unacceptable to liberalism due to the latter's emphasis on human dignity.[49] Thus, only one particular aim for torture is conceivable for liberals: intelligence gathering in order to prevent future harm. And when torture is used for this "purer" purpose, it may not even be considered torture and, indeed, there are limits to the nature of torture allowed.[50] Luban, of course, questions even this form of torture as being unacceptable because its basis—the ticking-bomb scenario—is never reliable and threatens to be unabashedly consequentialist.[51]

Luban and others also critique the Bybee/Yoo memo as a legal document, claiming that none of its arguments is very convincing and that all of them lack adequate support. For instance, Luban and Margulies critique the appropriateness of using a definition of "severity of pain" based on a health statute about an "emergency medical condition" to analyze U.S. protections against torture.[52] Jeremy Waldron also points to the faulty understanding of severity in the Bybee/Yoo memo, which considers the impact of an untreated condition leading to impairment or dysfunction as the meaning of severity itself.[53] Further, according to Luban, the emphasis on the "specific intent" requirement and the use of "self-defense" and "necessity" defenses were either misconstrued or had little precedent in U.S. law and were primarily meant to deliberately create a liberal ideology of torture. As Margulies explains, while a distinction between "intent" and "knowledge" can be made in the case of a surgeon who may know that pain would be caused by her actions but did not intend to cause it, in the case of interrogation this has little meaning because the point in interrogation is to inflict pain.[54] While all these arguments present effective critiques of the legal arguments in the Bybee/Yoo memo, portraying it as an example of bad lawyering, they underscore the aggressive hyperlegality in the memo rather than consider the memo as a lawless attempt.

Conversely, a focus on aggressive hyperlegality also allows us to note the limitations of this phenomenon vis-à-vis torture. In other words, while the memo did represent aggressive hyperlegality, not lawlessness, it did become a liability for the state, especially after the Abu Ghraib pictures were released. Thus, an additional question that is addressed neither by exception theorists nor by these critiques of bad lawyering is why, after creating and justifying the narrowing of protections against torture, the liberal state had to withdraw the egregious memo on torture from the realm of public discourse. In particular, I am referring to the need for the Bybee/Yoo memo to be withdrawn after the memo provided ways to narrow the protections against torture. In the new Levin memo, the section on necessity, self-defense, and the commander-in-chief powers was dropped in its entirety by the administration, which claimed that the "President's Commander-in-Chief power and the potential defenses to liability [were]—and [remain]—unnecessary."[55] The use of the term "unnecessary" is significant because it reveals the belief among state officials that the president can authorize methods in violation of the Federal Torture Statute. However, the fact remains that the blatant aspects of the torture memo were withdrawn in the Levin memo. Here I take the withdrawal of the Bybee/Yoo memo as an instance of the state taking deliberate actions to contain the torture controversy and explore its significance.[56]

As noted earlier, the symbolic act of withdrawal cannot be explained either by the exception argument or by a mere critique of bad lawyering. I suggest that the withdrawal of the memo became necessary because, first, it created a direct link between the U.S. policymakers and the perpetrators of violence and, second, the memo explicitly provided a framework for authorizing acts that exceeded the acceptable levels of violence in a liberal democracy.

In this context, the contributions by Robert Cover, Austin Sarat, and Timothy Kaufman-Osborn (as discussed in the introduction) on the ambivalent relationship of law to violence becomes useful.[57] Apart from pointing to ways in which mainstream theorists such as Hart and Dworkin focus on law as primarily rules, norms, and principles, leading to a "forgetting of violence," these scholars illustrate how the state tries to deny the role of violence in law despite its use.[58] According to Austin Sarat and Thomas Kearns, the dominant theory of legal violence suggests that "necessary" violence is primarily the action of agents who enforce the decisions made on the basis of abstract rules and principles. The emphasis of the mainstream legal theorists is on a bureaucratic structure of judicial decision making rather than on concrete acts of legal interpretation by the judges.[59] This, in turn, denies the important fact pointed out by Robert Cover that "legal interpretation takes place in a field of pain and death" and has physical implications.[60]

The example of the death penalty illustrates how the judges distance themselves from acts of violence. As Kaufman-Osborn explains, the violence is seen as being reflected only in the "deeds" of the executioner while carrying out the act of execution and not in the "words" of the judge proclaiming the execution, thereby allowing judges to ignore the integral relation between the two.[61] Thus, liberal states attempt to present violence as being marginal to law, rather than being integrally pervasive at both levels: legal interpretation and legal enforcement. In the post-9/11 context, the presence of the justificatory memos alongside the acts of torture in Abu Ghraib created a direct link between the interpreters of law (memo writers) and the acts of torture. When the pictures of torture confirmed the presence of these acts, the state started denying having authorized them, and when that tactic failed, withdrew the visible and explicit justificatory discourses. The symbolic significance of the act of withdrawal is that even at the height of the "war on terror" rhetoric, the Bush administration could not defend torture as torture, and when the leaked Bybee/Yoo memo appeared to be the genesis of the torture and abuse at Abu Ghraib (via Guantánamo), the memo had to be publicly withdrawn.

This was the case because the state always attempts to portray its own violence as "humane" in opposition to "inhuman" nonstate violence. This is most visible in the change in the methods of execution in the United States from hanging to gas chamber to electric chair and, finally, to lethal injection.[62] Each time the newer method was proclaimed as a less painful method of execution, and lethal injection was considered the most humane one. The withdrawal of the Bybee/Yoo memo, thus, has to be seen as the liberal state's attempt to ensure that the distinction between the humane "self" and the inhuman "other" is clearly maintained. If torture were allowed, this major distinction between the controlled state and the brutal other would have been questioned. Here again the parallel between methods of execution and methods of interrogation becomes important. Developing humane methods of execution, Austin Sarat notes, is not done out of concern for the executed; rather it is done to constantly ensure that the liberal state seems more humane than the other. The humane methods exist also to spare the witnesses from watching the pain and seeing the marks on the body of the condemned.[63] In fact, the recent debates on botched executions by lethal injections indicate the inability of the state to do away with pain even in its most humane method of killing.[64] In the case of interrogations, it is also the use of sanitized terms and comparisons to routine activities (as well as references to "harsh" or "enhanced" techniques), on the one hand, and the use of mental and less physically brutal methods of torture, on the other, that allowed the state to proclaim that it does not use torture (see chapter 3). Thus, the withdrawal of the memo became necessary because the Bybee/Yoo memo alongside the Abu Ghraib pictures explicitly linked the state to unacceptable levels of violence, creating a crisis in the legitimacy of the liberal state.

When does violence reach such a magnitude that it threatens the legitimacy of a state? Here the argument is not so much a particular identifiable or fixed threshold of violence that the state crosses but rather a combination of contingent circumstances that creates the anxiety for the state. In the post-9/11 context, it was the leak of the photos, the emergence of the memos and documents, and the Bybee/Yoo memo clearly articulating the overstepping of some boundaries of unacceptable violence (always negotiated, as a later section will illustrate) that required a withdrawal of this egregious document. The focus, therefore, is on the symbolic act of withdrawal that follows precisely because of a peculiar relationship that law has with violence in liberal states: the state cannot embrace its own violence when it is too explicit but still requires it and, hence, finds ways of reining in the violence to acceptable levels. The difficulties in doing so are illustrated in the death penalty debates mentioned earlier and also will be more specifically discussed in the last section of this chapter, which addresses the liberal state's innovative and constantly negotiated attempts to accommodate excess violence through, for example, the creation of a juridico-medical apparatus.

The question is whether with the withdrawal of the Bybee/Yoo memo, the liberal state's tension with excess violence during interrogations disappears. I argue that while the Bybee/Yoo memo, based on arguments advocating "unchecked and unbalanced" presidential power, explicitly narrows the protections against torture, its withdrawal does not represent the end of the torture debates.[65] To put it another way, the reason why the torture debate is better explained by analyzing law's relationship to violence is that the Bybee/Yoo memo's definition of torture is not an entirely new creation. I argue that while the Bybee/Yoo memo is significant to the extent that it narrowly reads the protections against torture, some of its arguments rely on torture debates in the pre-9/11 period, making it difficult for the liberal state to completely do away with the problem of dealing with this form of excess violence. This tension is articulated by the architect of the torture memos in the following way. When John Yoo was asked about his specific interpretation of the term "severity," he said,

> It's the phrase Congress used. The main criticism, which is certainly fair, is that statute is so different from this one, how can you borrow the language of one and include it in the other. On the other hand, that's the closest you

can get to any definition of that phrase at all. . . . The other thing I was quite conscious of was I didn't want the opinion to be vague so that the people who actually have to carry these things out don't have a clear line, because I think that would be very damaging and unfair to the people who are actually asked to do these things. The way I read what the department did two years later, was they just made the line blurry again.[66]

Thus, Yoo points to an existing lack of specificity regarding the definition of torture and the meaning of these terms that the memos pounce upon and aggressively interpret. And Yoo went on: "Yeah, so when they rewrote the memo, they made the lines less clear. They deleted that sentence. But it's not all that different in what it actually says and what it actually allows."[67] Is the statement made by John Yoo that nothing changed in the Levin memo actually true?

Definitional Ambiguities That Linger On

The Bybee/Yoo memo was presented by critics as an exceptional moment in the torture debate and its withdrawal as indicating that the liberal state could put to rest all suspicions regarding its reliance on illegitimate violence. However, in this section, I note how one of the more controversial sections of the Bybee/Yoo memo—namely, the narrow definition of torture—is not just a creation of the post-9/11 period. Rather, it is a reflection of a more ambiguous relationship that U.S. law has to the definition of torture that was present in the very formulation of the Federal Torture Statute. Analyzing the tensions regarding the definition of torture in the very ratification of the same statute indicates the constantly negotiated nature of law with excess violence even while the liberal state emphatically claims both legally and morally that torture is impermissible in a democracy. Further, the pre-9/11 debates also register ways in which the liberal state often struggles to find ways of accommodating excess violence even while trying to conform to its legal obligations. It is this tension that underlies the quotation from Judge Gonzales at a press briefing in 2004: "The administration has made clear before, and I will reemphasize today that the President has not authorized, ordered or directed in any way any activity that would transgress the standards of the Torture Convention or the Torture Statute, or other applicable laws."[68] The emphasis on legal obligations rather than a general denial of torture points to the ambiguities that remain from the pre-9/11 context in the laws regarding the definition of torture in the Federal Torture Statute.

The narrow definition of torture has, of course, not been the only area of concern as far as aggressive interrogation methods are concerned. Other strategies included the use of euphemisms or sanitized terms such as "sleep adjustment" or a "frequent flyer program" for sleep deprivation. While I discuss these additional strategies applied by the liberal state to mask its tension with excess violence in chapter 3, here I focus on the definition of torture in the Federal Torture Statute as an illustration of the liberal state's continued tension with excess violence. In particular, I point to the similarities between the definitions of torture in the U.S. Senate ratification debates in 1990 and the Bybee/Yoo memo. While the similarities themselves are not surprising given that the Bybee/Yoo memo is merely interpreting the same statute, they serve as a reminder that these definitional ambiguities troubled the Senate ratification debates as well and that the withdrawal of the Bybee/Yoo memo did not automatically resolve these tensions.

The definition of physical and mental torture was a subject of much concern in the U.S. Congress during the ratification of the UN Torture Convention. For instance, in 1990, Mark Richard, the then–deputy assistant attorney general in the Department of Justice, stated in his written and oral statement in front of the Senate Foreign Relations Committee, "Torture is understood to be that barbaric cruelty which lies at the top of the pyramid of human rights misconduct."[69] Richard goes on to explain what he calls a "relatively general definition." According to Richard, there seemed to be a "degree of consensus" on physical torture—"the mere mention of which send chills down one's spine: the needle under the fingernail, the application of electric shock to the genital area, the piercing of eye balls etc."[70] Indeed, he terms techniques that "inflict such excruciating and agonizing physical pain . . . as the essence of torture."[71] Hence, he writes, "the Convention chose the word 'severe' to indicate the high level of the pain required to support a finding of torture."[72] Thus, the 1990 Justice Department lists techniques that cause long-lasting physical injuries on the body as the "essence" of torture and link this to the term "severity," thereby exhibiting the origins of some of the arguments found in the Bybee/Yoo memo.

In fact, even the new Levin memo (that replaced the Bybee/Yoo memo) inherited this more ambiguous understanding of torture based on the 1990 Senate discussions. The Levin memo clarifies that the Department of Justice officials disagree with the statements made by the Bybee/Yoo memo that torture includes only acts causing "excruciating and agonizing" pain or suffering and reject the specific definition of severity given in the memo, which is based on the health statutes (pain in relation to death, organ failure, and impairment of bodily function).[73] The question is whether the Levin memo is able to explain the terms "severe pain" and "suffering" in a more encompassing way.

After stating the problem of objectively defining these terms, the Levin memo turns to the Torture Victim Protection Act cases to explicate the meaning of torture.[74] The cases primarily include "extreme" acts such as "electric shock, severe beating on genitals, cutting a figure on forehead," and "removal of teeth with pliers," although ostensibly "less [visibly] painful" acts such as "extreme limitations of food and water, sleep deprivation," and "shackling to a cot" were also included as forms of torture.[75] The question, however, is whether these "less visibly painful" forms by themselves are adequate to constitute torture, something not addressed by the cases and the memo. In other words, while the Levin memo distances itself from the Bybee/Yoo memo's emphasis on extreme acts, it does not clarify what its own interpretation of these terms is.

Thus, the Levin memo's own definition and citation of cases seem closer to what the Bybee/Yoo memo suggested because of the common source of these definitions being the Senate discussions on torture. There is, of course, a distinction to be made between the 1990 Senate discussions, which left room for ambiguity, and the Bybee/Yoo memo, which aggressively narrowed the protections against torture in the post-9/11 period. After all, even in the legal arena, the definition of torture is not clear. As Kim Lane Scheppele very aptly explains, "Torture does not have a clear legal meaning, in part because there have been no general and systematic attempts to map the border between 'torture' and 'not torture.'"[76] She further explains that in international law "torture is generally twinned with cruel, inhuman or degrading treatment or punishment," citing the definitions of these terms in the International Covenant on Civil and Political Rights (ICCPR) and the UN Convention against Torture.[77] But she goes on to state that in many instances the distinction between the two does not matter because both are legally prohibited. The United States did distinguish between the two to the extent that only torture was criminalized under the Federal Torture Statute.[78] The Yoo and Bybee memos utilize the distinction between the two terms to suggest that ostensibly cruel, inhuman, and degrading treatment could be used overseas as long as the methods do not constitute torture. Nonetheless, the discussions in the Levin and Bybee/Yoo memos and the 1990s Senate indicate that only the most brutal forms of physical torture were consensually considered as torture, leaving room for interpreting the less brutal methods (and/or mental torture) in different ways.

The debate on mental torture in the 1990s Senate thus has significant implications for the current context. According to Mark Richard, while there was some consensus on physical torture, it was mental pain that was seen as the "greatest problem" since it is "by its nature subjective."[79] He explains, "action that causes one person severe mental suffering may seem inconsequential to another person." Furthermore, he writes that "mental suffering is often transitory, causing no lasting harm."[80] Thus, the United States emphasized "prolonged mental harm" and the four predicate acts that would encompass the arena of mental torture. The predicate acts that led to "prolonged mental harm" were "infliction (or threat) of severe physical pain and suffering, administering (or threatening to administer) mind altering substances, threatening imminent death and threatening to do all these acts to a third person."[81]

One of the examples of the vagueness of the definition of mental torture mentioned by Mark Richard is the characterization by some international law treatises of "solitary confinement, or insulting language or . . . having been forced to strip naked" as mental torture.[82] In light of some of the methods of interrogation that have been used in the war on terror, namely, isolation, stress positions, removal of clothes, and sexual humiliation, it may be useful to note the lack of consensus on these methods even in the 1990s.

It is this emphasis on physical torture and a limited understanding of mental torture that allowed the Bush administration to claim not only that torture was never authorized but also that torture never took place in Guantánamo (or even Abu Ghraib).[83] The definitional ambiguities, particularly concerning acts of mental torture, especially in a context where Geneva conventions were not applicable, led to the authorization of certain methods, such as sleep deprivation, isolation up to thirty days, use of phobias, and removal of clothes, for the first few months at Guantánamo in November–December 2002.[84] But these methods were withdrawn because of their possible controversial nature and instead the methods that were authorized in 2003 were sleep adjustment, environmental manipulation, isolation, and dietary manipulation.[85] The criteria for determining whether a method was to be allowed or not was whether there was "an intent" to injure or not, whether "severe" physical or mental pain was involved or not, and, finally, whether there was a "legitimate government interest" or not, echoing the language of the Bybee/Yoo memo.[86] The military subsequently explicitly excluded some of the more controversial methods from its arsenal, but it is important to note that before the methods were rescinded, all of them were used both by the CIA and by the military interrogators at Guantánamo and, indeed, these methods have a longer history than that, at least for the CIA.[87]

Thus, the debates on the definition of torture in the 1990s Senate reflect a similar tension regarding the protections against mental torture that one observes in the withdrawn Bybee/Yoo memo and the Levin memo. While it is not surprising to note this similarity, given their common source, the significance of this analysis is that while the Bybee/Yoo memo may have been an example of aggressive hyperlegality (not a suspension), the ambiguities regarding definition cannot be said to disappear with the withdrawal of the Bybee/Yoo memo. Whether this was a conscious desire on the part of the United States is not the primary concern; rather, the concern is to point to a continuing struggle with excess violence that has preexisted the current period and continues to threaten the legal discourse as far as the detainees are concerned. The following question remains: did the absolute prohibition of torture primarily concern the most egregious of physical acts and was there a lack of clarity on methods permissible short of such acts?

Another question that has not been as carefully studied is whether in an era when the democratic branches were constantly, publicly, and proactively engaged in authorizing harsh interrogation methods (CIDT—cruel, inhuman, and degrading treatment—or torture) and some members within these branches were challenging them, how was the Supreme Court responding to the torture debate? While the Court has certainly responded consistently in the context of detention and the right to habeas corpus, as far as the torture debate was concerned, the Supreme Court responded mostly with silence.

Two Models of Governance and the Silence in the "Enemy Combatant" Cases

Immediately after 9/11, civil liberties activists in the United States identified a dual mode of governance in the "war on terror" in which a distinction was made between citizens with well-defined constitutional rights and noncitizens with few, if any, rights. As Michael Ratner from the Center for Constitutional Rights noted,

> I think one of the reasons we have seen so little opposition to some of these laws, apart from the fear factor . . . is that everybody (at least citizens) can say: "it's not me, it's someone else who will be treated badly." It is the other. It is not I as a citizen; it is a non-citizen. There has also been a tendency in the government to justify these laws by arguing that they are affecting non-citizens only.[88]

Thus, the president's military order of November 2001 explicitly stated that the detainees captured in Afghanistan and elsewhere would not be accorded the normal due process rights.[89] Meanwhile, within the United States, there was large-scale detention of noncitizens based on the material witness warrants and immigration laws.[90] Both these acts almost confirmed a parallel mode of governance for noncitizens. The clear government demarcations between citizens and noncitizens were severed when suspected terrorists turned out to be U.S. citizens (Yasser Hamdi, José Padilla, and John Walker Lindh).[91] However, the government was not willing to give up its dual mode of governance and instead created a new category of "enemy combatants" that would allow for citizen/enemy combatant and noncitizen/enemy combatant to be treated differently to some extent.

In this section, I discuss the response of the Supreme Court to the so-called exceptional policies introduced by the president in the post-9/11 period, with a special focus on its implications for the torture debate. I note that while the Supreme Court has upheld some important procedural and substantive rights for detainees, at times even challenging the executive and the Congress squarely, the Court's jurisprudence has stopped short of addressing the torture debate. Thus, I argue that the Court has primarily addressed what I term the "visible excesses" or only those actions that could not be hidden, namely, the detention of the actual bodies. In the process, what the Court managed to avoid were the implications of the visible (detention) for the invisible or partly visible excesses (torture and CIDT), as well as the intricate connection among detention, interrogation, and torture in the post-9/11 period. Despite numerous images, reports (official and unofficial), memos, testimonies, and, more importantly, direct requests to the Court from the amicus curiae and parties involved in the cases to address torture alongside detention, the Court somehow has managed to keep out of the torture debate.

The Supreme Court has intervened in five cases that have directly dealt with the "war on terror," namely, the Hamdi, Padilla, and Rasul cases in 2004 followed by the Hamdan and Boumediene cases in 2006 and 2008, respectively.[92] In the first three enemy combatant cases, the Supreme Court rejected some of the major arguments of the executive, especially the power to indefinitely detain citizens and noncitizens "based on nothing more than the president's word."[93]

José Padilla, a U.S. citizen, was arrested in the United States on a material witness warrant in relation to the 9/11 investigations, but in June 2002 the president designated him as an enemy combatant associated with al

Qaeda.[94] Padilla was detained at the Consolidated Naval Brig, Charleston, South Carolina, for nearly four years without charges or a trial until 2006, when he was charged and convicted in a federal criminal court.[95] In 2004, the only time when the Supreme Court discussed the Padilla case, the Court accepted the government's position that the habeas petition had been filed in the wrong jurisdiction and should be filed again. The Court argued that since Padilla had been moved from New York (where the material witness warrant was based) to South Carolina and the commander in charge was outside the jurisdiction of the Southern District Court of New York, the petition had to be filed again in South Carolina.[96] Thus, the Court decided the case primarily in terms of jurisdiction. Indeed, Ackerman reads this nonintervention in the case as indicating that the Court found it "too hot to handle" and notes that while perhaps a "strategic retreat" was better than "to capitulate to the war on terror," it did not bode well for protections of liberty.[97]

Yasser Hamdi was arrested in Afghanistan and initially taken to Guantánamo, but once it was discovered that he was an American citizen, he was brought to the United States. In Hamdi's case in 2004, the plurality of the Supreme Court agreed that Congress had authorized the detention of enemy combatants as a tool of war but also stated that as an American citizen, Hamdi had to be given "a meaningful opportunity to contest the factual basis for the detention before a neutral decision maker."[98] The Supreme Court, however, also stated that in order to reduce the burden on the executive, even "hearsay" could be admitted as the "most reliable available evidence" as long as the person had the right to rebut it. Thus, once the government gave adequate evidence for a person to be termed an enemy combatant, the burden of proof shifted to the enemy combatant to prove why he should not be termed as such, thereby radically changing the meaning of due process rights.[99] Ackerman criticizes the Hamdi Court for its use of a test (termed the Mathews test) to balance individual rights with government interests since the test in question was primarily used in public administration to determine pollution permits and welfare payments.[100] Cass Sunstein draws attention to Justice Thomas's dissent in Hamdi where he toes the executive's line, reflecting what Sunstein has called a "national security fundamentalism."[101]

In the third enemy combatant case and the first case concerning noncitizens, *Rasul v. Bush* (2004), the Supreme Court argued that enemy aliens held outside the United States did have access to U.S. courts, disagreeing with the lower courts on the issue. Differentiating this case from a previous U.S. case, Eisentrager, used to deny aliens a right to U.S. courts, the Court argued that in the Rasul case, the petitioners were not from countries at war, had denied their involvement in terrorism, and yet had been deprived of counsel, not charged, and detained for two years in an area that was under the United States' "exclusive jurisdiction and control."[102] The Supreme Court also stated that unless there were clear mention in a statute that it could not be used extraterritorially, the statute (in this case regarding habeas corpus) could be used in Guantánamo, especially since the base was within the "jurisdiction and control" of the United States.[103]

The Rasul decision, while welcomed by scholars and activists, was criticized for not clarifying the substantive rights available to the detainees in relation to U.S. and international laws.[104] As Chemerinsky put it, "I believe that the Supreme Court got it half right. They recognized a right of access to the courts. However, they do not go nearly far enough in specifying the rights that have to be accorded a detainee."[105] In that sense, by not elaborating on the rights available to noncitizen detainees (as compared to Hamdi's case), the Supreme Court continued to follow the two modes of governance based on citizenship. Of course, the distinction between the citizens and noncitizens was not as blatant as that observed in the lower courts in Rasul. As Gathhii notes, the lower courts' rejection of the access of detainees to U.S. courts was almost a continuation of previous colonial policies in which subjects were not given similar rights as citizens.[106]

My main point in considering the enemy combatant cases is to analyze the interventions of the Court in the torture debate. Here the brief discussion of the three cases suggests that while the Court did intervene in the detention cases, for the most part, it did not address the question of torture. The only place where torture was discussed was in the dissenting opinion in Padilla. Justice Stevens in his dissent (joined by Justices Souter, Ginsburg, and Breyer) pointed to the flexibility in the rules for filing habeas cases that could have allowed the court to accept and address the substantive questions of the Padilla case.[107] In addition, Justice Stevens noted,

> At stake in this case is nothing less than the essence of a free society. . . . Unconstrained executive detention for the purpose of investigating and preventing subversive activity is the hallmark of the Star Chamber. . . . Executive detention of subversive citizens, like detention of enemy soldiers to keep them off the battlefield, may sometimes be justified to prevent persons from launching or becoming missiles of destruction. It may not, however, be justified by the naked interest in using unlawful procedures to extract information. Incommunicado detention for months on end is such a procedure. *Whether the information so procured is more or less reliable than that acquired*

by more extreme forms of torture is of no consequence. For if this Nation is to remain true to the ideals symbolized by its flag, it must not wield the tools of tyrants even to resist an assault by the forces of tyranny.[108]

The dissent clearly found the very act of indefinite detention for prolonged interrogations unacceptable regardless of whether the information gained was reliable or not. Here the dissent did make a distinction between the methods used in the post-9/11 United States (incommunicado detention for months) and the more extreme forms of torture, but still determined the methods to be unacceptable.

Notwithstanding the dissenting opinion in the Padilla case, it is noteworthy that in all three enemy combatant cases there was a lack of discussion of the close linkages between detention and unlawful interrogation. After all, in the lower court proceedings of the same case, the government had accepted that the primary reason for the indefinite detention was information. The district court in the Padilla case noted this statement from the then–defense secretary, Donald Rumsfeld:

> It seems to me that the problem in the United States is that we . . . are in a certain mode. Our normal procedure is that if somebody does something unlawful . . . that the first thing we want to do is apprehend them, then try them in a court and then punish them. In this case that is not our first interest. . . . We are interested in finding out what he knows . . . our job, as responsible government officials, is to do *everything possible* to find out what that person knows, and see if we can't help our country or other countries.[109]

Thus, gaining information by doing "everything possible" was admittedly the primary purpose of the detention. In 2003, when the district court asked the government to grant Padilla access to counsel, one of the arguments made by the government in a subsequent hearing was that access to counsel would drastically affect the process of interrogating Padilla. The Jacoby Declaration made by Vice Admiral Lowell E. Jacoby, director of the Defense Intelligence Agency, stated the following:

> Developing the kind of relationship of trust and dependency necessary for effective interrogations is a process that can take a significant amount of time. Even seemingly minor interruptions can have profound psychological impacts on the delicate subject-interrogator relationship. Any insertion of

counsel into the subject-interrogator relationship, for example—even if only for a limited duration or for a specific purpose—can undo months of work and may permanently shut down the interrogation process. Therefore, it is critical to minimize external influences on the interrogation process.[110]

Despite such direct statements by the custodians of the detainees, it is surprising that the Supreme Court did not address the motivations behind the indefinite incommunicado detentions that were initially even denying counsel for the sake of gaining information at all costs. The psychological element of interrogation described by the administration was based on complete isolation and deprivation of contact with anyone for several months altogether (eerily close to the methods propounded by the CIA Kubark Manual that I discuss in the next section). Regardless of whether the domestic protections were considered applicable to suspected terrorists or not, the lack of discussion in the Court on the possible use of illegal methods of interrogation during the indefinite detentions remains noteworthy.[111]

Indeed, it was occasionally the lower courts that indicated the need for challenging the government's position. In the Rasul case, the district court wrote,

> [U]nless the Court assumes jurisdiction over their suits, they will be left without any rights and thereby be held *incommunicado*. In response . . . the government . . . conceded that "It is the government's position that the scope of those rights are for the military and political branches to determine. . . ." Therefore, the government recognizes that these aliens fall within the protections of certain provisions of international law. . . . While these two cases provide no opportunity for the Court to address these issues, the Court would point out that the notion that these aliens could be held *incommunicado* from the rest of the world would appear to be inaccurate.[112]

Yet, even while admitting that there was a serious concern regarding the possibility of the detainees being held incommunicado, the district court in Rasul accepted the government's theoretical suggestions that those concerns could be considered under international law, and the Supreme Court notably neither directly nor indirectly raised this issue.

This is despite the well-known fact that in a war situation, once the court accepts the fact of detention, the executive gets to determine the conditions of confinement entirely.[113] This point is reiterated by a report of the Association of the Bar of the City of New York in 2004:

Our whole tradition is opposed to coerced confessions, including by extended detentions designed to extract information. Once that Rubicon is crossed, the courts are poorly positioned to second-guess executive decisions as to the utility or necessity of extracting information from a particular detainee, or the tactics—including the length and conditions of the detentions—best calculated to perform the extraction.[114]

Thus, once the courts accept the general technique of indefinitely detaining an "enemy combatant," they lack the ability to control or oversee the conditions of detention and interrogation.[115]And sure enough, one observes the articulation of this deference toward the executive regarding the conditions of detention in *Odah v. U.S.* (2003), where the district court judge wrote,

> The level of threat a detainee poses to United States interests, the amount of intelligence a detainee might be able to provide, the conditions under which the detainee may be willing to cooperate, the disruption visits from family members and lawyers might cause—these types of judgments have traditionally been left to the exclusive discretion of the Executive branch, and there they should remain.[116]

Thus, what seemed missing from the discussions in the lower court decisions but more significantly in the Supreme Court were the implications of indefinite detention for illegal interrogations in either citizen or noncitizen enemy combatant cases.[117]

One could argue that the Supreme Court did not address the issue of torture in these cases because the torture debate had not assumed as much significance by then and the cases had not directly brought it up. After all, the Abu Ghraib pictures that brought the torture debate into public discourse were only exposed after the oral arguments in the cases (in fact, the same evening).[118] Further, the pictures created a crisis of legitimacy for the state only after the controversial memos regarding Guantánamo emerged. Thus, in 2004, the Court was more concerned with the actual questions raised in these cases that constituted the visible excesses of the "war on terror"— indefinite detention and lack of due process—and the Court's decisions did lead to some changes in executive policy.

The impact of the Hamdi case, in particular, was the implementation of some form of due process even in the Guantánamo cases. Combatant Status Review Tribunals (CSRTs) were set up to review the status of the detainees before they were subjected to the military commissions. The CSRTs were to ascertain whether the detainees could be considered enemy combatants. The latter was defined as "an individual who was part of or supporting Taliban or al Qaeda forces, or associated forces that are engaged in hostilities against the United States or its coalition partners."[119] Those who were declared enemy combatants were to be tried by the military commissions.

The question is, once the issue of torture became a nationwide and indeed worldwide concern and the courts were forced to take up additional cases clarifying their own previous decisions, did the Court respond more directly to the torture debate? In the Hamdan and the Boumediene cases, even though the Court was willing to challenge the democratically elected branches more directly, there was still no clear intervention in the torture debate despite the fact that the issue of coercion-tainted evidence had become a major point of contention.[120]

Salim Hamdan was captured in Afghanistan in 2001, transferred to Guantánamo in 2002, and subsequently charged with conspiracy by the president, who proclaimed him eligible to be tried by the military commissions.[121] Hamdan challenged the constitutionality of the military commissions, the charge of conspiracy, as well as the procedures that did not allow him to "see and hear the evidence against him."[122] The Supreme Court agreed with Hamdan that the president could not arbitrarily use military commissions in the absence of a specific congressional statute and that since conspiracy was not a violation of the laws of war, it could not be addressed by the military commissions. Further, the Court argued that even the procedures of the military commissions were a violation of American common law and the Uniform Code of Military Justice (UCMJ), particularly considering the fact that Hamdan, the accused, was on at least one occasion excluded from his own trial, along with his counsel.[123] Regarding the Geneva conventions that had very clearly been denied to the detainees by the executive, even though the Court did not clarify whether they had protections under the Third Geneva Convention (regarding the prisoner of war status), the Court did state unequivocally that Common Article 3 of all the Geneva Conventions was applicable to the detainees.[124] This was the case because the Court considered Common Article 3 applicable to any conflict that was not between nations, and that meant the detainees deserved a "regularly constituted court affording all judicial guarantees recognized as indispensable by civilized peoples."[125]

The Hamdan decision was possibly the most serious repudiation of the commander-in-chief by the Court. This is the case because the executive branch considered the CSRTs to be an adequate response to the Court's earlier decision requiring some due process, and yet the Court struck down the new procedures as unacceptable. Neal Katyal, who was then one of the lead counsels for Hamdan, wrote, "the real significance of Hamdan lies in its repudiation of the Administration's radical theory that the President has the ability to interpret creatively, and even set aside, statutes that he claims interfere with his war powers."[126] According to Katyal, the most significant evidence of the repudiation of the inherent power doctrine was the executive's acceptance of the suggestion by the concurrent opinion of the Court that the executive had to go to Congress to get authorization for the military commissions, and that is exactly what happened subsequently.

Yet, even in the landmark Hamdan case, the Court once again paid little attention to the issue of torture despite the fact that the torture debate was brought within the purview of the Court in the form of evidence linked to coercion. The plurality opinion as well as the concurring opinion in Hamdan did point out that the rules of evidence allowed by the military commissions were tainted by coercion. As the concurring opinion wrote, "they make no provision for exclusion of coerced declarations save those 'established to have been made as a result of torture.'"[127] It was left to the presiding officer to decide whether the evidence had "probative value to a reasonable person."[128] Thus, surprisingly, even while noting the unfair rules regarding coercive evidence, the Court's decision remained focused on ensuring that the accused in the trial be present and privy to the evidence against him.

One could, of course, claim that the Court was not responsible for ruling on all the defective rules of the military commissions, but to the extent that torture had been one of the most controversial policies (especially after the classified memos showed that they were not aberrant acts such that the only memo that was clearly repudiated was the torture memo), it was surprising that the Court did not take this opportunity to give a clear signal on the issue.

Hamdan was decided in 2006. By then not only were the Abu Ghraib abuses well known but so were the ones at Guantánamo. The implications of the statements regarding the tensions in the prohibitions against torture had become a part of the legal and political discourse. The Court even talked about the applicability of Common Article 3 to the detainees but stopped short of identifying the implications of it for the torture debate, namely, that acts of violence were potentially a violation of the War Crimes Act of 1996, meant to address "grave breaches" of the Geneva Conventions. One of the key provisions of Common Article 3 of the Geneva Conventions was that it disallowed "violence to life and person, in particular murder of all kinds, mutilation, cruel treatment and torture; . . . outrages upon personal dignity, in particular humiliating and degrading treatment."[129] This meant that acts less than torture that had permeated the post-9/11 context could have been addressed by the Court. Indeed, even if the Court did not want to confront the excess violence directly, it could have at least squarely addressed the issue of coercion-tainted evidence.

This is particularly significant when considered in the context of the military order that governed the first version of the military commissions (MC 1). Several amicus briefs had pointed to the fact that the president's military order in 2001 had stated that evidence shall be admitted if, "in the opinion of the Presiding Officer . . . the evidence would have probative value to a reasonable person."[130] According to the amicus, the wording implied that evidence derived as a result of torture was also not excluded by the president's order.[131] In fact, the ACLU read the language of the first military order as "an invitation to torture." The ACLU explains,

> The possibility that evidence secured through the methods described above might form the basis for a conviction—or even a sentence of death—infects the legitimacy of the entire commission process. Indeed, the absence of an express prohibition against the use of such tainted evidence creates an *irresistible incentive for the prosecutors of the detainees to become their torturers.*[132]

Even though the March 24, 2006, military commission instructions clarified that evidence gained from torture would not be used, they still did not explain whether evidence derived as a result of actions short of torture or in the realm of CIDT would be allowed. Thus, the lack of initiative on the part of the Court is significant also because torture and abuse were no longer invisible issues by the time the Court took up Hamdan. Even the amicus curiae and the petitioners in the case noted that Hamdan had been abused:

> Hamdan alleges—without contradiction—that while in the custody of U.S. forces, he was beaten, forced to sit motionless for days on end and exposed to sub-freezing temperatures without adequate clothing. After being transferred to the detention facility at Guantanamo Bay in 2002, he was held in solitary confinement in an eight-by-five-foot cell for ten months.[133]

Thus, the need for a clear signal from the Court on torture and CIDT was felt by the amicus groups both because of the narratives of abuse and torture and also because the groups saw a close link between the question of the constitutionality of the military commissions and the rules regarding coerced evidence. As the amici put it,

Amici believe that this Court should make clear that a trial system based on evidence gained by torture is not a legal proceeding at all. . . . Beyond the legal question of authority and its limits that are embraced within the question presented, there are pressing reasons for the Court to address the question of coerced evidence now.[134]

Even though the Court effectively challenged the Military Commissions (MC) as a violation of the UCMJ and Article 3 of the Geneva Conventions, pointing to other rules and procedures, it did not take this opportunity, despite the requests from amici, to send a clear signal on torture and CIDT, especially regarding the link between detention and interrogation. In fact, the amici even argued that the Court should not decide the case without clarifying the rules of evidence. "The legitimacy of future proceedings, the safety of those held at Guantanamo Bay, and adherence to basic standards of fairness and justice all depend on a clear statement that reliance on the fruits of torture will not be tolerated under law."[135]

Thus, the failure of the Court to send a clear signal on torture and the unacceptability of coercive evidence is significant and needs to be focused more. Despite the limitations in the Court's decisions, one could argue that the Hamdan case did lead to the executive's move to the Congress for authorization of some of its acts and ultimately led to a repudiation of the previous military order, resulting in the new Military Commissions Act in 2006.

The Military Commissions Act of 2006 (MC A), however, retained two very controversial aspects of the executive's position, namely, the suspension of habeas corpus for the detainees and a narrow definition of coercive acts, the latter giving the Court another opportunity to address the question of torture and coercive evidence when the case came up. In a landmark judgment in June 2008, the Supreme Court in *Boumediene v. Bush* claimed that the suspension of habeas corpus by the Military Commission Act was not acceptable and that the Detainee Treatment Act (DTA) review procedures were not an adequate substitute for habeas corpus.[136] The Court rejected the government's argument that only formal de jure sovereignty ensures the reach of the constitutional privilege of habeas corpus. Rather, the Court asserted that as long as there was a de facto control over the territory, the Constitution and the right to habeas corpus were applicable.[137] Furthermore, the Court asserted that the DTA did not provide adequate procedures required to substitute the right to habeas corpus due to some of its provisions, including the lack of counsel, limited knowledge of classified charges, and use of hearsay evidence—all leading to the conclusion that "even when all the parties involved in this process act with diligence and in good faith, there is considerable risk of error in the tribunal's finding of fact."[138]

While this is an extremely significant decision, hailed as being one of the most effective rebuttals of both the executive and the Congress for suspending a basic liberty that had always been available to citizens and noncitizens, the Court's silence on the question of torture and CIDT remains troubling. In one context, the Court writes, "in view of our holding we need not discuss the reach of the writ with respect to claims of unlawful conditions of treatment or confinement."[139] But one of the most significant aspects of indefinite detention has been the unlawful conditions of treatment or confinement that the Court clearly could have addressed but did not. Thus, even if the Hamdi, Padilla, and Rasul cases were more about the legality of detention, the two later cases—Hamdan and Boumediene—delved more deeply into the constitutionality of procedures that were directly or indirectly linked to torture and CIDT—either by omission (as in the president's military order and MC) or by being mentioned in some form (CSRT, DTA, and MC A).

The Court once again ignored a plea from the amici to address the issue of coerced statements. While torture was not the primary issue raised in the case, the DTA review process was attacked by amicus briefs filed by former federal judges precisely because "[t]he public record reveals that CSRT panels routinely made detention determinations without investigating torture allegations or excluding statements allegedly extracted through impermissible coercion, and the government maintains that the CSRT panels were authorized to rely on evidence extracted through such means."[140]

Thus, the entire review process was tainted by evidence derived from torture. Here, one of the caveats mentioned by many of the briefs is that regardless of whether these allegations were true or not, the more troubling issue was that there was no attempt by the CSRT review boards to assess the veracity of the claims. This is particularly significant given that the 2006 Military Commissions Act (MCA) had restricted the meaning of the protections provided by Common Article 3 of the Geneva Conventions. The grave breaches were limited to actions such as torture, rape, mutilating, maiming, or cruel and inhuman treatment.[141] The Military Commissions Act defined cruel and inhuman treatment

> as an act intended to inflict severe or serious physical or mental pain or suffering (other than pain or suffering incidental to lawful sanctions), including serious physical abuse, upon another within his custody or control. . . . [T]he term "serious physical pain or suffering" shall be applied

as meaning bodily injury that involves—(i) a substantial risk of death; (ii) extreme physical pain; (iii) a burn or physical disfigurement of a serious nature (other than cuts, abrasions, or bruises); or (iv) significant loss or impairment of the function of a bodily member, organ, or mental faculty.[142]

The narrow meaning of this term was interpreted by scholars such as Marty Lederman to point out that even a form of interrogation such as waterboarding, which many consider as torture or at least CIDT, would not be prohibited.[143] Similarly, Michael Matheson noted that the MCA did not clearly explain whether methods such as "beatings that do not cause permanent injury, exposure to cold or heat that does not cause permanent impairment, or deprivation of food, water, or medical treatment" would be prohibited.[144] Furthermore, Matheson writes, "Even more problematically, does the text apply to forcing a detainee to be naked or to commit sexual acts, or to the threatening use of dogs?"[145]

Thus, in the MCA, the broader protections provided by the original text of Common Article 3 of the Geneva Conventions against "humiliating" treatment or "outrages upon personal dignity" were deliberately removed from the scope of the War Crimes Act. Although the military specifically prohibited many of the abovementioned methods in its new field manual, the question is whether these limitations were applicable to the nonmilitary interrogators.[146] After all, some of the most controversial techniques, including waterboarding, were used against the high-value detainees, such as Abu Zubaydah and al Nashiri, who were kept at black sites.[147] Former president Bush answered this question by vetoing a bill that would have limited the CIA to using only those methods of interrogation mentioned in the army field manual.[148]

This was the broader political context of the Boumediene case, and the Court's silence was surprising also because even the petitioners in the Boumediene case, including five Bosnians, had alleged that they were subjected to "15 months of solitary confinement, sleep deprivation and extreme temperature conditions."[149] In fact, almost all the detainees who have approached the Supreme Court in the habeas cases have alleged that they have been tortured.

Thus, even if the Court were unwilling to take up torture and CIDT as a substantive due process issue, its focus on the constitutionality of the DTA and CSRTs as substitutes for the right to habeas corpus gave it adequate opportunity to make a direct intervention on torture and CIDT, and yet it did not. One has to keep in mind that the executive had asked the Court for avoidance or extreme deference in times of war.[150] The Court, however, rejected that request in some important respects, so it is intriguing that it did not extend its intervention to issues concerning torture. Here I do not attempt an in-depth analysis of why the Court did not intervene in the torture debate. Nonetheless, a couple of theorizations regarding the response of the courts to emergencies and war may be useful in explaining why the Court did not address the issue of torture directly. Neal Katyal, for instance, notes that the Court reflects some passive virtues, a notion pointed out by Alexander Bickel, which leads the courts to take a really long time to take up a case and decide on it. As Katyal explains, the "Court employed procedural and jurisdictional doctrines to produce a useful 'time lag between legislation and adjudication, as well as shifting the line of vision.'"[151] Of course, the adverse impact of this approach of the Court is the delay of due process rights for those concerned—a good example being Padilla.[152] So is the nonintervention just a reflection of the passive virtue of the Court? The question is, how long does it take the Court to address this issue?

In contrast to this empirical observation about the nature of the Court, Sunstein actually believes that the Court should follow a minimalist perspective. As Sunstein explains,

> Minimalists believe that, in the most controversial areas, judges should refuse to endorse any large-scale approach and should be reluctant to adopt wide rulings that will . . . bind the country in unforeseen circumstances. Instead, minimalists want judges to rule narrowly and cautiously. In the context of war, minimalists would like courts to avoid constitutional issues by, for example, holding that Congress has not authorized the executive to intrude into the domain of constitutionally protected interests. Minimalists also like to avoid broad judicial pronouncements about either presidential power or liberty, preferring instead close consideration of particular measures. In the aftermath of September 11, minimalists want courts to proceed in small steps, leaving the largest issues undecided as long as possible.[153]

To be fair, Sunstein does not directly analyze whether the courts should decide on torture and CIDT. Indeed, Sunstein is highly critical of the "national security fundamentalism" (reflected by Thomas in the Hamdi case) that does not challenge the executive power at all and reads the second circuit's rejection of Padilla's arbitrary detention as an example of minimalism. However, since he rejects "liberty perfectionism," it is not clear whether his framework would be open to a broader ruling on the substantive rights of the detainees, including a right not to be subject to harsh interrogations.

The unfortunate result of the Court's silence is that it ultimately ignored the issue of aggressive interrogations both in the pre–Abu Ghraib and the post–Abu Ghraib period. There was an expectation from a wide range of groups that the Court would respond to the torture debate in the Boumediene and Hamdan cases and reiterate the protections against torture and CIDT. The post–Abu Ghraib context did force the Supreme Court to accord certain due process rights to both citizens and noncitizen enemy combatants.[154] However, the interventions failed to address the conditions of detentions despite widespread discourses on the authorization of torture.[155] Significantly, the only cases on torture that did reach the Supreme Court were not taken up by the Court since they would involve issues of "state secrets" or because they were seen as already resolved.[156]

Apart from structural reasons that may explain why the Supreme Court did not address the issue of torture, I suggest that the reason may be that doing so would have led to uncomfortable conversations on excess violence that the Court as a normative institution would be less willing to take up. In particular, addressing the torture debate in the post-9/11 context would have meant not only defining torture clearly (beyond extreme physical violence) but also specifying the nature of violence acceptable in times of necessity. Thus, in extraordinary contexts, the Court hesitated to enter the conversation on excess violence and yet, as noted earlier, the focus on judicial authenticity in torture debates has been crucial historically.[157] The silence on the torture debate, however, reflects the continuation of the uneasy relationship that law has with excess violence in both routine and extraordinary times. Of course, even while the courts stay away from the question of excess violence, the state, in its own quest for legitimacy and control, continues to find ways of accommodating acceptable levels of excess violence within an art of government.

Excess Violence as a Part of Governmentality: Building the Juridico-Medical Complex

As the preceding discussion indicates, the continuing struggle of law with excess violence is an ongoing theme in a liberal democracy and is unaddressed by the dominant framework for understanding torture, namely, the state-of-exception analysis. Similarly, the Foucauldian paradigm assumes the disappearance of excessive violence in contemporary societies because of the emphasis on an art of government that controls individuals primarily by channeling their productive power. In particular, Foucault's notion of governmentality focuses on harnessing the productive capacity of individuals within a population: "government has as its purpose . . . the welfare of the population, the improvement of its condition, the increase of its wealth, longevity, health, etc."[158] Indeed, governmentality studies after Foucault have primarily been concerned with understanding how "liberal democracies developed technologies of governance which shifted away from 'top down' disciplinary and repressive controls to more indirect and persuasive controls."[159] As David Garland notes, it is the decentered state analysis emphasizing two poles of governance—how authorities govern and how individuals self-regulate—that is at the center of governmentality studies.[160] This framework largely seems to suggest an insignificant role for excess violence in modern societies. As Colin Gordon puts it,

> The idea of an "economic government" has, as Foucault points out, a double meaning for liberalism: that of a government informed by the precepts of political economy, but also that of a government which economizes on its own costs: a greater effort of technique aimed at *accomplishing more through a lesser exertion of force and authority.*[161]

Foucault's framework, from *Discipline and Punish* to his essay on governmentality, suggests that spectacular forms of violence, including torture, are rendered unnecessary because sovereignty based on obedience and fear is replaced by a decentralized power that works through disciplinary mechanisms and manages the conduct of populations. Foucault compares such a government to "the bumble bee who rules the bee hive *without needing a sting.*"[162]

In contrast to this Focauldian reading of state power, I reclaim certain key Foucaldian terms and concepts to account for the process of accommodation of excess violence by the modern state. This is significant because, while for the most part there is a transformation in the nature of state power such that direct reliance on physical pain and suffering is less visible in modern societies, there remains a space for what I call "excess violence." As noted earlier, "excess violence" is a term I reclaim from Foucaldian literature and define as violence that the state claims is unnecessary but still struggles to contain and in the process accommodates. Thus, even though Foucault underplays the role of excess violence in more modern societies, especially where the art of government emerges as a prominent mode of control, his notion of governmentality can actually be reinterpreted to allow for an understanding of how excess violence could be addressed within that framework. Here

I turn to Kevin Stenson's formulation that since liberalism always struggles to maintain sovereignty, it turns to "harsh despotic technologies of rule to bring government to areas and groups deemed to be most troublesome."[163] The emphasis by Stenson on these harsh technologies of rule easily fit within the Foucauldian framework if one understands the workings of sovereignty, discipline, and governmentality not in a chronological way, with the latter replacing the former two, but rather in a "synchronic" way, with all three working together.[164] Thus, even though governmentality studies for the most part have not focused on the role of excess violence in modern states, the Foucauldian framework does allow for such exploration.

Here I develop the Foucauldian notion of governmentality by indicating just one instance of the way excess violence is accommodated in the art of government. Using Foucault's concept of juridico-medical complex, I analyze how medical professionals have actually been drawn into the state's attempt to accommodate excess violence. In the post-9/11 context, there have been different kinds of allegations against medical professionals in the context of Iraq, Guantánamo Bay, Cuba, and Afghanistan, ranging from nonreporting of torture and ill treatment[165] to nonintervention in cases of torture[166] to actual participation in interrogations, including its "harsh" or "enhanced" forms. The latter allegation is of most interest to this argument because it notes a long-standing history of psychologists being involved in developing interrogation techniques.

Many scholars, including Alfred McCoy and Naomi Klein, have pointed out that the genesis of the "harsh" methods of interrogation used in the post-9/11 period lies in the experiments and studies conducted by psychologists during the Cold War.[167] The similarities between the methods used by the CIA from the 1960s till the present is so strong that Alfred McCoy writes, "Across the span of three continents and four decades, there is a striking similarity in U.S. torture techniques—from the CIA's original Kubark Manual, to the agency's 1983 Honduras training handbook, all the way to General Ricardo Sanchez's 2003 orders for interrogation in Iraq."[168]

During the Cold War, the CIA funded a number of studies that looked into the possibility of using psychological methods of control.[169] The first phase of these studies and experiments was focused on mind control with the help of "hypnosis and hallucinogenic drugs."[170] The experiments with drugs and hypnosis, however, failed. As Mark Bowden puts it, "fear and anxiety turned into terrifying hallucinations and fantasies, which made it difficult to elicit secrets, and added a tinge of unreality to whatever information was divulged."[171]

This led to a focus, in the second phase, on sensory deprivation and self-inflicted techniques, or what McCoy calls a "new approach to torture that was psychological, not physical, perhaps best described as 'no-touch torture.'"[172] Relating these methods to the current conflict, McCoy points out that the classic Abu Ghraib picture with the hooded Iraqi man with arms extended and wires attached to him exemplifies the methods of sensory deprivation (hooding) combined with extended arms as an example of the self-inflicted pain. Self-inflicted pain occurs when the subject's own action—extended arms—is responsible for the pain rather than an external force.[173] Well-known psychologists at famous universities, such as McGill in Canada, conducted many of these studies.[174] McCoy points to one such study in which student subjects were put in isolation, with reduced stimuli: "light 'diffused' by translucent goggles, 'auditory stimulation' limited by sound proofing and constant low noise, and 'tactual perception' blocked by thick gloves and a U-Shaped foam pillow about the head."[175] McCoy points to the similarities between these methods and the "goggled and muffled prisoners" at Guantánamo, thus illustrating the actual use of methods developed as a result of these studies and experiments.[176] What emerged from a number of studies and experiments funded and/or supported by the CIA was the Kubark Manual, produced in 1963, which emphasized the importance of using these psychological techniques to create "regression," "dependence," and "confusion" so as to make the situation "mentally intolerable" for the subjects.[177]

Even when CIA programs (exported to Asia and Latin America, among other parts of the world) were uncovered and U.S. congressional inquiries were held, according to McCoy, these inquiries did not look into the extent and source of psychological torture.[178] In fact, McCoy explains that the need to narrow the definition of mental torture was motivated by the state's desire to exempt some of these methods used by the CIA. As McCoy writes, "Strikingly, Washington's narrow definition of 'mental harm' excluded sensory deprivation (hooding), self-inflicted pain (stress positions) and disorientation (isolation and sleep denial)—the very techniques the CIA had refined at such great cost over several decades."[179] Thus, even while excluding egregious forms of physical torture and some forms of mental torture (limited to the four predicate acts), this narrow definition is another instance of the way the liberal state allowed for a limited understanding of torture that accounts for a number of psychological techniques in current times.

The development of these techniques, according to Darius Rejali, was not an accident of history but a necessity for democracies such as the United States. Rejali writes that these "clean" (nonscarring) "stealth techniques" are developed not by authoritarian governments, as is commonly believed, but rather have been the product of the main Western democracies—England, France, and the United States.[180] Indeed, one of the main reasons why these are primarily found in democracies is that their history of human-rights monitoring requires democracies to use torture techniques that leave fewer marks and can thus evade detection. As Rejali explains,

> *Public monitoring leads institutions that favor painful coercion to use and combine clean torture techniques to evade detection, and, to the extent that public monitoring is not only greater in democracies, but that public monitoring of human rights is a core value in modern democracies, it is the case that where we find democracies torturing today we will also be more likely to find stealthy torture.*[181]

Thus, Rejali forcefully illustrates that it was necessary for these states to develop less visible forms of torture in order to maintain their legitimacy. This further strengthens my central argument that not only is torture an ongoing issue for liberal states but there is in fact a long-standing history of these techniques being constantly developed in such a way as to evade detection by leaving fewer marks, further exhibiting a constant negotiation with excess violence. The question is the exact nature of this excess violence. Is it lawless? What are the parameters of its functioning? Taking the case of the juridico-medical complex, I suggest that the state constantly negotiates the boundaries of excess violence to ascertain what is permissible and the extent to which it can push those boundaries without explicitly appearing lawless.

In the post-9/11 context, the role of psychologists was not just restricted to conducting studies for the purpose of developing psychological techniques for the CIA; medical professionals actually became part of a juridico-medical complex. In 2002, Geoffrey Miller, who was in charge of Guantánamo, set up what is called a behavioral science consultant team (BSCT).[182] These BSCTs always had a psychologist and a psychiatrist who helped in developing strategies of interrogation. The strategies were based on psychological analyses of detainees, who were assessed by medical personnel who either participated in interrogations or observed the sessions and gave feedback to the interrogators. Many of these interrogation techniques were based on specific medical information about the detainees. This medical information was provided by caregivers ostensibly on the basis of a 2002 memo suggesting that privacy rights did not apply to detainees at Guantánamo and a 2005 memo that allowed for medical information to be used in interrogations.[183] Even when the Pentagon created guidelines regarding the involvement of medical caregivers in interrogations, prohibiting those directly engaged in caregiving from participating, they did not clarify whether noncaregivers could still be involved.[184]

While the BSCT developed customized methods for individual detainees, the base material appears to have been provided by the army's own program: SERE (Survival, Evasion, Resistance, Escape)—a program meant to train military personnel in ways of resisting torture when confronted by enemy forces. Mayer describes the SERE training as including the following: "trainees are hooded; their sleep patterns are disrupted; they are starved for extended periods; they are stripped of their clothes; they are exposed to extreme temperatures; and they are subjected to harsh interrogations by officials impersonating enemy captors."[185]

The link between SERE and Guantánamo is confirmed by the Department of Defense (DOD) inspector general's report that notes a meeting in Fort Bragg in September 2002 at which the members of the behavioral science consultation team from Guantánamo were familiarized with the SERE methods that they could potentially develop for use by the interrogators (JTF [Joint Task Force]-170) at Guantánamo. These methods eventually got used as counterresistance techniques in Guantánamo and later traveled to Iraq. The DOD continues to oppose the understanding that "SERE training was a determinate variable in the development of JTF-170 interrogation techniques."[186] However, it is important for our purpose to note the debate on the role of psychologists that has ensued as a result of these revelations. In other words, regardless of whether SERE methods were directly exported or not, the coincidental similarity between the methods used at Guantánamo, SERE, and the studies conducted in the past is striking, especially because of the central role of psychologists in all these contexts.

As a result, medical professionals seem to have emerged as central actors in the debate on interrogations, pointing to a key role of medicine in state power, as noted by Foucault. In an interview in 1976 Foucault remarked, "Medicine has taken on a general social function: it infiltrates law, it plugs into it, it makes it work. A sort of juridico-medical complex is presently being constituted, which is the major form of power."[187] Foucault notes how law and medicine work together in what he terms "the juridico-medical complex." The relationship between law and medicine in modern societies is of course an uneasy one, as illustrated in the dilemma faced by the doctors in another context of state power, namely, executions by lethal injections. Timothy Kaufman-Osborn eloquently writes about this paradox for state (law) and doctors (medicine) regarding executions:

On the one hand, the state has an interest in medicalizing capital punishment as fully as possible since it thereby assumes the character of a depoliticized humanitarian (non) event, a painless matter of putting someone "to sleep." . . . On the other hand, the medical profession has an obvious interest in resisting the conscription of its members for this purpose.[188]

Thus, as far as the doctors are concerned, the dilemma is that as healers they are unwilling to participate in state killing. However, as Kaufman-Osborn points out, they also risk being found guilty of violating their "code of ethics" by not providing suitable medical services during executions and in the process making the state look incompetent.[189]

The role of psychologists in the post-9/11 context has also raised similar questions about law and medicine. In response to the various criticisms of the role of psychologists in developing interrogation methods, there has been a very intense debate within the American Psychological Association (APA) on the role of psychologists in interrogations.[190] The APA set up a Presidential Task Force on Psychological Ethics and National Security (PENS) to look into the issue, especially since many of its members criticized psychologists for violating U.S. and international laws against torture and cruel, inhuman, and degrading treatment.[191] The PENS report, however, concluded that "[t]he Task Force believes that a central role for psychologists working in the area of national security–related investigations is to assist in ensuring that processes are *safe, legal, and ethical* for all participants."[192] The PENS report confirmed their commitment against torture and CIDT, stating that psychologists have a responsibility not only to stay away from these practices but to report them and to make sure that they do not get involved in situations where there could be a conflict between their role as consultants and their role as caregivers. Yet the report accepted a central role for psychologists in interrogations that was reiterated by the APA in 2007. Members of the APA, in contrast, criticized the report, claiming that members of the PENS were in fact directly involved in creating interrogation methods for Guantánamo, Iraq, and Afghanistan and that three members actually converted the SERE methods into harsh interrogation techniques for Guantánamo.[193] In 2008, the APA managed to find a majority willing to bar its members from participating in interrogations.[194] However, what this intense debate indicates in the post-9/11 context is yet another illustration of the uneasy relationship between law and medicine in the juridico-medical complex.

That the United States envisioned a role for medical professionals in interrogations was visible in the Report of the Working Group on Detainee Interrogations (DOD), which asked officials to ensure that the detainee is *medically and operationally evaluated as suitable* (considering all techniques to be used in combination); interrogators are specifically trained for the technique(s); a specific interrogation plan (including reasonable safeguards, limits on duration, intervals between applications, termination criteria and the *presence or availability of qualified medical personnel*) is developed; appropriate supervision is provided and appropriate specified senior approval is given for use with any specific detainee (after considering the foregoing and receiving legal advice).[195]

Indeed, medical professionals played a particularly visible role in justifying the use of "harsh interrogation techniques" on the high-value detainees. As the May 2005 memo on evaluating the legality of certain interrogation techniques stated,[196] "You have also explained that, prior to interrogation, each detainee is evaluated by medical and psychological professionals from the CIA's Office of Medical Services ('OMS') to ensure that he is not likely to suffer any severe physical or mental pain or suffering as a result of interrogation."[197] However, safety and evaluation here not only mean protecting the welfare of the detainee but more significantly refer to making it safe for the interrogator who is interested in gaining information even while trying to avoid violation of any laws against torture and CIDT. The psychologists then have to make sure that the interrogations continue as long as they do not reach the threshold of state definitions of torture, namely, the Federal Torture Statute (and CIDT if applicable). As the 2005 memo notes,

> At anytime, any on-scene personnel (including the medical or psychological personnel . . .) can intervene to stop the use of any technique if it appears that the technique is being used improperly, and on scene medical personnel can intervene if the detainee has developed a condition making the use of the technique unsafe. More generally, medical personnel watch for signs of physical distress or mental harm so significant as possibly to amount to the "severe physical or mental pain or suffering" that is prohibited by sections 2340-2340A.[198]

This is suggestive again of the anxiety of the liberal state. The state cannot stop relying on excess violence but has to ensure that the severity does not reach the levels that would constitute torture and CIDT under international and national laws. What the psychologists supporting a ban understand is that while formal laws against torture and CIDT would serve as some protection against illegal interrogations, they still allow for a great deal of flexibility and accommodation of excess violence, especially when these terms and laws are narrowly defined. Thus, the post-9/11 context brings to the fore another instance of negotiating excess violence where the psychologists are forced to balance their role as healers while responding to the state's need for excess violence. The juridico-medical complex thus formed is unstable and under attack and yet it indicates an instance of excess violence functioning within the art of government and not outside of it.

The recurrence of these acts, not as aberrations but as policies, at different moments of history suggests a constant negotiation with excess violence—an issue unsettled. The difference in the post-9/11 context is that these methods appear to be much more visible and, at least initially, explicitly defended. Yet what the withdrawal of the memo and the methods of interrogation exhibit is that even then the state has to ensure, both rhetorically and legally, that the terms being used are "enhanced or harsh interrogation techniques" and not a defense of torture by the all-powerful commander-in-chief in an exceptional context. The rhetoric and ambiguous laws work together to attempt a coherent state narrative that often breaks down and needs renegotiating. The constant negotiation and accommodation of excess violence lead to the assertion that excess violence is compatible with governmentality, not outside or in excess of it. Even if traditional forms of sovereignty are replaced by an art of government that focuses on populations, it is important to recognize that the very art of government includes certain excess forms of violence.

Torture in the TV Show *24*

Circulation of Meanings

Obviously, things like cutting off fingers, to me that sounds like
torture. . . .
— Former Attorney-General Alberto R. Gonzales, 2005[1]

In this chapter, I analyze the popular imagery of torture in the U.S. TV
show *24* to illustrate how the popular and the official legal and political debates
on torture inform and constitute each other. In other words, I point to a circulation of meaning of torture across all the different sites. I argue that the popular
imagery of torture, which emphasizes physical brutality, legitimizes a narrow
definition of torture that is visible in official discourses, and that the official
and popular discourses collectively use sanitized and routinized terminology
to make less severe forms of violence seem ordinary and acceptable. Thus, the
imagery not only helps government officials deny the presence of torture by
using narrow definitions but manages to present the current practice of coercive violence as an actual moment of progress from earlier, more brutal times.

The official discourse, then, cannot be understood independently of popular conceptions, and the relationship between the two further illustrates how
excess violence is denied and normalized. In contrast to the representation
of torture as physical brutality, human rights reports and scholars challenge
this imagery by pointing out the impact of the seemingly less severe forms of
violence and their context, namely, the custodial aspect of interrogations.

Imagery of Torture
Torture in U.S Popular Culture: Jack Bauer and the Ticking Clock

In recent years, the representation of torture in popular media has
increased phenomenally. Human Rights First has noted that the number of times torture is shown on television has grown from four times in a

year before 2001 to more than one hundred times per year in the post-9/11 period—24 having the most scenes of torture.[2] The show 24 concluded its eighth and final season on Fox in 2010. It won the Emmy Award for best drama series in 2006 and had about fourteen million viewers that year.[3] I focus on 24 not only because it was an extremely popular show but also, more significantly, because it has become a major site of debate on torture in recent years, among both academics and U.S. officials. In the show 24, Jack Bauer (Kiefer Sutherland) is a member of the Counter Terrorism Unit (CTU), and in each season of the show, Bauer saves the city, the nation, and, by implication, the world from some disaster, often relying on torture to attain his goal.

In 24, the use of torture is always in the context of the so-called ticking-bomb scenario. Episodes have ranged from "assassination plot against a presidential candidate and [Jack] has 24 hours to stop the murder" to "terrorists . . . have planted a bomb in Los Angeles" to "a high-profile drug dealer threatens to release a deadly virus on Los Angeles if his captured brother is not released."[4] Each of these plots reflects some version of the ticking-bomb scenario utilized by those in support of torture in the political and academic arena.[5] The plots requiring the use of torture have prompted a number of academics and activists to critique 24 for legitimizing torture in contemporary times.[6] Since each season enacts just one day in the life of the heroic Bauer, the crisis is both constant and immediate. In the show, one constantly watches the time passing, and the ticking clock is a reminder that "every minute that passes onscreen brings the United States a minute closer to doomsday."[7]

The show's producer, Joel Surnow, describes the direct relevance of the show in current times:

> The series, Surnow told me [Jane Mayer], is "ripped out of the Zeitgeist of what people's fears are—their paranoia that we're going to be attacked," and it "makes people look at what we're dealing with" in terms of threats to national security. "There are not a lot of measures short of extreme measures that will get it done," he said, adding, "America wants the war on terror fought by Jack Bauer. He's a patriot."[8]

Thus, Surnow connects the current fear (reflected in the terror alert code) among the American people with the need for using torture to save the people. "'Speaking of torture,'" he said, "'Isn't it obvious that if there was a nuke in New York City that was about to blow—or any other city in this country—

that, even if you were going to go to jail, it would be the right thing to do?"[9] Compare this to the language of justification for enhanced interrogation techniques by U.S. officials. In memos and documents written in the post-9/11 period on "coercive" techniques primarily for "high-value detainees," some of the most explicit justifications emerged.[10] The term "ticking-bomb scenario" is never used (as it is explicitly utilized in 24), but the language is very similar. As multiple memos written in 2002 and 2005 (that surfaced in 2009) regarding the CIA's use of enhanced interrogation techniques (henceforth EITS) noted, especially regarding waterboarding,

> the waterboard technique is used only if: (1) the CIA has credible intelligence that a terrorist attack is imminent; (2) there are "substantial and credible indicators the subject has actionable intelligence that can prevent, disrupt or delay this attack"; and (3) other interrogation methods have failed or are unlikely to yield actionable intelligence in time to prevent the attack.[11]

The ticking-bomb scenario thus becomes the justification for the use of torture and CIDT both on- and off-screen.

Even U.S. Supreme Court Justice Scalia has referred to the show and, indeed, defended Jack Bauer in a public forum. In a panel discussion on "torture and terrorism," a Canadian judge commented,

> "Thankfully, security agencies in all our countries do not subscribe to the mantra 'What would Jack Bauer do?'" [Justice Antonin Scalia in turn reacted by stating], "Jack Bauer saved Los Angeles. . . . He saved hundreds of thousands of lives." [He went on to ask], "Are you going to convict Jack Bauer?" Justice Scalia further challenged his fellow judges. "Say that criminal law is against him? . . . Is any jury going to convict Jack Bauer? I don't think so."[12]

While Justice Scalia may not explicitly take this line of argument in a Supreme Court opinion, he does articulate the logic of the argument of necessity that has been used to justify torture in the current war on terror. In fact, as discussed in chapter 1, Justice Scalia has raised the question of a "necessity exception" during the oral arguments in *Chavez v. Martinez* (2003), indicating the possibility of accepting excessive violence in some instances. More recently, the "public safety" exception emerging from the Quarles case has been invoked to question terror suspects without interrogators informing them of their Miranda rights.[13] The different versions of the ticking-bomb scenario, therefore, have been appearing in domestic cases as well. The debate is still more restricted in the context of the domestic laws protecting U.S. citizens, and the justices have not condoned the use of torture and CIDT even in emergency situations. However, these exchanges have significant implications for the war on terror, in which the laws are constantly being rewritten for primarily noncitizen detainees and extended to others, such as Times Square attempted bombing suspect Faisal Shahzad.[14]

In addition, the logic of necessity used by the Supreme Court justices and Department of Justice officials, such as in the Bybee/Yoo memo, is echoed in the popular discourse. Mayer points out that Bob Cochran (creator, with Surnow, of the show 24) believes that "[t]he Doctrine of Necessity says that you can occasionally break the law to prevent greater harm. . . . I think that could supersede the Convention Against Torture."[15] Similarly, in an early Republican presidential debate, journalist Brooks notes, "Tancredo brushed off 'theoretical' objections to torture as a luxury we can't afford: If 'we go under, Western civilization goes under.' And what's a little torture when Western civilization itself is at stake?"[16] Thus, the popular, legal, and political discourse on torture and the justifications for it, based either on necessity or on the ticking-bomb scenario, often feed into each other.

The popularity of the show even led to a conscious effort by the U.S. military to comment on its portrayal of torture. In a meeting between the show's producers and military officials, U.S. Army Brigadier General Patrick Finnegan told the show's producers to stop showing the use of torture by Jack Bauer. Finnegan claimed that his cadets at West Point Academy often referred to the show as evidence of the success of torture, and he argued that the use of torture created a negative image for the United States.[17]

Some producers of the show, however, claim that they expect viewers to be able to "differentiate between a television show and reality."[18] Similarly, 24 actor Carlo Rota commented, "at the end of the day, [24] is a fantasy. I would be quite surprised if a person wakes up in the morning and decides he knows how to torture people because he's just seen 24."[19] Echoing this sentiment, right-wing radio show host Rush Limbaugh said, "Torture? It's just a television show! Get a grip."[20] In fact, even Kiefer Sutherland (Jack Bauer), when told of the military's request to stop showing torture or, at least, occasionally show that torture backfires, said, "'The US army are worried about the sequences in our show? . . . They should be a lot more worried about their behaviour in Abu Ghraib than they should about our television show.'"[21] But he did state emphatically, in contrast to the main creators of the show, that 24 was not justifying torture and, in fact, he agreed that torture does not work. Rather, Sutherland said, "Within the context of our show, which is a fantastical show to begin with, the torture is a dramatic device to show you how desperate a situation is."[22]

The show's popularity is, however, taken by some as evidence that Americans accept the use of torture. As one conservative talk show host, Laura Ingram, put it, "They love Jack Bauer. . . . In my mind, that's as close to a national referendum that it's O.K. to use tough tactics against high-level Al Qaeda operatives as we're going to get."[23] Similarly, in one of the early 2008 Republican presidential debates, Colorado congressman Tom Tancredo said the following: "'We're wondering about whether waterboarding would be a—a bad thing to do? I'm looking for Jack Bauer at that time, let me tell you.'"[24] The journalist reporting on the event went on to say, "This remark was greeted by uproarious laughter and applause from the audience because, after all, who doesn't enjoy thinking about a hunky guy threatening to gouge out a detainee's eye with a hunting knife?"[25] Here again one observes the close linkages between the political and popular imagery of torture.

24's Definition of Torture

In this section, I explore the popular imagery of torture in contemporary U.S. culture. While acknowledging that there is no single image of torture, this chapter focuses on a particularly dominant set of images of torture in U.S. popular culture that informs and echoes the official discourses and legitimizes the attempts of U.S. state officials to maintain narrow definitions of torture.[26]

The point of reference for the popular imagery of torture still remains that of "torture as spectacle" in the Foucauldian sense—with the blood, marks, and pain visible on the body. Foucault wrote,

> Bouton, an officer of the watch, left us this account: "The sulphur was lit, but the flame was so poor that only the top skin of the hand was burnt, and that only slightly. Then the executioner, his sleeves rolled up, took the steel pincers, which had been especially made for the occasion, and which were about a foot and a half long, and pulled first at the calf of the right leg, then at the thigh, and from there at the two fleshy parts of the right arm; then at the breasts . . . ; the same executioner dipped an iron spoon in the pot containing the boiling potion, which he poured liberally over each wound.[27]

Even though Foucault is describing torturous executions in the eighteenth century, it is striking that the idea of torture in contemporary times continues to resemble this image. For instance, it is not surprising that Heather Macdonald reminds human rights activists about the "true" meaning of torture when she writes in defense of U.S. policies in Iraq and Afghanistan in the post-9/11 context,

> Human Rights Watch, the ICRC, Amnesty International, and the other self-professed guardians of humanitarianism need to come back to earth— *to the real world in which torture means what the Nazis and the Japanese did* in their concentration and POW camps in World War II; the world in which *evil* regimes, like those we fought in Afghanistan and Iraq, don't follow the Miranda rules or the Convention Against Torture but instead *gas children, bury people alive, set wild animals on soccer players who lose, and hang adulterous women by truckloads before stadiums full of spectators; the world in which barbarous death cults behead female aid workers, bomb crowded railway stations, and fly planes* filled with hundreds of innocent passengers into buildings filled with thousands of innocent and unsuspecting civilians.[28]

Here, one observes the replacement of certain technologies and methods prevalent in the eighteenth century by more recent "innovations," but the emphasis on physical brutality, involving excruciating pain, blood, and marks on the body, remains in both these contexts. Thus, it is the more egregious physical acts invoking the categories of "intense cruelty," "barbarity," and the "uncivilized," often associated with the past or with more totalitarian regimes or nonstate actors, that represent torture even in the popular imagination. I argue that this representation of torture in popular culture continues to provide the "imagination" that limits and delimits the legal and political interpretive debates on torture.

As noted earlier, the show 24 has emerged as an important site for discussions on torture in the contemporary United States. What is particularly relevant for the current chapter is that the common theme between those who criticize the show and those who admire it is that they focus only on the physically brutal aspects of torture. Thus, if we look at the various descriptions of torture on both sides of the debate over the show, we see that the debate is restricted to forms of torture that involve marks, blood, and, above all, extreme physical pain. Bauer is known to "shoot kneecaps, chop off hands, and bite his enemies to death."[29] As Mayer describes Bauer, "With unnerving efficiency, suspects are beaten, suffocated, electrocuted, drugged, assaulted with knives or more exotically abused."[30] Similarly, other weapons in the arsenal of Bauer are using a defibrillator paddle with feet inside the water, plunging a knife in the shoulder, breaking the suspect's fingers, using hypodermic needles that cause horrible pain, and shooting the suspect in the leg.[31] One of the former cast members of the show stated that 24 had over time become much more violent. He said, "It's become—for lack of a better word—a carnage hour."[32]

Although other methods are also used by Bauer, the dominant theme of the show is summarized in the following statement by lead writer Gordon: "Jack Bauer is a tragic character. He doesn't get away with it clean. He's got *blood on his hands*. . . . In some ways, he is a necessary evil."[33] There are no limits to the "carnage," and the Parents Television Council gave the show the strongest cautionary rating for physical violence.[34]

Regardless of whether the show 24 leads directly to an acceptance of torture or not (although the main creators of the show do support torture), it is significant that torture is represented primarily as physical brutality. Consequently, when there is no visible physical impact of an interrogation, the act comes to be characterized as "not torture." As noted earlier, the importance of physical markers of pain is also apparent in the U.S. debates on methods of execution.[35] In 2008, the U.S. Supreme Court was asked to decide whether the drug cocktail (sodium thiopental, or anesthesia, followed by a paralytic drug, pancuronium bromide, and, finally, the death-causing potassium chloride) used in lethal injection constitutes cruel and unusual punishment due to its impact on the executed.[36] This case is important because petitioners challenging the method claimed that the first drug (anesthetic) used by the execution process is sometimes inadequate. Consequently, the person may still be conscious when the final, painful drug, potassium chloride, is injected, but the second drug, which paralyzes the nerves, does not allow the person to exhibit any pain felt.[37] As Timothy Kaufman-Osborn explains it,

> lethal injection protocols currently in use in the United States should also be understood as a cosmetic, i.e., as a kind of make-up that gives the appearance of our distance from the irrationality associated with savagery. It achieves this end by paralyzing inmates whose bodies might otherwise give the lie to this cherished sentiment.[38]

Here Kaufman-Osborn points to the fact that the second drug merely serves to mask the pain associated with this form of execution, rather than ensuring a painless death. Indeed, the Supreme Court in its decision also seems to privilege the appearance of a painless death. As Michael Dorf explains, Chief Justice Roberts's emphasis on maintaining the "dignity of the procedure," which might be marred by "signs of consciousness or distress," suggests that the aesthetics of execution has become the primary focus of the Court rather than ensuring a painless death.[39]

While this debate continues to plague the most "humane" form of execution, it is interesting to contrast this form of execution with the representation of lethal injections by antitorture groups such as Human Rights First.[40] One of the examples used by the group to protest the increasing use of torture on TV comes from the popular show *Alias,* in which Jack Bristow (CIA agent on the show) injects a lethal chemical into the body of an informant.[41] In season 6 of *24,* as well, Jack Bauer uses a visibly painful injection on his brother in order to gain information. Lethal injection used for execution is justified because this method is portrayed as more humane than earlier methods, such as hanging or electric chair. But the representation of lethal injection as torture in these TV shows threatens the distinction drawn between these two contexts, especially at a time when the most "humane" method of execution has been challenged as flawed because it merely masks the pain and is not actually painless. Thus, the visibility of the pain and the signs of it on the body become the markers of the absence or presence of torture.

In the show *24,* there is also an attempt to differentiate between acts of torture committed by the protagonist, Jack Bauer, and those committed by his enemies. As Mayer explains, "The show's villains usually inflict the more gruesome tortures: their victims are hung on hooks, like carcasses in a butcher shop; poked with smoking-hot scalpels; or abraded with sanding machines."[42] If one analyzes the descriptions of the tortures used by Bauer, it is difficult to sustain this distinction. Indeed, the distinction actually seems to lie in the fact that Bauer appears to use torture only because of the "necessity" of the situation. To some extent, this echoes Justice Scalia's comments on BBC: "Is it really so easy to determine that smacking someone in the face to find out where he has hidden the bomb that is about to blow up Los Angeles is prohibited under the Constitution?"[43] Thus, Jack Bauer uses torture because there is no other choice under the circumstances. This is in contrast to (for instance) the Chinese, who routinely tortured Bauer when he was a prisoner.[44] The final effects of *24,* then, are to create a visual representation of torture as primarily physical and to justify Bauer's use of methods similar to his enemies' by establishing that nothing else will work.

Torture and Interrogations in U.S. Official Reports:
Legal Definitions, Sanitized Terms, Routine Methods, and
Alternate Imaginings

Does the popular imagery of torture as reflected in the show 24 have a bearing on the U.S. reports on torture and vice versa? In this section, I turn to two prominent official reports on Guantánamo, namely, the Schmidt Report and the Church Report, and to their representation of the interrogation techniques employed at this site. The Church Report is one of the most detailed reports on the "comprehensive chronology regarding the development, approval and implementation of interrogation techniques."[45] After a review of the various reports, testimony of state officials, and testimony of subject matter experts, the report concluded that there had been no evidence that torture or, indeed, any abuse had been authorized by U.S. officials.[46] The Church Report notes, "We found, *without exception*, that the DOD officials and senior military commanders responsible for the formulation of interrogation policy evidenced the *intent to treat detainees humanely*, which is fundamentally inconsistent with the notion that such officials or commanders ever accepted that detainee abuse would be permissible."[47] Here, the term "without exception" suggests that any incidents of abuse were aberrations or results of problems encountered in implementing policies and that state officials clearly intended to treat the detainees humanely. The findings of the Schmidt Report were even more surprising since the committee was specifically impaneled to investigate the abuse already witnessed and reported by FBI personnel based at Guantánamo. The report's executive summary notes, "the AR [Army regulations] 15-6 found no evidence of torture or inhumane treatment at JTF-GTMO."[48] In the case of only one high-value detainee does the report find that some methods used were degrading and abusive, though not inhuman.[49] These reports unequivocally concluded that no torture or cruel and inhuman treatment was either authorized or carried out at Guantánamo.

This official narrative is in complete contrast to the reports by human rights groups and the United Nations, which point out that torture has been allowed in the United States, especially in the context of the war on terror. In a section entitled "Has the U.S. Been Committing Torture in Guantánamo?" the Center for Constitutional Rights, a human rights group, states,[50] "Only an independent commission can fully address the nature and extent of the use of torture against Guantánamo prisoners. Yet, the evidence assembled in this report clearly points to a pattern and practice of torture and cruel, inhuman, and degrading treatment that implicates a policy encouraging its use."[51] This report is particularly significant because one of its primary sources is the testimony of the detainees themselves, gleaned from the prisoners' habeas cases and cleared for publication by the Department of Defense. The 2006 United Nations report on Guantánamo (by the Commission on Human Rights) also concluded that many of the methods authorized by the United States, when used "simultaneously," did constitute "degrading treatment," and in individual instances where there was "severe pain or suffering" involved, "amounted to torture."[52]

Here I argue that the official denials not only are based on the narrow definition of torture and CIDT that was adopted (as discussed in the last chapter) but also reflect an underlying popular imagery of torture as physical brutality. In the U.S. official reports, the popular imagery of torture leads to the characterization of other methods as "not torture."[53] A simultaneous use of sanitized terms for many of these "not torture" methods contributes to the acceptability of the apparently less severe forms of interrogation, especially when they are likened to routine methods of interrogation. Finally, the "absence" of torture and even cruel and inhuman treatment contributes to an alternate, more affirmative imagining of detention at Guantánamo.

The publicly available parts of the Church Committee Report block out the discussions on particular interrogation techniques and the incidents of abuse related to these methods, making it difficult to ascertain its central claim that "we can confidently state that based upon our investigation, we found nothing that would in any way substantiate detainee allegations of torture or violent physical abuse at GTMO."[54] The report pointed out that even the minor abuses invoked some action on the part of U.S. officials, illustrating that serious abuse would never have been tolerated by the strict command structure operating in the facility. Thus, the Church Committee Report proclaimed that the allegations of torture and CIDT were completely false (though investigated) and that no serious abuse actually took place. Even the possibility of serious abuse is preemptively denied by the Church Committee Report through its emphasis on the subjectivity of pain.[55] Further, the report calls into doubt the detainee narratives of torture by quoting an al Qaeda manual called the *Manchester Manual*, which explicitly asks its members to "'pretend that the pain is severe by bending over and crying loudly' in the event that an interrogator applies physical coercion."[56]

The narrow definition of serious abuse used in the Church Committee Report is also noteworthy. The Church Report writes, "we considered *serious abuse* to be misconduct resulting, or having the potential to result, in *death or grievous bodily harm*." Here the report uses the definition of "grievous bodily harm" found in the *Manual for Court Martial*—where "black eye" or "bloody nose" is not grievous but rather, grievous harms constitute incidents involving "fractured or dislocated bones, deep cuts, torn members of the body, serious damage to internal organs, and other serious bodily injuries."[57] This emphasis on long-lasting and visible physical injuries reiterates the focus on narrow definitions of torture apparent in other contexts.

The Church Report in 2004 found little evidence of serious abuse because it accepted only "long-lasting visible" injury as constituting the definition. If "cutting off the hand" and "the shooting of the leg," as shown in *24*, represent long-lasting injuries, then anything less than that is not torture, either in the show or in the reports. Thus, the narrow definitions of torture cut across not only the interpretations of the Federal Torture Statute and congressional legislations such as the Military Commissions Act in 2006, as discussed in the last chapter, but also official reports.

The Schmidt Report was specifically meant to look into the abuse reported by the FBI agents and, like the Church Report, it came to the conclusion that no torture or cruel and inhuman treatment took place at Guantánamo. The report noted that some of the allegations by the FBI included the use of "military working dogs during interrogation sessions to threaten detainees," the playing of loud music and yelling loudly, sleep deprivation, and "extremes of heat and cold."[58] The question is, how did the Schmidt Report conclude that these methods did not constitute torture or cruel and inhuman treatment, especially since these allegations were made not just by the detainees but also by the FBI officials? This was the case primarily because the report did not look into the legality of the methods that were authorized. As the Schmidt Report puts it, "The team did not review the legal validity of the various interrogation techniques outlined in Army Field Manual 34-52, or those approved by the Secretary of Defense."[59]

Indeed, both the Church and the Schmidt reports accepted the legality of all the interrogation methods that were authorized for the war on terror. In addition, while serious abuses were assumed to be absent, the reports explained away the "minor abuses" as mere variations of routine techniques of interrogation. The sanitized presentation of certain methods, such as sleep deprivation and gender-based coercion, in the U.S. official reports went a long way toward legitimizing them by undermining the pain and suffering associated with these methods.

The Schmidt Report's discussion of allegations of sleep deprivation is a perfect example of sanitization of terms. The Schmidt Report mentioned the "Frequent Flyer" program under which the detainee was shifted from one cell to another after every few hours. Here, the use of the term "Frequent Flyer," often used in reference to something consumers desire, is what I term sanitization of methods.[60] The sanitized term transforms the experience of the method for the detainees and undermines the impact of the method on them. At Guantánamo, there were also allegations of sixteen-hour interrogations in a twenty-hour cycle and of sleep deprivation for fifty days, used in the case of Qahtani.[61] But Schmidt does not attempt to explore the distinctions between the terms "sleep deprivation," "sleep adjustment," and "Frequent Flyer program." Schmidt did mention that the "Frequent Flyer" program was terminated in 2004 but accepted that sixteen-hour interrogations in a 24-hour cycle were allowed even after.[62] Thus, the converse of a popular imagery of torture as physical brutality is the sanitized presentation of other methods so that they appear to be completely distinct from the physical imagery. It is the sanitization of these terms that also explains why the official reports could so uncritically accept these methods.

In the show 24, one observes Jack Bauer similarly employing sanitized versions of impermissible methods. In season 2, Bauer asks the captured "terrorist" to disclose where the bomb is, while on a screen facing them the terrorist's two children are shown captive and bound in the Counter Terrorism Unit.[63] Bauer threatens to kill the terrorist's son if the information is not divulged. When the terrorist refuses to budge, the audience watches the terrorist's son being shot. When the agents threaten to kill his second son, the terrorist agrees to give the information. The Human Rights First rightly calls this method mock execution, which is disallowed under national and international law, but it is the representation of this method in 24 as "mere deception" that is pertinent. Just when the audience is shocked at the brutality of the situation, Bauer (known to use brutal torture unflinchingly) reassures the terrorist (and the viewer) that the execution was only staged and he had after all not crossed the line.

In the official U.S. reports, another instance of sanitization of terms appeared in the context of gender-based coercion. The Schmidt Report characterizes many of the "minor abuses" involving female interrogators as a creative use of some routine interrogation techniques from the regular (pre-9/11) army field manual. Thus, many of these abuses were analyzed as variations of "innocuous"-sounding methods such as "futility." In an instance where the female interrogator "rubbed against [a detainee's] back, leaned over the detainee touching him on his knee and shoulder and whispered in his ear that his situation was futile, and ran her fingers through his hair," the Schmidt Report considered her actions as being covered by the interrogation technique referred to as "futility."[64] The interrogator was admonished but mainly for not getting the method approved first. Similarly, in another incident, a woman told the detainee that the "red ink on her hand was menstrual blood and then wiped her hand on the detainee's arm."[65] This incident was also categorized as a variation of the futility technique, designed to emphasize the futility of the detainee's situation, though given the fact that the action was performed in retaliation for the detainee spitting on the interrogator, the female interrogator was verbally reprimanded. The Schmidt Report does recommend that gender coercion should not be used and, in this instance, agrees that inadequate action was taken, but the report still accepts that these are creative versions of regularly authorized techniques. Under this framework of analysis, when one of the authorized techniques, "[m]ild, non-injurious physical touching," occurred in the form of an interrogator rubbing perfume on the detainee and led the detainee to react (ostensibly to bite the interrogator) and fall down, breaking his tooth in the process, no action was required because the technique was an approved one.[66]

The 1998 film *Siege* illustrates a similar acceptance of gender-based coercion in popular culture. When FBI agent Anthony Hubbard (Denzel Washington) demands to see his prisoner, who is in military custody, he finds that his (Muslim) prisoner is naked and the female CIA interrogator (Annette Benning) questioning him has failed to get the answers. What follows is a serious contemplation of other models (sleep deprivation, shaking, and cutting) by Major General Devereaux (Bruce Willis) and the CIA agent because simple questioning failed. This is the moment when Hubbard gives a passionate speech against the use of torture. The unanswered question is whether the line is crossed only when the physical torture begins or is already crossed when the white female CIA agent started interrogating the naked Muslim detainee.

The show *24*, in more recent seasons, decided to tone down its representation of torture because the "writers are 'a little sick of it,'" though Katz, the executive producer of the show, argued that torture would "always be part of Bauer's 'arsenal.'"[67] Thus, in contrast to victims and even witnesses actually feeling sick as a result of intense pain and suffering that torture and CIDT cause, the producers of the show provide a different reason—boredom or consumer trends—for wanting to tone down the representation of physical torture in *24*. In addition, Gordon, one of the executive producers of the show, said that there would be fewer scenes of torture in the future not because of the various complaints by the human rights groups but rather because "[t]orture is starting to feel a little trite. . . . The idea of physical coercion or torture is no longer a novelty or surprise."[68] One wonders about the significance of the words in use here.[69] It is unlikely that physical methods of torture will simply be replaced by psychological torture in 24 and other shows, especially when the show's response to the military's suggestion for showing more routine methods of interrogation was that doing so would "'take too much time' on an hour-long television show."[70]

In the absence of torture (imagined as physical brutality) and use of sanitized terms (undermining the impact of the methods of interrogation), a new imagery of detention emerges in the Church Committee Report. The Church Report notes that "[i]n fact, detainees were more likely to suffer injury from playing soccer or volley ball during recreational periods than they were from interactions with interrogators or guards."[71] Thus, in contrast to the human rights reports, the Church Report presents a different narrative of detention, one in which sports injuries during recreation are the main problem. The impact of this popular imagery of torture as physical brutality is thus not only found in the official reports on Guantánamo but in addition continues to traverse the entire political discourse. In that sense, there is a meshing of legal, military, and political discourse with the popular imagery of torture.

Where Political and Popular Imaginings of Torture Coincide: Sanitized Terms and Routine Activities

In many public opinion polls, a majority of U.S. respondents oppose the use of torture even in the context of the "war on terror." For example, in a poll conducted in May 2004, 63 percent of the respondents were against the use of torture and 35 percent supported its use. For the same people, however, there was no clarity on whether specific methods constituted torture, CIDT, or abuse.[72] In that poll, 51 percent did state that the United States was using torture, but given a choice between terming these acts as torture or terming them as abuse, 60 percent said these acts were abuse, as compared to 29 percent who said they constituted torture.[73] In another poll, the discussion on particular interrogation techniques was also significant, revealing that respondents were more clearly opposed to some methods than to others.[74] Eighty-two percent of the people responded that the use of waterboarding was wrong, and 69 percent found threatening with dogs unacceptable.[75] The question, for our purpose, is why sleep deprivation does not get the same reaction as the two aforementioned methods. The response on sleep deprivation was evenly divided: 49 percent against and 48 percent in favor. One of the reasons for this distinction could be that sleep deprivation does not reflect the imagery of physical brutality associated with drowning and dog bites.

Consider how sleep deprivation is described in some of the narratives defending the interrogation techniques. Heather Macdonald, for instance, described why sleep deprivation was used by U.S. interrogators to question detainees in Afghanistan.

> If a type of behavior toward a prisoner was no worse than the way the army treated its own members, it could not be considered torture or a violation of the conventions. Thus, questioning a detainee past his bedtime was lawful as long as his interrogator stayed up with him. If the interrogator was missing exactly the same amount of sleep as the detainee—and no tag-teaming of interrogators would be allowed, the soldiers decided—then sleep deprivation could not be deemed torture. In fact, interrogators were routinely sleep-deprived, catnapping maybe one or two hours a night, even as the detainees were getting long beauty sleeps.[76]

Here, Macdonald is quoting Chris Mackey, an interrogator who worked at Bagram and Kandahar in Afghanistan. Mackey wrote in his narrative that the rule of thumb, in the absence of clear directives on the applicability of Geneva conventions to the conflict in 2002-2003, was that the interrogators could use methods of interrogation that they themselves would be able to endure.[77] Here, the interrogators saw their situation in the anxiety-prone conflict zone as comparable to the custodial context in which the detainees were being questioned. During the 2008 presidential campaigns, the routine nature of these methods was evoked as an argument even in contexts other than a conflict zone. Former Republican candidate for president Rudy Giuliani defended the practice of sleep deprivation in the following way: "They [Democrats] talk about sleep deprivation," he said. "I mean, on that theory, I'm getting tortured running for president of the United States. That's plain silly. That's silly."[78]

In this context, even the distinctions made in U.S. official reports on Guantánamo among sleep deprivation, sleep adjustment, and the so-called Frequent Flyer program are lost. The continued discourse on sleep deprivation is also a forgetting of previous U.S. reports in which sleep deprivation is characterized as a form of torture. The Wickersham Commission (1931), which confirmed the widespread prevalence of the third degree in the United States, wrote, "It has been known since 1500 at least that deprivation of sleep is the most effective torture and certain to produce any confession desired."[79] The confidence with which the report characterizes sleep deprivation as a method of torture or third degree is obviously not shared by others (then and now) who consider only brutally physical coercion as constituting torture and, therefore, either a thing of the past or extremely rare.

Similarly, the emphasis on physical brutality also exhibits amnesia about the history of mental torture or psychological torture.[80] In fact, as noted in chapter 2, Alfred McCoy points out that the methods used in the Abu Ghraib prison are the same methods of psychological torture used by the CIA in previous decades.[81] In particular, McCoy writes that a number of methods such as "outstretched hands" (as observed in the infamous Abu Ghraib picture) are found effective precisely because they are forms of "self-inflicted pain" that tend to affect the psychology of the victim more than externally inflicted pain.[82]

The war on terror reflects a continued inability to consensually describe psychological methods as torture despite the severity of the suffering involved. For instance, McCoy quotes Senator Jeff Sessions, a Republican from Alabama who "asked rhetorically if any Guantánamo prisoner 'suffered a broken bone or serious permanent injury,'" reiterating the focus on the body, not the mind, in characterizations of torture.[83] Thus, the sanitized methods of interrogation in popular and official discourses that do not conform to the images of torture as physical brutality serve another function: detracting attention from the history of psychological torture. The popular imagery of torture simultaneously undermines the protections against psychological torture in UN and U.S. laws.[84]

Given the history of mind-control techniques, including the category of "self-inflicted pain," it is not surprising to observe that one method of legitimizing certain techniques is to compare interrogation methods with normal day-to-day activities in what could be termed a routinization of methods. In the current conflict, the discussion on prolonged standing is a perfect illustration of this strategy. Former secretary of defense Donald Rumsfeld questioned "standing for 4 hours" as a proposed method of interrogation, stating that if he could stand for eight to ten hours, then why shouldn't the detainees.[85] Similar to the discussion on sleep deprivation, it is again the focus on the everydayness of the methods that is being used as a strategy of legitimation.

Further, even though waterboarding is opposed by large numbers of survey respondents, it is possible that their position will change when the term is sanitized and compared to routine activities. Recall again Vice President Cheney's remark about waterboarding in an interview. When he was asked, "Would you agree a dunk in water is a no-brainer if it can save lives?" he responded, "Well, it's a no-brainer for me. . . . But for a while there, I was criticised as being the vice president for torture. We don't torture. That's not what we're involved in."[86] Later the White House denied that he was referring to waterboarding, and there were distinctions made between waterboarding and "dunking."[87] Here again waterboarding becomes legally distinct from a "dunk in the water" and at the same time, likening a "dunk in the water" to waterboarding makes the latter self-evidently acceptable. As former White House press secretary Tony Snow said in relation to the term "dunk in the water," "the text speaks for itself."[88] In a moment of light-hearted banter between the questioners and Tony Snow, a questioner asked him what "dunk in the water" could mean.

> MR. SNOW: How about a dunk in the water?
> Q: So, wait a minute, so "dunk in the water" means what, we have a
>   pool now at Guantanamo, and they go swimming?
> MR. SNOW: Are you doing stand up? (Laughter.)[89]

Again, this is a sanitization and a comparison to a routine activity that otherwise could be considered a form of torture or CIDT, given that waterboarding refers to strapping a person to a board and pouring water on him.[90] But a "dunk in the water" does not appear that bad. The debate on waterboarding assumed even greater significance when former attorney general Michael Mukasey refused to consider waterboarding either illegal or torture, stating only that it was not a policy at the current time.[91] Thus, playing soccer and swimming in the pool are the alternative images that float about Guantánamo. After all, the characterization of these techniques reflects the subjective notion of "shock the conscience" that U.S. officials often believe in. As former vice president Dick Cheney states, "Now, you can get into a debate about what shocks the conscience and what is cruel and inhuman. And to some extent, I suppose, that's in *the eye of the beholder*."[92]

Furthermore, the sanitized and routinized methods serve as a way of making the American public feel better about themselves. Many Americans who are stuck in the rhetoric of 24, considering torture as necessary in the indefinite ticking-bomb scenario, can at least claim that these "harsh techniques" are not as bad as the "real" torture shown on that program. In the case of torture, the sanitized and routinized methods are meant not only to legitimize some of these methods of interrogation but also to help in creating a distance for the interrogators, the public, and even some U.S. officials from the impact of these methods.

Imagery, Excess Violence, and the Meaning of Custody

As stated earlier, analyzing the imagery of torture is important in revealing the circulation of discourses of torture across different sites. Only when one contrasts the popular, legal, and political imaginings of torture with human rights reports does one recognize the very different impact of these techniques. For example, according to the Center for Constitutional Rights, sleep deprivation can lead to "deterioration in cognitive abilities" and can "disorient and mentally weaken" detainees. Further, environmental manipulation such as sound and light adjustment can cause dizziness and affect the eyesight.[93] The report states, "Belkacem Bensayah lived under similar conditions for seventeen straight months and can no longer look at anything for long because he sees black spots."[94] Similarly, the analysis of gender-based coercion in the Schmidt Report is in direct contrast to the characterization of these acts in the nonstate reports. The Center for Constitutional Rights points out that some of the actions by the female interrogators were intended to inhibit the detainees' ability to pray during Ramadan—the holy month for Muslims.[95] The CCR report noted that many of these actions, including gender-based interrogations, forced grooming (shaving of facial hair), and removal of clothes (required to pray), had special significance at Guantánamo.[96] Similarly, the UN report contends, "It was also reported that these techniques were used before prayer times and that in some cases, detainees were not allowed to wash themselves before and therefore were not able to pray."[97] The UN report stated that some of these methods directly targeted the religious and cultural beliefs of detainees and, therefore, constituted a violation of international law.[98] Thus, the more serious abuses are by definition excluded from the reports and sanitized representation of other techniques is used to undermine the impact of the "less severe" methods of excess violence.

The critics of gender-based coercive methods and the use of religion as a tool of interrogation have noted that these methods are particularly abusive to Muslim men. Here one has to be cautious about what John Parry calls the urge to "exoticize the victims of torture."[99] He points out that critiquing these methods as being more humiliating for Muslim detainees in the process also presents these detainees as belonging to "'traditional' societies in which . . . religious practices are more 'profound,' and people hold strange and inappropriate views on issues of sexuality and gender.'"[100] However, regardless of whether one can assume that all these detainees had a homogenous "religious and cultural" sensitivity that was offended by these actions, the intent of the interrogators was clearly to "humiliate and degrade" what they perceived to be the religious and cultural beliefs of the detainees. The official reports thus undermine the intent of the interrogators by presenting these abuses as creative use of routine methods.

When a show such as 24 represents torture in ways that conform to the more brutal forms, the imagery coincides with the "aggressive hyperlegality" and the narrow official definitions chosen by the Bush administration in the post-9/11 period. In the process, the more expansive definitions of torture and CIDT that could be read into the formal laws are also obfuscated in the popular representation. It is important to note that while formal definitions themselves may include some gaps, clearly the entire gamut of laws could have been used to protect detainees from torture and CIDT in the immediate post-9/11 period. For example, the application of Common Article 3 of the Geneva Conventions alone would have been adequate to protect the detainees from many of these coercive techniques. However, in the Bybee or Yoo memos, discussed in the last chapter, the purpose precisely was to limit the boundaries of the protections. The limiting came through the combined use of a very narrow definition of "severity" and selective applicability of laws, and, as discussed here, through the use of sanitized and routinized terms, in both popular and official contexts, which becomes an additional strategy of denial of excess violence. In addition, one of the main ways in which these sanitized and routinized terms are used to normalize excess violence is by undermining the very meaning of custody in the context of interrogations.

A very good instance of the way the meaning of custody was undermined by U.S. state officials occurred in the context of the CIA-related memos (that surfaced in 2009) written for the high-value detainees such as Zubaydah and al Nashiri.[101] While there was a discussion of ten Enhanced Interrogation Techniquess (EITs) under consideration, here I discuss just one of the techniques—waterboarding—as an illustration of the way questions of custody were undermined through invocation of the SERE (Survival, Evasion, Resistance, Escape) programs.

Waterboarding as an EIT was largely justified as not violating laws such as the Federal Torture Statute not only because of "aggressive hyperlegality" but also because state officials made the argument that the technique was being used in the training of navy and other armed forces under the SERE program without any problem. In other words, comparing the use of the same technique in the training of U.S. armed forces became the main tactic for defending it. In the 2002 Bybee memo sent to the CIA, waterboarding in the context of SERE programs was presented as being completely free of any problems.[102] As the memo put it, "It was also reported to be almost 100 percent effective in producing cooperation among the trainees. . . . [Redacted] also indicated that he had observed the use of the waterboard in Navy training some ten to twelve times. Each time it resulted in cooperation but it did not result in any physical harm to the student."[103]

However, with the withdrawal of the Bybee/Yoo memo and the issuance of the CIA inspector general's report by 2004, it was clear that there were serious problems with the way waterboarding was actually being used, and there was a need to distinguish between the SERE and CIA programs' use of this technique. The reasons why armed forces other than the navy gave up waterboarding in their SERE training was a major source of debate. The inspector general's report that looked into the counterterrorism detention and interrogation activities from September 2001 to October 2003 directly contradicted the idea that forces other than the navy gave up the waterboarding technique due to its success.[104] In a footnote, the report notes that many individuals familiar with the SERE training stated that the waterboarding program was withdrawn due to "its dramatic effect on the students who were subjects."[105] In another footnote, the report notes that the efficacy of the CIA program was exaggerated and comparison with SERE was actually difficult due to the different nature of waterboarding in the context of the CIA, and even the Office of Medical Services was not consulted on the use of this technique despite the possible adverse medical effects of this act.[106] The difference in the way waterboarding was conducted was important because while in the SERE program, a damp cloth with a small amount of water was used, in the CIA program, large amounts of water were continually applied over the nose and mouth. The inspector general's report noted that one of the psychologists/interrogators acknowledged the difference, stating that the CIA program was "'for real'" and "more poignant and convincing."[107] In view of these concerns about effectiveness and safety, the 2005 memos on the use of the EITS become particularly significant since they continued to allow for the use of the waterboard in the context of the high-value detainees despite the criticisms by the inspector general's report.

While I discussed the role of the psychologists and medical personnel in monitoring the application of these techniques earlier (chapter 2), here I point to the way in which the comparison between the SERE and CIA programs continued to play a justificatory role for waterboarding. The 2005 CIA memo, based on the 2004 Levin memo that replaced the Bybee/Yoo memo, recognized the distinction between training and real-life application of the technique. There was even a suggestion that "undue reliance" on SERE should be avoided, but still there continued to be insistence that the SERE program "is nevertheless of some value in evaluating the technique"[108] and an emphasis that some changes had been made in light of the criticisms. However, the justificatory narrative for the use of the technique continued. Perhaps one of the best illustrations of the fact that the SERE programs continued to provide the framework for justification appears in the memo that considers whether these techniques violate Article 16 of the UN Convention regarding Cruel, Inhuman, and Degrading Treatment and comes to the conclusion that they do not.[109] The memo states, "Although there are obvious differences between training exercises [SERE] and actual interrogations, the fact that the United States uses similar techniques on its own troops for training purposes strongly suggests that these techniques are not categorically beyond the pale."[110]

Thus, the larger implication of these memos is not only that they interpret laws with aggressive hyperlegality but also that they represent interrogation techniques in their sanitized and routinized forms and, above all, that they undermine the significance of these techniques in a hostile custodial situation. The meaning of custody and the adverse impact of a technique in this particular context is completely absent in the discussions of the EITs.

In this context, Elaine Scarry's point that each and every object and method could be an instrument of torture in a custodial situation becomes useful. Scarry, for instance, points to how the room (the basic form of shelter) itself and all the objects within are or can be transformed into instruments of torture. Scarry writes,

> The torture room is not just the setting in which the torture occurs; it is not just the space that happens to house the various instruments used for beating and burning and producing electric shock. It is itself literally converted into another weapon, into an agent of pain. All aspects of the basic structure—walls, ceiling, windows, doors undergo this conversion. . . . Just as all aspects of the concrete structure are inevitably assimilated into the process of torture, so too the contents of the room, its furnishings, are converted into weapons: the most common instance of this is the bathtub that figures prominently in the reports from numerous countries.[111]

Here Scarry is primarily describing the torture rooms in contexts such as Spain, Syria, and the Philippines, where these torture rooms existed, but the import of her argument is broader. Her framework suggests an ability to recognize the ways in which traditionally defined instruments of torture may not be the only source of torture. Rather, torture can be the result of ordinary things and familiar techniques in custodial contexts. Thereby,

Scarry's argument challenges not only the narrow definition of torture but also the sanitization and routinization of methods by her reminder that in a custodial situation, anything and everything can be an instrument of torture, let alone a technique that has traditionally been known to affect detainees adversely. The fact that a training program such as SERE, which has been controversial and not free of negative impact, was used to defend techniques used on detainees in custody actually exhibits a particular lack of understanding of the meaning of custody and further compounds the impact of this technique.

Conclusion

As seen in this chapter, a range of actors, from the military to scholars to human rights activists, pointed to the impact of the TV show *24* on soldiers and on Americans in general and sought changes from the show's producers. In a sense, these explicit strategies directly address the question of whether "just a TV show" could have so much impact. Furthermore, the use of Bauer as a metaphor for antiterror state agents by a range of legal and political actors has magnified the impact of this show. In addition, when the producers themselves claimed to be intervening in the torture debates, the power of the image got magnified. While popular culture always has an impact on policies and perceptions, *24* both reflects that trend and represents an excellent example of an explicit attempt to do so. The argument here is thus to point to a circulation of meanings of torture across the popular, legal, and political spectrum.

By focusing on the most brutal aspects as torture and justifying it, *24* represents an excess in the old Foucauldian spectacular sense that ostensibly disappeared in modern democracies, thereby making the show a "fantastical" one as Sutherland (Bauer) claimed, making "torture" a "dramatic device to show how desperate a situation is." However, the emphasis on this excess masks the ways in which the main arena of the debate—the space between coercion and torture—is not focused as such. As I have discussed earlier, that space is a constantly negotiated one, and there is considerable accommodation of excess violence—violence that the state claims as unnecessary yet holds onto. The violence is in the realm of not-torture and the official and popular discourses make efforts to sanitize and routinize it. The debate then shifts to the extreme forms of violence, whether in terms of justifications or condemnations or even prohibitions, while the space in between remains inadequately addressed.

--- 4 ---

Jurisprudence on Torture and Interrogations in India

> I do not want my house to be walled in on all sides and my win-
> dows to be stuffed. I want the cultures of all lands to be blown
> about my house as freely as possible. But I refuse to be blown off
> my feet by any.
>
> —Mahatma Gandhi, 1921[1]

Like any liberal democracy, the Indian state claims either that torture does not occur in India or that it is never authorized as a policy. The
Indian state backs this claim by pointing to the strong legal safeguards against
the use of torture. Yet in India the number of cases of custodial torture and
deaths is extremely high, to the point where torture is a subject of serious
concern for human rights scholars and activists. The National Human Rights
Commission (hereafter NHRC), a statutory institution created under the
Protection of Human Rights Act (1993), recorded 1,597 incidents of custodial deaths in its annual report of 2006-2007.[2] One hundred and eighteen
of these deaths took place in police custody and the rest in judicial custody.
Further, this number only includes custodial deaths that have been reported
to the NHRC.[3] Official and unofficial reports note that these statistics do not
reflect the actual number of incidents of torture and inhuman and degrading
punishment and treatment meted out by police and prison officials to those
in custody.[4] More recently, the Asian Center for Human Rights (ACHR) col-
lated the NHRC figures of custodial deaths from 1994-2008 and came up
with an astounding figure of 16,836 custodial deaths, or 1,203 persons per
year.[5]

Despite these figures, the ACHR notes,

> India is in a worrying state of denial. The Home Minister attributes cus-
> todial deaths to "illness/natural death, escaping from custody, suicides,
> attacks by other criminals, riots, due to accidents and during treatment

or hospitalization." These attitudes are widespread and explain in part the inadequacy of India's actions to combat torture in the legal, political and institutional domain.[6]

Thus, torture as a cause for custodial deaths is continually denied by the Indian state. The paradox here is that postcolonial India is a liberal democracy with very clearly articulated constitutional and statutory provisions against torture. This raises the question, how does torture continue to persist in India? The debates on torture in India have primarily focused on the institution of the police to explain the continuing presence of torture. However, in the process, there has been inadequate focus on the existing tensions within the jurisprudence on torture and interrogations.

In this chapter, I examine the jurisprudence of interrogations developed by the Indian Supreme Court to analyze its response to torture. I focus on the major constitutional and procedural safeguards against torture in interrogations and conclude that while the jurisprudence has been extremely innovative in addressing custodial deaths and torture, prompting a focus on the perpetrators of torture, an exclusive emphasis on the latter distracts attention from the continuing ambivalence of the Court toward excess violence.

Situating the Debate on Torture in India: Protections against Torture

The Indian state signed the UN Convention against Torture in 1997. However, using the excuse of state sovereignty, it has still not ratified the convention despite repeated recommendations and demands from the NHRC and from human rights groups and scholars.[7] Nonetheless, even those demanding the ratification of the convention acknowledge that it would primarily strengthen preexisting domestic safeguards against torture.[8] There is an effort currently to pass an antitorture bill intended to legislatively define torture and specify the punishments associated with it.[9] In the absence of any national law on torture, a combination of constitutional, statutory, and judicial precedents have collectively created a formal legal regime against the use of torture in India.

Over the years, the Indian Supreme Court has played an important role in developing a rich jurisprudence on interrogations using the formal legal safeguards on torture. The constitutional provisions under which cases of torture have been addressed are Articles 21 and 20(3). Article 21 notes the importance of not depriving persons of life and liberty except by following a procedure established by law. Even though Article 21 does not explicitly refer to torture or any other form of state violence, over time the judiciary has extended its meaning in such a way as to protect citizens from several forms of illegal state violence, including custodial violence.[10] Article 20(3) represents the right against self-incrimation or the right for a person not to be "compelled to be witness against himself."[11] Apart from these constitutional safeguards, there are also many statutory provisions in the Indian Penal Code (hereafter IPC), the Criminal Procedure Code (hereafter CrPc), and the Indian Evidence Act (hereafter IEA), particularly those provisions related to the recording of confessions, to protect people from torture.[12] While addressing cases of torture, the judiciary often refers to these statutory provisions since they constitute a uniform criminal code throughout most of the country.[13] The early 1990s also saw the Court having formulated custody jurisprudence by creating innovative responses to instances of custodial deaths. Thus, not surprisingly, given the rich jurisprudence in this arena, the Supreme Court has not been the focal point of criticism as far as custodial violence is concerned, and the continuing high levels of torture and custodial deaths have been attributed mostly to the perpetrators of the violence: the police.[14]

In the following section, I analyze the explanations commonly provided for the persistence of torture in India, which can be broadly discussed under the following categories: the role of the media, the colonial history, and institutional weaknesses. While there is some attempt in the literature on torture to point to the shortcomings of the Indian government (Parliament in particular) in addressing some of the gaps within existing laws, primarily, the persistence of torture is attributed to the police.[15]

If Torture Appears to Exist in a Democracy, Here's Why!
The Role of Media and of Perception

Despite the recognition in most of the governmental and nongovernmental reports that cases of custodial torture are extremely high in India and have, in fact, increased over the years, much of the literature claims that these reports are exaggerated by the media.[16] Although there is no systematic discussion on the role of the media, several commentators hold the media responsible for the negative perceptions of the police and of the state of human rights in India. Commentators criticize the media for exaggerating the reports and making false accusations, even for falling prey to the "fake" reports propagated by the "neighboring country."[17]

According to some commentators, the negative representation of the police by the media, in turn, leads to an adverse impact on the morale of the police force.[18] Nirman Arora writes that the media often exaggerate even a minor "aberration" out of proportion and ignore the positive contributions of the police.[19] Venugopal mentions the work of American sociologists William Westley and A. Neiderhoffe, who point out that negative attitudes exhibited toward police actions lead to their further alienation from the public. As a result, the police start behaving like a "fraternity" and end up taking the law into their own hands.[20]

One of the few empirical studies on the "perceptions of various strata of the Criminal Justice System and the Academics" of custodial deaths in India had a question in its survey on "the role of the media in projecting the problem before the society."[21] Officials, including senior police officials, judicial officers, and civil servants, mostly agreed that the "media was exaggerating the problem," and in each category, only a few said that the media was playing a positive role in efforts to control custodial deaths. Most of the academics interviewed in this study also agreed with the officials about the negative role of the media.[22]

It is perhaps prudent to note here that many (though not all) of these articles emphasizing the role of the media in exaggerating tales of torture are written by police officials themselves.[23] In fact, holding the media responsible for exaggerating the violation of human rights appears repeatedly in reports and surveys on torture and reflects a classic form of official denial that I discussed in chapter 1. A focus on media exaggeration, of course, seeks to downplay the enormity of the problem, the reality of the high numbers of custodial deaths, and the everyday prevalence of custodial torture recorded by human rights activists. The narrative constructs a congruence of anti-state forces—media and human rights groups—working together to undermine the police.[24] Exaggeration and falsity appear as categories used almost to blame the media and human rights groups for the very creation of the problem. Thus, if the narrative is successful, the liberal state could claim that the problem is less systemic than it appears in human rights reports, thereby containing or shaping, however unsuccessfully, the discourses on torture.

Historical Context: Colonial Dependencia

Many contemporary laws and institutions in India originated in the British colonial period and have continued in exactly the same manner in contemporary times, and the impact of their continuity has been the subject of much debate.[25] In explaining police brutality, several scholars and reports have pointed to the functioning of the police force during British times as an explanatory cause. Arora argues that torture existed all throughout Indian history but that it was during the British colonial period when these forms of violence got connected to the police for use in furthering the colonial state's interests.[26] Indeed, one of the most systematic inquiries into the causes of torture, the Madras Commission Report, was conducted by the British East India Company in 1855. However, one of the ironic and noteworthy aspects of this report is that, on one hand, it remains one of the most systematic documentations of torture in either colonial or postcolonial India while, on the other hand, it was primarily meant to absolve the British of any role in the persistence of torture despite the use of violence to ensure the continuation of the colonial regime. In reality, torture and human rights violations were a corollary to the "rule of law"–based legal system introduced by the British. While the British prided themselves on being the exception in the history of judicial torture in Europe, this account completely denied British accommodation of torture and excessive force in places such as India.[27]

The Madras Report ended up becoming a key moment of reformation, transformation, and legitimization of a new administrative legal structure for India. This was the case despite the fact that by absolving the British of any role in torture, the Madras Report became another example of a colonial policy that oscillated between an assumed "liberal" ideology (expressed in the establishment of the commission) and colonial imperatives (seen in its absolution of itself), thereby reflecting what Ranajit Guha calls the limits of bourgeois culture. As Guha writes, "Bourgeois culture has its historical limit in colonialism."[28] For him, all the liberal notions of "democracy, liberty and rule of law" are not achievable in a colonial context primarily because the consolidation of state power through dominance is the key element in colonial rule. Thus the Madras Report reflected the tension between upholding the "ideology of the rule of law" and supporting the colonial need to retain state power through any means necessary.

In postindependent India, despite the apparent change in the role of the police from colonial instruments to "servants of the people," there was neither a radical break from the colonial origins of police institutions nor a transformation of the legal system as a whole. B. Hydervall writes that there was no effort by the framers of the Indian Constitution to envisage a new "crime and control model suitable to freedom and democracy."[29] Thus, scholars argue that the current police still suffer from the impact of their origins as repressive instruments of the police *raj*.[30] As a result, the "police mindset is steeped into [sic] colonial era when the police were supposed to treat every Indian as an enemy of the state."[31] Others argue that the colonial origins of the police may not explain the persistence of torture because, after all, the colonial period has been followed by "forty [now sixty-four] years of adherence to a democratic pattern of government and a liberal Constitution ought to have imbued the police system with a higher sense of responsibility and humanity."[32]

The colonial origins of the police continue to be referred to as an important cause of the persistence of torture. In most of the contemporary discourse on torture, however, there is no systematic analysis of the impact of these colonial origins—only statements that the colonial policies have left their residual impact on police behavior in the postcolonial context. In this regard, there seems to be a wide gap between the postcolonial literature and the legal literature on the issue of torture. Upendra Baxi, in one of the few notable formulations, writes that even while recognizing the colonial-repressive nature of the police, one has to acknowledge that the continuity with colonial policies has remained primarily because of the desire of the governing elites. He notes, "Indian police is basically a colonial police, both in its organization and operations: it is basically a repressive force."[33] However, he goes on to explain, "But if the police retain its repressive colonial profile, it is due to the fact that the governing elites wish it so."[34] Indeed, Baxi notes that while police are often seen as supporting the status quo in other contexts as well, what is different in the postcolonial context is a lack of initiative, indeed a resistance, on the part of the elites to change the institution of the police. Thus, he points to the presence of not only a "colonial-repressive police organization" but also a "colonial-repressive political regime."[35] Perhaps that is the reason why a number of the institutional weaknesses of the police noted in the next section have not been addressed by the state and do contribute to the persistence of torture.

Institutional Reasons: Police Reforms, Training, and Politics

Apart from the focus on colonial history for explaining the persistence of torture in India, institutional reasons have also been recognized for its continuation. One of the reasons highlighted by scholars to explain the use of the third degree by the police is the constant pressure on them from all quarters, including politicians and bureaucrats.[36] The dilemma faced by the police is that, on the one hand, the public as well as higher officials expect instant results from them, and, on the other hand, they are bound by the legal parameters of investigation and the fear of sanctions. According to commentators, lack of adequate facilities, fewer personnel for investigation, extremely high case load, and an inefficient supervisory structure hinder the ability of the police to produce the results required of them, prompting them to take shortcuts.[37]

Not surprisingly, police reforms have been on the agenda for the past several decades. But the continued commissions and reports assembled since the 1979 National Police Commission, set up to conduct a comprehensive review of the functioning of the Indian police at the national level, have meant little until the more concerted efforts in the last few years.[38] A more recent initiative in this regard has been the 2006 *Prakash Singh v. Union of India* case, in which the Supreme Court issued directives asking for immediate action by the states and national government to improve the structure and functioning of the police.[39] The Court asked the governments to ensure the autonomy of the police by making them structurally independent on questions of tenure, appointments, and transfer even while recommending more accountability from the police individually and as a group with the help of independent review committees. How successful these reforms will be will become clear in the coming years.

Apart from police reforms, the lack of training in human rights has been identified as an important focus area. Scholars recommend adequate training for the police in order to raise their consciousness about human rights and to ensure that they are more respectful toward the population.[40] Formal training in human rights, particularly in the curriculum, is definitely important, but this emphasis on training simultaneously implies that in the absence of it, there is a tendency to use illegal methods of violence against the accused, especially the marginalized sections in society. The focus on lack of training in the case of U.S. soldiers at the Abu Ghraib prison in Iraq indicated a similar assumption that in the absence of clear directives on what not to do, the values of a liberal democracy are not enough to inculcate a consciousness that would prevent a state official from indulging in a "culture of violence."[41] In that sense, the police are in fact a part and indeed a reflection of the violence that already exists in society, and the emphasis on training reminds scholars that the police have to be trained out of this "culture of violence."[42]

As the discussion in this section indicates, the literature on torture in India focuses mostly on the police or the enforcers of law to explain the persistence of torture and points to the need for changes in police institutions. Indeed, some of the significant changes that are required to check torture at the level of enforcement do entail structural reforms in the institution of the police compatible with a more democratic postcolonial India. In addition, other reforms require improving the wages and conditions of the bulk of the police force, providing more resources for training and investigations, and actually acknowledging the interests of the police as a group.[43]

While institutional weaknesses do contribute toward an understanding of why torture may continue to persist in India, an exclusive focus on the police distracts attention from the question of whether the jurisprudence itself is ambivalent toward the infliction of pain and suffering in the context of interrogations. This lack of focus on the jurisprudence may be due either to the fact that Supreme Court decisions are considered by scholars to be extremely effective in addressing cases of custodial violence and/or to the fact that the police are involved in such glaring illegalities that there is a lesser scrutiny of the jurisprudence.[44] Just to give one example, Deva Prasad M., in his excellent survey on torture and law in the Indian context, points out, "The Supreme Court has been quite forward-thinking regarding the views on rights of the accused and ways to curb torture."[45] Similarly, the Asian Center for Human Rights emphasizes the powerful nature of the judicial interventions: "The Indian judiciary despite powerful rulings on torture and other human rights violations is restricted by a number of factors" such as judicial delays, impunity, and lack of a specific law for compensation.[46] While this assessment is correct, an unfortunate and unintended consequence of such statements is that the focus then becomes entirely or mostly on enforcement or implementation of the laws by the police.

However, as noted earlier, the jurisprudence of interrogations or legal interpretation is integrally linked to enforcement of the laws and needs to be further scrutinized as far as the state's and law's relationship to excess violence is concerned. Thus, I focus on three formal legal regimes that constitute the jurisprudence of interrogations in the Indian context, namely, the right against self-incrimination, procedural safeguards, and custody jurisprudence. I argue that in each arena of the particular protections that are developed by the Supreme Court, the Court constantly struggles in its response to cases of torture and custodial deaths. I note that despite its innovations, the inability of the legal discourse to completely contain torture is a reflection of a liberal democracy's failure to distance itself from excess violence.

Three Legal Regimes: Self-Incrimination, Procedural Safeguards, and Custody Jurisprudence

Theorization of Violence in the Absence of a Definition: Indian-ized Miranda and beyond the "Lodestar"

Despite many formal safeguards and judicial initiatives against torture, there is no single definition of torture in Indian jurisprudence.[47] Yet there have been occasional attempts by the Indian Supreme Court to specify their understanding of illegal violence, for instance, in the *Nandini Satpathy v. P. L. Dani* case (1978). The discourse on custodial violence in India has historically developed fairly independently of the jurisprudence on self-incrimination, although there are a few notable exceptions.[48] One of the most significant cases in this regard is *Nandini Satpathy v. P.L. Dani*, which relies heavily on the logic of the U.S. Miranda case and in the process gives an innovative interpretation of Miranda.[49] The Satpathy case is thus a classic example of the ways in which U.S. jurisprudence has influenced the jurisprudence in India even as the Indian Court's own interpretation (theorization of violence) surpasses what the Court ostensibly "depended" on. The Court writes, "The *Miranda* ruling clothed the Fifth Amendment with flesh and blood and so must we, if Article 20(3) is not to prove a promise of unreality. . . . [W]e seek light from *Miranda* for interpretation, not innovation, for principles in their settings, not borrowings for our conditions."[50] The judges thus relied on the reasoning of the Miranda decision—which they referred to as "the lodestar"—in order to formulate principles that would be meaningful and applicable to the Indian context.

In this case, the former chief minister of the eastern Indian state of Orissa, Nandini Satpathy, was accused of corruption, and she refused to answer certain questions, claiming a constitutional and statutory right to silence.[51] This case is generally read as a major defense of the constitutional right against self-incrimination (Article 20[3]) and a right to counsel (Article 22[1]), but here I focus on another important aspect of the opinion that is not adequately focused, namely, the Court's theorization of violence.

Both sides in the Satpathy case used U.S. jurisprudence to debate whether the right against self-incrimination could be extended to pretrial proceedings, and the Court, following Miranda, concluded in the affirmative.[52] Quoting extensively from the Miranda decision about the three distinct forms of violence elaborated by the U.S. Court, namely, physical violence, mental violence, and inherent coercion, the Indian Court adopted the reasoning of the majority in the Miranda case and even extended it, one could argue, to its logical conclusion. For instance, in contrast to the U.S. courts, which did not clarify how the methods mentioned in the interrogation manuals would be characterized, the Indian Court defined all the methods of interrogation mentioned in the American manuals as torture. The Indian justices wrote, "A thorough and intimate sketch is made of the versatility of the *arts of torture* developed officially in American country calculated to break, by physical or psychological crafts, the morale of the suspect and make him cough up confessional answers."[53]

The Indian Court seemed to follow the Miranda Court's reasoning that since the methods of interrogation were meant to "create an atmosphere of domination" and force the person to speak, these methods constituted "torture." One could argue that the Indian Supreme Court actually conflated the distinctions between the different kinds of violence, ranging from physical third degree to mental torture to inherent coercion, that the U.S. Supreme Court differentiated in the Miranda case. In contrast, I suggest that the Indian Court recognized that once one accepts a broad definition of coercion, as the Miranda Court attempted to do, it is difficult to determine when a particular act actually constitutes excess violence or even torture, an issue that haunts the post-Miranda jurisprudence in the United States. Even if there is a lack of unanimity on what exactly constitutes torture, the Indian Supreme Court, while following the framework of Miranda, recognized the slipperiness of defining and distinguishing between acceptable and unacceptable forms of violence in interrogations.

The Indian Court further notes, "Police sops and syrups of many types are prescribed to wheedle unwitting words of guilt from tough or gentle subjects. The end product is involuntary incrimination, subtly secured, not crudely traditional. Our police processes are less 'scholarly' and sophisticated, but . . . ?"[54] Thus, if the intention of the interrogators in using these methods is to finally get an "involuntary incrimination," the act is by definition an illegal form of violence. According to the Indian Court, the difference between the third degree and other methods of interrogation mentioned in the manuals seems to be the difference between the "crudely traditional" (physical?) methods and the more "subtle" (yet coercive?) ones. Here the Indian Court, similar to the Miranda Court, recognizes the significance of inherent coercion (which Peter Brooks brilliantly addresses) in forcing confessions but, in addition, the Indian Court recognizes the continuum between the different forms of excess violence.

Consequently, in the Satpathy case, not only was the third degree completely disallowed as a procedure for gaining confessions but any kind of compulsion was prohibited by the right against self-incrimination. Here the Indian Court sets forward, more clearly than its American counterpart, the forms of violence that would be disallowed. Compulsion includes not only "physical threats or violence" but also "psychic torture, atmospheric pressure, environmental coercion, tiring interrogative prolixity, overbearing and intimidatory methods and the like."[55] The Satpathy case, as a result, represents one of the most systematic understandings of torture and other forms of excess violence, including physical and mental violence, as separate from inherent coercion.

The Satpathy case shows the attempt of the Indian Court to develop substantial formal safeguards against the possibility of using violence in interrogations. Furthermore, the definition of the violence disallowed seemed to be broad enough to exclude a range of violence, regardless of whether it leaves marks on the body or not. However, although this case jurisprudentially developed a comprehensive perspective on custodial violence, there were two major shortcomings. First, there was a very limited impact of the decision on cases of confessions and custodial violence. Despite the Court's recognition that the warnings regarding a right to silence and a right to counsel during interrogation were established by the Constitution, the lack of a well-developed public defender system (as the Court seemed to acknowledge) made the impact of the case substantially less significant in practice.[56]

The second limitation was that while the Miranda case connected the right against self-incrimination to the issue of voluntariness in custodial interrogations in the United States, the Indian Supreme Court did not use the *Satpathy v. Dani* case as a precedent in the custodial violence cases. Instead, the Indian jurisprudence focused on different paths to deal with custodial violence: instituting procedural safeguards on recording of confessions and broadening the scope of Article 21.[57] Although there is little discussion on why the Supreme Court did not use the Satpathy case in custodial violence cases, a couple of the reasons are apparent in particular statutory and constitutional provisions in India. First, some of the warnings established under Miranda in the U.S. context were already a part of the procedural safeguards in place for the recording of confessions in India (as will be discussed in the next section). Second, the Indian Court found the expansion of rights under Article 21, which prevents state officials from depriving persons of life and liberty unless they are following "procedure established by law," as a more effective way to intervene in custodial violence cases, especially custodial death cases. Thus, in practice, the Satpathy case neither had much impact on the high levels of custodial violence nor did its theorization of violence carry forward the jurisprudence on custodial violence.

Policing the Police: Safeguards against Torture in Recording of Confessions

The second major legal regime against torture in India has been institutionalized first and foremost in the recording of confessions specified in Section 164 of CrPc and Sections 24-27 of the IEA. The entire process of recording confessions is based on the premise that voluntariness can be ensured only if these statutory provisions are followed.[58] The statutory provisions disallow the police from recording confessions in routine cases. In fact, confessions recorded by police officers are not admissible as evidence against the accused (Section 25 of IEA). Section 26 of IEA states that only a confession made in front of a judicial or metropolitan magistrate is admissible as evidence.[59] In accordance with Section 164 of the CrPc, the magistrate has to ensure that the confession is voluntary by following an elaborate procedure of providing warnings and also signing a certificate stating that he or she believes the confession to be voluntary; otherwise the evidence is excluded.[60] Thus, some of the safeguards in the form of warnings ensuring voluntariness that did not develop in the United States until the Miranda case (1966) were always present in the form of statutory safeguards against torture in the Indian criminal procedure itself. The stringent standards regarding confessions are most visible in *Sarwan Singh v. State of Punjab* (1957).[61] In this case, even a mechanical fulfillment of procedural safeguards was unacceptable to the Court since it did not respect the underlying substantive principle of removing all possibilities of pressure during confessions.

This was a murder case in which one of the accused appealed his conviction by claiming that his confession was involuntary.[62] In its decision, the Supreme Court reiterated the need for confessions to be free from any "inducement, threat or promise," a requirement similar to the Bram standard discussed in the U.S. context.[63] In addition, the Court also considered warnings inadequate unless there was meaningful distancing between the police and the accused, achieved by sending the latter to jail custody—outside police influence—to reflect over whether they wanted to confess at all.[64] The magistrate's uncritical acceptance of Sarwan Singh's explicit desire to confess was also rejected since it reflected "casualness" and a "mechanical" element to the magistrate's inquiry, rather than a more substantive one. The Court wrote, "This insistence on the part of Sarwan Singh to make a confession immediately should have put the learned Magistrate on his guard because it obviously bore traces of police pressure or inducement."[65] Thus, the Court set an extremely high standard for ensuring the voluntariness of confessions and disallowed any possibility of coercion. However, the sheer inconsistency of the Court in a later case delayed any emergence of a systematic jurisprudence on the issue of procedural safeguards. In *Shankaria v. State of Rajasthan* (1978), where the accused was arrested for mass murders, the Supreme Court took a very different approach to the question of recording confessions.[66] In this case, the accused was arrested and sent by the magistrate to judicial lockup for two days. Subsequently, he was produced in front of the magistrate who gave him warnings and fifteen minutes for reflection, after which the magistrate started recording the confession in this and another case.

Shankaria contended that his confession was the result of torture and that he had not been given adequate time for reflection. The Supreme Court, however, determined that the confession was voluntary mainly based on the magistrate's assertion that he had ascertained voluntariness. A major lacuna in the case is that Shankaria was given only fifteen minutes' time *after* the warnings were given by the magistrate. The Supreme Court read the fifteen minutes as adequate by mechanically reading its previous decision in Sarwan Singh. In the earlier Sarwan case, the Court had said,

> It would *naturally be difficult to lay down any hard and fast rule* as to the time which should be allowed to an accused person in any given case. However, *speaking generally, it would, we think, be reasonable to insist upon giving an accused person at least 24 hours to decide whether or not he should make a confession.* Where there may be reason to suspect that the accused has been persuaded or coerced to make a confession, [an] even longer period may have to be given to him before his statement is recorded.[67]

Clearly, while the Supreme Court in the Shankaria case is technically right that there is no hard and fast rule set by the Sarwan Court, it is important to note the language used by the Court in the Sarwan case.[68] The Court in the previous case had recognized the importance of reflection outside police control and suggested twenty-four hours as a reasonable period. Thus, by considering fifteen minutes an acceptable time for reflection (after warnings were issued), the Court in Shankaria completely rejected the sentiment behind the earlier decision.[69] Finally, in the two cases, a "totality of facts" test determined whether the confessions were admissible or not.[70] For instance, even in the Sarwan case, where the Court rejected the confession, the Court focused on other factors such as the unreliability of the witness, inconsistencies in the confession, and the illegality of his detention. Similarly, in the case of Shankaria, the Court focused on the truth of the confession and even tried to iron out any contradictions the justices noted in the medical testimonies.[71]

This emphasis on factors such as reliability and the truth of a confession, rather than procedural errors, is addressed more squarely in the *Shivappa v. State of Karnataka* (1995) case, where the accused was charged with murder and the only evidence was the confession made by him, which was retracted subsequently. While determining whether the confession was "voluntary, true and trustworthy," the Court wrote, "unless the Court is satisfied that the confession is voluntary in nature, it cannot be acted upon and no further enquiry as to whether it is true and trustworthy need be made."[72] Here the Court appeared to be more concerned about voluntariness during the recording of confessions not just "in form" but also "in essence" and considered the confession involuntary because warnings were not adequately conveyed to the suspect.[73] The Shivappa case thus upholds voluntariness as being the most important element in confessions but reliability and truth continue to be determinants. In fact, in a 2001 case, the Court wrote that voluntariness and truth are both important for the admissibility of confessions, leaving the issue wide open for further interpretation.[74]

The procedural safeguards for recording confessions were enforced to address the reality of illegal violence and the impossibility of knowing what goes on in interrogation rooms and police custody. Yet the tension between the existence of these safeguards and the Court's focus on the "totality of facts" is a major source of contention. Since the Court has allowed the bypassing of these safeguards in some instances, the justices open themselves to criticism. The question is especially pertinent for India, where the number of custodial deaths and instances of torture has been extremely high. In recent years, it is also this very safeguard regarding the recording of confessions by magistrates that has been bypassed in so-called extraordinary laws (TADA and POTA) by allowing senior police officials to record confessions, thereby creating further murkiness in the torture debates in India.[75]

The interpretation of statutory safeguards has only been one other legal regime in the Indian jurisprudence on custodial torture. The Indian legal system has over the years developed what can be termed "custody jurisprudence" in an attempt to address the incidents of custodial torture and deaths. The formal safeguards were unable to contain the physical and psychological violence used by state officials and became a major concern for the judiciary, especially when custodial death cases came up repeatedly and prompted the need for some response, becoming the basis of the third major legal regime.

Confronting Custodial Violence

The Erratic Phase: Custodial Deaths, Torture, and the Supreme Court

Until the 1990s, the Supreme Court's intervention in custodial violence cases reflected extremely erratic decisions despite the rising number of cases of torture and custodial deaths. The significant numbers of unexplained deaths of citizens in the custody of state officials could have prompted the Supreme Court of a liberal democracy to develop a strong, consistent jurisprudence. However, in the absence of a framework for dealing with custodial violence, the Court decided on a case-to-case basis. While the post-1990s custody jurisprudence has been the focus of most scholarly analysis, the Supreme Court's response to the custodial death and torture cases in the 1970s and 1980s are significant for four reasons. First, during this period, the Court often disbelieved and delegitimized narratives of torture by unduly focusing on "inconsistencies" in the stories of what the Court termed "shady" and "unreliable" characters. Second, the Court's belief in the police versions of the custodial death and torture cases was not just an uncritical defense of state institutions but also a complete denial of the unequal power relations that exist between the police and the accused in custodial interrogations. Third, the tension between a strong rhetoric against torture and an inadequate jurisprudence is most palpable in this phase. Finally, the eventual significance of the systematic custody jurisprudence becomes apparent only by noting the absence of clear guidelines in this period.

In many of the cases, the justices did express a general concern about the rise of custodial deaths and articulated their shock that law enforcers indulged in acts of torture. However, ironically, this rhetoric, when contrasted with some of the actual decisions, makes it seem as if torture exists in a parallel universe, the result of invisible actors, in spaces where the Court cannot intervene except in a very few instances.[76] For instance, in *Ram Chander v. State of Haryana* (1983), the detained Balwant Singh was tortured during a theft investigation and died in police custody. The dead body had approximately thirty-three external injuries and four internal ones. His relatives, who were sitting outside the police station, heard his cries while he was being tortured.[77] Despite the fact that the Haryana High Court found the injuries, especially the ones on his soles and buttocks, similar to the ones caused by police use of rulers, the Supreme Court disagreed. The Court went out of its way to reverse the convictions by pointing to several other injuries that could have been inflicted by the public while the thief was fleeing.

Sometimes, the Court even accepted the veracity of the claim of torture but was hesitant to make the system accountable. In *Maiku v. State of U.P.* (1989), Bharat, who was suspected of bicycle theft, was beaten by the police when he tried to escape and died subsequently.[78] The Court wrote,

> The general nature of evidence is that torture was done. . . . It is true that Bharat has lost his life. It is also true that he had some injuries by hard and blunt weapon on his body but it is not clear under what circumstances it happened and how present appellant Sub-Inspector Sarjoo Singh could be connected with those injuries.[79]

Even in cases where there was evidence of torture leading to death, the Supreme Court declined to intervene in any effective manner.

Thus, despite custodial death cases giving the Court an opportunity to intervene in this universe concretely, the Court failed to come up with either an effective means of redress or a systematic jurisprudence. The rhetoric against torture in general, thus, stepped in to occlude the failure to intervene in the particular cases.

If the Supreme Court's response to custodial *death* cases was so unpredictable, cases where there were only allegations of torture and no dead bodies, unsurprisingly, received even more arbitrary treatment by the Court. In fact, in some of the murder cases that came before the Court, it just seemed to dismiss the issue of torture entirely, primarily by claiming that the accusations of torture came belatedly.[80]

A perfect illustration of the response of the Supreme Court toward illegal violence in the pre-1990s period is a case where there were not only allegations of torture but even a bypassing of the procedural safeguards regarding recording of confessions. Here the normalization of torture and the articulation of "unreliability" of witnesses reflect a structural bias exhibited by the Court during this time. In *Dagdu v. State of Maharashtra* (1977), the case concerned one Maharashtrian (western Indian state) village, where five small girls (ten years old), a one-year-old, and four women in their thirties were murdered and twenty people were arrested for the ten murders. In the course of the decision, the Supreme Court casually mentioned that Shankar (a witness) was charged for attempted suicide because he "struck his head against a wall while in police custody and sustained a head injury."[81] Shankar said that "he was driven to break his head as a result of the torture inflicted upon him by the police."[82] However, the Court was little concerned in its opinion with these injuries that occurred in police custody. Elsewhere in the opinion, the Court even accepted the possibility that torture took place against another witness:

> Ganpat the approver, was driven to admit that he was tortured while in the lock-up and we have serious doubts whether the injury caused on his head was, as alleged by the police, self-inflicted. . . . We have resisted the failing which tempts even judicially trained minds to revolt against such methods and throw the entire case out of hand. But we must, with hopes for the future, utter a word of warning that just as crime does not pay, so shall it not pay to resort to torture of suspects and witnesses during the course of investigation.[83]

The horrific nature of the case possibly made the Court decide in this manner. After, all, even the magistrate's inability to apply the procedures to ensure voluntariness of confessions is explained by the Court in the following manner: "The magistrate was either overcome by the sensation which the case had aroused in Maharashtra or perhaps he blindly trusted the high police officers who were frantically looking out for a clue to these mysterious murders."[84]

According to the Court, the "tendency" and "temptation" of the police to use a "strong arm" must be "nipped in the bud," yet even in an instance where torture was actually used, the Court has not intervened and has fallen back on a general concern against torture. The Court did exclude the evidence of one witness, but it was not the alleged torture (which may have occurred during the one and a half months of interrogation before he confessed) that led to the exclusion of his evidence but rather his "unreliability" as a person. Shankar was considered an "utterly worthless witness" because he used to deceive women about having the powers to find a cure for diseases or to discover treasure troves.[85] Thus, the Court's opinion about admitting confessions seemed to relate not so much to preventing torture (as being the basis of including safeguards) but rather to the "unreliability" of these witnesses.

In many of these cases, the "character" of the witnesses is a category that constantly reappears and often reflects the structural class bias against many of the witnesses.[86] In the Dagdu case, for instance, the Court trusted the two main suspects because they were more educated and, consequently, less superstitious. One of the suspects was an influential man, described as a "man of some means" and for some time president of the local municipality office (local government). In contrast, the other suspects, who were his servants, were easily characterized by the Court as unreliable and superstitious. The fact that superstition could be shared by people across the class and educational spectrum is completely denied in this "objective" assessment of the Court.

The structural class bias is not just visible in court cases such as Dagdu. Rather, it is integrally related to routine custodial violence cases, since it is mostly the marginalized sections of society who are targeted by the police. As the People's Union for Democratic Rights (henceforth PUDR) reports have repeatedly pointed out in the context of Delhi, many of the custodial deaths involve "poor migrants" who are young (less than thirty years old), work in occupations such as auto driver, rickshaw puller, vendor, and watchman, and reside in slums and resettlement colonies.[87] Witnesses in these custodial violence cases are also hard to find because they come from similar backgrounds and live in constant fear of the police. In fact, PUDR reports state that since the victims of custodial deaths are often "minor lawbreakers" and "social dropouts" and are considered "habitual bad characters," their deaths (and, one could add, torture) are considered of "little consequence."[88] The Supreme Court's erratic responses during this period thus reinforced some of these narratives on the unreliability of the witnesses by focusing on their shady character and their lack of education and status. The Court's approach fed into the police arguments and collectively delegitimized the voices of torture victims and characterized their experiences as false and unworthy of further exploration.

Coincidentally, during the same period, the campaign against custodial rape in India faced similar challenges when the state brought up the past sexual history and character of the rape survivors to discredit them.[89] In addition, just as visible injuries were considered the only proof that torture took place, the absence of injuries on a rape survivor was considered evidence of consent and as proof that the woman failed to resist during the rape. After the protests in the Mathura case (1983), where a tribal woman was raped by two policemen and the police were acquitted by the Supreme Court using some of these arguments, a campaign by legal activists and feminist groups challenged these conceptions regarding consent and the relevance of women's sexual history in rape cases.[90] The campaigns led to significant changes in custodial rape laws such that the onus of proof about consent was put on the accused and the character and past sexual history of the rape survivor was considered irrelevant. Despite the change in the rape laws, Rakesh Shukla points out that in practice women's immorality and lack of resistance due to absence of visible injury continue to be the two main arguments used to challenge the credibility of the woman.[91] Regardless, there were at least some judicial and legislative interventions that conceptually rejected these emphases in custodial rape cases, and, in contrast, during the same period the jurisprudence on (nonsexual) custodial torture/deaths continued to focus on the "unreliabilty" and "shady character" of the witnesses and on visible injuries.[92]

Thus, the pre-1990s era exhibits a peculiar response on the part of the Supreme Court. On the one hand, the Court came up with a strong defense of the right against self-incrimination that conceptually excluded the use of almost any violence in the context of interrogations.[93] The Court was also willing to respond to the grievances of prisoners in the Sunil Batra and Charles Sobhraj cases as a natural extension of the right to life and liberty under Article 21.[94] On the other hand, it refused the opportunity to take up the issue of custodial death in a systematic way, let alone address the issue of custodial torture. This is particularly noticeable because the Supreme Court rejected a petition filed by PUDR on custodial deaths in 1992.[95] As a result, the Court ended up responding to the cases in an unpredictable way, and was unable to deal with the issue of custodial violence in any meaningful manner until the Behera and the Basu cases in the 1990s. In the process, incidents of custodial violence continued to grow and challenged the political and legal discourses that stated that torture was unequivocally impermissible in a liberal democracy.

Emergence of Custody Jurisprudence in India

Torture is a wound in the soul so painful that sometimes you can almost touch it, but it is also so intangible that there is no way to heal it. Torture is anguish squeezing in your chest, cold as ice and heavy as a stone, paralyzing as sleep and dark as the abyss. Torture is despair and fear and rage and hate. It is a desire to kill and destroy including yourself.[96]

It was only in the 1990s that the Supreme Court finally acknowledged the peculiar nature of custodial deaths and the difficulty in getting any evidence regarding torture or deaths in custody. The emergence of this systematic custody jurisprudence coincided with the consolidation of the civil liberties and democratic rights movement in India, which highlighted and countered the Indian state's repressive response to voices of discontent.

During the period right after independence in 1947, India witnessed broad-based support for the Congress Party (a dominant party in the anticolonial struggle) and a belief in the Nehruvian vision of democracy and development.[97] The Indian Constitution that was the result of significant debates in the Constituent Assembly led by the *dalit* leader B. R. Ambedkar did seek to represent the aspirations of the newly emergent nation.[98] However, civil liberties activists and scholars G. Haragopal and K. Balagopal point out that the Constitution ultimately did not represent the interests of the Indian masses since it differentiated between the fundamental rights (life, liberty, and property) that were made judicially enforceable and the directive principles (socioeconomic rights) that were included as "normative declarations."[99]

By the 1960s, the faith in the Nehruvian (Mahanolobis) development model of big dams and Green Revolution was waning, particularly because of the growing poverty, rising prices, and disparities between the rich and the poor. The growing discontent manifested itself in movements such as the armed struggles—the Naxalite movement (1967)—on the one hand and the Gandhi-inspired Jay Prakash Narayan movement (1974) on the other.[100] The Indian state responded to these movements with highly repressive laws and actions, and in 1975, Prime Minister Indira Gandhi imposed the emergency, which witnessed some of the worst state excesses in postcolonial India. As Balagopal and Haragopal note, "The torture, the encounter deaths, the illegal detentions, the killing of prisoners were the manifestations of the extent to which naked physical force was being used at the time. The total choking of the throat and the voice of the society was the essence of the emergency."[101]

The excesses during the emergency did lead Indian liberals and the Left to appreciate the need to preserve the Constitution, and eventually this realization led to the consolidation of the civil liberties groups.[102] Even though groups such as the Association of Protection of Democratic Rights (APDR) and Andhra Pradesh Civil Liberties Committee (henceforth APCLC) formed before the emergency to counter the state repression of the Naxalites, a wider network of civil liberties groups emerged only after the emergency, collectively emphasizing the need to preserve democratic institutions. There was perhaps an indirect realization of the provocative point made by Baxi in this regard that even though the movements challenging the state were responding to the economic and political crisis, the call for total transformation, whether peacefully or through armed struggle, had the unfortunate effect of weakening the liberal institutions in the process.[103]

The emergency (1975–1977) witnessed the complete suspension of fundamental rights, violations of human rights, and continuing increases in poverty and unemployment. The civil liberties and democratic rights movement in India, consequently, struggled with whether to focus primarily on civil liberties (fundamental rights enshrined in the Constitution) or democratic rights (socioeconomic rights beyond those guaranteed in the Constitution).[104] Groups emphasizing the protection of civil liberties wanted to strengthen the "fragile institutions of democracy" while those focusing on democratic rights believed that the realization of civil liberties for all depended on going beyond this paradigm. As Balagopal and Haragopal explain, "the democratic rights perspective asserts that the deprived and starved have a right to organise and struggle even for the total change of the system as they do not find solutions to their problems in the given socio-economic system."[105] This conflict between the civil-liberties and democratic-rights perspectives was most visible in the context of the debates within the People's Union for Civil Liberties–Democratic Rights, which eventually became two organizations: the People's Union for Civil Rights (henceforth PUCL) and PUDR. As Ajay Gudavarthy explains, for the PUCL, "the state's constitutional framework guaranteed certain basic freedoms and they need to be effectively and progressively realised," while PUDR found that framework inadequate.[106]

In the context of custodial violence, the effect of this debate has been largely theoretical. Both the PUDR and the PUCL (alongside others such as the APCLC) focus on the fundamental rights of the victims of custodial violence while noting that these victims are often the marginalized sections in society and the latter overlap with those resisting the systemic socioeconomic inequalities.[107] Thus, there is recognition among the groups that even while structural inequalities have to be focused, the fundamental rights enshrined in the Constitution and reiterated by judicial decisions have to be preserved and utilized.[108]

In that sense, the domestic civil liberties groups emphasize the routineness of the custodial violence, as compared to international groups such as Amnesty International, which also highlighted the incidents of torture in India but in more extraordinary contexts. In 1973, Amnesty International brought out a seminal international report on torture that highlighted its widespread prevalence in the world.[109] The report's section on India mostly focused on torture, detention, and killings by the Indian state in conflict areas occupied by Naxalites (Maoists) in Bengal and the secessionist movements in Nagaland and Kashmir. Noorani, in his review of the Amnesty report, makes reference to "the bad treatment inflicted on revolutionaries when they are arrested—tortures, burnings with cigarettes—or during their detention—absence of medical treatment, beatings, etc."[110] Even though the Amnesty report mentioned the routine cases of torture and killings, the focus was on state violence in the conflict areas. As the report notes, "the pattern that emerges is that although incidents of police and prison warden brutality continue to occur, the worst period was in 1970-71, when the threat from the Naxalites was judged to be greatest."[111] Undoubtedly, the excesses affecting the political detainees in conflict areas were considerable, but the Amnesty report's focus on the extraordinary had the unfortunate effect of obfuscating the widespread torture and deaths in routine murder investigations and theft cases. In contrast, domestic human rights groups such as PUDR and PUCL have been focusing on custodial deaths in both routine and extraordinary contexts. PUDR has, for example, brought out a fact-finding report on each and every case of custodial death since 1980 in Delhi, the capital of India, pointing to the routineness of the phenomenon and its relationship to the extraordinary.[112]

The emergence of systematic custody jurisprudence not only coincided with the consolidation of the civil liberties and democratic rights movement in India but also corresponded with a new era of judicial activism termed "public interest litigation or social action litigation" (PIL or SAL). In the 1970s and 1980s, the Supreme Court encouraged the emergence of a new institutional mechanism to make the judicial system more accessible for activists focusing on violations of fundamental rights. As Ramanathan notes, "PIL was a process which . . . recognised rights and their denial which had been invisibalised in the public domain . . . and led to 'juristic' activism. . . . The potential for reading a range of rights into the fundamental rights was explored."[113] The Court made the rules of locus standii more flexible such that anyone could bring a case to the Supreme Court on behalf of those who were unable to, and simplified the litigation process by allowing even a letter to be considered as a writ petition.[114]

A range of rights concerning the environment, education, freedom, and dignity were jurisprudentially expanded through PIL or what Baxi terms "social action litigation." Indeed, Baxi considers SAL as a further expansion of the human rights movement. "[P]eople participate, through activation and legitimation of adjudicatory power, in fashioning an expansive regime of rights converting the Supreme Court of India into a permanent Constituent Assembly of India, sculpting the nature and future of rights movement, steadily converting the Directive Principles of State Policy into judicially enforceable rights."[115] The Court in many cases utilized Article 21 to enunciate some of these rights.[116] This article of the Indian Constitution is deliberately worded differently from the Fourteenth Amendment due process clause of the U.S. Constitution. As Sathe points out, the Indian framers were concerned about the "unpredictability and vagueness" of the concept of due process, and feared constant judicial review of legislative policies.[117] Therefore, they decided that Article 21 would consider a procedure for depriving a person of life and liberty to be valid as long as it was established by law.[118] Gradually, particularly in response to the suspension of fundamental rights during the emergency and the protests of the civil liberties and democratic rights movement, the judiciary clarified that under Article 21 a procedure not only had to be legal but also had to be "reasonable, just and fair."[119] Thus, over the years, the expansion of the scope of Article 21 has led to the establishment of many rights, including the "right to be free from torture," through the use of public interest or social action litigation.

The combined significance of the rise of civil liberties groups and the power of social action litigation is best reflected in two key decisions of the Supreme Court on custodial deaths: *Nilabati Behera v. State of Orissa* in 1993 and *D. K. Basu v. State of West Bengal; Ashok K. Johri v. State of Uttar Pradesh* in 1996.[120] Even before these cases, the Supreme Court had started formulating some of the principles of custodial jurisprudence, for instance rejecting its own previous emphasis on "unreliable witnesses" and putting the onus of explaining custodial deaths on the police, thereby shifting the burden of proof in favor of the person in custody.[121] These specific principles found a more systematic exposition in two landmark cases: *Behera* and *Basu*.

The Nilabati Behera case involved a 22-year-old man, Suman, who was suspected of theft, picked up by the police, and found dead the next day on the railway tracks, his body bearing the signs of multiple injuries.[122] The police claimed that he had escaped from custody in the middle of the night and been hit by a passing train. The Court, however, converted a letter from the mother into a writ petition and stated,

> The burden is, therefore, clearly on the respondents to explain how Suman Behera sustained those injuries which caused his death. Unless a plausible explanation is given by the respondents which is consistent with their innocence, the obvious inference is that the fatal injuries were inflicted to Suman Behera in police custody resulting in his death, for which the respondents are responsible and liable.[123]

The Supreme Court relied on the doctor's postmortem report, which attributed the fatal injuries to "merciless beating" with a *lathi* (stick). The Court rejected a range of other improbable evidence, such as a second doctor's report and a joint inquiry by the magistrate and senior police suggesting that Suman had escaped from the police by chewing off his rope and subsequently died in a train accident.

The most significant outcome of this case is the elaboration of the right to compensation for violation of Article 21 in custodial death cases. Even the state did not deny that there was a right to compensation for a violation of Article 21 but refused to accept the death as a custodial one.[124] Disagreeing on the facts of the case, the Court went on to explain the particular significance of a right to compensation in such instances:

> The defence of sovereign immunity being inapplicable and alien to the concept of guarantee of fundamental rights, there can be no question of such a defence being available in the constitutional remedy. It is this principle which justifies award of monetary compensation for contravention of fundamental rights guaranteed by the Constitution, when that is the only practicable mode of redress available for the contravention made by the State or its servants in the purported exercise of their powers, and enforcement of the fundamental right is claimed by resort to the remedy in public law under the Constitution by recourse to Articles 32 and 226 of the Constitution.[125]

The Supreme Court stated that while there was sovereign immunity for officers in private law cases, there was no such immunity with respect to a right to compensation for violation of fundamental rights in public law.[126] The Court also considered the traditional methods of redress—civil and criminal proceedings or disallowing illegal detentions with the help of writs—inadequate and emphasized the need to ensure compensation. An amount of 150,000 rupees was accorded to the victim's mother in this case; this figure was calculated according to the amount the victim Suman earned and some additional money for legal expenses.

The Court took a substantial and uniquely creative step in improving the safeguards against torture by imposing the monetary burden on the state for its inability to protect the human rights of citizens. Even though this was not the first case where the right to compensation was given by the Court for violation of fundamental rights or custodial deaths, the Court certainly went to great lengths to explain and justify the principle behind it.[127] Nonetheless, even in this landmark case, the Court continued to assume the general adequacy of existing procedural mechanisms to contain custodial deaths and torture.

It was not until 1996 that the Supreme Court actually addressed the procedural mechanisms required to deal with custodial deaths.[128] In fact, this lacuna was pointed out by the Legal Aid Services in Bengal, which articulated a need for "custody jurisprudence" from the Court. The Legal Aid Services drew the Court's attention to news items about custodial deaths in lockups and asked for their letter to be treated as a writ petition to inquire into why custodial deaths were being hushed up by the police and also to ask for the development of mechanisms for compensating the victims. The Court, in turn, asked the various states of India to submit reports on custodial deaths and violence. Although most of the states that replied denied the extent of the problem, they eventually did participate in the process of coming up with some mechanisms to deal with the issue of custodial violence. As noted earlier, the denial of torture by governments is a recurring feature in democracies and is often issued despite the well-documented government and nongovernment reports on torture (and the particular PIL filed in this case). The Indian state governments eventually cooperated with the Supreme Court, almost indicating a realization that an abstract concern for torture could be expressed without accepting their own specific complicity in the persistence of torture.

In *D. K. Basu v. State of West Bengal*, the Court, first and foremost, acknowledged the peculiar nature of custodial violence and the "helplessness" of the victim in custody.[129] The Court, while accepting the lack of any definition of torture in the law, describes it in the following manner.

> "Torture" has not been defined in [the] Constitution or in other penal laws. "Torture" of a human being by another human being is essentially an instrument to impose the will of the "strong" over the "weak" by suffering. The word torture today has become synonymous with the *darker side of human civilization*. . . . "Custodial torture" is a naked violation of human dignity and degradation which destroys, to a very large extent, the individual personality.[130]

Thus, the Supreme Court emphasizes the unequal power relationship between the "strong" and "the weak," the impact of torture on "human dignity," and the relationship between torture and "the darker side of civilization." The Court further wrote, "Any form of torture or cruel, inhuman or degrading treatment would fall within the inhibition of Article 21 of the Constitution, whether it occurs during investigation, interrogation or otherwise."[131]

The Court does write elsewhere that "reasonable restrictions" can be applied to the protections under Article 21 but does not clarify the nature of these restrictions. The detailed analysis of methods of interrogation or forms of violence is also missing in this case, and it appears as if the Satpathy case (on self-incrimination), where the Court elaborated on its understanding of violence, and the Basu case continue to exist in parallel universes.[132]

Apart from a powerful rhetoric and enunciation of the legal safeguards against torture and CIDT, the D. K. Basu Court was also willing to acknowledge a crisis in legitimacy being created by the widespread use of custodial violence. The Court wrote,

> Experience shows that [the] worst violations of human rights take place during the course of *investigation, when the police with a view to secur[ing] evidence or confession often resorts to third degree methods including torture. . . . The increasing incidence of torture and death in custody has assumed such alarming proportions that it is affecting the creditibility of the Rule of Law and the administration of [the] criminal justice system.* The community rightly feels perturbed. Society's cry for justice becomes louder.[133]

Here, in noting the modus operandi of custodial violence as taking place during investigations, the Court finally recognized (without acknowledging them, of course) the findings of several human rights groups about the methods used by the police to hide custodial deaths. The police often arrested people without any record of the arrest and subjected them to torture during interrogations. If a person died in custody, the police "disposed of the body," denying that the person was ever detained in the first place.[134] If custody could not be denied in some cases, the police subsequently claimed that the person died after she or he was let go or escaped from the custody of the police.

Decades of PUDR reports have recorded the numerous myths perpetuated by the police to hide custodial torture and deaths.[135] For instance, a PUDR report narrated the story of Surat Lal, whose body was found on the railway tracks. The police insisted that they had released him and he either committed suicide or was accidentally hit by a train.[136] Another official story of death in police custody is "suicide" accomplished by means of all kinds of improbable instruments and techniques. For instance, in the case of Vikal Kumar Adhana, the police claimed that he committed suicide despite the fact that he apparently died by tying "a rope fashioned from a floor mat and suspended from a vertical bar of the cell."[137] Previous ill health was an additional excuse provided in some cases. The police claim that the person had previous health problems and died as a result.[138] The PUDR fact-finding reports pointed out not only that most of these accused were in perfect health (according to their family) but also that lack of medical attention in custody needed investigation. The pattern of explanations of custodial deaths has been quite consistent in the decades that PUDR has been investigating the cases, and these reports have persuasively pointed to the contradictions in the police narratives.[139]

The D. K. Basu case clearly admitted that the preexisting legal safeguards had failed to check the increasing incidents of custodial violence and did not spare even the judiciary from their share of blame in the increasing cases of torture. The Court wrote,

> The Courts are also required to have a change in their outlook and attitude, particularly in cases involving custodial crimes, and they should exhibit more *sensitivity and adopt a realistic rather than a narrow technical approach*, while dealing with the case of custodial crime so that as far as possible within their powers, the guilty should not escape so that the victim of crime has the satisfaction that ultimately the Majesty of Law has prevailed.[140]

In order to further strengthen the custody jurisprudence, the Court reiterated the recommendation of the Law Commission that the Indian Parliament change the burden of proof in custodial violence cases: if a person is injured or dies in custody, the police should be presumed to be responsible for the injury.[141]

Finally, recognizing the need to check illegal arrests and detentions, the Court sought "transparency" and "accountability" by introducing an arrest memo or custody memo to be signed by the arrestee and a witness (relative or respectable person) at the time of arrest.[142] The arrestee is to be informed of this right and examined medically if he or she requests, and the facts are to be recorded in an "inspection memo" signed by both the officer and the arrestee. The Court also required the arrestee to be examined by a recognized doctor every forty-eight hours and asserted the need for counsel during a part of the interrogation. Records of all documents are to be sent to the district magistrate and a police control room in a state or district to monitor all arrests and detentions.[143]

The weakest intervention in the Basu case was perhaps its lack of emphasis on prosecutions in custodial deaths.[144] The Court did suggest certain punitive measures in the form of contempt of court in case of violations, but as in the Behera case, the Supreme Court's emphasis in the Basu case was on the right to compensation.[145] The Court explained,

Mere punishment of the offender cannot give much solace to the family of the victim—civil action for damage is a long drawn [out] and cumbersome judicial process. *Monetary compensation for redressal by the Court finding the infringement of the indefeasible right to life of the citizen is, therefore, useful and at times perhaps the only effective remedy* to apply balm to the wounds of the family members of the deceased victim who may have been the breadwinner of the family.[146]

The Court reiterated its commitment to a right to compensation and, in fact, occasionally considered monetary compensation as the most "suitable remedy for redressal."[147]

The Behera and Basu Courts, thus, for the first time developed systematic custody jurisprudence. The Supreme Court explained the specificity of the custodial crimes, reemphasized the measures required to effectively intervene against the violence, and highlighted the right to compensation as an important remedy for the violation of fundamental rights. The police strategy of bypassing existing safeguards led the Court to involve the public as witnesses of arrest. Since most cases of custodial torture and deaths occurred when the police just informally arrested someone, the Court's insistence on the arrest memo was an extremely creative remedy. The absence of the "public gaze" from the police process had been a major obstacle both at arrest and during interrogations. Involving the public directly in the process was significant also because the Court acknowledged, indirectly of course, that an incident of custodial death and torture became an issue only when the public protested against it.[148]

The Impact of Custody Jurisprudence and the Dilution of Safeguards

The extremely innovative custody jurisprudence developed by the Supreme Court heralded a new phase in dealing with custodial violence. Indeed, in the immediate post–Behera and Basu phase, there were some strong interventions by the Court, as in the Hailakandi and Sahadevan cases. *Secretary, Hailakandi Bar Association v. State of Assam and Another* (1995) was a classic case of a custodial death in which the police tortured Nurul Haque, initially blamed the public for beating him up, and, finally, attributed the cause of his death to heart ailments.[149] In this case, the Court not only issued an independent Central Bureau of Investigation inquiry but, in addition, in a subsequent followup of the case, the Court ordered a three-month simple imprisonment for the superintendent for falsifying the report regarding Nurul Haque.[150] The superintendent was charged with contempt of court, and his unconditional apology was declined. The Court based its decision on the CBI report that the superintendent had deliberately misled the court and Nurul did die as a result of torture, lack of food, and lack of sleep. This case reflects a serious effort on the part of the Court to address custodial deaths and occasionally to hold even higher officers responsible for hushing up cases of custodial violence.[151]

Further, despite the Parliament's failure to amend the Indian Evidence Act (to change the burden of proof in custodial violence cases), the Court continued to follow this rule in some custodial death cases. In *Sahadevan v. State* (2003), Vadivelu was arrested in a murder case and was beaten by the police with a ruler in the presence of witnesses.[152] Later, the police told the family that Vadivelu had escaped. When a body with the head crushed was found soon after, the family filed a writ petition in the High Court and the Court asked for charges to be filed in the case. The district judge accepted the body as that of Vadivelu and convicted the policemen accordingly, but the High Court disagreed and, in the absence of the body, asked for other evidence linking the accused with the deceased. The Supreme Court, however, concluded that the body found was indeed Vadivelu's, pointing to other identification marks. The Court further noted that the onus was on the police to explain the disappearance of a person if he was last seen in the company of the police and subsequently upheld the convictions in the case. Thus, the Supreme Court took extremely seriously the responsibility of intervening in some custodial death cases and even tried to monitor the implementation of their previous orders.

Overall, however, the impact on custodial violence cases of the 1996 D. K. Basu judgment and the custody jurisprudence has been limited. As the recent report by the Asian Center for Human Rights notes, between 1994–2008, 2,207 of the 16,836 deaths took place in police custody and 14,629 of these deaths, in judicial custody.[153] Even though the NHRC closely monitors cases of custodial deaths (reported to them within twenty-four hours) and can send in investigative teams and recommend compensations, it has not been very effective in reducing custodial violence.[154] PUDR reports also reiterate that over the twenty-five years that it has been monitoring the issue, there has been continued custodial violence, lack of convictions, and hardly any compensation. In a report on capital crimes regarding deaths in police custody in Delhi from 1980 to 1997, it notes that there were only two convictions in about ninety-three cases.[155] By 2000, the number of deaths increased to 109 and the number of convictions increased by one.[156] The same myths about the causes of death are perpetuated by a continuing collusion of doctors, police, and executive magistrates working together to mask custodial deaths as marginalized sections keep getting targeted by routine custodial violence.[157] More recent initiatives by groups such as the ACHR to focus on state institutions such as the NHRC for accountability regarding torture and extrajudicial executions have led to some action in terms of both compensation and punishment.[158]

While these reports do not specifically deal with the impact of the D. K. Basu case, a 2003 report of the Law Commission on the IEA notes that the jurisprudence developed in the Basu and Behera cases has not been that effective. The Law Commission Report on Review of IEA (1872) noted in 2003,

> Till today, the guidelines or precautions indicated in D. K. Basu have not been implemented by the police. In fact, most police officers are ignorant of them. Question also is whether in India we can accept the statement of any police officer that these precautions were indeed taken. In our view, today courts in our country cannot accept any such assertion on the part of the police. In a pending public interest case when the Supreme Court asked the States to submit whether D. K. Basu guidelines were being followed by the police in various States, the amicus curiae is reported to have stated that the reports from States are that the said guidelines were not being followed.[159]

The report notes that the D. K. Basu guidelines are not being followed in many of the states and the police often lack or withhold information about these rights. However, as stated earlier, the focus in this study is not the implementation of laws and decisions per se since that would require a more detailed analysis of the arena of enforcement.[160] The question, for our purpose, is whether, in the face of increasing incidents of custodial violence, the Court has consistently upheld and further developed its innovative custody jurisprudence in recent years.

Interestingly enough, in more recent cases, while the Court continues its grave concern for custodial violence, it has simultaneously introduced qualifications or dilutions that echo the weaknesses of the pre-1990s jurisprudence. In *Shakila Abdul Gafar Khan v. Vasant Raghunath Dhoble and Anr.* (2003), for instance, the Supreme Court does express grave concern that custodial torture is on the increase.[161] The Court even notes that the custody jurisprudence developed from 1990 onward "seems to have caused not even any softening attitude to the inhuman approach in dealing with persons in custody."[162] Noting the few convictions in custodial violence cases, the Court emphasized (once again) the necessity of changing the burden of proof and avoiding a *technical* view in dealing with cases of custodial violence. This aspect of the Court's opinion reiterates the aggressive attitude of the Supreme Court toward custodial crimes in the 1990s. A closer reading reveals that this is actually a reproduction of the statements made in previous Banjara and Basu cases.[163] The use of exactly the same language in referring to custodial violence is reflective of the sense of despair that even the Supreme Court feels about the issue. Yet, surprisingly, these recent cases also reflect a newly expressed concern about avoiding any encouragement of false cases. As the Court writes,

> But at the same time there seems to be [a] disturbing trend of increase in cases where *false accusations of custodial torture* are made, trying to take advantage of the serious concern shown and the stern attitude reflected by the courts while dealing with custodial violence. It needs to be carefully examined whether the allegations of custodial violence are genuine or are sham attempts to gain undeserved benefit masquerading as victims of custodial violence.[164]

The Court provided a strong note of caution about "false cases." The Gafar Khan case involved the arrest and torture (the instruments used were hockey sticks) of Abdul Gafar, which was witnessed by his family. Later he was released on bail and taken to the hospital, where he died. The Supreme Court agreed with the acquittal by the High Court, citing a delay in complaint and contradictions in the testimonies of the witnesses. However, the Supreme Court still decided to award compensation to the family for the death and asked for an inquiry. Thus, even though the particular evidence in the case did not lead to convictions, the Court did leave room for further action, which was a major change from the pre-1990s jurisprudence. However, the Court also returned to the unclear "totality of circumstances test" in the case rather than the more stringent standards that place the burden of proof on the police to explain their role in the death. Furthermore, an argument of the pre-1990s jurisprudence about "unreliability of the witnesses" reappears, bringing back the problems from the erratic phase of the Court.[165]

While false cases could be a legitimate concern, the increase in the number of cases of torture and deaths over the years makes the current emphasis on falsity (primarily based on police allegations) surprising. This is especially significant given that allegations of torture in murder trials are still not addressed by the Court. In that limited sense, in both the pre- and the post-

1990s, the exclusive focus on custodial death cases actually diverts attention away from custodial torture cases. These allegations of torture are either not even discussed in the Court opinion or are explained away in a myriad of ways. On the one hand, this could actually be proof that there are several false allegations of torture, but on the other hand, it might illustrate the continued emphasis on visible injuries and death by the Supreme Court, which emphasis allows for torture to continue in less visible ways. Given the high numbers of custodial deaths, the absence of a procedure for dealing with allegations of torture suggests a continuing lacuna in the jurisprudence. The inability of the Supreme Court to see the clear continuum between custodial torture and custodial death is noteworthy.

The inadequacy of the Court in addressing custodial torture is most visible in a 2006 case, *Sube Singh v. State of Haryana and Others*, where Sube Singh was picked up in connection with an investigation regarding his son, who was accused of killing a police official.[166] The family members alleged illegal detention and torture on more than one occasion. The Court did order several inquiries in the case, but its final assessment reflects the limitations of its approach. The Court, in its decision, not only denied that there was any "incontrovertible evidence" of torture but also significantly reduced the scope of the right to compensation in Article 21 cases. The Court suggested that the right to compensation should be restricted to exceptional cases and that Sube Singh should pursue civil and criminal redress. In a situation where the right to compensation as a public-law remedy had been one of the primary ways, and often the only way, of redressing those affected by custodial violence, this is a tremendous step backwards on the part of the Court.

The inconsistency in the Court's opinion is visible in its handling of the assertions of torture in this case. The Court, for instance, wrote,

> The report of the CBI shows that there is prima facie evidence about petitioner and some of his relatives being illegally detained in Police Station/Post and *subjected possibly to some third degree methods*, to extract information regarding the whereabouts of Joginder Singh. At the same time, the report makes it clear that neither the illegal detention nor the alleged torture (if true) was of [the] extent . . . alleged by the petitioner and his relatives. The claims were *clearly exaggerated and many a time false* also.[167]

Even while accepting the difficulties in getting proof, the Court here decided not to provide compensation precisely by relying on the lack of evidence. As the Court explains,

Where there is no independent evidence of custodial torture and where there is neither medical evidence *about any injury or disability*, resulting from custodial torture, *nor any mark/scar*, it may not be prudent to accept claims of human rights violation, by *persons having criminal records* in a routine manner for awarding compensation.[168]

The Court even accepts elsewhere that the police routinely use the third degree, acknowledges the CBI's observation that it may have been used in the case, and at the very least accepted that beating and some illegal detention undoubtedly took place. Yet clearly the persons were not tortured enough to get compensation since they lacked the visible marks and dead bodies to show it. Thus, once again, the Court failed to recognize the logic of its own previous jurisprudence, the difficulty in finding evidence against the police, and the need to acknowledge that many of these forms of violence exist on a continuum ranging from custodial deaths to physical third degree to beating to mental torture, all of which are closely related to illegal detention. An emphasis on falsity and exaggeration in a context where custodial deaths and torture continue unabatedly makes the situation worse for survivors. The Court's statement about carefully deliberating before giving a right to compensation to those with a criminal record is even more striking since it almost allows for a regime of custodial violence against criminals as long as it does not reach the levels that would leave scars and/or produce an unexplained dead body in custody.

Thus, the Supreme Court in recent years has clearly undermined its own emphasis on the uniqueness of custodial death and torture cases and threatens to dilute the custody jurisprudence that it had developed in the Basu and Behera cases. The long-term pattern of the Supreme Court response in custodial torture and death cases will emerge over time. However, the discussion of some recent cases does indicate one emerging feature of the jurisprudence of interrogations in India. A landmark case such as the D. K. Basu case that attempts to theorize custodial violence and generate innovative ways of dealing with it immediately leads to an actual or perceived challenge by the liberal state regarding its ability to maintain law and order. The Court subsequently exhibited a desire to mediate the carefully thought out safeguards and build a certain amount of flexibility into the safeguards. This flexibility, however, means that there is a dilution of the safeguards to some extent and, more significantly, threatens to bring back the same uncertainties that existed earlier in the Court's ability to contain custodial violence.

The Indian State, Jurisprudence, and Interrogations: The Way Forward

The implementation of formal legal safeguards against torture is not the sole responsibility of the judiciary and clearly reflects a lack of will at different levels of the Indian state. Just to give some examples, despite the Court's insistence, the Parliament has not changed the rules of evidence concerning the burden of proof in custodial violence cases. Similarly, reforms in the structure and functioning of the police remain unaddressed in spite of several reports and recommendations. Section 197 of the Criminal Procedure Code, which requires prior approval to prosecute a public official, continues to be unchallenged. Finally, despite repeated demands by the NHRC and human rights groups, the Indian government, regardless of regimes, has refused to ratify the UN Convention against Torture.

In a slightly more encouraging vein, recently the government of India has proposed a Torture Bill that has passed the Lok Sabha (the lower house of Parliament), but critics have raised a number of questions about the scope, purpose, and parameters of the act. The main purpose of this act is to move a step forward in ratifying the UN Convention against Torture. As the bill notes, "Ratification of the Convention requires enabling legislation to reflect the definition and punishment for 'torture.'"[169] However, there are significant limitations to this four-page-long bill. First, the definition of torture itself is too narrow and focuses on physical more than mental torture since the bill specifies an "intentional act that causes grievous hurt to any person" or "danger to life, limb or health (whether mental or physical) of any person."[170] As Tarunabh Khaitan explains,

> Grievous hurt is defined under Section 320 of the Indian Penal Code to include extremely serious injuries such as permanent loss of eye or ear, emasculation, bone fractures, or hurt which causes severe and debilitating pain for twenty days or more. In other words, a very high threshold has been set for an act to qualify as "torture." . . . The term "danger" implies a certain level of seriousness, while mental and physical "health" has frequently been interpreted by courts in civil cases to only include medically recognised illnesses.[171]

Second, a serious limitation is the fact that the bill requires complaints to be filed within six months of the alleged incident, totally ignoring the difficulties in dealing with custodial torture, especially for marginalized sections of the population who are often surrounded by the perpetrators. Third, the bill asks for prior sanction from the government for prosecuting a public servant, which had been a major problem in prosecuting torture cases even earlier. Finally, despite critiques by civil liberties groups of a previous bill that contained no reference to cruel, inhuman, and degrading treatment or any acknowledgment of the peculiarly high number of custodial deaths in India, the present version continues to be silent on these fronts.[172] In that sense, there appears to be a complete disjuncture between the custody jurisprudence developed by the Court and the provisions of the antitorture bill.

Notwithstanding the critique of other state institutions, the Court has distinguished itself by its insistence on a custody jurisprudence that recognizes the unequal power relationships in interrogations and gives the benefit of the doubt to the accused in cases of deaths in police custody. Yet, the dilution in recent times suggests that even the jurisprudence is unable to distance itself from some accommodation of excess violence. Furthermore, an interesting paradox has emerged in the debate on the antitorture bill. The debates on the bill show that the government does acknowledge the incidents of torture, but by failing to ackowledge that deaths resulted from torture, they can bypass the Court's jurisprudence on custodial violence, which would force the legislators to include a discussion of the deaths as well as the CIDT. The Court in turn has acknowledged custodial deaths due to torture but has not adequately addressed the issue of torture itself. Thus, neither the government nor the Court has completely adopted a framework of custody jurisprudence that recognizes the continuum of violence between torture and custodial deaths regardless of whether there is a body or marks.

There is also a growing emphasis in the Indian legal and political discourse on developing scientific means of investigation as a way to deal with custodial violence.[173] There seems to be an assumption that the modern means of investigation will do away with the need for the third degree and custodial violence of any kind. As Justice Katju noted, "In western countries scientific methods of investigation are used. . . . Hence, in western countries torture is not normally used during investigation and the correct facts can be usually ascertained without resorting to torture."[174]

As shown in the previous chapter, Western experiments in the context of interrogations actually allowed for the emergence of psychological techniques of torture in place of physical ones. While some forms of scientific investigation may be useful, the path specified by the Indian discourses raises significant questions for future modes of interrogation. One of the main questions this raises is as follows: does the desire for scientific methods of interrogation in Indian legal discourses reflect a desire for less visibly painful and, more importantly, less crude methods, rather than a desire to do away with excess violence altogether? In the last few years, the use of lie detectors, brain scans, and narco analysis in criminal investigations exhibits a nascent juridico-medical apparatus emerging even in the Indian context.[175] While the Supreme Court has rightly struck down the involuntary use of these techniques, the techniques themselves are not ruled out, keeping the path open in the future.[176]

5

Contemporary States of Exception

Extraordinary Laws and Interrogation in India

On December 13, 2001, the Indian Parliament was attacked by five heavily armed "Islamic militants" while the Parliament was in session.[1] All five attackers and nine security men were killed in the firing between the two sides. This attack on the Indian Parliament is politically significant for a number of reasons. Since it occurred three months after the September 11, 2001, U.S. attacks, the Indian state represented it as part of the global threat to liberal democratic institutions.[2] It also became an opportunity for the state to pass a new antiterrorism law, namely, the previously mentioned Prevention of Terrorism Act (POTA), which had been in the works even earlier. Several media reports made comparisons between the U.S. PATRIOT Act, passed in the 9/11 context, and the POTA, passed in the 12/13 context, and suggested that India followed the lead of United States in this regard.[3]

POTA was repealed by the Indian National Congress–led United Progressive Alliance (UPA) government, which took over power from the Hindu right-wing Bharatiya Janata Party (BJP)-led National Democratic Alliance (NDA) in 2004.[4] Yet the saga of extraordinary legislations continued, as seen in the amendment in 2004 to the UAPA (Unlawful Activities Prevention Act) and the introduction of regional laws such as the CSPSA (Chhatisgarh Special Public Security Act) in 2005.[5] The shocking terrorist attacks in Mumbai in November 2008 also led to a strengthening of the UAPA in 2008, making such legislations a permanent feature of Indian democracy.[6]

In this chapter, I study the jurisprudence of interrogations related to the extraordinary legislations in India. Unlike in the United States, the *recent* debates on exceptional laws in India are not linked to any one event (9/11 or 13/12) but rather have always existed as a parallel system of governance from colonial to postcolonial times. While extraordinary laws were integral to the very functioning of colonial rule, in postcolonial India, many extraordinary legislations were introduced in response to several internal conflicts/struggles within the Indian context, such as in Kashmir, the North East, Punjab, and Andhra Pradesh, which have gradually been linked to a global threat of terrorism. In this chapter, I focus on two major national legal regimes that have represented the extraordinary legislations on interrogations and confessions in contemporary India:[7] the previously mentioned Terrorism and Disruptive Activities (Prevention) Act (TADA), introduced in 1985, and POTA, introduced in 2002—both all-India-based extraordinary legislations. In addition, I focus on a British Report on Torture (1855) that highlights the origins of the peculiarly Indian routine safeguard against torture disallowing the police from recording confessions. This particular safeguard has been bypassed in the extraordinary laws, thereby transforming the Indian discourse on torture and interrogations in recent times.

A study of the jurisprudence of interrogations related to extraordinary laws points to the integral relationship between the routine and exceptional contexts. The Indian state has defended the extraordinary laws as temporary measures necessary for dealing with crisis situations. In response, a number of scholars have challenged these laws on two grounds. First, they have focused on the unfair and undemocratic nature of extraordinary laws. Second, scholars have also noted the ways in which these laws have a tendency to remain even after the so-called crisis has passed and thereby threaten to change the very functioning of the ordinary laws by a "permanence of the temporary."[8] While these analyses are extremely significant, I additionally focus on how the ordinary or routine laws help constitute the extraordinary laws. I point to the ways in which the ambivalence in the routine jurisprudence of interrogations regarding torture and excess violence plays a constitutive role in the formation of exceptional laws. Indeed, one could argue that there is far greater acceptance of extraordinary provisions regarding interrogations precisely because they are seen as a resolution of, not a break from, the preexisting tensions in the routine contexts and thereby less resisted in this less protected/scrutinized arena. Consequently, even if one successfully challenges the continuation of the extraordinary laws, some of these preexisting tensions continue in the routine context and allow excess violence to persist. This excess violence then gets further institutionalized by the phenomenon of "permanence of the exception."

Situating Indian Extraordinary Laws in the Glocal (Global + Local) Discourse on Terrorism

In recent years, a number of states have introduced antiterrorism laws in their countries, thereby transforming the global debate on national security and human rights. Resolution 1373, adopted by the United Nations Security Council immediately after 9/11, played an instrumental role in prompting many of these countries to adopt antiterrorist legislations. The post-9/11 initiatives include, for example, the USA PATRIOT Act, the Anti-terrorism, Crime, and Security Act in the United Kingdom, Bill C-36 in Canada, and the Terrorism Suppression Act in New Zealand.[9]

In its push for POTA, the then-ruling party in India, the BJP, also referred to the UN resolution as requiring India, a member state, to take specific steps to deal with terrorism. However, this use of the UN resolution has been criticized by scholars and activists, such as Anil Kalhan, who point out that there was no effort to distinguish between the requirements for a law under the UN resolution and the specifics of the legislation adopted by the state.[10] To take the example of India, the concerns within India about the impact of the proposed legislation on human rights were set aside by the government in power, which used the UN resolution as a pretext for quickly passing the antiterror legislation it desired. The situation was worsened by the lack of effective intervention from the UN Counter-Terrorism Committee to ensure that these legislations did not simultaneously undermine human rights.[11]

The multiple initiatives in the post-9/11 context coalescing around the UN resolution did create and strengthen a global discourse on terrorism, and scholars such as Jayanth Krishnan specifically note a strong resemblance between the provisions in POTA and the PATRIOT Act.[12] Nonetheless, it is important to note that POTA did not come up only as a result of the global discourse on terrorism, although 2001 gave the Indian government an opportunity to pass this law in a rare joint seating of the two houses of Parliament.[13] Rather, extraordinary legislations have been recurring features of both colonial and postcolonial India. In fact, the focus on POTA as primarily a part of the global discourse on terrorism distracts attention from this specific colonial and postcolonial Indian history.

During the colonial period, the British primarily introduced three kinds of extraordinary policies in India.[14] First, within the governance structure itself (established by the Indian Governance Act, 1861) there was the built-in ability of the governor general to pronounce an emergency and to use extraordinary powers during that time. Second, the British introduced several special emergency legislations such as the Defense of India Act of 1915, passed during World War I. Third, the British continued these efforts in nonemergency periods either by introducing new laws or by extending the emergency legislations. An excellent example of the nonemergency laws is the infamous Rowlatt Act (Anarchical and Revolutionary Crimes Act) of

1919.[15] In all these situations, preventive detentions and bypassing of procedural safeguards, such as lower standards of evidence and longer periods of detention, were allowed since the defense of the colonial state overpowered the need to maintain the "rule of law."[16] As human rights scholar, lawyer, and activist K. G. Kannabiran explains, many of the British laws were meant to legitimize their rule and consolidate their power. He writes, "It is evident that a legal system structured to rule colonies can never square with a constitutional scheme."[17] Ironically, when the Congress Party, which was at the forefront of the anticolonial struggle, came into power in some provinces under the 1935 act, it was also willing to use the same preventive detention laws even though many of these laws had been used to target and detain them (and others) earlier.[18]

Given the willingness of the Congress Party to retain preventive detention laws in pre-independent India, unsurprisingly, a number of extraordinary provisions remained in the constitutional framework in postindependent India. The Indian Constitution makers retained the powers of the executive to proclaim emergencies, which allowed the executive enormous centralized powers, including the ability to suspend fundamental civil liberties.[19] As with British colonial policies, even though some of these extraordinary powers were introduced during emergencies, they had a tendency to continue even after the crisis passed. This was the case in the Defense of India Act, 1962, which was introduced during the Indo-China war but continued till 1968, long after the war was over.[20]

The Indian Constitution also retained a provision for preventive detention in nonemergency contexts that was used to introduce laws such as the Preventive Detention Act (1950), the Maintenance of Internal Security Act (1971), and the Unlawful Activities Prevention Act (1967).[21] Kannabiran points out that this uncritical continuation of several repressive colonial laws, ideologies, and institutions directly contradicts the egalitarian visions of the Indian Constitution makers and the democratic aspirations of the Indian people.[22] Given this long tradition, TADA and POTA actually follow a substantial history of extraordinary legislations in India. Here I do recognize that the post-9/11 developments have connected initiatives such as POTA and the PATRIOT Act. The point to note, however, is that these commonalities ironically do not reflect a "copycatism" of the Western states, but rather may point to the influence of the global South on the antiterrorism initiatives introduced by the United States.[23] Of course, if we analyze more carefully the significance of the global South becoming the model for extraordinary laws for the West, we begin to go in circles, for the groundwork for India's extraordinary laws was established by a Western colonial regime. Regardless, the continuation of extraordinary laws in independent India clearly reflects what Upendra Baxi calls the compatibility of a "reign of terror" with a rule of law.[24]

Jurisprudence on TADA and POTA

As discussed in the last chapter, the three main safeguards against torture in India have been the right against self-incrimination, the requirement that the judicial (or metropolitan) magistrate follow an elaborate process of recording confessions, and the development of a custodial jurisprudence by the Supreme Court. These and other safeguards that form the backbone of due process in the routine Indian criminal justice system were systematically eroded in the two extraordinary laws introduced and designed primarily to try terrorism-related offenses.

Even though the introduction of extraordinary legislations was not a new phenomenon in postcolonial India, what was different about TADA was its gradual extension to most of India and its attempt to bypass the routine criminal justice system in a radical way.[25] The law itself defined a terrorist and disruptionist in an extremely broad and vague manner, allowing for its misuse in many instances.[26] There were several other provisions in TADA that diluted the existing procedural safeguards. For example, TADA allowed for an extended duration of the detention period, as well as extremely stringent bail provisions.[27] Furthermore, even though TADA was meant to introduce a parallel system of trying terrorists and disruptionists, the Indian state ended up using it randomly against a broad section of people, often as a means of preventive detention.[28] The normal remand period in the criminal procedure code is fifteen days, extendable to a maximum of sixty or ninety days only with the permission of a judicial magistrate. The act, however, allowed for an extended period of remand, even up to one entire year.[29] Indeed, Kannabiran characterizes the remand provision in TADA as "akin to introducing the provisions of preventive detention laws through the back door," without even the safeguards, such as a review, associated with preventive detention.[30] The bail provisions also indicated a deviation from a central safeguard of the adversarial system, namely, a presumption of innocence. In TADA, bail could depend on the public prosecutor's opposition to the application and the court's ability to ensure that "he [the accused] is not guilty of such offence and that he is not likely to commit any offence while on bail."[31] Unsurprisingly then, under TADA (till 1994), about seventy-six thousand people were detained, 35 percent were tried, 25 percent were released, and 95 percent of those tried were acquitted, making the conviction rate only 1 percent.[32] Many of these provisions individually and collectively violated the right to a fair and speedy trial.[33]

The second major extraordinary law was POTA, which also introduced many stringent provisions that bypassed the routine safeguards regarding arrest, detention, and bail procedures. The definition of terrorism under POTA was also very broad. As Jayanth Krishnan explains, "The heart of the problem is how the statute define[d] the words 'terrorist,' 'terrorist acts,' and 'terrorist activities.' Under section 3, a terrorist act is an act done 'with intent to threaten the unity, integrity, security or sovereignty of India or to strike terror in the people or any section of the people.'"[34] POTA also allowed for remand for ninety days without producing the detained in front of a court, extendable to another three months and then, without bail, to a period of one year. Also, as with TADA, the presumption of guilt attached the moment a person was charged with POTA, with little meaningful opportunity for due process.[35] Most crucial for our purposes is that both the acts transformed the procedure for recording confessions and allowed senior police officials to record confessions in TADA and POTA cases, thereby completely altering the safeguards against torture.

Upholding Parallel Regimes of Governance: The Exceptionality of TADA

TADA was first introduced in India in 1985, one year after the assassination of the then prime minister, Indira Gandhi. The immediate impetus for TADA may have been the assassination, but it gained support across political parties primarily because it was useful in dealing with the militant movements in different parts of the country, namely, Kashmir, the North East, and Punjab.[36]

The response of the Indian state in all these areas of conflict was either to introduce armed actions against the militants and/or to target these regions with extraordinary laws. In the case of Punjab, which was the stage for the introduction of TADA, the Indian state responded to the militant movements (which were demanding a separate state of Khalistan) by sending the army into the Golden Temple—the holy place for the Sikhs—in Operation Blue Star. As a result of the attack, alongside the Sikh militants and the members of the armed forces, a number of pilgrims were also killed, alienating the Sikhs further from the Indian state. The assassination of Indira Gandhi by her Sikh bodyguards, while tragic, has to be understood in the context of the brutal state repression in Punjab, particularly Operation Blue Star.[37] Human rights groups documented thousands of deaths and disappearances in Punjab as a result of the counterinsurgency state operations. The Indian state introduced many local laws in Punjab, such as the Armed Forces (Punjab and Chandigarh) Special Powers Act of 1983 and the National Security Act of 1984 and 1987, and also enforced President's Rule (wherein the president of India governs the state directly, dissolving the state government).[38] However, the legislation having the most long-lasting impact at this time, both in Punjab and at the all-India level, was TADA.[39]

TADA was extended four times and then was allowed to lapse in 1995 due to large-scale protests.[40] Despite its lapsed status, TADA remains an important point of reference for the legal discourse in many ways. First, trials continued under the act even after its lapse under a clause that allowed for the completion of proceedings initiated while the act was still in operation. As Ujjwal Singh puts it, there is a "life after death" quality to this law that allowed thousands of detainees to remain in jail.[41] Singh notes a remarkable statistic that in 2000, five years after the law lapsed, there were almost five thousand cases where the trials had not been completed.[42] Second, despite protests by human rights activists and scholars in India and abroad against the draconian law, the Supreme Court upheld the constitutionality of TADA in *Kartar Singh v. State of Punjab* in 1994.[43] The reasoning of the Court in upholding the law went a long way toward legitimizing extraordinary legislations in India and, among other things, normalizing the transformation of the safeguards on recording confessions.

In the Kartar Singh case, the defense lawyers questioned the constitutionality of TADA (1984, 1985, and 1987) on two main grounds.[44] First, the lawyers challenged the ability of the central government—the Indian Parliament—to pass this law since terrorism was a state subject concerning "control of public order."[45] Second, the lawyers argued that many of the provisions of the acts were "draconian, ugly, vicious and highly reprehensible" since they were in direct violation of both the Indian Constitution and the International Covenant on Civil and Political Rights (ICCPR).[46] The lawyers used international and national human rights reports to show that the police were using TADA to indulge in a "witch hunt against innocent people and suspects . . . thereby unleash[ing] a reign of terror [like the] institutionalized terror perpetrated by Nazis on Jews."[47] Alongside the extrajudicial killings or encounters prevalent in the conflict areas, the de facto preventive detention regime emerged as a new form of state violence: a parallel form of governance no longer in the shadow of law.

In contrast to this stinging critique, the main position of the Indian state was that not only were the provisions constitutional but also TADA was introduced by the Parliament because the existing criminal—procedural and penal—system was found inadequate to deal with the "astronomical" increase of "inhuman" terrorist actions. The state lawyers pointed to the "sense of fear and helplessness among the civilians" created by the terrorists, which had led to a loss of faith in "Government's ability to protect them" and an assumption of "impotence among government officials." The state thus articulated a deep-seated "crisis" in Indian society being caused by the terrorists and requiring an extraordinary response.[48]

The state's understanding of the crisis in Indian society is in stark contrast with other kinds of analyses regarding the accentuated crisis in India since the late 1960s.[49] As noted in the last chapter, much of the violence by non-state actors emerged out of the inability of the postcolonial state to address the socioeconomic, political, and cultural problems of the people in many regions and in India as a whole.[50] As Balagopal writes,

> Paradoxically, political militancy calls for harsh laws not because it is ter-
> ror, but precisely because it is not just terror, but is a politics. It is a politics,
> right or wrong, with a social base of people—well guided or misguided—
> supporting it and its armed activity, which makes it difficult in the extreme
> to deal with it, if dealing with it means policing it.[51]

According to Balagopal, the state needed to recognize that many of the armed movements—regardless of their ideology and strategy—represented politics, not "terror," and required a political solution rather than further repressive action. In this interpretation, the crisis was mainly a result of the state's inability to respond to the grievances and demands of marginalized people, and it was made worse by the increasing state repression of the movements. As Amnesty International put it, "Wherever movements for autonomy or secession have appeared to threaten the Indian state, the Government of India has responded with harsh and aggressive methods. These have included arbitrary arrests, torture, deaths in custody and 'disappearances' of those believed to be connected with insurgency."[52]

Thus, apart from the already ever-present high levels of custodial deaths and torture in the routine criminal justice system (discussed in the last chapter), numerous human rights reports have pointed to excessive abuses carried out in extraordinary contexts.[53] The extent of the crisis, especially in the conflict-ridden states, was (and is) apparent in the increasing number of reports of the "extrajudicial killings" or encounters, "disappearances," and the continual spiral of violence in many regions of India.[54] The state, for the most part, has continued to refuse to deal sociopolitically and economically with the underlying problems that gave rise to the crises (at least in part). Instead, the main response of the postindependent state has been to generally characterize most of the militant movements as "terrorists" and/or "disruptionists" and to introduce repressive laws to contain them, thereby removing the specific political contexts of all these actions and movements. As Singh puts it, the focus on "terrorism" and "disruption" has "depoliticised identity struggles, dismembering them into specific acts of violence, demanding extraordinary legal solutions, procedures and punishments."[55] The crisis created by violent societal actions required an unprecedented violent state response, both legal and extralegal.

The Supreme Court, in its entry into the debate, accepted the Indian state's analysis of the crisis at face value—that the violence in Indian society was primarily due to the increase in terrorist acts—and consequently upheld the right of the Parliament to impart an extraordinary response to combat the violence and support the "Defense of India." Apart from steering clear of the underlying causes of this violence, the Court also failed to see the role of the state in perpetuating a spiral of violence. Finally, by upholding the constitutionality of the extraordinary law, the Court legitimized the notion that exceptional provisions could extend to nonemergency situations, thereby reinforcing a colonial tactic but taking refuge in specifically postcolonial state constructions.

TADA and Confessions: "An Implicit Sanction of Police Torture?"[56]

As noted in the previous chapter, one of the most important safeguards against torture in India has been the procedure of recording confessions, which can only be performed by a judicial or metropolitan magistrate after ensuring the voluntariness of the admission in an atmosphere free from police coercion. This protection regime, which by no means was completely effective, was directly challenged and transformed by TADA, and the change was upheld as constitutional by the Supreme Court in the Kartar Singh case. Section 15 of TADA allowed confessions to be recorded by police officials not lower in rank than superintendent of police "either in writing or on any mechanical device like cassettes, tapes or sound tracks."[57] The confession could be admissible in the trial of the accused, the co-accused, abettor, or conspirator. Before recording the confession, the police official had to warn the person that "he is not bound to make the confession and if he does so, it may be used as evidence."[58] Thus, a member of the police force may record the confession only if he or she is convinced that the confession is made voluntarily and must certify as much.[59]

Ram Jethmalani—the defense lawyer in the Kartar Singh case—termed this particular provision "atrocious and totally subversive of any civilized trial system."[60] There were two main objections. First, the new rule on confessions under TADA went against the criminal law provisions that existed precisely because the police were considered "untrustworthy." Second, the use of mechanical devices for recording was criticized since they could easily be tampered with. Thus, Section 15 of TADA was termed by the lawyers as both "unjust" and "unreasonable" and as violation of Articles 14 (right to equality) and 21 (procedure established by law) of the Indian Constitution.[61]

The state counsel, however, claimed that since TADA only allowed the recording of confessions by a *superior* police officer, it served as a protection against misuse.[62] Here the state's assumption clearly is that it is only the lower-level (read poorly paid, untrained, and "ignorant") police rather than the elite police (primarily civil servants from the Indian Police Service, who constitute the upper echelons of the bureaucracy) who indulge in misuse of power.[63] The articulation of a class/education-based distinction within police actions echoes a similar focus on the reliability and unreliability of torture narratives produced by the victims, noted in the previous chapter. Thus, just as the dishonest tortured and their witnesses were often from the lower echelons of society, so were the torturers. Furthermore, the distinction between the two kinds of police officials denies the endemic nature of custodial torture noted by human rights groups (and analyzed in the previous chapter), which could not have continued without the participation or, at the very least, sanction of higher police officials.

In response to these contending arguments, the Supreme Court, while acknowledging the significance of the safeguard, especially for the right against self-incrimination, decided to uphold the constitutionality of the new rule of confessions on the basis of two arguments: the reasonableness of the distinction and the right of Parliament to introduce a new mode of proof. First, the Court argued that Section 15 of TADA was not a violation of the right to equality protected under Article 14 of the Constitution. This was determined to be the case because Indian jurisprudence allowed "legislative classification" of distinct groups of persons for differential treatment as long as the basis of the distinction was "rational and scientific" and fulfilled the specific objective of the legislation. According to the Court, since

TADA focused on a "distinct group of persons" who engaged in "aggravated and incensed . . . offences," distinct from those committed by ordinary criminals, the classification was reasonable and the different procedure did not violate Article 14 of the Indian Constitution. The Court specified that if the classification of people had been left to the discretion of the central government, it would have been arbitrary, but here the act itself made a distinction among terrorists, disruptionists, and ordinary criminals, and this constituted a rational reason for classification. The reasonableness of the classification also made the act compatible with Article 21 of the Indian Constitution.[64] The difficulty in defining and distinguishing among a terrorist, a disruptionist, and an ordinary criminal was, of course, ignored by the Court despite the fact that the arbitrary application of TADA was a major source of contention and discrimination.[65]

Second, the Kartar Singh Court decided to defer to the Parliament's right to introduce a new mode of proof in terrorism cases despite its misgivings about the police use of torture. The Court readily acknowledged the presence of custodial deaths and torture but upheld the constitutionality of the change by taking refuge, to an extent, in two conflicting opinions put forward by the police and the judicial commissions. The National Police Commission (NPC) in its 1980 report had noted the dissatisfaction of the police with the prevalent practice of disallowing them to record confessions (that could be admissible) on the basis of an 1872 colonial law (Indian Evidence Act). The NPC report argued that while in colonial times the police did use torture, in modern times they had greatly reduced the practice and therefore should be allowed to record confessions that could at least be used as supplementary evidence.[66] The Court compared this report to the one submitted by the National Judicial Commission, which confirmed the ongoing use of torture by the police even at the "supervisory" level.[67]

The discussion of conflicting reports about the continued use of torture makes the final decision of the Court with regard to recording of confessions very surprising. The Court even stated that its first instinct was to conclude that the police should not be allowed to record confessions, but the justices decided against this conclusion because they believed in the right of the legislature to introduce a new "mode of proof" in the given circumstances. The Court stated,

> Though we—having regard to the legal competence of the legislature to make the law prescribing a different mode of proof, the meaningful purpose and object of the legislation, the gravity of terrorism unleashed by the

terrorists and disruptionists endangering not only the sovereignty and the integrity of the country but also the normal life of citizens, and the reluctance of even the victims as well as the public in coming forward at the risk of their life, to give evidence—hold that the impugned section cannot be said to be suffering from any vice of unconstitutionality. In fact, if the *exigencies of certain situations* warrant such a legislation then it is constitutionally permissible as ruled in a number of decisions of this Court, provided none of the fundamental rights under Chapter III of the constitution is infringed.[68]

Thus, the Court decided that the extraordinary situation of terrorism warranted bypassing the usual safeguards and upheld the right of the Parliament to determine the new "mode of proof." The Court did recognize the possibility of misuse and cautioned police officers against it but mostly found the rules for recording confessions in Section 15 of TADA to be adequate and not a violation of Articles 14 and 21 of the Indian Constitution. Overall, therefore, in the Kartar Singh case, the Supreme Court accepted the dilution of a major routine protection against torture, which in any case had not been able to effectively contain the use of custodial violence, and enabled a new mode of proof for a "different" set of people rendered easily distinguishable from others despite evidence provided by human rights groups to the contrary.

The Court did suggest the incorporation of additional guidelines into TADA to prevent the use of coercion—a suggestion either embodying their own apprehension about the less protective regime or responding to the two strong dissents written by Justice K. Ramaswamy and Justice Sahai (dissents not being such a common occurrence in Indian jurisprudence as compared to the U.S. Court). [69] In his dissent, Justice Ramaswamy pointed to the long history of separation of powers between the judiciary (magistrate) and the executive (police) in recording confessions that had been established precisely to check police misuse. The justice, therefore, found the change in procedure to be "unfair, unjust and unconscionable, offending Articles 14 and 21 of the constitution," and questioned whether the procedure could be termed a "civilized procedure."[70] For him, the involvement of senior officers was not enough to remove the suspicion of misuse of powers, especially given that the police officers (as a whole) were responsible for law and order at all costs. Justice Sahai agreed with Justice Ramaswamy, reiterating that this section was a constitutional violation of Articles 20(3) and 21 since it did not provide the same protections to the accused as was available in the routine context. Thus, he insisted that all accused were entitled to such fundamental rights regardless of the nature of the offence.

Prominent human rights activist, scholar, and lawyer K. Balagopal also criticized the reasoning of the majority in the Kartar Singh case. He not only pointed out that Article 21 required a rational basis for classification of persons but also reminded the Court of its own jurisprudence, that a test under the article was meant to ensure that the procedures being followed were just and fair.[71] He criticized the Court for completely letting the Parliament determine the nature of these procedures, rather than ensuring their fairness. Thus, fairness was given an entirely new meaning in this parallel regime in terms of its absence.

Ironically, even while the same Supreme Court was developing a two-pronged custody jurisprudence (custody or arrest memos and right to compensations) to deal with state violence in the routine context, it was simultaneously undermining one of the most crucial protections against torture in the extraordinary context, namely, the recording of confessions. While each instance of bypassing safeguards did not necessarily mean the use of torture, the removal of the safeguards did increase the chances of torture under TADA, particularly when the new procedure was used in conjunction with several other extraordinary provisions in the law noted earlier. By upholding the provision, the Court also undermined the other safeguards against torture such as the right against self-incrimination and the perspective about the unequal power relations between the police and the detained reflected by custody jurisprudence (discussed in the last chapter).

In the TADA case, torture was not authorized explicitly, but as K. Balagopal puts it, the Supreme Court decision clearly did lead to the "implicit sanction of police torture."[72] If the U.S. Supreme Court's role in the post-9/11 context has been one of absence in the torture debate, the Indian Supreme Court frontally addressed the dilution of the safeguards against torture only to uncritically accept the logic of the extraordinary law to such an extent that it undermined its own concurrently developing custody jurisprudence in the routine context.

Sliding the Slippery Slope: The Post–Kartar Singh Phase

Once the Indian Supreme Court upheld the constitutionality of TADA, the cases thereafter observed a further dilution of even the minimal safeguards applicable to confessions. In fact, any notion of voluntariness in confessions was completely undermined in subsequent cases, illustrating the slippery slope that appears when procedural and substantive safeguards are radically changed. Kannabiran terms this post-TADA jurisprudence the "weird jurisprudence of a dead act," referring to the ways in which the act continued after its death in much more dangerous ways.[73] Yet this jurisprudence escaped much scrutiny from the legal community even though this was the exact time when the Supreme Court was being heralded for its custody jurisprudence in the routine context.

The casualness toward the voluntariness of confessions in the TADA cases is most visible in the *Gurdeep Singh v. State (Delhi Administration)* (1999), when the Supreme Court was even willing to accept the confession of a person in handcuffs, while the police holding the chains were standing near him and armed guards were standing just outside the room.[74] The counsel in the case argued that the confession could not be considered voluntary under the circumstances. The Court described the reasons behind the objections in the following way:

> To substantiate this he [the counsel] refers to the facts that his [the accused's] confession was recorded by S. P. Raj Shekhar Shetty, PW 13, when he was in handcuffs, there was another policeman in the same room holding the chain of his handcuff, and even outside the room, in which his confession was recorded, there were armed guards. Such set up reveals by itself that threat perception existed which was hanging over his head, thus such confession cannot be construed to be . . . voluntary under Section 15 of the TADA Act, contended the counsel.[75]

However, despite noting the circumstances in which the confession was recorded, the Court considered it voluntary primarily because all the "formal" safeguards had been ensured by the police superintendent and "no other threat or inducement" was used in the case. The Court, in fact, stated that the handcuffing and the presence of guards was necessary for ensuring security and did not in any way affect the voluntariness of the confession. Pointing to the obvious contradictions in this situation where the prisoner was subject to prolonged detention and interrogation in chains, Kannabiran wrote,

> Arrest and confinement would be coercive enough; but the denial of freedom of movement, the freedom to meet people and talk to them for long periods, were sufficient to destroy both volition and will. . . . Classifying the accused as a high-security prisoner and parading him in chains dehumanized him and destroyed his volition and will. Thereafter, nothing remained of his person that could perform a voluntary act.[76]

Thus, according to Kannabiran, voluntariness in any case had very little meaning in custody, and under TADA, even less, but the process became visibly coercive in the current instance. In addition, one could argue that this case merely followed the logic upheld by the Kartar Singh Court. Once the Court agreed that under TADA, the higher-ranked police officials could record confessions despite the well-documented evidence of police abuses in routine cases, the Court demolished the very backbone of the safeguards against torture. Not surprisingly, then, the subsequent courts did not consider "minor" bypassing of safeguards as indicating involuntariness of confession.[77] In other words, the Gurdeep Singh case went a step further by "rightly" applying the logic of the Kartar Singh case that once a higher police official was allowed to record confession and ensure voluntariness, the handcuffing by a lower-ranked police official under his/her supervision during the confession process was permissible.[78]

As noted earlier, the Supreme Court in Kartar Singh had suggested certain additional guidelines to be added to TADA in order to ensure protections against custodial violence. These guidelines included the production of the accused in front of a chief metropolitan or chief judicial magistrate, to whom the confession would have already been sent under TADA. The magistrate was to ask the accused to sign the statement and in case of any complaint of torture, to ensure that the accused was examined by a medical officer. However, the dilution of the procedural safeguards became so entrenched in the Supreme Court jurisprudence that in a subsequent case, *Lal Singh v. State of Gujarat,* the Court argued that even if the Kartar Singh Court's guidelines were not accepted, the evidence would not be considered inadmissible.[79]

In *Lal Singh v. State of Gujarat,* 2001, the Court stated that since the guidelines were not included in the act by the Indian Parliament, and the Kartar Singh decision had not ruled that noncompliance with the guidelines led to inadmissibility of confessions, the guidelines had little relevance. Technically, the Court was correct in stating that the Kartar Singh guidelines had not been included either in the act or in the rules. Yet, the Court ignored the rationale behind the guidelines, particularly the need to ascertain whether torture or coercion had taken place or not. In TADA cases, the confession was already being recorded by those traditionally known to use and/or sanction torture, and the Kartar Singh Court suggested the production of the accused in front of a magistrate as a minimal safeguard. Given that one of the usual ways of hiding police torture was to keep a person detained until the marks of torture were completely obliterated, the response of the Court in this case was surprising. The allegations of severe physical torture in the case, including cutting the tongue and injury on the head, could have at least prompted a more complex jurisprudential decision than that adopted by the Court. But in the post–Kartar Singh cases, the Court was willing to overlook not only the reasoning of the safeguards in routine cases but even the caution suggested by the earlier Kartar Singh case.

In a case where there were not only severe allegations of torture but also procedural irregularities, S. N. Dube v. N. B. Bhoir (2000), the Court determined that "in the absence of any specific act suggested by the defense it is not possible to accept the belated allegation made by those accused that their confessions were obtained in that manner."[80] The Court noted that Deputy Superintendent of Police Shinde had tried to inquire into the allegations of torture but had found the confessions voluntary. The Court explained that the accused did not deny that the DSP (Shinde) recorded the confessions in accordance with TADA. However, "The only suggestion that was made in his cross-examination was that he had obtained those confessions after exerting influence, coercion, and physical and mental torture."[81] In its narrative, the Court failed to acknowledge the irony that the allegations of torture were made precisely against those officers who had been given the responsibility of ascertaining the voluntariness of the confessions and recording them.[82] The case was clearly reflective of the excessive violence that TADA allowed and the Court's acceptance of the fruits of that violence. Thus, in the post–Kartar Singh jurisprudence, the Court not only ended up accepting the procedural irregularities but also ignored the basic framework of approaching custodial violence in terms of the unequal power relationships that exist in prolonged interrogation.

TADA lapsed in 1995 despite the Court's intervention and attempt to uphold the constitutionality of the act. On the one hand, the end of the extraordinary law was definitely a result of the concerted campaigns by human rights groups in India and abroad. After all, it was primarily used against the poor, the marginalized, and the dissenting. On the other hand, the act's end may also point to an inability of the liberal state to uphold a law that was held constitutional despite its gross violation of fundamental rights and the critiques of the act by human rights activists and scholars explicitly highlighting the contradiction between the routine and exceptional contexts. The end of TADA could, therefore, also be considered as a necessary act on the part of the liberal state to contain a crisis in its legitimacy as a rule-of-law based system.

After TADA lapsed, there were failed attempts to draft another law, namely, the Criminal Law Amendment Bill in 1995. But it was only in the aftermath of 9/11 and 12/13 that the Indian Parliament was able to introduce another all-India antiterrorism legislation, namely, the Prevention of Terrorism Act (POTA). Interestingly enough, the same Kartar Singh safeguards that were not considered essential by the Supreme Court in some of the post–Kartar Singh TADA cases were taken as a way of justifying the legitimacy of the next all-India-level antiterrorist legislation.

POTA: Responding to a New Axis of "Terrorism"—
"Indian," "South Asian," and "Global"

As noted earlier, the immediate context for POTA was the attack on the Indian Parliament on December 13, 2001. However, POTO (Prevention of Terrorism Ordinance) had been promulgated prior to that, failing in the Rajya Sabha (upper house of Indian Parliament) twice, once before the attack and again when repromulgated after the attack.[83] Finally, POTA was passed in a rare joint seating of the Parliament on March 26, 2002, reflecting the undemocratic nature of the process through which it was finally passed. Jayanth Krishnan notes that the joint seating allowed the law to be passed with a simple majority in the entire Parliament rather than requiring a majority in the individual houses of Parliament.[84] The rhetoric of a need for stringent laws in the face of a terrorist attack has often led to a fast-track action that bypasses the usual deliberative process required in the passage of laws. This was observed both in the case of POTA in India and with the PATRIOT Act in the United States.[85] The amendments to the Unlawful Activities Prevention Act (UAPA) made only a couple of weeks after the Mumbai attack in 2008 also reflect a similar haste in passing such laws. The hasty passing of new laws, of course, presumes a complete absence of any routine laws to try terrorist offenses, which is almost never the case in these legal systems.

The introduction of POTA, another extraordinary law, despite the lapse of TADA a few years earlier, led civil liberties activists and lawyers to once again question it in the Supreme Court. In *People's Union for Civil Liberties and Another v. Union of India*, 2004, the highest court once again upheld the constitutionality of the new law—this time unanimously considering it as necessary for responding to the war on the "territorial sovereignty and integrity of India."[86]

As in the TADA case, the Supreme Court declared that the Parliament had the "legislative competence" to create POTA under the subject heading "Defense of India." But one of the most significant formulations had to do with its own role in reviewing the new law. Responding to critics who pointed to the evidence of abuses under TADA as a reason for opposing

POTA, the Court stated that its role was not to look into whether there was a "need" for this statute since that was a policy decision. Rather, the Court considered its responsibility to be restricted to analyzing the constitutionality of the act.[87]

Even though the Court claimed that it was not responsible for looking into the need for the statute, that clearly did not stop the justices from providing the ideological justifications for the act (as they did in the TADA case). According to the Court, the act was necessary to combat the multipronged attempts of terrorists to "destabilize" the nation, create "fear . . . among the people," and affect the social, economic, and secular fabric of India.[88] The ideological justification for TADA had also been on similar grounds. However, what distinguished the justification of POTA from that of TADA was the explicit reference made to the global discourse on terrorism, with special mention of the UN resolutions on terrorism.[89]

The Indian discourse on terrorism post-2001 thus saw the convergence of the global discourse with the specific concerns of the ultranationalist Hindu government that was in power during the time. The BJP-led government had always used an anti-Muslim, antiminority rhetoric to strengthen its support among the majority Hindu community and had been demanding an antiterror law even before the Parliament attack. The 2001 events prompted the BJP-led government to connect the global discourse on "Islamic terrorism" directly to the "proxy war" with Pakistan in Kashmir.

Historically, the antiterror laws in India have always been very selectively applied against minorities, political dissidents, and other marginalized sections. The state used TADA to target many innocent Muslims in the name of focusing on a nebulous category of "terrorists." K. Balagopal notes that in contrast, Hindu fundamentalist groups and their terrorist actions were not focused as much.[90] Just to give one example, under TADA, the attacks by Islamic terrorists in Mumbai in 1993 were focused and targeted more than the organized killing of Muslims by the right-wing Hindus with state complicity in the same city after December 1992.[91] Thus, TADA, which had been introduced to check Sikh militancy in Punjab, not only targeted innocent Sikhs but was also used disproportionately against Muslims in Kashmir and elsewhere. As Krishnan notes, out of those detained under TADA in Rajasthan, Maharashtra, and Gujarat, 80 percent were Muslim.[92] Navlakha notes a similar pattern in the case of POTA, where most of those arrested under this law in regard to the train-burning case in Godhra were Muslims.[93] In contrast, those involved in the state-supported/planned genocide of Muslims in Gujarat were not subjected to POTA. The targeting of minorities worsened under the BJP-ruled POTA regime. The specific targeting of Muslims in many of these laws is so striking that Singh aptly calls it the creation of a "suspect community" wherein "the entire community is seen as potentially dangerous and a threat to national-security."[94] Thus, both in terms of their conceptualization as parallel systems of governance and their implementation, these legal regimes have been extraordinary.

The Indian state further connects the global and South Asian regional struggles against "Islamic terrorism" to what they consider the "internal terrorist actions" or the armed movements. Thus, these extraordinary laws focused on containing any form of movement seen as challenging the state, often allowing for the apprehension and detention of activists or sometimes even persons who just happened to be in a targeted area. Consequently, identity movements in the North East of India, social-transformative Naxalite movements in Andhra and Bihar, and struggles in forest-rich areas in Central India have all been subjected to these extraordinary laws.[95]

Bollywood films are also notorious for reiterating this axis of evil. For instance, in *Sarfarosh* (1999), a film on combating terrorism, the title song itself shows how guns and drugs are transported from the Pakistani border to the Indian state of Rajasthan.[96] The weapons are then put in large sacks of red chilies and sent to Mumbai and finally transported to the Naxalite (Maoist) leader who uses them to kill the members of a wedding party. Thus, in the span of one song, *Sarfarosh* links all forms of criminality and defiance to terrorism and all forms of terrorism to Pakistan and by implication to global terrorist threats. In the context of POTA, India's own "axis of evil" was explicitly created, connecting "terrorism" of all kinds, internal and external.

POTA and Confessions

As noted earlier, POTA continued to allow higher-level police officials to record confessions, but Sections 32 and 52 of POTA did attempt to include additional safeguards, drawn both from the TADA constitutionality case and the famous D. K. Basu guidelines. Under Section 52 of POTA, the police had to prepare a custody memo as soon as a person was arrested, inform him or her of the right to counsel, and inform a relative about the arrest. Similarly, under Section 32, after recording the confession, the accused had to be produced in front of a magistrate within forty-eight hours so that the magistrate could ensure the voluntariness of the confession—and in case there was any complaint of torture, the person had to be sent for medical examination. Those challenging the act questioned the additional step of the police recording the confession if the person was to be presented in front of a magistrate anyway.[97] The human rights scholar and activist A. G. Noorani, in fact, claimed that the additional step was difficult to explain, "[u]nless, of course, the game [was] to pin the man down to an extracted confession first and, next, get it legitimized through a magistrate."[98]

The Supreme Court, however, felt that the additional safeguard would give the accused a chance to rethink the confession, although this was substantially different from the routine context, which allowed the accused to rethink his or her confession outside of police influence. Accepting the necessity of special procedures for terrorism cases, the Court justified the section on confessions in POTA despite the well-documented misuse of TADA. The Court went on to uphold not only Section 32 of POTA regarding confessions but also most of the other provisions regarding bail, detention, and related provisions applicable in the course of pretrial investigations.[99]

The main test for the application of POTA and its implications for confessions has been the Parliament attack case *State (N.C.T. of Delhi) v. Navjot Sandhu* (2005). Although the five attackers were killed during the course of the attack, a few days later, four people were arrested in the case and tried: Mohammad Afzal (a former Jammu Kashmir Liberation Front member who had surrendered to the government in 1994), Shaukat Hussain Guru (Afzal's cousin), S. A. R. Geelani (a faculty member at Delhi University), and Afsan Guru (Shaukat's wife, known as Navjot Sandhu before marriage).[100] The special trial court set up in the case sentenced the first three of the accused to death, and the fourth was sentenced to five years of rigorous punishment.[101] The High Court found the evidence against Geelani and Afsan Guru inadequate and acquitted them, but it confirmed the death sentences of the other two. Eventually, the Supreme Court confirmed the death sentence of Mohammad Afzal, commuted Shaukat Guru's sentence to ten years of imprisonment, and acquitted Afsan Guru and the university professor, S. A. R. Geelani. This case became the test case not only for POTA but also for the human rights and democratic movements in India, particularly with respect to the way in which these laws could be used against innocent people (as confirmed subsequently by the higher courts). On the one hand, S. A. R. Geelani's and Afsan Guru's acquittals demonstrate the tremendous power of human rights groups and democratic groups in India in ensuring justice for innocents.[102] On the other hand, the case chillingly reflects the impossibility of standing up to extraordinary laws on an individual level, especially in the face of the erosion of traditional safeguards. One of the reasons indicated for Afzal Guru's continued death sentence is the lack of adequate counsel, especially since there is very little evidence against him.[103] It is also important to mention that even in Geelani's case, his allegations of torture never figured in the Supreme Court's consideration, for the case fell apart mainly due to lack of adequate evidence.[104] Indian human rights activists used several discrepancies in telephonic interceptions, translations of telephone conversations, and the identification of the accused to illustrate the hollowness of the case. Some of these factors eventually led to the acquittal of two of the accused.[105]

I, however, focus here on the Court's discussion of confessions, which represents a remarkable moment in Supreme Court jurisprudence where introspection regarding exceptional provisions leads not to a rejection of the provisions but rather to an eventual argument that extraordinary laws are even more protective of custodial rights than routine contexts. In the Parliament attack case, the Court noted that even the majority in the Kartar Singh (TADA) case had been wary of the "inhuman treatment" and "third degree" used by the police during confessions and suggested detailed guidelines to prevent these practices. Perhaps as a result of the majority's concerns and the dissent's stinging attacks in the TADA case, which were completely vindicated by the jurisprudence that followed, the Court in the Parliament attack case exhibited an unusual moment of introspection regarding confessions. The Court wrote,

> It is perhaps too late in the day to seek reconsideration of the view taken by the majority of the Judges in the Constitution Bench. But as we see Section 32, a formidable doubt lingers in our minds despite the pronouncement in Kartar Singh's case. . . . *That* [doubt] *pertains to the rationale and reason behind the drastic provision, making the confession to [a] police officer admissible in evidence in a trial for POTA offences.* Many questions do arise and we are unable to find satisfactory or even plausible answers to them. If a person volunteers to make a confession, why should he be not produced before the Judicial Magistrate at the earliest and have the confession recorded by a Magistrate? . . . The doubt becomes more puzzling when we notice that in practical terms, a greater degree of credibility is attached to a confession made before the judicial officer.[106]

Many of the questions that had been asked since the very inception of the section on confessions in TADA were asked by the Supreme Court in this case, especially regarding the provision of allowing police rather than magistrates alone to record confessions. By posing these fundamental questions about the rationale behind this process, the Court momentarily echoed the concerns of civil libertarians. However, the very next moment it disappoints the civil libertarians and undermines its own custody jurisprudence when it goes on to say, "However, we refrain from saying anything contrary to the legal position settled by TADA and POTA constitutionality cases. We do no more than [express] certain doubts and let the matter rest there."[107] The justices even acknowledge that given the reality of police violence, "We have serious doubts whether it would be safe to concede the power of recording confessions to the police officers to be used in evidence against the accused making the confession and the co-accused."[108] However, the Court stopped short of overturning the precedent and upheld the process of recording of confessions by senior police officials.

In fact, later in the judgment, the justices go a step further, actually praising POTA for including the additional safeguards, thereby suggesting that even if the confessions under TADA had been flawed, the process had been rectified under POTA. The Court hailed not only the direct involvement of the chief judicial magistrate in the confession process but also the inclusion of the famous D. K. Basu guidelines on creating an arrest or custody memo. It is at this moment that the Court made a remarkable observation about the routine jurisprudence, invoking the famous Nandini Satpathy judgment on the right against self-incrimination. The Court wrote,

> Perhaps, Nandini Satpathy does not go so far as Miranda in establishing access to [a] lawyer at [the] interrogation stage. But, Section 52(2) of POTA makes up this deficiency. It goes a step further and casts an imperative on the police officer to inform the person arrested of his right to consult a legal practitioner, soon after he is brought to the police station. Thus, the police officer is bound to apprise the arrested person of his right to consult the lawyer. To that extent, *Section 52(2) affords an additional safeguard to the person in custody. Section 52(2) is founded on the MIRANDA rule.*[109]

The Court's statement that the extraordinary law was more protective of the rights of the criminal defendants seems surprising, especially since the Court's interpretation of the Satpathy case is questionable. In the 1978 Satpathy case, the Supreme Court had written,

> The right to consult an advocate of his choice shall not be denied to any person who is arrested. This does not mean that persons who are not under arrest or custody can be denied that right. The spirit and sense of Art. 22 (1) is that it is fundamental to the rule of law that *the services of a lawyer shall be available for consultation to any accused person under circumstances of near-custodial interrogation.*[110]

Thus, the Satpathy Court clearly accepted a right to counsel in the interrogating phase, but the Court in the Parliament attack case interpreted it in an extremely limited manner, perhaps to overemphasize the protections available under POTA. Yet in the process, the Court was willing to admit that the routine contexts were more vulnerable to excess violence than had been acknowledged earlier.

Of course, the limitation in both the routine and extraordinary context is that the introduction of safeguards, even theoretically, always appears to represent an absolute right that is undermined in subsequent discourse. For instance, the Court in the Parliament attack case, invoking the "totality of circumstances" test, notes that while Sections 32 and 52 were important safeguards, violations of these sections may not necessarily lead to a rejection of evidence, though they may be used as factors in determining the admissibility of a confession.[111] As suggested in previous chapters, the Court's emphasis on a "totality of circumstances" test has proved to be unpredictable in both the Indian and U.S. contexts.[112] The violations of Sections 32 and 52 did lead to the inadmissibility of confessions in the case of Afzal and Shaukat, mainly because of the glaring violations. In this case, the senior police official who had recorded the confessions just took the accused to the officer's mess to remove them from the "coercive" influence and gave them five to ten minutes for reflection.[113] As Kannabiran, the counsel for Shaukat, put it in his brief to the Court, "All that he did was to give the statutory warning, somewhat in the spirit of cigarette manufacturers, that the accused was not bound to make the confession, and that if made it would be used against him."[114] Thus, although confessions were thrown out in the case, the Parliament attack is atypical in the way it was focused by the human rights groups in India, and the fact that the same scrutiny has not been possible in all cases is apparent in the history of cases under TADA.

In any event, even if the extended protections in POTA theoretically seem to be in consonance with or better than the criminal law protections against torture, they become less meaningful both in terms of how they are followed and in terms of the overall context of extraordinary laws that allow for arrests based on suspicion, long-term detention, and stringent bail provisions. The protections then merely become a way of claiming that POTA is more legitimate precisely because, as the Hindu right-wing leader L. K. Advani put it, "POTO [Prevention of Terrorism Ordinance] is different than TADA."[115]

Thus, a close analysis of the jurisprudence on TADA and POTA indicates that even though the extraordinary laws claim to be completely distinct and disconnected from the routine in terms of their emphasis and scope, they are integrally connected. Since the rationale behind the exceptional provisions in extraordinary laws relies on the clear separation between the former (temporary, for a separate purpose) and the routine (well-defined rights of criminal defendants of a liberal democracy), a moment such as the invocation of a routine case (such as the Satpathy case) shatters the clear demarcation between the two contexts and raises the fundamental question of why extraordinary laws are required in the first place.

The formal bypassing of safeguards in TADA and POTA cases does not seem completely surprising also due to the slippage or dilution of safeguards even within the routine discourses. Thus, rather than considering the bypassing of a safeguard in the TADA and POTA cases as completely exceptional, linking it with the tensions in the routine (as illustrated in the last chapter) allows us to recognize that the Court found it easier to bypass a safeguard in extraordinary contexts precisely because safeguards against torture were never completely followed even earlier. In other words, the Court in the extraordinary cases mainly resolves the tensions within the routine context, finding it of course easier to justify the change in the less scrutinized context.

The discourse on torture in India has been closely related to the recording of confessions by the police. Why does India have this particular safeguard regarding confessions, especially since most Anglo-American Western democracies allow the police to record confessions? This particular safeguard has to be understood in the context of its origins in the colonial period as described in one of the most systematic studies of torture, namely, the 1855 Madras Commission Report on Torture. In the last chapter I mentioned the significance of the colonial context in understanding custodial violence in contemporary India. As an illustration of the way colonial policies play a constitutive role in postcolonial torture debates, I bring attention to just one aspect of the colonial discourse that led to the formation of the very safeguards that are being bypassed in extraordinary laws: recording of confessions by the police.

The Colonial and the Postcolonial
Colonial Legacies on Confessions and Torture: Constructing the Indian Policeman

The universal existence of torture as a financial institution of British India is thus officially admitted, but the admission is made in such a manner as to shield the British Government itself. In fact, the conclusion arrived at by the Madras commission is that the practice of torture is entirely the fault of the lower Hindoo officials, while the European servants of the Government had always, however unsuccessfully, done their best to prevent it —Karl Marx, 1857.[116]

In this section, I discuss the Madras Commission Report on Torture (1855) (hereafter "the Madras Report") for the very specific purpose of historically contextualizing the characterization of the Indian police and the origin of some of the laws concerning their powers. I argue that the Madras Report played a formative role in the way the Indian police were and continue to be viewed. Furthermore, the discourse in the Madras Report and its aftermath possibly explains the Court's occasional expressions of desire to change procedural safeguards regarding the recording of confessions in the routine context and its actual acceptance of the transformation in extraordinary laws. Allowing the police to record confessions increases the vulnerability of the accused to the practice of torture. Nonetheless, the colonial context gives a sense of the particular history of this safeguard and makes this question more complex than it appears in the jurisprudence on ordinary and extraordinary laws.

As mentioned earlier, the Madras Commission on Torture was set up in the 1850s to look into complaints of torture in the southern Indian province of Madras.[117] While the Madras Report represented a remarkable attempt to systematically document widespread cases of torture, it simultaneously created a very specifically colonial discourse on torture.[118] In a nutshell, as the quotation from Karl Marx at the beginning of this section suggests, the Madras Report concluded that torture took place in a systemic manner but that the "native Indian servants" alone were responsible for the torture, with no relation to British policies.[119] The natural proclivity of the native policemen to commit acts of violence for their own benefit was pronounced as the primary cause of torture. The conclusions of the Madras Report fed directly into the colonial desire to modernize and civilize India through the institution of procedural and substantive legal codes, including the Indian Evidence Act, the Indian Penal Code, the Criminal Procedure Code, and the Police Act, which were introduced soon after.[120]

The Madras Report does refer to the structural reasons for the increase of torture in revenue matters, namely, the inadequate laws for punishment and redress for torture as well as the new arrangements for revenue collection.[121] The British had given the responsibility of revenue collection to the police officials under the *tehsildar*.[122] Douglas Peers states that while the British thought the merger would be a good administrative move due to its "cheapness" and the creation of a "direct channel" between the state and the people, it became a "decentralized" system with "an unintended amount of discretionary power."[123] Yet even the administrative decision of the British in 1816 to give the task of revenue collection to precisely those natives who had police functions and were known to use torture was not considered an example of a policy decision to allow the persistence of torture. Rather, it was considered to be a benign policy decision made by the British at the time and easily rectified later by dividing the revenue and police functions.

The Madras Report's confirmation of a systematic pattern of torture in the revenue and police functions of the colonial administration should have created a sense of crisis for British rule. Instead, the report ended up absolving the British administration of any blame for torture by creating an artificial separation between the natives and the colonials.[124] Indeed, by holding only the native policemen responsible for the acts of torture, the Madras Report exhibited the classic "rule of colonial difference" that Partha Chatterjee powerfully illustrates. Chatterjee explains that the universality of principles such as the "rule of law" and the institutions of police, army, and judiciary were denied to the natives precisely due to the "colonial difference." The colonial system was "a modern regime of power destined never to fulfill its normalizing mission because the premise of its power was the preservation of the alienness of the ruling group."[125]

Thus, even though the native police worked for the British, they were always considered outside the system as well as within it.[126] In other words, they had to follow colonial orders, but their actions did not represent the essence of the colonial rule. Even when the Madras Report found evidence of torture in revenue collections, as well as in police functions, the report used testimonies from former Indian revenue officials as evidence that torture was not used for the collection of revenues per se but rather to fulfill the illicit demands of revenue officers.[127] As Anupama Rao wrote, "The police were understood as a cultural institution compromised by the fact of being 'native,' and hence fundamentally irrational and prone to excess."[128] Since the use of torture in police matters predated the British, it could easily be distanced from any British policy decision.[129]

The Madras Report's denial of the use of torture as a state policy, whether for the extraction of revenues or for social control, also reflects a tension between the use of excess violence on one hand and an inability to openly accept its use on the other.[130] Nasser Hussain notes a similar tension in the Jallianwalla Bagh inquiry report between the colonial state's need to consolidate and establish state power during moments of crisis and the necessity to do so without acknowledging excessive violence.[131] In one of the most horrific incidents of colonial brutality, in 1919, a British general, Reginald Dyer, ordered the firing of 1,650 rounds on a peacefully protesting crowd without any warning, which resulted in the death of about 379 people and the injury of thousands (according to official records).[132] The state, on the one hand, could not uphold the use of excess brutal force by the general. On the other hand, it could not deny the reasoning behind the use of this force, which was ostensibly to maintain and in fact establish colonial authority. According to Hussain, the Hunter Committee set up to inquire into the Jallianwalla Bagh massacre thus could neither deny that "firing" was necessary nor uphold the use of "excessive force."[133]

In the case of England, the need to distance itself from torture was even more urgent due to the British claim of exceptionality in the history of torture in Europe. Thus, when systematic incidents of torture were confirmed, the colonial state found a way of distancing itself from them in two ways. First, the state ensured that torture was not seen by the colonial subjects or the liberals in England as being the result of a colonial policy. Second, the perpetrators of torture were understood to be only those who enforce the law, in this case the native policemen. One way to avoid a crisis was to take some action, such as instituting an inquiry or occasional punishment for an errant policeman.[134] Consequently, the British instituted the safeguards against the recording of confessions by the main perpetrators of torture in the colonial context: the native police.[135] As a result, the Indian police force was held responsible for all the excesses in the colonial regime, and it is this peculiarity that has significant implications for the debates on interrogations and confessions in both routine and extraordinary contexts.

Connecting the Dots: The Colonial to the Postcolonial

One of the major consequences of the Madras Report was the codification of the very provision that has been the subject of much debate in the postcolonial routine and exceptional contexts, namely, the provision disallowing the Indian police from recording confessions.[136] The conclusion and recommendation of the report was, of course, based on a colonial discourse that constructed the "native" Indian police as having a natural proclivity to use excess violence. If, however, one were to accept that torture was not used by the native police for (only?) their own interests but rather to secure the colonial enterprise, then in postindependent India, disallowing the police to record confessions was merely an uncritical acceptance of the Madras Commission's conclusions. After all, the colonial analysis ignored the central fact that the torture used by the native police played an important role in maintaining the power of the state.

Consequently, the question that has simmered in independent India is whether the police have the right to demand a change in their role in recording confessions. In other words, if one of the criticisms of the Indian legal system has been the lack of radical transformation in the laws and institutions from colonial times, the response would involve asking difficult questions about the role of the police in contemporary India. After all, the colonial safeguards were put in place precisely to prevent the "native" police from recording confessions, a rule not followed either in the English or the American context and thus clearly reflecting a "colonial difference." Unsurprisingly, the Indian police themselves have demanded a change in the colonial safeguards and have argued that disallowing the police to record confessions affects their morale negatively.[137] Eminent legal scholar Upendra Baxi also points to the continuing paradox in not allowing police to record confessions in India. Baxi writes "Paradoxically, this very attempt to protect the dignity of the accused tends to create a situation of loss of dignity for the police profession, real or apperceived."[138]

Thus, the question remains: does a need to reject colonial ideology and institutions then require a change in the police role in recording confessions? To answer this question, however, one has to recall the perspectives provided by scholars such as Baxi and Kannabiran, whose point is not to mechanically reject all things colonial. Rather, the goal of any radical restructuring of the laws and institutions is a desire to make them compatible with the democratic vision of the Constitution makers of India. It is the lack of a critical attitude toward repressive colonial institutions that Kannabiran points to.[139] In the absence of a rethinking of the legal institutions, the laws, and the police, and in the presence of widespread custodial violence, a critique of the colonial characterization of the native police alone cannot be used to concede to the demands of the modern police to be given the right to record confessions.

Even though the colonial origin of this safeguard does not justify changing the role of the police in recording confessions, it does explain a more fundamental tension regarding the role of the police that mediates and occasionally appears in the Indian jurisprudence on interrogations. On the one hand, the Supreme Court has been wary of allowing the police to record confessions in the routine context, but on the other hand, the Court periodically refers to the need to trust the police more in order to break with colonial perceptions of the police.

The Indian Court's skepticism regarding the police is reflected in the fact that despite relying heavily on the Miranda decisions, it decided not to allow the police to record confessions even though (as noted earlier) the demand for such a change has been traversing the legal discourse. In other words, the justices in India followed Western precedents in terms of the reasoning but stopped short of instituting similar functions of the police. This reflects the ability of the Indian justices to recognize the continuing reality of police torture in custodial interrogations in India, which could get even worse if the formal safeguards were to be further removed.

Yet, despite recognizing this reality, the Court has occasionally appeared to be conflicted about the role of the police. The Court wrote in a 2001 case,

> We feel that it is an archaic notion that the actions of the police officer should be approached with initial distrust. We are aware that such a notion was lavishly entertained during [the] British period and policemen also knew about it. Its hangover persisted during post-independence years but it is time now to start placing at least initial trust on the actions and documents made by the police. At any rate the court cannot start with the presumption that police records are untrustworthy. As a proposition of law the presumption should be the other way around.[140]

The courts thus also recognize a need to break away from the colonial distrust toward the police. It is this conflict within the jurisprudence that to some extent finds its resolution, whether justified or not, in the arena of extraordinary laws when some members of the police are finally allowed to record confessions.

One must note that even in the extraordinary laws, the state attempts to limit the recording of confessions to senior police officials. In that sense, as noted earlier, torture is often seen as a function of the subordinate officials in the arena of enforcement, whether in colonial, postcolonial, and/or contemporary situations. For instance, just as the colonial state focused on the native Indian police, the extraordinary laws target the lower rung of the police, and the United States primarily held lower-level officials responsible for the torture at Abu Ghraib, Iraq. It appears as if the difference between colonial times and contemporary discourses is that race has been replaced by a "lack of training" and/or lower class/educational background.

The significance of this distinction between the different tiers of police is fascinatingly reflected in the making of the 2009 Oscar hit *Slumdog Millionaire*. As noted in the introduction, in the film one observes a constable beating up the boy while the inspector watches. The Indian government's request to change the role of the torturer in the film has a special significance in the context of the extraordinary laws. Recall again the narrative provided by *New York Times* reporter Sengupta: "The Indian authorities told Mr. Colson to take out the police commissioner. No police officer above the rank of inspector should be shown administering torture, they said."[141] Here it is difficult to ascertain whether the use of the term "commissioner" is deliberate. However, the coincidence in the terms between the Indian government's request and extraordinary laws is striking, and if this is true, it appears that instead of asking for torture scenes to be removed per se, the Indian government appears to be more concerned that no senior police officer be implicated in an act of torture, even in a film.

Thus, even while being critical of the Indian Court for diluting the safeguards against torture in the extraordinary laws, one has to recognize the broader context provided by the particular colonial and postcolonial discourse on the role of the police. In other words, the change in the role of the police in extraordinary laws has to be understood as emerging not only in the context of terrorism but also in the preexisting tensions in the routine context and, by extension, in the colonial understanding of the native policemen. The larger significance of this genealogy is that it puts into perspective some of the recent state attempts not just to legitimize extraordinary laws but also to transform routine laws.

Theorizing the Ordinary and the Extraordinary

Extraordinary laws pose a special dilemma for liberal states because, by definition, they represent a radical shift from routine jurisprudence. The reason why they do not immediately interrupt the self-definition of states as liberal is precisely that extraordinary laws appear as an exception and ostensibly never traverse the spaces represented by the routine criminal discourse. Thus, one of the primary conditions of successful narratives about exceptional discourses relies on maintaining a clear distinction between the laws of the ordinary and those of the extraordinary. The way in which a liberal state legitimizes the extraordinary laws is to claim that these are temporary measures, specifically targeted to that moment, that event or crisis, and to those directly involved in creating the crisis, thus making a clear separation between the routine and the extraordinary.

In either routine or exceptional times, liberal democracies claim that torture is not authorized as a policy under any circumstances. In routine contexts, the strong framework of legal safeguards and the jurisprudential remedies are pointed out as indictors of that commitment to protect citizens from torture. In terms of extraordinary laws, the state puts forward almost a parallel system of laws that are still upheld as compatible with the democratic system because they are temporary and controlled. However, this particular claim of the liberal state about the parallel systems of governance in the Indian context, especially in the context of interrogations and torture, appears unsustainable since the routine and the extraordinary laws are integrally connected and together constitute the discourse on torture in India.

The relation between the two is visible not only in the ways the jurisprudence intersects but also in the identification of the sections of Indian society that are affected by the state violence, whether in everyday custody or in extraordinary contexts. The reports on custodial violence point out that in both the ordinary and the extraordinary contexts, similar groups of people are affected. The PUDR reports note that custodial deaths in routine contexts impact the people from the most marginalized sections—the working classes, *dalits* (previously termed untouchable castes), Muslims, and dissident communities in general. Similarly, POTA and the TADA have also focused on minorities such as Muslims and Sikhs as well as landless *dalit* and *adivasi* (scheduled tribes) and agricultural workers, often the state claiming the latter to be Naxalites (Maoists) or other militants.[142] Even the courts are unable to distinguish between the different sections of people targeted by the routine and extraordinary laws. In the famous D. K. Basu case, the justices wrote,

> We are conscious of the fact that the police in India have to perform a difficult and delicate task, particularly in view of the deteriorating law and order situation, communal riots, political turmoil, student unrest, terrorist activities, and among others the increasing number of underworld and armed gangs and criminals. Many hardcore criminals like extremists, terrorists, drug peddlers, smugglers who have organized gangs, have taken strong roots in the society. . . . To deal with such a situation, a balanced approach is needed to meet the ends of justice.[143]

By referring to all these different sections together, the Court itself opened up the possibility of connecting the ordinary and extraordinary contexts directly. This is despite the fact that the state and the courts have always disagreed with most civil liberties groups and activists, who claim that existing laws are adequate for dealing with terrorism.[144] In other words, if there is no distinction between the "criminals" and the "terrorists," then why introduce different laws for the terrorists? The state and the Supreme Court have always upheld the need for separate laws for the ordinary and extraordinary criminal contexts, yet in terms of who and what they target, there seems to be an intricate connection.

Further, the relation between the routine and extraordinary is visible in the concerns of civil libertarians about the long-term implications of these exceptional policies, or the possibility of their survival beyond the temporary. Just to give one example, the trend of long-standing impact of extraordinary laws is particularly visible in the recommendations of the report of the Malimath Committee, a committee set up to look into the reform of the Indian criminal justice system.[145] The overall framework of the report is to move away from an adversarial system toward a more inquisitorial system where the judge plays a greater role in the "quest for truth." The committee was primarily set up to deal with two major malaises of the Indian legal system, namely, the low rate of convictions and the high criminal case loads caused by the delay in resolution of cases.[146]

The report suggests that apart from increasing the time allowed in police custody, the law of confessions within the Indian Evidence Act should be changed in accordance with Section 32 of POTA, allowing for senior police officials to record confessions.[147] In addition, the report suggests an abridgement of the right to remain silent enshrined in Article 20(3) of the Indian Constitution. The committee states that since the accused is the "best source of information," he or she should be questioned, and if he or she remains quiet, the court should be allowed to draw "adverse inferences."[148] Pressuring or "tapping" the accused in this context was also assumed by the Court to be "noncoercive." The report has been rightly criticized by many human rights groups and notable legal scholars such as Upendra Baxi as being highly undemocratic in its inception and provisions because it bypasses a number of safeguards in the criminal justice system.[149]

This report has also led some scholars to point to the long-term impact of the extraordinary laws on routine laws in India. Ujjwal Singh suggests that while antiterrorist laws have always been a part of the Indian landscape, after 9/11 there was a "distinct shift." He wrote, *"In particular the POTA and TADA judgments that have come after September 11, as well as the report of the . . . Malimath Committee on Reforms of the Criminal Justice system, show how the extraordinary and the ordinary have come to traverse common ground, bringing about a permanence of the temporary."*[150] Many of the changes suggested by the Malimath Committee Report are, unsurprisingly, based on the provisions of POTA and related Court judgments. Thus, even though the extraordinary laws are meant to address more specific concerns, they are being used to reform the entire routine criminal justice system, leading to a "permanence of the temporary."[151]

However, even while recognizing that the extraordinary laws are a more blatant bypassing of routine safeguards, it is also important to note the ways in which the routine discourses on interrogation had always been in tension vis-á-vis some of the laws. In other words, it is simultaneously significant to focus on how the extraordinary contexts also make the tensions within the routine contexts more explicit and represent the resolution of the dilemma for the state in some instances. To put it another way, scholars such as Singh point to the "interlocking of the ordinary and extraordinary" in the functioning of POTA and TADA such that evidence gained under exceptional provisions was used in convicting the accused in ordinary law.[152] Here again the emphasis is on the impact of the extraordinary on the ordinary, but instead I focus on another kind of interlocking in which the tensions within the ordinary itself perform a constitutive role in extraordinary laws. The significance of this phenomenon is that even when the extraordinary laws are repealed or allowed to lapse, the routine laws continue with some of the tensions.

In colonial times, the tension between the rule of law and state authority in times of apparent crisis was resolved in favor of the colonial powers, although even the British could not entirely defend torture or excessive force. In postindependent India, the liberal state can never directly uphold the use of torture even in extraordinary laws because the rule-of-law-based liberal democracy would run amok. But the tension between law's need to use excess violence and an attempt to control it emerges in different ways in the extraordinary context, and the jurisprudence resolves the tensions by either denying the violence or accommodating it in uniquely creative ways.

6

Conclusion:
Unraveling the Exception

Torture in Liberal Democracies

Impermissibility and the Politics of Denial

One of the primary themes of this study is the status of torture in liberal democracies or, more specifically, the notion of impermissibility of torture in democracies. In his speech on Afghanistan on December 2, 2009, President Obama said,

> And finally, we must draw on the strength of our values—for the challenges that we face may have changed, but the things that we believe in must not. That's why we must promote our values by living them at home—which is why I have prohibited torture and will close the prison at Guantánamo Bay.[1]

The question is, since President Obama has prohibited torture, is torture no longer an issue in the United States? Is it now an issue of the past? When President Obama made this statement, it indicated an understanding that torture had reemerged for a brief moment in the immediate post-9/11 period but had been made by his administration a subject of the past (the immediate past, perhaps, but the past nonetheless).

This statement could be challenged empirically by reference to the myriad ways in which torture continues to be an issue in the United States: after all, criminal and civil cases filed by torture survivors are still going on despite courts continually throwing them out,[2] arrest warrants based on convictions of CIA officials have been authorized in Italy,[3] there are continuing incidents of torture in American prisons and detention centers, and regardless of the legal status of their cases, there is the enduring impact of torture on the survivors. Even if one takes the president's statement to mean not that torture is no longer an issue in the United States but just that torture is no longer an authorized policy (which was of course never admitted by President Bush either), it bypasses many of the vexing questions that were raised in the post-9/11 context regarding the difficulties that law and liberal states face in containing excess violence. In addition, one of the main arguments of this book is that discussions of torture in liberal democracies are characterized by a politics of denial or, more specifically, that the notion of impermissibility of torture masks a lack of clarity about the nature of violence allowed or disallowed.

In the context of India, the denial has appeared most recently in the Lok Sabha (Lower House of Parliament) discussions on the antitorture bill in May 2010. During the parliamentary debates on the bill, parliamentarian Shashi Tharoor stated,[4]

> I have often felt that the issues here go to two fundamental problems in our country. The first is how we treat our own people; and the second is the image of our country in the world at large. We were also excited around the world about the huge success of "Slumdog Millionaire" but, yet, none of us seem to make anything of the fuss. There was no public uproar about the fact that this film opens with a scene of *astonishing police brutality where the Indian police-man is . . . [shown] torturing the hero* including with electric shocks to get him to confess . . . [to] cheating in a quiz show. What was startling with that, it seems to me, was that the mindset of our public has become such that we are immune to it. We took these scenes for granted. No one said how outrageous it is that our country should be shown in this way because, in fact, the assumption appears to be, well, this happens all the time.[5]

Here one observes the acceptance of torture as pervasive in India, the pervasiveness of torture being reiterated by quite a few ministers during the parliamentary debates on the antitorture bill.[6] However, the tension between the very introduction of this antitorture bill and the lack of a comprehensive perspective behind it is visible in the fact that there is an attempt to focus the problem entirely either on the police, as Tharoor does, or on torture as a remnant of colonial rule. As Panna Lal Punia, another legislator, put it, "Aaj thanon mein wohi angrezi hukumat ki boo aati haih." (From today's police stations, the same stink of English rule can be smelled.)[7] However, the torture bill itself makes no reference to the realities of custodial deaths or CIDT, which are integrally related to the issue of torture, and the Home Ministry even denies that custodial deaths occur as a result of torture (as noted in chapter 3). In such a context, the emphasis of the law appears to be on strengthening the image of India, not so much on how the Indian people are treated. As Tharoor put it,

> Indeed, the next time if somebody wants to make an Oscar-winning movie showing an Indian policeman behaving in that way, we can surely hope that they will also show him being punished and sentenced for his actions. That is indeed what India should stand for and be seen as standing for around the world.[8]

Again, as noted earlier, the bill continues to require prior approval from the government for prosecuting officials, which had been an issue even earlier, thereby limiting prosecutions and making Tharoor's words and the act itself more symbolic than substantive. Thus, the denials in India continue not so much in terms of officials denying that acts of torture exist as in terms of their refusal to address the issue systematically and comprehensively on the basis of decades of documented experiences of Indian realities.

Why is the discussion of impermissibility and/or denial so crucial? It is crucial because, first and foremost, it contributes towards the self-definition of these states as liberal democracies. Note the emphasis on values in President Obama's statement: "we must draw on the strength of our values."[9] The political discourse on "inherent values" plays an important role in defining the status of torture. Denial and impermissibility furthermore detract attention from a close examination of the law's and the state's relationship with violence and its constant negotiation and accommodation of excess violence, which continues to be an ongoing challenge in a liberal democracy.

Circulation of Discourses: Jurisprudence in Liberal Democracies

In this work, I move away from two primary assumptions of comparative and theoretical work on the state, the law, and violence. First, theoretical work on liberal democracies has often relied on Western experiences that are then generalized or presented as universal. Conversely, non-Western experiences are often read as case studies with little to contribute apart from their own specific experiences. Here, I take inspiration from postcolonial scholars such as Rajeswari Sunder Rajan. In her book *The Scandal of the State: Women, Law, and Citizenship in Postcolonial India*, Sunder Rajan oscillates between the terms "the state," connoting the theoretical concept, and the "postcolonial Indian state," reflecting the specific experiences of the "context and history of contemporary India," and writes,

While I have been confronted by this as a methodological predicament, its source lies equally in the disciplinary classification of studies of/from regions or nation-states in the non-West as "area studies." There is a case, nonetheless, to be made for recognizing postcolonial studies as not simply case studies of this kind but increasingly representative modes of a critical and theoretical understanding of democracy in the modern nation-state. Such an understanding has relevance beyond the immediate context of the region, but also, more crucially, it ought to unsettle the paradigmatic status of Western political theory.[10]

Thus, in my work I focus on India and the United States as two illustrations of liberal democracies. Furthermore, in the spirit of using empirical illustrations to theorize the state, I also join the ranks of political theorists who do not restrict themselves to traditional normative political theory.[11]

The framing of this study reflects a particular moment in my biography: I was in the United States on September 11, 2001, and was witness to some of the vitriolic media debates on torture in the United States (and the world). However, focusing on India brings attention to structural patterns regarding the state's relationship to violence and the way in which democracies respond to undeniable cases of torture deaths. Unlike in the United States, where for the most part custodial deaths take place rarely and on the margins (for example, in immigration detention centers) or outside the borders (in Afghanistan and Iraq), making the routine jurisprudence on interrogations appear less blemished, in India custodial deaths still infect the routine criminal justice system. Consequently, the Indian Supreme Court has responded to custodial deaths by coming up with a very substantial understanding of violence and custody. In turn, this meaning of custody jurisprudence is an extremely useful theorization for understanding state violence and distinguishing it from other kinds of violence.

While there has been a focus on the way U.S. jurisprudence has informed, indeed dictated, Indian jurisprudence, this study points to ways in which there is a complex circulation of discourses. For instance, extraordinary laws, which have been a hallmark of the Indian system, are increasingly being incorporated into the U.S. system with the antiterrorism initiatives and recent discussions on preventive detention laws.[12] In contrast, the Indian Court's interpretation of Miranda and a comprehensive understanding of violence had few reverberations in the U.S. discourse, which has only moved further away from addressing the issue of violence (since violence is no longer considered an issue) in the routine jurisprudence. Thus, the influence appears to be highly selective.

The insights emerging from the Indian jurisprudence, especially about the notion of custody, could contribute significantly to Western jurisprudence. While the U.S. Miranda decision famously points to certain keys elements of interrogation—its incommunicado nature, its impact on more marginalized sections in society, and its inherently coercive nature—the Indian jurisprudence goes a step further by pointing to the continuum between the different forms of excess violence and the difficulties in distinguishing and thereby disallowing certain forms of violence. This recognition is significant for any debates on the law, the state, and violence and has particular significance for U.S. debates on torture in the post-9/11 period. Furthermore, the particular guidelines emerging from the Indian jurisprudence to deal with custodial violence—including a presumption that the police (or any state official) have to explain the fate of a person if last observed in their custody, the necessity for a custody memo (for all detained), and a right to compensation for violation of fundamental rights by the state—are significant contributions to theorizations of custodial violence in any liberal democracy. Most of all, the very meaning of custody and the conceptual category of custody jurisprudence is a reminder of the power relations during interrogation that are undermined in justificatory comparisons in post-9/11 memos between SERE (voluntary training) and the CIA (forced) renditions of waterboarding.[13]

Finally, studying Indian jurisprudence alongside that of the United States points to the ways in which the exception and the routine are on a continuum and not a complete break from each other. The only way in which liberal democracies claim to hold on to their self-definition as liberal is to point to the temporary nature of the exception and its break from the routine. But this study notes the ways in which the routine and the extraordinary traverse common spaces in terms of law's tension with excess violence, which manifests differently according to the state's relationship to its citizens/noncitizens/subjects.

Courts, Law, and Politics

In debates on law and violence, the emphasis has been on the realm of enforcement—on how there is a gap between "ideal law" and the enforcement that results in excessive violence. Undoubtedly, there continue to be several problems at the level of enforcement due to a variety of causes, including lack of supervision, training, and resources. While these studies have undoubtedly contributed tremendously to the understanding of legal violence, the point of intervention of this study is on the integral relationship between the enforcement and the official legal discourse itself. Here I demonstrate the inability of the liberal state to contain excess violence in precisely the most authoritative judicial and legal discourse. Thus, the emphasis is not at the level of enforcement but rather at the level of the jurisprudence itself.

I emphasize the jurisprudence as an authoritative discourse not because I privilege the positivistic formal understanding of law. I focus on this tension within the jurisprudence to illustrate the relationship of the dominant conception of law to violence. Here I note the significance of what Paul Kahn suggests:

> Much of the cultural studies of law movement has been an effort to shift the location at which we study law from the opinions of the appellate courts to the expressions of ordinary people carrying out the tasks of everyday life. Because of my focus on the constitutional rule of law, my work moves in an opposite direction.[14]

Here Kahn points to the need to continue studying the "language of law's rule," which he considers as "our dominant, although not exclusive, language of legitimacy."[15] As noted earlier, the Court is observed as a major site of authentication of torture. Thus, the absence of a discussion on torture (as in the post-9/11 United States) or, in other instances, illustrations of the tension in the jurisprudence toward excess violence have crucial implications for understanding the liberal state's relationship to violence. However, the dominant conception of law, of course, is not the sole site of study within my work since I also note how a range of actors, such as the human rights groups and popular culture, help constitute the law and reinforce (TV show *24* or *Slumdog Millionaire*) or challenge (human rights reports) this dominant conception.[16]

Governmentality: Theorizing the Law, Violence, and State Power

My main argument has to do with the relationship among the law, violence, and state power, and I argue that torture has to be understood as a manifestation of the law's and the state's constant negotiation and accommodation of excess violence. In my study of the state and violence, I draw upon many of the significant contributions of Foucauldian governmentality studies but move away from one of the primary foundations of contemporary governmentality studies, which focused precisely on deprivileging the state as the main locus of power.[17]

Foucault has famously criticized the field of "political thought and analysis" for not yet "cut[ting] off the king's head" and has argued that "[w]e must eschew the model of Leviathan in the study of power."[18] As Nikolas Rose and Peter Miller noted in their 1992 essay "Political Power beyond the State," "From this perspective on political power, Foucault suggested, one might avoid over-valuing the 'problem of the State,' seeing it either as a 'monstre froid' confronting and dominating us, or as the essential and privileged fulfillment of a number of necessary social and economic functions."[19] Thus the famous phrase "governmentalization of the state" emerged as a way to point out that the state is only one of the many institutions in the art of governing. As Rose and Miller write,

> Within the problematics of government, one can be nominalistic about the state: it has no essential necessity or functionality. Rather, the state can be seen as a specific way in which the problem of government is discursively codified, a way of dividing a "political sphere," with its particular characteristics of rule, from other "non-political spheres" to which it must be related, and a way in which certain technologies of government are given a temporary institutional durability and brought into particular kinds of relations with one another.[20]

This framework is pathbreaking in many ways. First, it focuses attention on ways in which the state works with many other nonstate and private institutions. Second, it identifies the different modes of social control, including the "political rationalities," technologies of governance, and discourses, thereby pointing to the less visible ways in which power works in modern society. However, the question is whether in the process, governmentality studies deprivileged the significance of the state such that it fails to observe the ways in which the state itself is reconstituted by these different technologies of governance. In other words, what this framework does not explain is the continuing dominant significance of the state and the utilization of excess violence by the law and the state even in a modern liberal democracy.

Here I turn to Timothy Kaufman-Osborn's work to further explain this claim. Kaufman-Osborn writes that theorists have often found Michel Foucault's work to be incompatible with Max Weber's work—the latter focusing on the state as representing the monopoly of legitimate violence. As Kaufman-Osborn puts it,

From the perspective of Foucault, some say, Weber represents the state as a privileged monopolist of the means of violence, and that in turn distracts inquiry from the web of extrastate disciplinary controls that render it an ever less significant locus of political power. From the perspective of Weber, some say, Foucault's antipathy toward the state as an object of inquiry distracts attention from its coercive role in securing the order that is the political presupposition of the spread of various technologies of discipline.[21]

In contrast, Kaufman-Osborn explains how he finds the two theorists complementary by demonstrating, in the context of the "technological and organizational history" of the governmental practice of hanging (as a method of execution), "how transformations internal to that practice [in a Foucauldian sense] contribute to the formation of a state that is well understood in qualified Weberian terms."[22] For him, an exclusive focus on Foucauldian contributions would not be adequate to explain the workings of political power and, more relevant for our purpose, the state and legal violence. This is the case because, as Kaufman-Osborn puts it,

> What Foucault cannot do as well as Weber is to show how various incremental changes sometimes coalesce into larger structures of domination, how transformed modalities of practice, although neither intended nor foreseen by anyone, sometimes come together to create obdurate formations of power that are more than the sum of their individual parts.[23]

Thus, the state remains a primary mode of control through its monopoly over legitimate violence even if its functions are increasingly being performed by nonstate and private actors alongside state ones.

In my study, I note the liberal state's continued reliance on excess violence as a mode of control in modern society. Here I introduce this new concept of excess violence, which is a constantly negotiated category that exists on a continuum of acts ranging from coercion to torture. There is no uniformity in the way the actual negotiation and accommodation of excess violence occurs. In fact, the actual modes vary according to the context. For instance, in the two liberal democracies I study, it emerges differently in distinct historical periods, the sections it affects are varied at times though often with overlaps, and it may change with a new regime. While all these specific circumstances are significant and have been focused in the various chapters of the book, what my work shows is the commonality that despite the assertion that torture and excess violence are impermissible in a liberal democracy, the state is engaged in a constant struggle, a negotiation, and even an accommodation of excess violence in both routine and extraordinary contexts.

Since excess violence is a constantly negotiated category, the attempt is always to define it within the law, rather than on the basis of an exceptional sovereign decision. Yet due to its slippery nature and the inability of the law to clearly define it, there is always a tentativeness to it. There are just two benchmarks of this negotiation: one is that it illustrates the constant struggle of law with violence in liberal states and the second is that the nature of violence is such that it cannot appear to exceed the acceptable levels of violence in a society. In each of the chapters, I suggest that the state constantly negotiates the boundaries of excess violence to ascertain what is permissible and the extent to which it can push them without explicitly appearing lawless. The threshold of that violence depends on a range of factors, including the success of the rhetoric, the transparency of the act, the legal loopholes, the subjects of control, and the political climate of a particular moment.

The emphasis on excess violence is not meant to indicate that there has been no transformation in the nature of state power. Rather, it is to indicate that the art of government does not work only through disciplinary mechanisms and the conduct of populations but also by the use of excess violence. Thus, even though Foucault does undermine the role of excess violence in more modern societies, especially where the art of government emerges as a prominent mode of control, his notion of governmentality can actually be reinterpreted to allow for an understanding of how excess violence could be addressed within that framework. Even though governmentality studies for the most part have not focused on the role of excess violence in modern states, the Foucaldian framework does allow for such exploration, as illustrated in the discussion on the juridico-medical apparatus in chapter 2.[24]

Mitchell Dean in his study on governmentality rejects the traditional questions of "who rules?" "what is the source of that rule?" and "what is the basis of its legitimacy?" in an effort to focus on "how different locales are constituted as authoritative and powerful, how different agents are assembled with specific powers, and how different domains are constituted as governable and administrable."[25] However, this study seeks to bring together the traditional questions regarding state power with the technologies of governance in an effort to analyze what Kaufman-Osborn calls the "structured pattern of effects."[26] For Foucault, "Law cannot 'help but be armed' but this feature is increasingly encased in new normalizing and regulatory functions."[27] However, in this study, I note this emphasis in liberal democracies on law as continually being armed with excess violence, which has been not adequately focused in governmentality studies.

The larger significance of this illustration of law's tension with excess violence is that even when the so-called exceptional policies are withdrawn (as evident in the Obama era or across the different political regimes in India), the liberal state and the law continue to confront the preexisting tensions with excess violence. The continuing tensions of law with violence indicate that state power in liberal democracies has to be understood in relation to the negotiation with and accommodation of excess violence. While the state and the law constantly try to define the limits of this violence, the process is slippery, making it difficult to demarcate the boundaries of this relationship. What prevents violence from appearing in the most brutal forms is precisely the need for the state to portray its own violence as more humane than the violence used by the "other." This study thus argues that the liberal state, while engaging in multiple forms of social control, still retains its ability to engage in excess violence within its art of government, a reality pointing to the continued centrality of violence in liberal democracies.

Notes

INTRODUCTION

1. *Slum Dog Millionaire*, 2008, Danny Boyle, director, Loveleen Tandan, codirector of the film in India.

2. Somini Sengupta, "Extreme Mumbai, without Bollywood's Filtered Lens," *New York Times*, November 11, 2008. http://www.nytimes.com/2008/11/16/movies/16seng. html?scp=4&sq=slum%20dog%20millionaire&st=cse (last visited January 15, 2009).

3. See chapter 5.

4. David Edwards and Stephen C. Webster, "Cheney Admits Authorizing Detainee's Torture," December 15, 2008. http://rawstory.com/news/2008/Cheney_admits_authoriz-ing_detainees_torture_1215.html (last visited January 15, 2009).

5. Thomas Hobbes, *Leviathan*, edited by Richard E. Flathman and David Johnston (New York: Norton, 1997); John Austin, *The Province of Jurisprudence Determined and the Uses of the Study of Jurisprudence* (New York: Noonday Press, 1954); H. L. A. Hart, "A New Conception of Law," in *Philosophy of Law*, edited by Joel Feinberg and Hyman Gross, 54-68 (Belmont, CA: Wadsworth, 1986); Ronald M. Dworkin, "The Model of Rules," *University of Chicago Law Review* 35 (1967): 14-46.

6. Robert Cover, "Violence and the Word," in *Narrative, Violence, and the Law: The Essays of Robert Cover*, edited by Austin Sarat, Michael Ryan, and Martha Minow, 203-38 (Ann Arbor: University of Michigan Press, 1995); Austin Sarat and Thomas R. Kearns, "A Journey through Forgetting: Towards a Jurisprudence of Violence," in *The Fate of Law*, edited by Austin Sarat and Thomas R. Kearns, 209-73 (Ann Arbor: University of Michigan Press, 1991); Timothy Kaufman-Osborn, *From Noose to Needle: Capital Punishment and the Late Liberal State* (Ann Arbor: University of Michigan Press, 2002).

7. Michel Foucault, *Discipline and Punish: The Birth of the Prison*, translated by Alan Sheridan (New York: Vintage Books, 1995).

8. Darius Rejali, *Torture and Modernity: Self, Society, and State in Modern Iran* (Boulder, CO: Westview, 1994).

9. Rejali points out that in modern societies such as Iran, torture continues to play an important part. Ibid.

10. Talal Asad, "On Torture, or Cruel, Inhuman, and Degrading Treatment," in *Social Suffering*, edited by Veena Das, Margaret Lock, and Arthur Kleinman, 285-308 (Berkeley: University of California Press, 1997), 296.

11. The term "war on terror" has been used a number of times in the book primarily because this phrase was frequently used by the post-9/11 Bush administration. However, the current president, Barack Obama, has deliberately rejected this language. "Obama

Scraps 'Global War on Terror' for 'Overseas Contingency Operation.'" *FOXNews.com*, March 25, 2009. http://www.foxnews.com/politics/elections/2009/03/25/report-obama-administration-backing-away-global-war-terror/ (last visited April 1, 2009).

12. *Consideration of Reports Submitted by State Parties under Article 19 of the Convention: Initial Reports of the State Parties Due in 1995 (United States of America) to the United Nations Committee against Torture*, October 15, 1999, 6.

13. *India: Torture, Rape, and Deaths in Custody* (New York: Amnesty International, 1992), 1.

14. Michael Ignatieff, *The Lesser Evil: Political Ethics in an Age of Terror* (Princeton, NJ: Princeton University Press, 2004), 2.

15. Steven Lukes, "Liberal Democratic Torture," *British Journal of Political Science* 36 (2005): 1-16, 12-13, emphasis added.

16. John Locke, "*The Second Treatise of Civil Government*" and "*A Letter Concerning Toleration*" (Oxford: Blackwell, 1966), 9, emphasis added.

17. Ibid., 10, emphasis added.

18. Max Weber, "The Economic System and the Normative Orders," in *Law in Economy and Society*, edited with an introduction and annotations by Max Rheinstein,11-40 (Cambridge, MA: Harvard University Press, 1966), 14.

19. Ibid., 14, emphasis added. Weber does consider legal orders to be constituted not just by the state but by any entity backed by coercive power, but still, the state has a particular significance among all these institutions. Ibid., 17. See David M. Trubek, "Max Weber on Law and the Rise of Capitalism," *Wisconsin Law Review* 3 (1972): 720-53.

20. Ignatieff, *The Lesser Evil*, 15, emphasis added.

21. Ibid., 17.

22. See Edward Peters, *Torture* (Philadelphia: University of Pennsylvania Press, 1996). Despite a worldwide condemnation and development of a legal regime against torture, there is a widespread persistence of torture, which assumes significance also because more than 136 countries have signed and ratified the UN Convention against Torture. Duncan Forrest, ed., *A Glimpse of Hell: Reports on Torture World Wide* (*Amnesty International*) (New York: New York University Press, 1998).

23. Torture is often considered in popular discourse as well as mainstream literature (at least prior to the post-9/11 United States) as a feature of ancient regimes and medieval times. Certain forms of torture, such as whipping, flogging, pillorying, and duckstooling, were considered as forms used in the premodern era in the United States. Bertil Duner, ed., *An End to Torture: Strategies for Its Eradication* (London: Zed, 1998). Alice Morse Earle, *Curious Punishments of Bygone Days* (New York: Macmillan, 1896).

24. Jeremy Waldron, "Torture and Positive Law: Jurisprudence for the White House." *Columbia Law Review* 105 (2005): 1681-1750, 1719-20.

25. Historically, Egyptians, Persians, Greeks, and Romans used torture, and rank and citizenship had a close relationship to the use of torture. See Edward Peters, *Torture*, 11-39. See George Ryley Scott, *The History of Torture throughout the Ages* (London: Kegan Paul, 2003) on the history, techniques, and impact of torture. Also see Page Dubois, *Torture and Truth* (New York: Routledge, 1991).

26. Ibid.

27. Lynn Hunt, *Inventing Human Rights: A History* (New York: Norton, 2007) 33-34.

28. Ibid., 112.

29. Karl Shoemaker, "The Problem of Pain in Punishment: Historical Perspectives," in Austin Sarat, ed., *Pain, Death, and the Law* (Ann Arbor: University of Michigan Press, 2001), 15-42, 35.

30. Lisa Silverman, *Tortured Subjects: Pain, Truth, and the Body in Early Modern France* (Chicago: University of Chicago Press, 2001).

31. Ibid.

32. Peters, *Torture*.

33. Langbein uses the phrase "fairy tale" of abolition. John Langbein, *Torture and the Law of Proof: Europe and England in the Ancien Regime* (Chicago: University of Chicago Press, 1997), 10-11. Peters writes that in twelfth-century Europe, confession became the "queen of proofs" while torture became the "queen of torments." Peters, *Torture*, 40. According to the law, torture could not be used to extort confessions directly. It could only be utilized to gain corroborative evidence from the accused to confirm what was already indicated by other independent evidence. From the thirteenth to the eighteenth century, torture became a part of the "ordinary criminal procedure of the Latin Church and most of the states of Europe." Peters, *Torture*, 54. According to Foucault, judicial torture at the time was a "judicial game" with strictly worked out rules. Foucault, *Discipline and Punish*, 35-46. See discussion on Foucault and punishment in David Garland, *Punishment in Modern Society* (Chicago: University of Chicago Press, 1990).

34. Langbein, *Torture and the Law of Proof*.

35. Peters, *Torture*, 85.

36. Silverman, *Tortured Subjects*, 9. See also Cesare Beccaria, *Of Crime and Punishment and Other Writings*, edited by Richard Bellamy (Cambridge: Cambridge University Press, 1995).

37. In contemporary language, torture is also described in more sentimental terms—with torture being anything that is not pleasant or acceptable in any sphere of society. See Peters, *Torture*, 2-3. Rejali, *Torture and Modernity*.

38. W. L. Twining and P. E. Twining, "Bentham on Torture," *Northern Ireland Legal Quarterly* 24 (1973): 305-56, 306.

39. Waldron, "Torture and Positive Law," 1683-84.

40. Walter Pincus, "Silence of Four Terror Suspects Poses Dilemma for FBI," *Washington Post*, October 21, 2001. http://www.washingtonpost.com/ac2/wp-dyn/A27748-2001Oct20 (last visited March 21, 2003).

41. Edward Greer, "'We Don't Torture People in America': Coercive Interrogation in the Global Village," *New Political Science* 26 (2004): 371-87, 386.

42. *D. K. Basu v. State of West Bengal; Ashok K. Johri v. State of Uttar Pradesh* (1996). http://judis.nic.in/supremecourt/qrydisp.asp?tfnm=14580 (last visited June 23, 2005), emphasis added.

43. Foucault, *Discipline and Punish*.

44. Ibid., 7.

45. Ibid, chapter 2.

46. For Foucault, the sovereign is the "master" of life and death in this context. Even the pardon by the sovereign shows the ability of the sovereign to suspend both law and vengeance. Ibid., 53.

47. Ibid., 16.

48. Ibid., 177.

49. Damiens's execution in Foucault, *Discipline and Punish*.

50. Austin, *Province of Jurisprudence*, 24.

51. Ibid.

52. Dworkin, "The Model of Rules," 19. See discussion on Hart and Dworkin in the context of judicial decision making in Howard Gillman. "What's Law Got to Do with It? Judicial Behavioralists Test the 'Legal Model' of Judicial Decision Making," *Law and Social Inquiry* 26 (2001): 465-504.

53. Carole Pateman rightly points out that the story of the social contract is primarily a contract among men and prefaced by a sexual contract and consequently women are excluded from this original act, thereby lacking access to the rights of liberty and equality in the newly formed society. Carole Pateman, *The Sexual Contract* (Stanford: Stanford University Press, 1988).

54. Hobbes, *Leviathan*, 95-96, emphasis added.

55. Sarat and Kearns, "A Journey through Forgetting," 223.

56. K .G. Kannabiran, "Repealing POTA: Some Issues," *Economic and Political Weekly* 39 (2004): 3794-95, 3795.

57. Dworkin, "The Model of Rules," 22.

58. Ibid.

59. Sarat and Kearns, "A Journey through Forgetting," 245-46.

60. Ibid., 246-47.

61. Austin Sarat, "Situating Law between the Realities of Violence and the Claims of Justice: An Introduction," in *Law, Violence, and the Possibility of Justice*, edited by Austin Sarat, 3-16 (Princeton, NJ: Princeton University Press, 2001), 3-4.

62. Waldron, "Torture and Positive Law," 1687.

63. Ibid., 1726. Emphasis added.

64. Phillipe Nonet and Philip Selznick, *Law and Society in Transition: Towards Responsive Law* (New York: Harper and Row, 1978), see chart on 16.

65. Ibid.

66. Sarat, "Situating Law," 3-4. Sarat and Kearns, "A Journey through Forgetting."

67. Due to the influence of critical theory and deconstruction, law's violence has become a broadly defined term ranging from that experienced in language to its representation to denial of experience. As a result, the focus on physical violence is often lost. See Cover, "Violence and the Word." Here one can place the work of Jacques Derrida and Drucilla Cornell. Drucilla Cornell, ed., *Deconstruction and the Possibility of Justice* (New York: Routledge, 1992).

68. Cover, "Violence and the Word," 203. Sarat and a number of scholars in the last couple of decades have focused on the issue of law and violence, especially emphasizing the work of Robert Cover. See Austin Sarat, ed., *Pain, Death, and the Law*; Austin Sarat, *Law, Violence, and the Possibility of Justice*; Austin Sarat and Thomas R. Kearns, eds., *Law's Violence* (Ann Arbor: University of Michigan Press, 1992); Austin Sarat, Michael Ryan, and Martha Minow, eds., *Narrative, Violence, and the Law: The Essays of Robert Cover.* Their work has also been influenced by Walter Benjamin's work on violence; Walter Benjamin, "Critique of Violence," in *Reflections*, ed. Peter Dementz, 277-300 (New York: Harcourt, Brace, 1978).

69. Cover, "Violence and the Word," 208.

70. Sarat, *Law, Violence, and the Possibility of Justice*, 6.

71. Timothy Kaufman-Osborn, *From Noose to Needle: Capital Punishment and the Late Liberal State*.

72. Austin Sarat, *When the State Kills: Capital Punishment and the American Condition* (Princeton, NJ: Princeton University Press, 2001).

73. Upendra Baxi, *Marx, Law, and Justice* (Bombay: N.M. Tripathi, 1993), 19, emphasis added. In comparison to the state's violence, the nonstate actors lack what Baxi calls the "authoritative language with which to camouflage their behavior; their violence is for all to see and feel." Ibid.

74. Jayanth K. Krishnan, "Lawyering for a Cause and Experiences from Abroad," *California Law Review* 94 (2006): 575-615; S. P. Sathe, *Judicial Activism in India: Transgressing Borders and Enforcing Limits* (New Delhi: Oxford University Press, 2002); Gary Jacobsohn, "Three Models of Secular Constitutional Development: India, Israel, and the United States," *Studies in American Political Development* 10 (1996).

75. Krishnan, "Lawyering for a Cause."

76. Rajeev Dhavan, *The Supreme Court of India: A Socio-Legal Critique of Its Juristic Techniques* (Bombay: Tripathi, 1977), 1-6.

77. Upendra Baxi, *The Crisis of the Indian Legal System* (New Delhi: Vikas Publishing House, 1982), 42-44.

78. Here he is obviously referring to the formulations of dependencia by Latin American theorists. Ibid.

79. Baxi, *The Crisis of the Indian Legal System*, 43.

80. Some prison reform cases refer to the continuation of colonial laws that penalize even the wearing of a Gandhi cap. See *Sunil Batra etc. v. Delhi Administration and Ors etc.*, 1978. http://judis.nic.in/supremecourt/qrydisp.asp?tfnm=5022 (last visited August 5, 2005).

81. *Satpathy v. Dani* (1978) 2 SCC 424, 431.

82. Baxi, *The Crisis of the Indian Legal System*, 42-43.

83. Scholars have not only made comparisons between India and the United States but have also referred to the debates in Israel on the legality of torture. The Justice Landau Commission looked into the allegations of torture by the General Security Service (GSS) interrogators and upheld the use of "moderate physical pressure" if based on necessity, making Israel the only democracy that upheld torture for a while. Under tremendous national and international pressure, the Supreme Court of Israel gave a judgment that moderate physical pressure could not be used under existing law although they did say that if the legislature wanted, it could pass a law specifically for that. The Israeli debate really contributed to the discussions in the United States regarding the legality of torture—especially with Alan Dershowitz being an important participant in both contexts. *Commission of Inquiry into the Methods of Investigation of the General Security Service Regarding Hostile Terrorist Activity (Justice Landau Commission Report)* (1987). Excerpts (and other critical engagements) published in *Israel Law Review* 23 (1989): 146-92. Alan Dershowitz, "Is It Necessary to Apply Physical Pressure to Terrorists and to Lie about It?" *Israel Law Review* 23 (1989): 193-200; Dershowitz, "Let America Take Its Cues from Israel Regarding Torture," *Jewish World Review* (Jan. 30, 2002). http://www.jewishworldreview.com (last visited December 28, 2003).

84. Asad, "On Torture, or Cruel, Inhuman, and Degrading Treatment"; Abdul-
lahi Ahmed An-Naim, "Towards a Cross-Cultural Approach to Defining International
Standards of Human Rights: The Meaning of Cruel, Inhuman, or Degrading Treatment or
Punishment," in *Human Rights in Cross-Cultural Perspectives,*edited by Abdullahi Ahmed
An-Naim, 19-43 (Philadelphia: University of Pennsylvania Press, 1992). On colonial concep-
tions of "inhuman" acts see Nicholas B. Dirks, "The Policing of Tradition: Colonialism and
Anthropology in Southern India," *Comparative Studies in Society and History* 39 (1997): 182-
212. For critiques of Western notion of pain, see Veena Das et al., *Social Suffering.*

85. Ibid.

86. David Garland, *The Culture of Control: Crime and Social Order in Contemporary
Society* (Chicago: University of Chicago Press, 2002), ix.

87. This was how Sutherland was introduced for the Golden Globe award nomination
in 2008. *Redemption* was actually released as a film between the sixth and seventh seasons.

88. See *Investigation into FBI Allegations of Detainee Abuse at Guantanamo Bay, Cuba
Detention Facility (Schmidt Report)* (April 2005). http://balkin.blogspot.com/Schmidt%20
Furlow%20report.pdf (last visited December 20, 2005).

89. Jean Elshtain, "Reflection on the Problem of 'Dirty Hands,'" in *Torture: A Collection,* edited by Sanford Levinson, 77-92 (New York: Oxford University Press, 2004), 77,
emphasis added.

90. Ariel Dorfman, "Foreword: The Tyranny of Terror; Is Torture Inevitable in Our
Century and Beyond?" in *Torture: A Collection*, edited by Sanford Levinson, 3-18 (New
York: Oxford University Press, 2004).

91. Article 2 states, "No exceptional circumstances whatsoever, whether a state of war
or a threat of war, internal political instability or any other public emergency, may be
invoked as a justification of torture." http://www.unhchr.ch/html/menu3/b/h_cat39.htm
(last visited, March 22, 2006).

92. Dorfman, "The Tyranny of Terror," 17.

93. Žižek, quoted in Lukes, "Liberal Democratic Torture," 1. Slavoj Žižek, *Welcome to
the Desert of the Real* (London: Verso, 2002), 103-4.

94. See Steven Lukes, who does not start off with the assumption of an absolutist
stance but comes to the conclusion that torture, even in the rarest of cases, cannot be used
since it is incompatible with a liberal democracy. Ibid.

95. See Baxi's reading of Bentham scholars like Twining, Upendra Baxi, *The Crisis of
the Indian Legal System*, 140.

96. Henry Shue, "Torture," in *Torture: A Collection*, edited by Sanford Levinson, 47-60
(New York: Oxford University Press, 2004).

97. Ibid.

98. Ibid., 57. See critiques of the "ticking bomb scenario" by Scheppele and Rejali. Kim
Lane Scheppele, "Hypothetical Torture in the War on Terrorism," *Journal of National Secu-
rity Law & Policy* 1 (2005): 285 – 340; Darius Rejali, *Torture and Democracy* (Princeton, NJ:
Princeton University Press, 2007).

99. Alan Dershowitz, *Why Terrorism Works* (New Haven, CT: Yale University Press,
2002).

100. Dershowitz, "Is There a Torturous Road to Justice?" *Los Angeles Times*, November
8, 2001. http://proquest.umi.com/pqdweb?did=88868293&sid=1&Fmt=3&clientId=523
9&RQT=309&VName=PQD (last visited May 15, 2006). See also Michael Levin, "The

Case for Torture, 2001." http://ontology.buffalo.edu/smith//courses01/rrtw/levin.htm (last visited December 30, 2003).

101. Alan Dershowitz, "Tortured Reasoning," in *Torture: A Collection*, edited by Sanford Levinson, 257-80 (New York: Oxford University Press, 2004), 259.

102. Shue, "Torture," 57.

103. Scarry, "Five Errors in the Reasoning of Alan Dershowitz," in *Torture: A Collection*, edited by Sanford Levinson, 281-90 (New York: Oxford University Press, 2004), 285.

104. Ibid., 282-83.

105. Michael Walzer, "Political Action: The Problem of Dirty Hands," in *Torture: A Collection*, edited by Sanford Levinson, 61-76 (New York: Oxford University Press, 2004).

106. Ibid., 71-74.

107. Henry Shue, "Torture in Dreamland: Disposing of the Ticking Bomb," *Case Western Reserve Journal of International Law* 37 (2006): 231-39, 238.

108. Ibid., 236.

109. See Ray and Ratner for the argument that existing laws are adequate for addressing the problem of terrorism. Michael Ratner and Ellen Ray, *Guantánamo: What the World Should Know* (White River Junction, VT: Chelsea Green Publishing, 2004). For a discussion on suspension of laws, see Mark Tushnet, "Emergencies and the Idea of Constitutionalism," in *The Constitution in Wartime: Beyond Alarmism and Complacency*, edited by Mark Tushnet, 39-54 (Durham, NC: Duke University Press, 2005).

110. Bruce Ackerman, *Before the Next Attack: Preserving Civil Liberties in an Age of Terrorism* (New Haven, CT: Yale University Press, 2006).

111. Ibid., 42.

112. Ibid.

113. David Cole, "The Priority of Morality: The Emergency Constitution's Blind Spot," *Yale Law Journal* 13 (2004): 1753-1800, 1758.

114. Ibid., 1768.

115. Eric A. Posner and Adrian Vermeule, *Terror in the Balance: Security, Liberty, and the Courts* (New York: Oxford University Press, 2007), 184.

116. Ibid., 5.

117. Richard A. Posner, *Not a Suicide Pact: The Constitution in a Time of National Emergency* (New York: Oxford University Press, 2006), 85.

118. Ibid., 81-82.

119. Ackerman, *Before the Next Attack*, 109. Ackerman accepts the necessity of detention in some instances, but he completely rejects the use of torture, even during emergencies. Thus, for Ackerman, the Emergency Constitution (despite its extraordinary nature) has to be compatible with the "principles of liberal democracy." Interestingly, for him, liberal democracy is represented by the absence of torture and yet not affected by the use of mass detentions, once again reinforcing the argument made earlier that torture is by definition seen as impermissible in a democracy. Ibid., 109-12.

120. Posner, *Not a Suicide Pact*, 83.

121. Thomas P. Crocker, "Book Review: Torture, with Apologies of *Terror in the Balance; Security, Liberty, and the Courts*, by Eric A. Posner and Adrian Vermeule (New York: Oxford University Press, 2007) and Richard A. Posner, "Not a Suicide Pact," *Texas Law Review* 86 (Feb. 2008): 569-613, 611.

122. Ibid., 612.

123. Giorgio Agamben, *State of Exception*, translated by Kevin Attell (Chicago: University of Chicago Press, 2005).

124. Ibid.

125. Ibid., 3.

126. Michelle Brown, "'Setting the Conditions' for Abu Ghraib: The Prison Nation Abroad," *American Quarterly* 57 (2005): 973-98, 975-76.

127. Judith Butler, "Indefinite Detention," in *Precarious Life: The Powers of Mourning and Violence*, 50-100 (New York: Verso, 2004), 53.

128. President's Memo, "Humane Treatment of al Qaeda and Taliban Detainees" (February 7, 2002), in *Torture and Truth: America, Abu Ghraib, and the War on Terror*, edited by Mark Danner, 105-6 (New York: New York Review of Books, 2004), 105.

129. Memorandum for the President from Alberto R. Gonzales, "Decision re Application of the Geneva Convention on Prisoners of War to the Conflict with al Qaeda and the Taliban" (January 25, 2002), in Danner, ed., *Torture and Truth*, 83-87, 84. It is important to note that even scholars critical of this position do recognize the limitations in the Geneva Conventions in providing protections to all. See Scott Michaelson and Scott Cutler Shershow, "The Laws of War and Sovereign Exception," 2004. http://usa.mediamonitors.net/layout/set/print/content/view/full/3849 (last visited April 22, 2006). See also Judith Butler, "Guantánamo Limbo," *Nation*, April 1, 2002.

130. Carl Schmitt, *Political Theology: Four Chapters on the Concept of Sovereignty*, translated by George Schwab (Cambridge: MIT Press, 1985), 5.

131. Joseph Margulies, *Guantanamo and the Abuse of Presidential Power* (New York: Simon & Schuster, 2006), 40.

132. Ibid., 45.

133. Fleur Johns, "Guantanamo Bay and the Annihilation of the Exception," *European Journal of International Law* 16 (2005): 613-35, 620.

134. While many adopting this framework of exception have asked for a return to the law nationally and internationally, Johns suggests that the very conception of the Schmittian exception in this context is flawed because it relieves the sovereign from agonizing about decisions in an exception. Ibid., 631.

135. Ujjwal Kumar Singh, *The State, Democracy, and Anti-Terror Laws in India* (New Delhi: Sage, 2007), 18.

136. Note the language of "exceptional" being used here even though Suresh does look at the relationship between the ordinary and the extraordinary. Mayur Suresh, "Exposing the Repressive Potential of 'Ordinary' Law." Alternative Law Forum, Bangalore. www.altlawforum.org/Resources/Humanrights/seminar proceedings.doc (last visited March 30, 2009).

137. Ananya Vajpeyi, "The Bare Life of S. A. R. Geelani," *Outlook*, February 11, 2005.

138. See Giorgio Agamben, *Homo Sacer: Sovereign Power and Bare Life*, translated by Daniel Heller-Roazen (Stanford: Stanford University Press, 1995).

139. Peter Fitzpatrick, "Bare Sovereignty: *Homo Sacer* and the Insistence of Law," *Theory and Event* 5 (2001). http://muse.jhu.edu/journals/theory_&_event.

140. Jonathan Simon, "The Vicissitudes of Law's Violence," in *Law, Violence, and the Possibility of Justice*, edited by Austin Sarat, 17-48. (Princeton, NJ: Princeton University Press, 2001).

141. Ibid. Simon, for instance, points toward the change in penal history in the United States from an emphasis on torture to the emergence of the prison system along with a general disciplining of society (as Foucault suggests happened in Europe). Another phase within the penal system was the emphasis on rehabilitation, especially in the 1950s and 1970s. This was replaced by retributivist notions and, in recent times, the reemergence of revenge. By failing to look at the relationship between law and violence historically, Cover failed to address the possibilities and impossibilities with which this project was fraught.

142. Waldron, "Torture and Positive Law," note 207.

143. Sarat, *When the State Kills*; Kaufman-Osborn, *From Noose to Needle*. See critique in Jinee Lokaneeta, "Revenge and the Spectacular Execution: The Timothy McVeigh Case," in *Studies in Law, Politics, and Society* 33, edited by Austin Sarat and Patricia Ewick, 201-21 (Oxford: Elsevier, 2004). Even if they do not argue that explicitly, their framework assumes that.

144. Ibid.

145. Sarat, ed., *Law, Violence, and the Possibility of Justice*; and Kaufman-Osborn, *From Noose to Needle*.

146. *Report on Torture: Amnesty International* (New York: Farrar, Straus, Giroux, 1975).

147. Nigel S. Rodley, *The Treatment of Prisoners under International Law* (New York: Clarendon, 1999).

148. *Torture Worldwide: An Affront to Human Dignity* (New York: Amnesty International, 2000). *Broken Bodies, Shattered Minds: Torture and Ill Treatment of Women* (New York: Amnesty International, 2001). On torture in the United States, see Human Rights Watch release, "The Legal Prohibition against Torture." http://www.hrw.org/press/2001/11/TortureQandA.htm (last visited January 15, 2004). Even before Amnesty and other groups highlighted the issue of torture, Rejali notes that it was writers, lawyers, and intellectuals who first started writing about the presence of torture, whether it was Pierre Vidal-Naquet in the context of France using torture in Algeria (and within France) or Noam Chomsky and Edward Hermann in the context of U.S. distribution of torture techniques. Darius Rejali, *Torture and Democracy*. See Winston P. Nagan and Lucie Atkins, "The International Law of Torture: From Universal Prescription to Effective Application and Enforcement," *Harvard Environmental Law Review* 14 (2001): 87-121.

149. Ibid.

150. Sarat and Kearns, *Law's Violence*, 8.

151. According to Rejali, the national security model was most visible in the context of the French in Algeria, where the bureaucrats in the form of the French army took over the use of torture to hold onto Algeria at all costs and all democratic institutions, including the press, the legislature, and the judiciary, failed to stop them. Darius Rejali, *Torture and Democracy*, 49.

152. Rejali takes Japan as an example of this model in contemporary times due to a "legal environment, reinforced by cultural dispositions, [that] creates an overreliance on confessions" strengthened by the use of torture in some instances, particularly in the case of long-term preventive detention centers. Ibid., 55.

153. Rejali writes, "What drives torture in these cases is neither war nor a permissive legal environment, but informal arrangements among police, residents, and businesses to shape the urban landscape." Ibid., 60.

154. Ibid, 63.

155. John T. Parry, *Understanding Torture: Law, Violence, and Political Identity* (Ann Arbor: University of Michigan Press, 2010), 12.

156. Article 1 of the UN *Convention against Torture and Other Cruel, Inhuman, or Degrading Treatment or Punishment*, 1985. http://www.unhchr.ch/html/menu3/b/h_cat39.htm (last visited, March 22, 2006).

157. The UN definition is criticized by international law scholars for not defining torture clearly and for failing to focus on "negligence of the government" and "private individuals," and in particular for not clarifying the meaning of "lawful sanctions." Ahcene Boulesbaa, *The UN Convention on Torture and the Prospects for Enforcement* (The Hague: Martinus Nijhoff, 1999).

158. If absence of torture and unnecessary violence is such a distinguishing feature of democracies, the presence and, indeed, as I argue, the consistent space for excess violence do raise the question whether these two countries can continue to be called liberal democracies. I thank sociologist Anand Chakravarti and feminist historian Uma Chakravarti (both also active in the civil liberties movement in India) for pushing me toward this question, particularly in the context of India, and even though my conclusions differ somewhat from theirs, they did force me to articulate what exactly makes me conceptualize these two countries as liberal democracies.

159. Cover, "Violence and the Word"; Elaine Scarry, *Body in Pain: The Making and Unmaking of the World* (New York: Oxford University Press, 1985); John T. Parry, "The Shape of Modern Torture: Extraordinary Rendition and Ghost Detainees," *Melbourne Journal of International Law* 6 (2005): 516-33.

160. Waldron, "Torture and Positive Law," 1727.

CHAPTER 1

1. *Brown v. Mississippi*, 297 U.S. 278, 282 (1936).

2. Jonathan Alter, "Time to Think about Torture," *Newsweek*, November 5, 2001. http://proquest.umi.com/pqdweb?did=86957963&sid=2&Fmt=3&clientId=5239&RQT=309&VName=PQD (last visited May 10, 2006).

3. Mail Call, "Torture and the Modern World," *Newsweek*, December 17, 2001. http://proquest.umi.com/pqdweb?did=96371833&sid=2&Fmt=3&clientId=5239&RQT=309&VName=PQD (last visited May 10, 2006).

4. See news stories that highlight the use of torture in nondemocracies, for instance, "China Torture 'Still Widespread,'" BBC News, December 2, 2005. http://news.bbc.co.uk/2/hi/asia-pacific/4491026.stm (last visited December 30, 2008); "Iran: Torture Used to Suppress Dissent," *Human Rights Watch*, June 6, 2004. http://www.hrw.org/en/news/2004/06/06/iran-torture-used-suppress-dissent (last visited December 30, 2008).

5. Cruel and unusual punishment is primarily an issue in the arena of punishment—penal torture. Here I will restrict myself to discussing the question of torture during interrogations.

6. The United States Constitution. http://www.law.cornell.edu/constitution/constitution.billofrights.html#amendmentv (last visited May 15, 2006).

7. William Hawkins's *Pleas of the Crown*, 1787, quoted in *Bram v. United States*, 168 U.S. 532, 547 (1897), emphasis added.

8. M. K. B. Darmer, "Beyond Bin Laden and Lindh: Confessions Law in an Age of Terrorism," *Cornell Journal of Law and Public Policy* 12 (2003): 319-72.

9. The Fifth Amendment self-incrimination clause was incorporated in *Malloy v. Hogan*, 378 U.S. 1 (1964).

10. Joshua Dressler, *Cases and Materials on Criminal Law* (St. Paul, MN: Thomson/West, 1999).

11. Michael J. Klarman, "The Racial Origins of Modern Criminal Procedure," *Michigan Law Review* 99 (2000): 48-97.

12. *Brown v. Mississippi*, 297 U.S. 278, 285 (1936).

13. Ibid., 285-86.

14. Klarman, "The Racial Origins of Modern Criminal Procedure," 82-83.

15. *Ashcraft v. Tennessee*, 322 U.S. 143, 154 (1944).

16. Ibid.

17. Darmer, "Beyond Bin Laden and Lindh," 329-31.

18. *Spano v. New York*, 360 U.S. 315 (1959) on the will being overborne; see also *Blackburn v. Alabama*, 361 U.S. 199 (1960) on "rational intellect and a free will," at 208.

19. See Richard A. Leo and George C. Thomas III, *The Miranda Debate: Law, Justice, and Policing* (Boston: Northeastern University Press, 1998).There were other attempts made by the Court, including using the McNabb (and Mallory) rules regarding taking the suspect to the nearest magistrate "without unnecessary delay" as the basis of rejecting the confession. *McNabb v. United States*, 318 U.S. 332 (1943). The Mallory decision strengthened this protection by interpreting unnecessary delay as meaning no "eliciting damaging statements" before taking a suspect to the magistrate. *Mallory v. United States*, 354 U.S. 449 (1957). Despite the standards regarding voluntariness and its effects on reliability of confessions, even in 1964, in the Escobedo case, the Court stated that "history has shown us that a system that relies on confessions will be less reliable and more subject to abuses than one which depends on extrinsic evidence independently secured through skillful investigation." *Escobedo v. Illinois*, 378 U.S. 478, 488-89 (1964).

20. Miranda warnings: A person has the right to remain silent and be informed that anything that the person says can and will be used against the individual in court. The person has to be made aware of the right to counsel and the right to have an attorney present during questioning if desired. If the person cannot afford an attorney, an attorney will be appointed by the state. *Miranda v. Arizona*, 384 U.S. 436 (1966).

21. The four cases were *Miranda v. Arizona* (where the defendant was subject to interrogation in a special room and a confession gained), *Vignera v. New York* (where the defendant signed an inculpatory statement after an oral confession), *Westover v. United States* (involving a lengthy interrogation conducted during the night and morning and given over to the FBI), and *California v. Stewart* (suspect interrogated for five days in station on nine separate occasions and inculpatory statement signed).

22. *Malloy v. Hogan*, 378 U.S. 1, 8 (1964).

23. *Grunewald v. United States*, 233 F.2d 556, 581-82 (1956).

24. *Miranda v. Arizona*, 384 U.S. 436 (1966), 460.

25. See Austin Sarat, *When The State Kills: Capital Punishment and the American Condition* (Princeton, NJ: Princeton University Press, 2001).

26. *Gregg v. Georgia*, 428 U.S. 153 (1976). This is only one example of the wide variety of cases that elaborate on the degree of pain that can be allowed in an execution.

27. Ibid., 173.

28. See *Baze v. Rees*, 128 S. Ct. 1520 (2008).

29. See Austin Sarat on the attempts by the Court to determine whether executions involved unnecessary pain or not and the problems in determining the distinctions. "Killing Me Softly: Capital Punishment and the Technologies for Taking Life," in Sarat, *When the State Kills*, 60-84.

30. Stanley Cohen, *States of Denial: Knowing about Atrocities and Suffering* (Cambridge, England: Polity Press, 2001), 104.

31. See supra note 4.

32. Zechariah Chafee Jr., Walter H. Pollak, and Carl Stern, *The Third Degree: Report to the National Commission on Law Observance and Enforcement (June 1931)* (New York: Arno Press and The New York Times, 1969).The 1931 report was reprinted in the form of a book titled *The Third Degree*. In an online introduction to the report on lawlessness, Samuel Walker writes that the origin of this particular report was mysterious. This is the case because there seemed to be no particular interest group lobbying for an inquiry into police conduct. The three authors were well-known civil-liberties activists, and this was reflected in their report, which was in contrast to other reports on criminal procedure that advocated further liberties for police actions. Samuel Walker, "Introductory Note on the Wickersham Commission Report," 1997. http://www.lexisnexis.com/academic/guides/jurisprudence/wickersham.asp (last visited May 15, 2004).

33. The Wickersham Commission Report referred to three main reasons why the third degree was illegal. First of all, it was against the principle of assuming a person to be innocent until proved otherwise. Secondly, the use of the third degree was violative of the right against self-incrimination. Finally, there was a rule that compelled confessions could not be introduced as evidence in a trial. Chafee Jr., Pollak, and Stern, *The Third Degree*, 24-37.

34. Ibid.

35. Ibid., 19.

36. For instance, the report considered questioning by itself as a justified interrogation method, but the same was termed as third degree by the authors of this report if the interrogation consisted of protracted relay questioning. Ibid. See, in contrast, the discussion on definitions of torture in chapter 2.

37. See influence of British police on the American model. Edward Peters, *Torture* (Philadelphia: University of Pennsylvania Press, 1996), 109-14. See also Samuel Walker, *The Police in America: An Introduction* (Boston: McGraw Hill College, 1999).

38. Ibid.

39. Cohen, *States of Denial*. Cohen has a broader project that considers not just official denials but also personal denials by bystanders and observers, but here I primarily draw upon his formulation of state denials.

40. Ibid.

41. Richard A. Leo, *Police Interrogation and American Justice* (Cambridge, MA: Harvard University Press, 2008), 70.

42. Chafee Jr., Pollak, and Stern, *The Third Degree*, 38-44.

43. Ibid., 42-43.

44. Duncan Matheson, "The Technique of the American Detective," *Annals of the American Academy of Political and Social Science* 146 (1929): 214-18, 218.

45. Cohen, *States of Denial*, 106.

46. Ibid., 108.

47. Greer, "'We Don't Torture People in America': Coercive Interrogation in the Global Village," *New Political Science* 26 (2004): 371-87, 386.

48. Leo, *Police Interrogation and American Justice*, 46.

49. Theodore A. Bingham, "Administration of Criminal Law: Third Degree System,"*Annals of the American Academy of Political and Social Science* 36 (1910): 11-15, 13.

50. Ibid., 15, emphasis added.

51. In 1930, a Committee on Lawless Enforcement of Law wrote that the third degree was being used throughout the United States. While the law stated that the arrested person should be taken before the magistrate as soon as possible, in reality the person was kept in detention incommunicado in order for the police to use the third degree to gain confessions. The police and other officials "work" on the prisoner, which could imply just "severe cross-examination" but could actually range from keeping detainees in a cold, dark cell or a sweat box (heated until he or she confessed) to whipping and beating with rubber hose or fists to kicking to threats. The 1930 report also mentions the use of electric chairs and bright lights on the suspect's face as methods of gaining confessions. Quoted in Chafee Jr., Pollak, and Stern, *The Third Degree*, 46-47.

52. Michael T. Taussig, *Defacement: Public Secrecy and the Labor of the Negative* (Stanford: Stanford University Press, 1999), 5.

53. Richard A. Leo, *Police Interrogation and American Justice*, 55.

54. Samuel Walker, "Introductory Note on the Wickersham Commission Report." The Wickersham Commission's *Report on Lawlessness in Law Enforcement*, in conclusion, provides very few recommendations for remedying the situation except creating a will of the community. "The real remedy lies in the will of the community. If the community insists upon higher standards in police, prosecutors, and judges, the third degree will cease to be a systematic practice." Chafee Jr., Pollak, and Stern, *The Third Degree*, 191.

55. Welsh S. White, *Miranda's Waning Protections: Police Interrogation Practices after Dickerson* (Ann Arbor: University of Michigan Press, 2003), 20.

56. Chafee Jr., Pollak, and Stern, *The Third Degree*.

57. Martin Shapiro, *Courts: A Comparative and Political Analysis* (Chicago: University of Chicago Press, 1986).

58. Ibid., 2.

59. Ibid., 37.

60. There is a major debate within the fields of law and political science between those scholars who consider judicial decision making as being based on political attitudes (Jeffrey Segal and Harold Spaeth) and those who consider justices as strategic actors (Lee Epstein). See a brief discussion in Lee Epstein and Thomas G. Walker, *Constitutional Law for a Changing America* (Washington, DC: CQ Press, 2004). For an analysis of the weaknesses of these approaches and an articulation of an alternative approach to judicial decision making, namely, the historical interpretive approach, see Howard Gillman, "What's Law Got to Do with It? Judicial Behavioralists Test the 'Legal Model' of Judicial Decision Making," *Law and Social Inquiry* 26 (2001): 465-504.

61. *Brown v. State*, 173 Miss. 542, 563 (1935).

62. Judge Griffith in ibid., 579, emphasis added.

63. Chafee Jr., Pollak, and Stern, *The Third* Degree, 21.

64. *Miranda v. Arizona*, 384 U.S. 436, 448 (1966).

65. Susan Bandes, "Patterns of Injustice: Police Brutality in the Courts," *Buffalo Law Review* 47 (1999): 1275-1341; John T. Parry, "Escalation and Necessity: Defining Torture at Home and Abroad," in *Torture: A Collection*, edited by Sanford Levinson, 145-64 (New York: Oxford University Press, 2004). John T. Parry, "What Is Torture, Are We Doing It, and What If We Are?" *University of Pittsburgh Law Review* 64 (2003): 237-62.

66. J. E. Reid and Fred Inbau, *Criminal Interrogations and Confessions* (Baltimore, MD: Williams and Wilkins, 1986).

67. *Miranda v. Arizona*, 384 U.S. 436, 445 (1966).

68. Ibid., 455.

69. Ibid., 457.

70. Quoted in White, *Miranda's Waning Protections*, 44.

71. Ibid., 45.

72. Joseph D. Grano, *Confessions, Truth, and the Law* (Ann Arbor: University of Michigan Press, 1996), 104-6.

73. See in contrast *Lisenba v. California*, where a murder suspect, James, was interrogated for prolonged periods of time, up to forty-eight hours, and over different days deprived of sleep without a formal warrant, and even though there was conflicting testimony about whether he had been beaten up, everyone did agree that he was slapped. However, the Court in that case decided that there was no due process violation because there was conflicting testimony about the coercion and neither the coercion nor the threats and promises were extreme. *Lisenba v. California*, 314 U.S. 219 (1941).

74. *Chambers v. Florida*, 309 U.S. 227, 239 (1940), emphasis added.

75. Ibid., 239.

76. *Miranda v. Arizona*, 384 U.S. 436, 445, 507 (1966), emphasis in original.

77. Ibid., 515, emphasis in original.

78. Ibid., 505.

79. Ibid., 508. Yale Kamisar, *Police Interrogations and Confessions: Essays in Law and Policy* (Ann Arbor: University of Michigan Press, 1980); Darmer, "Beyond Bin Laden and Lindh," 329-31.

80. White, *Miranda's Waning Protections*, 48.

81. Peter Brooks, *Troubling Confessions: Speaking Guilt in Law and Literature* (Chicago: University of Chicago Press, 2000).

82. This term is taken from Yale Kamisar's famous essay and formulation questioning why the protections in the courtroom were not available at the police station before Miranda. Yale Kamisar, "Equal Justice in the Gatehouse and Mansions of American Criminal Procedure: From Powell to Gideon, from Escobedo to...," in *The Miranda Debate: Law, Justice, and Policing*, edited by Richard A. Leo and George C. Thomas III, 15-34 (Boston: Northeastern University Press, 1998).

83. See Grano on how the laws on police interrogations can be considered "overly restrictive and formalistic." Grano, *Confessions, Truth, and the Law*, 3. See critique of Grano in White, *Miranda's Waning Protections*.

84. White, *Miranda's Waning Protections*; Kamisar, *Police Interrogations and Confessions*.

85. Liva Baker, *Miranda: Crime, Law, and Politics* (New York: Atheneum, 1985).

86. *Dickerson v. United States*, 530 U.S. 428, 432 (2000).

87. This act of Congress took courage from the dissents in Miranda as well. In fact, the dissenting justices (Justices Harlan, Clark, and White) in Miranda had emphasized the due process clause of the Fourteenth Amendment as well the "totality of circumstances test" rather than the Fifth Amendment and Bram as the basis of excluding coerced confessions. *Miranda v. Arizona*, 384 U.S. 436, 502 (1966).

88. See Justice Scalia's dissent that the only way Miranda could have been upheld was by clearly stating that the act of Congress was unconstitutional. However, since the majority could not state that position due to previous cases claiming Miranda rights as prophylactic rights, not constitutional ones, he argued that the violation of Miranda was not a violation of the Fifth Amendment and that the Court had overreached its power and become antidemocratic. *Dickerson v. United States*, 530 U.S. 428, 432 (2000).

89. Yale Kamisar, "William Pedric Lecture: Miranda Thirty-Five Years Later; A Close Look at the Majority and Dissenting Opinions in Dickersonm," *Arizona State Law Journal* 33 (2001): 387-428.

90. Ibid., 396.

91. In an earlier case, *Michigan v. Tucker*, 417 U.S. 433 (1974), the Miranda rights were stated to be prophylactic rights rather than rights protected by the Constitution.

92. George C. Thomas III, "The End of the Road for *Miranda v. Arizona*? On the History and Future of Rules for Police Interrogation," *American Criminal Law Review* 37 (2000): 1-39, 9.

93. Ibid., 39.

94. Richard Leo, "Miranda's Revenge: Police Interrogation as a Confidence Game," *Law and Society Review* 30 (1996): 259-88.

95. White, *Miranda's Waning Protections*, 122.

96. Ibid., 122-23.

97. Peter Brooks, *Troubling Confessions*, 4.

98. Ibid., 6.

99. Ibid., 81.

100. Leo, *Police Interrogation and American Justice*, 5-6.

101. Peter Brooks, *Troubling Confessions*, 6.

102. Ibid., 86.

103. *Miranda v. Arizona*, 384 U.S. 436, 457-58 (1966).

104. Justice White in ibid., 533.

105. Brooks, *Troubling Confessions*, 87.

106. Marianne Constable, *Just Silences: The Limits and Possibilities of Modern Law* (Princeton, NJ: Princeton University Press, 2005), 156.

107. Using Austin's work, Constable refers to the constative and the perlocutionary effects of the Miranda decision while ignoring the illocutionary aspect of the warnings as speech act. See discussion in ibid., 164-65.

108. Many scholars agree that after Miranda, only "deception" or "trickery" is allowed. Richard A. Leo, "From Coercion to Deception: The Changing Nature of Police Interrogation in America," in Leo and Thomas, ed., *The Miranda Debate*, 65-74; Leo does question the morality of these "soft" methods. Jerome H. Skolnick, "American Interrogation: From Torture to Trickery," in Levinson, ed., *Torture*, 105-27.

109. Tony Karon, "Times Square Bomb Arrest Raises U.S. Security Questions," May 5, 2010. http://www.time.com/time/nation/article/0,8599,1987126,00.html (last visited May 25, 2010).

110. *Haynes v. Washington*, 373 U.S. 503 (1963).

111. Ibid., 519, emphasis added.

112. *New York v. Quarles*, 467 U.S. 649 (1984).

113. In this case, the accused was apprehended in a supermarket for attempted rape. The officer found an empty gun holster on him and asked him the whereabouts of the gun without giving him the Miranda warnings. After the gun was found, the suspect was given the Miranda warnings and then asked certain questions. Chief Justice Rehnquist stated that since there was a gun somewhere in the supermarket, there were reasonable grounds for bypassing the safeguards. Ibid.

114. Ibid., 657.

115. Ibid., 658-59, emphasis added.

116. Ibid., 685, emphasis added.

117. Ibid., 686, emphasis added.

118. See discussion in introduction.

119. Thomas P. Crocker, "Overcoming Necessity: Torture and the State of Constitutional Culture," *SMU Law Review* 61 (Spring 2008): 221-79, 249.

120. See Alan Dershowitz. *Why Terrorism Works* (New Haven, CT: Yale University Press, 2002). In this case, a cab driver, Louis Gachelin, was requested by passengers to take their luggage to their apartment. He was then taken hostage at gunpoint and gagged and his family was asked for ransom. The brother, accompanied by the police, agreed to meet Leon, and when Leon drew a gun, the police caught hold of him and asked him about Gachelin's location. *Leon v. Wainwright*, 734 F.2d 770 (1984).

121. Ibid., 771.

122. Ibid., 773, emphasis added.

123. *Chavez v. Martinez*, 538 U.S. 760 (2003).

124. Qualified immunity entails immunity from being sued for damages for constitutional or statutory violations (42 U.S.C. § 1983), if the behavior is not a violation of established constitutional rights that a "reasonable person" may be aware of. *Chavez v. Martinez*, 538 U.S. 760, 855 (2003).

125. *Martinez v. City of Oxnard*, 270 F.3d 852, 854 (2001).

126. *Chavez v. Martinez*, 538 U.S. 760 (2003), 773.

127. Ibid., 775.

128. Ibid., 775.

129. Ibid., 776.

130. John Parry, "Escalation and Necessity," in Levinson, ed., *Torture*, 158-60.

131. *Chavez v. Martinez*, 538 U.S. 760, 783-84 (2003), emphasis added.

132. Ibid., 789-90.

133. Skolnick, "American Interrogation," in Levinson, ed., *Torture*, 121.

134. Oral argument in *Chavez v. Martinez*, 2002. http://www.oyez.org/cases/2000-2009/2002/2002_01_1444/argument/ (last visited December 20, 2007).

135. Ibid.

136. Ibid.

137. Ibid.

138. Ibid.

139. Skolnick, "American Interrogation," in Levinson, ed., *Torture*, 123.

140. Coleen Rowley's memo to FBI director Robert Mueller, May 21, 2002. http://www.time.com/time/covers/1101020603/memo.html.

CHAPTER 2

1. The quotation used as the first part of the chapter title can be found at Mail Call, "Torture and the Modern World," *Newsweek*, December 17, 2001. http://proquest.umi.com/pqdweb?did=96371833&sid=2&Fmt=3&clientId=5239&RQT=309&VName=PQD (last visited May 10, 2006).

2. Mike Dorning, "Prisoner Abuse Poses Peril for Bush," *Chicago Tribune*, July 12, 2004.

3. Daniel Benjamin, "Perils of the Dark Side: U.S. Excesses in the Terror War Are Causing a Self-Defeating Backlash," *Time International*, December 12, 2005.

4. Lynne Cheney, wife of former U.S. vice president Dick Cheney, gave the *Daily Show* host, Jon Stewart, a Darth Vader statue as a gift, clearly acknowledging the fact that the former vice president was being compared to the *Star Wars* character. http://starwarsblog.wordpress.com/2007/10/11/darth-vader-gift-on-the-daily-show/ (last visited January 30, 2008).

5. George Bush's Nomination Acceptance Speech, Republican Convention, 2004. http://www.presidentialrhetoric.com/campaign/rncspeeches/bush.html.

6. Giorgio Agamben, *State of Exception*, translated by Kevin Attell (Chicago: University of Chicago Press, 2005).

7. The torture memo is the memo signed by Jay S. Bybee though written by John Yoo. Lisa Hajjar had very early on noted the significance of actors such as John Yoo, who had written this memo and who had also been the main state official to put forward the arguments about the nonapplicability of Geneva Conventions to the "war on terror." Lisa Hajjar, "What's the Matter with Yoo? The Crime of Torture and the Role of Lawyers," paper presented at Law and Society Association Annual Meeting, Las Vegas, 2005. Bybee worked as an assistant attorney general in the Office of Legal Counsel at the U.S. Department of Justice from 2001 to 2003. John Yoo worked as a deputy assistant attorney general in the Office of Legal Counsel at the U.S. Department of Justice from 2001 to 2003. Memorandum for Alberto R. Gonzales, Counsel to the President, from U.S. Department of Justice, Office of the Attorney General, Jay S. Bybee (August 1, 2002), "Re: Standards of Conduct for Interrogation under 18 U.S.C. §§2340 – 2340A," in *Torture and Truth: America, Abu Ghraib, and the War on Terror*, edited by Mark Danner, 115 – 66 (New York: New York Review of Books, 2004).

8. Kim Lane Scheppele, "Hypothetical Torture in the War on Terrorism," *Journal of National Security Law & Policy* 1 (2005): 285-340, 289.

9. Agamben, *State of Exception*, 3.

10. Judith Butler, "Guantánamo Limbo," *Nation*, April 1, 2002.

11. Nasser Hussain, "Beyond Norm and Exception: Guantanamo," *Critical Inquiry* (Summer 2007): 734-53, 739.

12. Ibid., 741.

13. Ibid.

14. Fleur Johns, "Guantánamo Bay and the Annihilation of the Exception," *European Journal of International Law* 16 (2005): 613-35, 618.

15. Hussain, "Beyond Norm and Exception," 735.

16. Danner, ed., *Torture and Truth*. Diane Marie Amann, "Abu Ghraib," *University of Pennsylvania Law Review* 153 (2005): 2085-2141.

17. Memorandum for Commander, Joint Task Force 170, "Request for Approval of Counter-Resistance Strategies" (October 11, 2001), in Danner, ed., *Torture and Truth*, 167-68. Memorandum for the Commander, U.S. Southern Command, "Counter Resistance Techniques" (January 15, 2003) (Signed by Secretary Rumsfeld), in Danner, ed., *Torture and Truth*, 183.

18. Press Briefing by White House Counsel, Judge Alberto Gonzales, DOD General Counsel, William Haynes, DOD Deputy General Counsel, Daniel Dell'Orto, and Army Deputy Chief of Staff for Intelligence, General Keith Alexander, June 22, 2004. http://www.whitehouse.gov/news/releases/2004/06/20040622-14.html (last visited July 6, 2004).

19. See Paul Kahn, *Sacred Violence: Torture, Terror, and Sovereignty* (Ann Arbor: University of Michigan Press, 2008), 9.

20. Indeed, one could argue that the Bybee memo was more crisis generating than even the recent memos precisely because now a lot of documents are emerging as representing moments of the past rather than as representing the policies of a government in power.

21. This is the case because many of its sections did not explain why military interrogators would not be inhibited by the Uniform Code of Military Justice and other laws concerning the military. Marty Lederman, "Heather MacDonald's Dubious Counter-'Narrative' on Torture," January 1, 2005. http://balkin.blogspot.com/2005/01/heather-macdonalds-dubious-counter.html (last visited, June 26, 2007).

22. The Yoo memo is even more egregious because it went beyond the Bybee/Yoo memo and argued that the president, on the basis of commander-in-chief powers, could bypass all laws regarding interrogations—the Fifth and Eighth Amendments of the U.S. Constitution, as well as federal criminal laws—if the interrogations are "properly authorized interrogations of enemy combatants." Here I primarily focus on the commander-in-chief powers, the necessity defenses, and the definitions on torture that are common to both the Bybee and the Yoo memos. Memorandum for William J. Haynes II, General Counsel of the Department of Defense, from John Yoo, "Re: Military Interrogation of Alien Unlawful Combatants Held outside the United States," March 14, 2003. http://graphics8.nytimes.com/packages/pdf/national/OLC_Memo1.pdf (last visited January 30, 2008).

23. "Torture Memo Author John Yoo Responds to This Week's Revelations," Esquire.com, April 3, 2008. http://www.esquire.com/the-side/qa/john-yoo-responds (last visited December 30, 2008).

24. Memorandum for John A. Rizzo, Senior Deputy General Counsel, Central Intelligence Agency, from Steven Bradbury, Principal Deputy Assistant Attorney General, "Re: Application of 18 U.S.C. §§ 2340-2340A to Certain Techniques That May Be Used in the Interrogation of a High Value al Qaeda Detainee," May 10, 2005. http://luxmedia.com.edgesuite.net/aclu/olc_05102005_bradbury46pg.pdf (last visited January 23, 2011).

25. Memorandum for William J. Haynes II, General Counsel, Department of Defense, from John C. Yoo and Robert J. Delahunty, "Application of Treaties and Laws to al Qaeda and Taliban Detainees (January 9, 2002)," in *The Torture Papers: The Road to Abu Ghraib*,

edited by Karen J. Greenberg and Joshua L. Dratel, 38-79 (New York: Cambridge University Press, 2005), 43-47.

26. *Consideration of Reports Submitted by State Parties under Article 19 of the Convention: Initial Reports of the States Parties Due in 1995 (United States of America) to the United Nations Committee against Torture,* October 15, 1999. More discussion on the definitional issues in the Bybee memo will come later.

27. Bybee/Yoo Memo, in Danner, ed., *Torture and Truth.*

28. Bybee/Yoo Memo, in Danner, ed., *Torture and Truth,* 149.

29. Yoo, "Re: Military Interrogation of Alien Unlawful Combatants Held outside the United States," 1.

30. John Yoo, *The Powers of War and Peace: The Constitution and Foreign Affairs after 9/11* (Chicago: University of Chicago Press, 2005), 5.

31. David Schultz, Book Review of John Yoo, *The Powers of War and Peace: The Constitution and Foreign Affairs after 9/11* (Chicago: University of Chicago Press, 2005). http://www.bsos.umd.edu/gvpt/lpbr/subpages/reviews/yoo0106.htm (last visited January 30, 2008).

32. Yoo, *The Powers of War and Peace,* 18.

33. Yoo, "Re: Military Interrogation of Alien Unlawful Combatants Held outside the United States," 5.

34. Justice Thomas criticized the plurality for not being deferential enough to the rights of the executive, the president, and, more importantly, the commander-in-chief and stated that the Court should not second guess his actions. *Hamdi v. Rumsfeld,* 542 U.S. 507 (2004).

35. The inherent powers doctrine has been used a number of times in the war on terror, such as in the context of the NSA wiretapping. The Court's decisions in old and new cases are also used to bolster this argument. See Department of Justice Defense on NSA wiretapping, December 2005. http://www.sinc.sunysb.edu/Class/pol325/DoJ%20 Letter%20on%20NSA%20Eavesdropping.htm (last visited, October, 2006); John Yoo, "Commentary: Behind the 'Torture Memos'; As Attorney General Confirmation Hearings Begin for Alberto Gonzales, Boalt Law School Professor John Yoo Defends Wartime Policy." January 2005. http://www.berkeley.edu/news/media/releases/2005/01/05_johnyoo. shtml (last visited July 5, 2007).

36. Here the congressional authorization was for Afghanistan and, later, for Iraq. Fisher points out that even though George Bush Jr. did go to the Congress before attacking Afghanistan and Iraq, there were two caveats. The first was that the administration still insisted that, under the "inherent" powers doctrine, they need not have gone to the Congress for authorization, and the second was that the Iraq resolution did not clearly indicate use of force. Louis Fisher, *Presidential War Power* (Lawrence: University Press of Kansas, 2004).

37. Yoo, "Re: Military Interrogation of Alien Unlawful Combatants Held outside the United States," 4.

38. While Fisher cannot deny that the past presidents have not necessarily gone to the Congress in order to get their consent (in terms of declaration or authorization), he disagrees with Yoo that this was the intent of the founders (Fisher, *Presidential War Power,* preface, xi). One of Fisher's most powerful critiques of the unilateral commander-in-chief inherent powers doctrine is that even in a new nation that was in the process of formation

and faced various crises, the founders chose to reject the British model of resting all powers in the executive and asked for statutory authorization, not relying on inherent powers. Fisher, *Presidential War Power*.

39. In its ratification of the UN convention, the United States limited the protections against cruel, inhuman, and degrading treatment to violations disallowed by the Fifth, Fourteenth, and Eighth Amendments of the U.S. Constitution. Further, since the Fifth Amendment was not considered applicable outside the United States, there was an assumption that there was no prohibition on CIDT abroad. The John Yoo memo actually argues that the "Fifth Amendment Due Process Clause does not apply to the President's conduct of a war" and that, even if it does, the "Fifth Amendment does not apply extraterritorially to aliens." Yoo, "Re: Military Interrogation of Alien Unlawful Combatants Held outside the United States," 6. See critique of this position in Seth F. Kreimer, "'Torture Lite,' 'Full-Bodied' Torture, and the Insulation of Legal Conscience," *Journal of National Security Law & Policy* 1 (2005): 187-229. Kreimer's analysis suggests that the basis for some of the constitutional protections against torture, namely, to defend "bodily integrity" from "pain and suffering" and "cruelty," are equally applicable to cruel, inhuman, and degrading treatment, therefore making such distinctions redundant. In contrast to Kreimer, Parry states that existing laws are inadequate to deal with torture primarily because the laws do not provide a broader definition of torture that includes not only inflicting "severe pain and suffering" for information gathering or punishment but also "domination" and "blaming the victim for the pain." John T.Parry, "'Just for Fun': Understanding Torture and Understanding Abu Ghraib," *Journal of National Security Law and Policy* 1 (2005): 253-84, 260.

40. Yoo, "Re: Military Interrogation of Alien Unlawful Combatants Held outside the United States," 32. The 2003 Yoo memo does try to argue that the Federal Torture Statute may not even be applicable to Guantánamo since it was "within the territorial United States or on [a] permanent military [base] outside the territory of the United States." Yet it still needs to make sure that the definition of torture is narrow in case the statute is seen as applicable, especially when Yoo argued elsewhere that the aliens at Guantánamo Bay didn't have access to U.S. courts and constitutional protections.

41. Bybee/Yoo memo in Danner, ed., *Torture and Truth*, 108; Memorandum for James B. Comey, Deputy Attorney General, from Daniel Levin, Acting Assistant Attorney General, "Re: Legal Standards Applicable under 18 U.S.C. §§ 2340-2340A" (December 30, 2004) (hereafter Levin Memo, 2004) http://www.usdoj.gov/olc/dagmemo.pdf (last visited March 3, 2006), 3.

42. Statement of Mark Richard, Deputy Assistant Attorney General, U.S. Department of Justice, in *Convention against Torture*, Hearing before the Senate Committee on Foreign Relations, 101st Congress, 1990.

43. See discussions on definition of torture in Ahcene Boulesbaa, *The UN Convention on Torture and the Prospects for Enforcement* (The Hague: Martinus Nijhoff, 1999).

44. *Black's Law Dictionary* quoted in Bybee/Yoo memo, in Danner, ed., *Torture and Truth*, 117. Also, Joan Dayan's work points to the fact that specific intent has been an important requirement in the applicability of the protections under the Eighth Amendment in recent years. Joan Dayan, "Cruel and Unusual: The End of the Eighth Amendment," *Boston Review* (October/November, 2004). http://bostonreview.net/BR29.5/dayan.html (last visited March 31, 2006).

45. Bybee/Yoo Memo, in Danner, ed., *Torture and Truth*, 119-20, emphasis added.

46. Jeremy Waldron, "Torture and Positive Law: Jurisprudence for the White House," *Columbia Law Review* 105 (2005): 1681-1750, 1708.

47. See Hajjar, "What's the Matter with Yoo?"

48. David Luban, "Liberalism, Torture, and the Ticking Bomb," in *The Torture Debate in America*, edited by Karen J. Greenberg, 35-83 (Cambridge: Cambridge University Press, 2005).

49. Ibid., 38-42.

50. Ibid., 43-44.

51. Ibid., 44-45.

52. Ibid., 57; Joseph Margulies, *Guantánamo and the Abuse of Presidential Power* (New York: Simon & Schuster, 2006), 91.

53. Waldron, "Torture and Positive Law."

54. Margulies, *Guantánamo and the Abuse of Presidential Power*, 92.

55. Levin Memo, 2004, 2.

56. In September 2006, the military introduced a new manual that explicitly prohibited certain methods of interrogation, including hooding, electric shocks, food deprivation, mock executions, waterboarding, use of military dogs, and sexual humiliation. Field Manual No. 2-22.3, 2006. http://www.fas.org/irp/doddir/army/fm2-22-3.pdf (last visited December 25, 2007).

57. Austin Sarat, "Situating Law between the Realities of Violence and the Claims of Justice: An Introduction," in *Law, Violence, and the Possibility of Justice*, edited by Austin Sarat, 3-16 (Princeton, NJ: Princeton University Press, 2001). Timothy Kaufman-Osborn, *From Noose to Needle: Capital Punishment and the Late Liberal State* (Ann Arbor: University of Michigan Press, 2002).

58. Here, of course, I refer to the well-known essay by Austin Sarat and Thomas R. Kearns, "A Journey through Forgetting: Towards a Jurisprudence of Violence," in *The Fate of Law*, edited by Austin Sarat and Thomas Kearns, 209-73 (Ann Arbor: University of Michigan Press, 1991).

59. Sarat, "Situating Law between the Realities of Violence and the Claims of Justice," 3.

60. Robert Cover, "Violence and the Word," in *Narrative, Violence, and the Law: The Essays of Robert Cover*, edited by Austin Sarat, Michael Ryan, and Martha Minow, 203-38 (Ann Arbor: University of Michigan Press, 1995), 203.

61. Kaufman-Osborn, *From Noose to Needle*, chapter 2.

62. Austin Sarat, "Killing Me Softly: Capital Punishment and the Technologies for Taking Life," in Sarat, *When the State Kills: Capital Punishment and the American Condition*, 60-84 (Princeton, NJ: Princeton University Press, 2001).

63. Ibid.

64. Kate Randall, "Executions on Hold in Two U.S. States," *World Socialist Website* 18 (December 2006). http://www.wsws.org/articles/2006/dec2006/leth-d18.shtml (last visited, May 1, 2007).

65. Frederick A. O. Schwarz and Aziz Z. Huq, *Unchecked and Unbalanced: Presidential Power in a Time of Terror* (New York: New Press, 2007).

66. "Torture Memo Author John Yoo Responds to This Week's Revelations."

67. Ibid.

68. Press Briefing by White House Counsel, Judge Alberto Gonzales (June 22, 2004). http://www.whitehouse.gov/news/releases/2004/06/20040622-14.html (last visited July 6, 2004).

69. Statement of Mark Richard, 13.

70. Ibid., 16.

71. Ibid.

72. Ibid.

73. Levin Memo, 2004, 8.

74. Claims for civil damages are allowed under the TVPA (Torture Victim Protection Act) but are primarily for torture committed by non-U.S. officials or foreigners.

75. Levin Memo, 2004, 9-10.

76. Scheppele, "Hypothetical Torture," 289. Even legal scholars, while being extremely critical of the narrow definitions of torture adopted by the Bush administration, are seldom unanimous on the parameters of the term. For instance, John Parry suggests that torture and CIDT should not be considered different because that distinction allows officials to claim that "no matter what they do, at least it was not torture." He argues that torture should be considered on a continuum with a number of other forms of "violent and coercive state practices." John T. Parry, "Just for Fun," 258. Sanford Levinson, in contrast, disagrees with Parry that the distinction between terms such as "torture" and "cruel, inhuman, and degrading treatment" should not be maintained. For Levinson, making that distinction does not mean that CIDT is being allowed or accepted. Levinson writes, "To say that something is 'not torture' is not to commend or even to tolerate it." But he adds, "I think it is especially important to differentiate between 'degrading treatment' and 'torture,' lest one end up trivializing the concept of torture and diminishing the special horror attached to that term." Sanford Levinson, "In Quest of a 'Common Conscience': Reflections on the Current Debate about Torture," *Journal of National Security Law & Policy* 1 (2005): 231-52, 242.

77. See definitions of torture and CIDT in ICCPR and UN Convention, Scheppele. "Hypothetical Torture."

78. Ibid. and Federal Torture Statute, 1994. http://caselaw.lp.findlaw.com/casecode/uscodes/18/parts/i/chapters/113c/sections/section_2340.html (last visited December 15, 2007).

79. Statement of Mark Richard, 17.

80. Ibid.

81. When the United States signed and ratified the treaty in 1994, it put forward this particular understanding of the definition of torture. This specific version of the UN convention subsequently became the basis of the Federal Torture Statute. U.S. Report to CAT, 1999, 25.

82. Statement of Mark Richard, 17.

83. *Review of Department of Defense Detention Operations and Detainee Interrogation Techniques (Church Report)*, 2005. http://humanrights.ucdavis.edu/resources/library/documents-and-reports/ChurchReport.pdf (last visited January 23, 2011).

84. For Secretary of Defense from William Haynes, "Counter Resistance Techniques" (November 27, 2002) (Signed by Secretary Rumsfeld, December 2002), in Danner, ed., *Torture and Truth*, 181-82.

85. Memorandum for the Commander, U.S. Southern Command, from Secretary of Defense, "Counter Resistance Techniques in the War on Terrorism" (April 16, 2003), in Danner, ed., *Torture and Truth*, 199-204.

86. Memorandum for Commander, Joint Task Force, from Diane Beaver, "Legal Review on Aggressive Interrogation Techniques" (11 Oct. 2002), in Danner, ed., *Torture and Truth*, 169-177.

87. Field Manual No. 2-22.3, 2006. http://www.fas.org/irp/doddir/army/fm2-22-3.pdf (last visited December 25, 2007).

88. Michael Ratner, "Moving Away from the Rule of Law: Military Tribunals, Executive Detentions, and Torture," *Cardozo Law Review* 24 (2003): 1513-22, 1515.

89. President Bush, Military Order of November 13, 2001, in Danner, ed., *Torture and Truth*, 78-82.

90. Frank H. Wu, "Profiling in the Wake of September 11," *Criminal Justice Magazine* 17 (2002).

91. Walker Lindh (the "American Taliban") was arrested in Afghanistan and initially detained but was immediately given access to lawyers once his U.S. citizenship was revealed. Subsequently, he was tried in the civilian court. In the case of Lindh there were allegations of torture that may have come up in a U.S. court had there not been a bargain made between Lindh and the government. However, some scholars argue, using the *New York v. Quarles* case, that the public safety exception would allow the use of coercion in case of Lindh. M. K. B. Darmer, "Lessons from the Lindh Case: Public Safety and Fifth Amendment," *Brooklyn Law Review* 68 (2002): 241-87.

92. *Padilla v. Rumsfeld*, 542 U.S. 426 (2004); *Hamdi v. Rumsfeld*, 542 U.S. 507 (2004). *Rasul v. Bush*, 542 U.S. 466 (2004); *Hamdan v. Rumsfeld*, 548 U.S. 557 (2006); *Boumediene v. Bush* 128 S. Ct. 2229 (2008).

93. Margulies, *Guantánamo and the Abuse of Presidential Power*, 157.

94. On September 18, 2001, the U.S. Congress passed a joint "Authorization for Use of Military Force" allowing the president "to use all necessary and appropriate force against those nations, organizations, or persons he determines planned, authorized, committed, or aided the terrorist attacks that occurred on September 11, 2001, or harbored such organizations or persons, in order to prevent any future acts of international terrorism against the United States by such nations, organizations or persons." http://news.findlaw.com/wp/docs/terrorism/sjres23.es.html (last visited May 10, 2006). Also see President's Military Order in Danner, ed., *Torture and Truth*.

95. *Padilla v. Rumsfeld*, 233 F. Supp. 2d 564 (2002) and *Padilla v. Rumsfeld*, 243 F. Supp. 2d 42 (2003).

96. *Jose Padilla v. Rumsfeld*, 542 U.S. 426 (2004). A few days before the government was supposed to file its response to Padilla's appeal to the Supreme Court (again), the government stated that they were transferring his case to a federal criminal court for materially supporting the terrorists and moved him to civilian custody, and finally he was tried and convicted in the domestic system. In April 2006, the Supreme Court decided not to take up the Padilla case and as a result did not rule on the extremely significant aspect of the Padilla case regarding the issue of indefinite detention of American citizens. Linda Greenhouse, "Justices Decline Terrorism Case of a U.S. Citizen," *New York Times*, April 4, 2006.

97. Bruce Ackerman, *Before the Next Attack: Preserving Civil Liberties in an Age of Terrorism* (New Haven, CT: Yale University Press, 2006), 26-27.

98. *Hamdi v. Rumsfeld*, 542 U.S. 507, 533 (2004).

99. The Court's decision is nonetheless extremely significant because of the highly divided nature of the Court in the case. While the plurality (O'Connor, Rehnquist, Kennedy, and Breyer) found this balance between individual and government interests, Scalia disagreed that the Court should have dealt with it this way. He believed that Hamdi should have been tried either for treason or for another crime. If that was not possible,

the writ should have been suspended. In the absence of both these options, Hamdi should be released. *Hamdi v. Rumsfeld*, 542 U.S. 507 (2004).

100. Ackerman, *Before the Next Attack.*

101. Cass R. Sunstein, "Recent Decisions of the United States Court of Appeals for the District Court: National Security, Liberty, and the D.C. Circuit," *George Washington Law Review* 73 (2005): 693 – 709.

102. *Rasul v. Bush*, 542 U.S. 466 (2004).

103. The dissent, however feels that by deciding the case this way, "the court boldly extends the scope of the habeas statute to the four corners of the earth" since it allows anyone "captured in active combat" from any part of the world to be able to file a *habeas* petition against the secretary of defense. The dissent concludes by stating strongly that the action of the Court is a "clumsy counter textual reinterpretation that gives wartime prisoners greater habeas rights than domestic detainees," mentioning specifically Padilla. *Rasul v. Bush*, 542 U.S. 466, 498-505 (2004).

104. Indeed, Chemerinsky points out that the government did achieve major victories during this time. Hamdi did allow for detention of an American enemy combatant, Rasul did not specify the due process available, and Padilla was asked to go back to the courts. Erwin Chemerinsky, "Wartime Security and Constitutional Liberty: Detainees," *Albany Law Review* 68 (2005): 1119-26.

105. Ibid., 1122.

106. James Thuo Gathii writes that the extraterritoriality argument, used in the Rasul case in district court, was primarily an excuse used by the government not to intervene in cases where the United States could be using torture against noncitizens. He points to other cases outside the United States involving destruction of U.S. property, commercial agreements, and torture by others that had not been considered outside the jurisdiction of the U.S. courts. According to Gathii, the ruse of extraterritoriality has not only been used previously by the United States in the case of Haitian refugees but also constitutes a more modern version of a typical colonial strategy of denying rights on the basis of citizenship to the colonial subjects and territories under their control. James Thuo Gathii, "Torture, Extraterritoriality, Terrorism, and International Law," *Albany Law Review* 67 (2003): 335-70.

107. In the oral arguments for the Hamdi case, there is a brief mention of the Torture Convention by Justice Ginsburg but it is not explored much. http://www.oyez.org/cases/2000-2009/2003/2003_03_6696/argument/ (last visited January 30, 2008).

108. *Jose Padilla v. Rumsfeld*, 542 U.S. 426 (2004), 465, emphasis added.

109. *Padilla v. Rumsfeld*, 233 F. Supp. 2d 564, 574 (2002), emphasis added.

110. *Padilla v. Rumsfeld*, 243 F. Supp. 2d 42, 49 (2003). The government, for its part, argued that the Mobbs and Jacoby declarations (based on some interviews and interrogations by state officials) used to confer the status of "enemy combatant" to Padilla were adequate to fulfill the "some evidence" test.

111. Some indication of what the justices were thinking in the Padilla case was apparent in the oral argument. There was concern about constraints on the use of torture that the state actually accepted and also discusson on whether there was precedent of incommunicado detention for information gathering. The majority, however, did not finally concern itself with this explicitly in the opinion, and only the dissent pointed to the integral relation between detention and interrogation. See oral arguments in Padilla case. http://www.oyez.org/cases/2000-2009/2003/2003_03_1027/argument (last visited January 30, 2008).

112. *Rasul v. Bush*, 215 F. Supp. 2d 55, 56-57 (2002).

113. Gathii, "Torture, Extraterritoriality, Terrorism, and International Law."

114. "The Indefinite Detention of 'Enemy Combatants': Balancing Due Process and National Security in the Context of the War on Terror," *Record of the Association of the Bar of the City of New York* 59 (2004): 41-169, 105.

115. Ibid.

116. *Odah v.U. S.*, 321 F.3d 1134, 1150 (2003), emphasis added.

117. There is a brief moment in the Padilla case when during the oral arguments, Justice Ginsburg does bring up the question of what prevents the executive from using torture during these detentions, and while the deputy solicitor general, Paul Clement, does mention the treaty obligations, he also ultimately takes refuge in the fact that torture is not being authorized by the executive and that the court should trust the executive in times of war. See http://www.oyez.org/cases/2000-2009/2003/2003_03_1027/argument/ (last visited January 30, 2008).

118. It is of course ironic that the day the Supreme Court finished the oral arguments for the Hamdi and Padilla case, April 28, 2004, is also the day when the Abu Ghraib pictures were shown by the press.

119. *Hamdi v. Rumsfeld*, 542 U.S. 507, 516 (2004).

120. *Hamdan v. Rumsfeld*, 344 F. Supp. 2d 152 (2004); *Hamdan v. Rumsfeld*, 367 U.S. App. D.C. 265 (2005). See also criticism of initial tribunals by scholars. David D. Caron and David L. Sloss, "International Decision: Availability of U.S. Courts to Detainees at Guantánamo Bay Naval Base—Reach of Habeas Corpus—Executive Power in War on Terror," *American Journal of International Law* 98 (2004): 788 – 98. There was also a presumption of guilt that the detainees were enemy combatants, and the detainees had to prove they were not. Jameel Jaffer, "Dispatches from Guantánamo," November 4, 2004. http://www.aclu.org/SafeandFree/SafeandFree.cfm?ID=16924&c=206 (last visited April 4, 2005).

121. Here I differentiate between the military commissions introduced before Hamdan (MC) and the military commissions introduced under the act in 2006 (MCA).

122. *Hamdan v. Rumsfeld*, 548 U.S. 557 (2006).

123. Ibid.

124. Ibid.

125. There has been discussion among scholars and officials about whether the Geneva Conventions were being used as a part of treaty law within the Uniform Code of Military Justice or as customary international law. See implications of this in John B. Bellinger III, legal advisor to the U.S. secretary of state, "Symposium on the New Face of Armed Conflict: Enemy Combatants after Hamdan v. Rumsfeld; Transcript of Remarks, October 20, 2006," *George Washington Law Review* 75 (2007): 1007-20.

126. Neal Kumar Katyal, "*Hamdan v. Rumsfeld*: The Legal Academy Goes to Practice," *Harvard Law Review* 120 (2006): 65-123, 98.

127. *Hamdan v. Rumsfeld*, 548 U.S. 557 (2006), 2807-8.

128. Ibid.

129. Convention (III) Relative to the Treatment of Prisoners of War. Geneva, 12 August 1949. http://www.icrc.org/ihl.nsf/0/e160550475c4b133c12563cd0051aa66?OpenDocument (last visited July 6, 2007).

130. President Bush, Military Order of November 13, 2001, in Danner, ed., *Torture and Truth*, 80.

131. The brief filed by the Bar Human Rights Committee of the Bar of England and Wales and the Commonwealth Lawyers Association added that in a recent case regarding international terrorists, the House of Lords clearly stated that evidence gained as a result of torture, even in a foreign state without the involvement of the English, would not be accepted in the proceedings. Bar Human Rights Committee of the Bar of England and Wales and the Commonwealth Lawyers Association, 2005 U.S. Briefs 184.

132. Amicus Curiae Brief of the American Civil Liberties Union in Support of Petitioner, 2005 U.S. Briefs 184, 8, emphasis added.

133. Brief of Amicus Curiae Human Rights First, Physicians for Human Rights, Center for Victims of Torture, Advocates for Survivors of Torture and Trauma, Boston Center for Refugee Health and Human Rights, and a number of human rights groups against torture, 2005 U.S. Briefs 184, 29-30. Brief for Petitioner Salim Ahmed Hamdan, 2005 U.S. Briefs 184.

134. Brief of Amicus Curiae Human Rights First, Physicians for Human Rights, Center for Victims of Torture, Advocates for Survivors of Torture and Trauma, Boston Center for Refugee Health and Human Rights, and a number of human rights groups against torture, 2005 U.S. Briefs 184, 2, emphasis added.

135. Ibid.

136. *Boumediene v. Bush*, 128 S. Ct. 2229 (2008).

137. Ibid.

138. Ibid., 2270.

139. Ibid., 2274.

140. Brief on Behalf of Former Federal Judges as Amici Curiae in Support of Petitioners, Boumediene, 2006 U.S. Briefs 1195, 5.

141. Military Commissions Act, 2006, http://thomas.loc.gov/cgi-bin/query/D?c109:3:./temp/~c109LgPKpw (last visited, July 6, 2007). Since there were attempts by the United States to take advantage of the possible gaps in the existing laws prohibiting torture and CIDT abroad, it was not surprising that (despite the U.S. Supreme Court's insistence on the application of Common Article 3 to the conflict) one of the major concerns of the United States was to limit Common Article 3's broad protections. The administration was concerned that American soldiers and commanders could be held in violation of the War Crimes Act of 1996 for committing "grave breaches" of the Geneva Convention.

142. Military Commissions Act, 2006. http://thomas.loc.gov/cgi-bin/query/D?c109:3:./temp/~c109LgPKpw (last visited, July 6, 2007). See critique in David Glazier, "Full and Fair by What Measure: Identifying the International Law Regulating Military Commission Procedure," *Boston University International Law Journal* 24 (2006): 55-122.

143. See Marty Lederman, "Yes, It's a No-Brainer: Waterboarding *Is* Torture," October 28, 2006. http://balkin.blogspot.com/2006/10/yes-its-no-brainer-waterboarding-is.html (last visited April 21, 2007). Marty Lederman, "Three of the Most Significant Problems with the 'Compromise,'" September 22, 2006. http://balkin.blogspot.com/2006/09/three-of-most-significant-problems.html (last visited April 21, 2007).

144. Michael J. Matheson, "Agora: Military Commissions Act of 2006; The Amendment of the War Crimes Act," *American Journal of International Law* 101 (2007): 48-55, 52.

145. Ibid. Also, the MCA does not clarify whether evidence gained as a result of humiliating treatment would be allowed and may even allow for some evidence tainted by torture if it was gained before December 2005. See Jack M. Beard, "Agora: Military Commissions Act

of 2006; The Geneva Boomerang; The Military Commissions Act of 2006 and U.S. Counter-terror Operations," *American Journal of International Law* 101 (2007): 56-73.

146. See note 56.

147. Memorandum for John A. Rizzo, Senior Deputy General Counsel, Central Intelligence Agency, from Steven Bradbury, Principal Deputy Assistant Attorney General, "Re: Application of United States Obligation under Article 16 of UN Convention against Torture That May be Used in the Interrogation of High Value al Qaeda Detainees," May 30, 2005. http://luxmedia.com.edgesuite.net/aclu/olc_05302005_bradbury.pdf (last visited January 23, 2011).

148. Deb Riechmann, "Bush Vetoes Waterboarding Bill," March 8, 2008. http://news.yahoo.com/s/ap/20080308/ap_on_go_pr_wh/bush_torture (last visited March 14, 2008).

149. Petition for Writ of Certiorari, 2006 U.S. Briefs 1195, 5.

150. Yoo, "Re: Military Interrogation of Alien Unlawful Combatants Held outside the United States."

151. Katyal, "*Hamdan v. Rumsfeld*," 84.

152. These passive virtues, however, were taken into account by Hamdan's counsel by educating the Court early on about all the issues. Ibid.

153. Sunstein, "National Security, Liberty, and the D.C. Circuit," 694-95.

154. See Steven R Shapiro, "Defending Civil Liberties in the War on Terror: The Role of the Courts in the War against Terrorism; A Preliminary Assessment," *Fletcher Forum of World Affairs Journal* 29 (2005): 103-16.

155. Similar to the Court, scholars such as Ackerman also seem to ignore this relationship between detention and torture. Rejecting torture as Ackerman does may not be adequate to ensure the protections in a context where the very definition of torture and CIDT and excess violence in general is being debated. Here, framing the need for the state to reconstitute effective sovereignty both symbolically and functionally by allowing the state to take extraordinary measures precludes a discussion on some of these historically linked relations between detention and torture and between detention and race, citizenship, and ethnicity. Thus, Ackerman underestimates the power of the panic that will ensure that detentions are not just neutral, egalitarian measures that affect all but rather have very particularized impact based on preexisting stigmas that often result in violent measures against specific sections. Ackerman, *Before the Next Attack*.

156. *El-Masri v. United States,* 128 S. Ct. 373 (2007); *Arar v. Ashcroft,* 2010 U.S. LEXIS 4750 (2010).

157. See page 48.

158. Michel Foucault, "Governmentality," in The *Foucault Effect: Studies in Governmentality,* edited by Graham Burchell, Colin Gordon, and Peter Miller, 87-104 (Chicago: University of Chicago Press, 1991), 100.

159. Kevin Stenson, "Crime Control, Governmentality, and Sovereignty," in *Governable Places: Readings on Governmentality and Crime Control,* edited by Russell Smandych, 45-73 (Aldershot, England: Ashgate/Dartmouth, 1999), 47.

160. David Garland, "'Governmentality' and the Problem of Crime," in *Governable Places: Readings on Governmentality and Crime Control,* edited by Russell Smandych, 15-43 (Aldershot, England: Ashgate/Dartmouth, 1999), 15.

161. Colin Gordon, "Governmental Rationality: An Introduction," in Burchell, Gordon, and Miller, eds., *The Foucault Effect: Studies in Governmentality,* 1-51, 24 (emphasis added).

162. Foucault, "Governmentality," 96 (emphasis added) using physiocrat La Perriere's work.

163. Stenson, "Crime Control, Governmentality, and Sovereignty," 46.

164. Ibid.

165. Lifton writes that there were instances when nurses and doctors saw injuries such as dislocated shoulders as a result of detainees being handcuffed or forced to hold their hands over their head but did not report it. Robert Jay Lifton, "Doctors and Torture," *New England Journal of Medicine* 351 (2004): 415-16.

166. Physicians for Human Rights points out that apart from issues of quality and access that were really problems in Iraq and Afghanistan, doctors did not try to intervene when they saw the use of torture. Sometimes they were present and actually revived the detainee so that the torture could continue. And even when they saw the impact of torture on the detainees, they did not intervene. Physician for Human Rights, *Broken Laws, Broken Lives* (2008), 86. http://brokenlives.info/?page_id=69 (last visited January 23, 2011).

167. Alfred W. McCoy, *A Question of Torture: CIA Interrogation from the Cold War to the War on Terror* (New York: Metropolitan Books, 2006); Naomi Klein, *The Shock Doctrine: The Rise of Disaster Capitalism* (New York: Metropolitan Books, 2007).

168. McCoy, *A Question of Torture*, 12. These methods traveled from the United States to different parts of the world. In fact, there were actual training schools in the United States. Timothy J. Kepner, "Torture 101: The Case against the United States for Atrocities Committed by School of the Americas Alumni," *Dickinson Journal of International Law* 19 (2001): 475-529.

169. I emphasize that the relationship of law and state to violence is a constant negotiation because the argument is not that excess violence is an unchanging part of governmentality. Rather, it is a historically variable relationship and the exact nature of the excess violence also differs in varied circumstances at different moments in time. For instance, even the role of doctors and medical professionals in state power has transformed over different periods of history. During the Second World War, doctors, psychologists, and psychiatrists had been involved in actual human experiments and in the process caused immense pain and suffering (Nazi doctors' experiments, for example). However, that was transformed in the post–World War II context, when certain medical protocols were introduced, as reflected in the Geneva Conventions but most specifically in the Declaration of Tokyo in 1973 and UN principles in 1982 prohibiting the involvement of doctors in torture and CIDT. And yet the participation of medical professionals in different forms in the current context is significant.

170. McCoy, *A Question of Torture*, 26.

171. Mark Bowden, "The Dark Art of Interrogation," *Atlantic Monthly*, October 2003. http://www.theatlantic.com/magazine/archive/2003/10/the-dark-art-of-interrogation/2791/ (last visited January10, 2011); ibid., 57.

172. McCoy, *A Question of Torture*, 7.

173. Ibid., 8.

174. In fact, Naomi Klein points out that one of the reasons the experiments may not have been conducted in the United States was their potential impact, but there is adequate evidence to show that these studies were clearly funded and utilized by the CIA. Naomi Klein, *The Shock Doctrine*.

175. McCoy, *A Question of Torture*, 35.

176. Ibid.

177. KUBARK Counterintelligence Interrogation, Central Intelligence Agency (July 1963). http://www.gwu.edu/~nsarchiv/NSAEBB/NSAEBB122/ (last visited March 3, 2006). For instance, strikingly reminiscent of present debates, the CIA Kubark Manual back in 1963 suggested that the best way to ensure compliance is to use environmental manipulation and sensory deprivation in less intense ways. Minor changes in sleep patterns and food timings were considered more effective methods of interrogation than more drastic measures that could lead to hallucinations and delusions. KUBARK Counterintelligence Interrogation, Central Intelligence Agency, July 1963. http://www.gwu.edu/~nsarchiv/ NSAEBB/NSAEBB122/ (last visited March 3, 2006), 92.

178. McCoy, *A Question of Torture*. Indeed, the highly controversial Kubark Manual was replaced by the 1983 Honduras Manual with little change as far as the psychological methods were concerned. As Kaufman-Osborn writes, while the more explicit provisions were removed from the 1983 manual and the current army manual, "there is little reason to believe that the basic logic of these disciplinary practices has changed in any significant way." Timothy V. Kaufman-Osborn, "Gender Trouble at Abu Ghraib?" *Politics & Gender* 1 (2005): 597-619, 608.

179. McCoy, *A Question of Torture*, 100. This may have also been possible because, according to Naomi Klein, the discourse in the 1970s and 1980s had primarily been on mind control and brainwashing. "The word 'torture' was almost never used." Naomi Klein, *The Shock Doctrine*, 38.

180. Rejali uses the term "nonscarring" to note that the distinction between physical and psychological is not adequate to explain the nature of some of these techniques. He notes that many of these are physical techniques except that they do not leave marks. Darius Rejali, *Torture and Democracy* (Princeton, NJ: Princeton University Press, 2007), 4.

181. Ibid., 8.

182. M. Gregg Bloche and Jonathan H. Marks, "Doctors and Interrogators at Guantanamo Bay," *New England Journal of Medicine* 353 (2005): 6-8.

183. Ibid.

184. Jane Mayer, "The Experiment: The Military Trains People to Withstand Interrogation; Are Those Methods Being Misused at Guantánamo?" *New Yorker*, July 11, 2005. http://www.newyorker.com/archive/2005/07/11/050711fa_fact4?printable=true (last visited September 25, 2008).

185. Other methods mentioned are Bible trashing, noise stress, waterboarding, and sexual humiliation. Some of these were used in the Qahtani case and the log shows the participation of a psychologist. Ibid.

186. Review of DOD-Directed Investigations of Detainee Abuse, Office of the Inspector General of the Department of Defense, August 25, 2006. See appendix, 107. http://human-rights.ucdavis.edu/projects/the-guantanamo-testimonials-project/testimonies/testimonies-of-the-defense-department/dod_inspector_general.pdf (last visited January 23, 2011).

187. Michel Foucault, *Foucault Live: Collected Interviews, 1961-1984*, edited by Sylvere Lotringer (New York: Semiotext, 1996), 197.

188. Kaufman-Osborn, *From Noose to Needle*, 199.

189. Ibid. The inability of the state to visibly use pain in its executions reflects the basic instability between the state's punitive functions (sovereignty) and its welfare functions (juridico-medical complex in the realm of governmentality).

190. Here I focus on the psychologists because the American Psychiatric Association and the American Medical Association bar their members from participating in interrogations. http://www.psych.org/MainMenu/Newsroom/NewsReleases/2008NewsReleases/APAStatementonInterrogation.aspx (last visited September 25, 2008).

191. "How Pentagon Report Contradicts APA Statements Q&A," June 9, 2007. http://www.scoop.co.nz/stories/WO0706/S00114.htm (last visited September 25, 2008).

192. Report of the American Psychological Association, Presidential Task Force on Psychological Ethics and National Security, June 2005, 2. http://www.apa.org/pubs/info/reports/pens.pdf (last visited January 11, 2011).

193. "How Pentagon Report Contradicts APA Statements Q&A."

194. In 2008, the American Psychological Association banned its members from participating in interrogations. "Psychologists Ban Role in Interrogations," September 18, 2008. http://www.cbsnews.com/stories/2008/09/18/terror/main4457822.shtml (last visited September 30, 2008).

195. Working Group Report, "Detainee Interrogations in the Global War on Terrorism: Assessment of Legal, Historical, and Policy and Operational Considerations" (April 4, 2003), in Danner, ed., *Torture and Truth*, 187-98, 197. This was subsequently approved by the defense secretary. Memorandum for the Commander, U.S. Southern Command, from Secretary of Defense, "Counter Resistance Techniques in the War on Terrorism" (April 16, 2003), in Danner, ed., *Torture and Truth*, 199-204, 203.

196. Memorandum for John A. Rizzo, Senior Deputy General Counsel, Central Intelligence Agency, from Steven Bradbury, Principal Deputy Assistant Attorney General, "Re: Application of 18 U.S.C. §§ 2340-2340A to Certain Techniques That May Be Used in the Interrogation of a High Value al Qaeda Detainee," May 10, 2005. http://luxmedia.com.edgesuite.net/aclu/olc_05102005_bradbury46pg.pdf (last visited January 23, 2011).

197. Ibid., 4.

198. Ibid., 6.

CHAPTER 3

1. *Senate Judiciary Committee's Hearings on the Nomination of Alberto R. Gonzales to Be Attorney General*, January 2005. http://www.humanrightsfirst.com/us_law/etn/gonzales/statements/gonz_testimony_010604.htm (last visited March 5, 2006).

2. Human Rights First, "Torture on TV Rising and Copied in the Field." http://www.humanrightsfirst.org/us_law/etn/primetime/index.asp#impact (last visited March 15, 2008).

3. Jesse Holcomb, "Tortured Logic," *Sojourners Magazine*, June 2007.

4. Yahoo show description of *24*. http://tv.yahoo.com/show/28479/castcrew;_ylt=As.DV2gEEtrhwxiV5w9BN53Ev9EF.

5. Dershowitz often starts his discussion on torture by invoking the "ticking bomb scenario." Alan Dershowitz, *Why Terrorism Works* (New Haven, CT: Yale University Press, 2002).

6. For example, see Slavoj Zizek, "The Depraved Heroes of 24 Are the Himmlers of Hollywood," *Guardian*, January 10, 2006.

7. Jane Mayer, "Whatever It Takes: The Politics of the Man behind '24,'" *New Yorker*, February 19, 2007. http://www.newyorker.com/reporting/2007/02/19/070219fa_fact_mayer (last visited January 13, 2011).

8. Ibid.

9. Ibid.

10. The identification of certain methods as "coercive" is also very significant here since then there is a need to distinguish these techniques from standard criminal enforcement protections, state reports on other countries, and army field manuals, and here coercion is directly linked to the necessity of the act.

> Coercive techniques "place the detainee, in more physical and psychological stress" than the other techniques and are generally "considered to be more effective tools in persuading a resistant [detainee] to participate with CIA interrogators." . . . These techniques are typically not used simultaneously. The Background Paper lists walling, water dousing, stress positions, wall standing, and cramped confinement in this category. We will also treat the waterboard as a coercive technique.

Memorandum for John A. Rizzo, Senior Deputy General Counsel, Central Intelligence Agency, from Steven Bradbury, Principal Deputy Assistant Attorney General, "Re: Application of United States Obligation under Article 16 of UN Convention against Torture That May Be Used in the Interrogation of High Value al Qaeda Detainees," May 30, 2005, 14. http://luxmedia.com.edgesuite.net/aclu/olc_05302005_bradbury.pdf (last visited January 23, 2011).

11. Memorandum for John A. Rizzo, Senior Deputy General Counsel, Central Intelligence Agency, from Steven Bradbury, Principal Deputy Assistant Attorney General, "Re: Application of 18 U.S.C. §§ 2340-2340A to Certain Techniques That May Be Used in the Interrogation of a High Value al Qaeda Detainee," May 10, 2005, 14. http://luxmedia.com.edgesuite.net/aclu/olc_05102005_bradbury46pg.pdf (last visited January 23, 2011).

12. Steve Benen, "Scalia Asks, 'Are you going to convict Jack Bauer?'" June 19, 2007. *crooks and liars.com* (last visited September 28, 2007).

13. Tony Karon, "Times Square Bomb Arrest Raises U.S. Security Questions," May 5, 2010. http://www.time.com/time/nation/article/0,8599,1987126,00.html (last visited May 25, 2010).

14. Ibid.

15. Mayer, "Whatever It Takes."

16. Rosa Brooks, "Pro-Torture Republicans Betray Their Country's Highest Ideals," *San Jose Mercury News*, May 21, 2007. http://www.mercurynews.com/opinion/ci_5946789 (last visited July 5, 2007).

17. Stephen Armstrong, "Rough Justice," *New Statesman*, March 19, 2007.

18. Mayer, "Whatever It Takes."

19. Bill Keveney, "'24' Actor Gets Full-Bore into Torture Scene," *USA Today*, February 19, 2007.

20. Mayer, "Whatever It Takes."

21. Armstrong, "Rough Justice."

22. Ibid.

23. Mayer, "Whatever It Takes."

24. Brooks, "Pro-Torture Republicans."

25. Ibid.

26. *24* is only one of the range of shows on terrorism. Some of the others include *Alias* and films such as *Siege*.

27. Michel Foucault, *Discipline and Punish: The Birth of the Prison*, translated by Alan Sheridan (New York: Vintage, 1995), 3-4.

28. Heather MacDonald, "How to Interrogate Terrorists: Don't Believe the Charges; American Troops Treat Terrorists with Geneva-Convention Politeness—Perhaps Too Much So," *City Journal*, Winter 2005. http://www.city-journal.org/html/15_1_terrorists. html (last visited, June 26, 2007), emphasis added.

29. Jon Wiener, "Keifer Sutherland, Torture Guy: This Ain't Your Father's 'MASH'; How Tommy Douglas's Grandkid Became Poster Boy for US Anti-Terror Tactics," January 18, 2007. http://thetyee.ca/Entertainment/2007/01/18/24/ (last visited, July 4, 2007).

30. Mayer, "Whatever It Takes."

31. Ibid.

32. Terry Armour, "'24' Isn't a Must-See for Its Former President," *Chicago Tribune*, March 25, 2007.

33. "Fictional '24' Brings Real Issue of Torture Home: TV Hero's Tactics Debated in World after Abu Ghraib," *USA Today*, March 15, 2005, emphasis added. http://www. infowars.com/articles/ps/torture_tv_24_brings_torture_home.htm (last visited, July 6, 2007).

34. Parents Television Council, http://www.parentstv.org/ptc/shows/main. asp?shwid=1538.

35. Austin Sarat, *When The State Kills: Capital Punishment and the American Condition* (Princeton, NJ: Princeton University Press, 2001).

36. *Baze v. Rees*, 128 S. Ct. 1520 (2008).

37. Timothy Kaufman-Osborn, "The Paradox of Lethal Injection," paper presented at the Law and Society Association Annual Meeting Conference, Berlin, Germany, 2007.

38. Ibid., 37.

39. Michael Dorf, "How the Supreme Court's Lethal Injection Ruling Elevates Appearances over Reality," April 21, 2008. http://writ.news.findlaw.com/dorf/20080421.html (last visited April 29, 2008).

40. Human Rights First, "Torture on TV Rising."

41. Ibid.

42. Mayer, "Whatever It Takes."

43. "Scalia Defends Torture: It's 'Absurd' to Say the Gov't Can't 'Smack' a Suspect 'in the Face,'" *Think Progress*, February 12, 2008. http://thinkprogress.org/2008/02/12/scalia-torture/ (last visited March 14, 2008).

44. Patrick Day, "C'mon, Jack Bauer; It's Time to Get Real; The '24' Hero Isn't Very Rational at the Moment; Take Him at His Word? Or Did Life Alter Him?" *Los Angeles Times*, April 18, 2007.

45. *Review of Department of Defense Detention Operations and Detainee Interrogation Techniques (Church Report)*, 2005, 23. http://humanrights.ucdavis.edu/resources/library/documents-and-reports/ChurchReport.pdf (last visited January 23, 2011).

46. Even for the abuses at Abu Ghraib (such as physical and sexual assault) that are commonly understood as mental and physical torture, the term "torture" is not easily used. For example, the Schlesinger Report set up to review the detention operations of the Department of Defense did not term the acts of U.S. soldiers as torture. Rather, they were defined as "acts of brutality and purposeless sadism." Final Report of the Independent Panel to Review DOD Detention Operation (Schlesinger Report) (August 2004), in

Torture and Truth: America, Abu Ghraib, and the War on Terror, edited by Mark Danner, 329-402 (New York: New York Review of Books, 2004).

47. *Church Report*, 3, emphasis added.

48. *Schmidt Report*, 1. http://balkin.blogspot.com/Schmidt%20Furlow%20report.pdf (last visited December 2005).

49. Ibid., 1.

50. The Center for Constitutional Rights is a nonprofit group based in New York City that has been at the forefront of ensuring due process rights and protections for the detainees under U.S. and international laws. Center for Constitutional Rights (CCR), *Report on Torture and Cruel, Inhuman, and Degrading Treatment of Prisoners at Guantanamo Bay, Cuba,* July 2006 (hereafter *CCR Report).*

51. Ibid., 31.

52. UN Report on Guantánamo, 2006, 37. The UN Report found many of the methods authorized by the Department of Defense to be violations of Article 7 of ICCPR and Article 16 of the Convention against Torture. Arbitrary and extended detention and "prolonged solitary confinement" were also termed "inhuman treatment" by the report. United Nations Commission on Human Rights, *Situation of Detainees at Guantánamo Bay,* February 15, 2006, 36-38 (hereafter *UN Report).*

53. Kim Lane Scheppele, "Hypothetical Torture in the War on Terrorism," *Journal of National Security Law & Policy* 1 (2005): 285-340, 289.

54. *Church Report*, 177.

55. This reminds one of Scarry's arguments about how it is impossible to know of the other's pain: the inexpressibility of pain. Elaine Scarry, *The Body in Pain: The Making and Unmaking of the World* (New York: Oxford University Press, 1985), introduction.

56. *Church Report*, 108.

57. Ibid., 88-89.

58. *Schmidt Report*, 2.

59. Ibid., 4.

60. Another instance of this sanitization that compares an interrogation method with an act that consumers desire is the comparison between dietary manipulation (where the calorie intake is reduced) to commercial weight loss programs. The memo does note that they are not equating the two, but the imagery is still important. Memorandum for John A. Rizzo, May 10, 2005, footnote on p. 7.

61. *Schmidt Report*, 18.

62. Ibid., 10-11.

63. Human Rights First, "Torture on TV Rising."

64. *Schmidt Report*, 7.

65. Ibid., 8.

66. Ibid., 7.

67. Maureen Ryan, "'Entourage' Actor, Garofalo Join Cast of '24,'" *Chicago Tribune,* August 24, 2007.

68. Rosa Brooks, "America Tortures (Yawn)," *Los Angeles Times,* February 23, 2007.

69. As noted in the introduction, in the last couple of seasons, there was an attempt to echo some of the real debates within the intelligence agencies. In the eighth season, while there was a lot of bloody violence, it was not necessarily in the context of custodial interrogation; for instance, to get an informer out of parole, his hand is cut.

70. Mayer, "Whatever It Takes."

71. *Church Report*, 178.

72. May 20-23, 2004, *Public Opinion Online*, University of Connecticut, Roper Center. Right after 9/11, people were predominantly against the use of torture against terrorists. This confirms the observation by theorists such as Scheppele that initially the reaction to 9/11 was more measured. Kim Lane Scheppele, "Law in a Time of Emergency: States of Exception and the Temptations of 9/11," *University of Pennsylvania Journal of Constitutional Law* 6 (2004): 1001-83. However, by March 2002, the response to the possibility of using torture became less oppositional. Overall, there seemed to be a growing consensus that torture or torturelike methods could be used by the United States. See March 12-13, 2002, *Public Opinion Online*, University of Connecticut, Roper Center, where the polls shows that 41 percent supported torture while 44 opposed. Again the opinion seemed to change when the images of torture appeared in the press—59 percent said that they opposed torture even if the terrorists had knowledge about the attacks. *USA Today/CNN/Gallup Poll Results*, January 12, 2005 (from a survey of 1,008 American adults conducted January 7-9, 2005). http://www.usatoday.com//news/polls/tables/live/2005-01-10-poll.htm.

73. The question asked was, "Do you think what American soldiers did to prisoners at the Abu Ghraib prison in Baghdad amounts to torture, or do you think it was abuse, but not torture?" Roper Center at University of Connecticut, May 20-23, 2004, *Public Opinion Online*, University of Connecticut, Roper Center.

74. *USA Today/CNN/Gallup Poll Results*, January 12, 2005 (from a survey of 1,008 American adults conducted January 7-9, 2005). http://www.usatoday.com//news/polls/tables/live/2005-01-10-poll.htm.

75. Ibid.

76. MacDonald, "How to Interrogate Terrorists."

77. Chris Mackey and Greg Miller, *The Interrogators: Task Force 500 and America's Secret War against Al Qaeda* (Boston: Little, Brown, 2004).

78. "Giuliani Questioned on Torture," *New York Times*, October 25, 2007.

79. Zechariah Chafee Jr., Walter H. Pollak, and Carl Stern, *The Third Degree: Report to the National Commission on Law Observance and Enforcement (June 1931)* (New York: Arno Press and The New York Times, 1969), 47.

80. While the state continued to insist that only a few bad apples were responsible for the abuse (not torture), Eisenman writes that the acceptance of the Abu Ghraib images of torture by the wider public was also due to a familiarity with these images as exhibited in ancient Roman and Greek architecture and the classical Western tradition in general. The representation of "cruelty of the Battle of Gods and Giants" (16) on the beautiful Pergamon altar and the coexistence of pain and eroticism in James Bond movies show this continuity in representation of eroticized violence by the oppressor over the subordinated. Eisenman suggests that the "Abu Ghraib effect," or moral blindness, is precisely attributable to the familiarity with these images. Using the Freudian concept of the uncanny he explains that the uncanny is a familiarity that one feels simultaneously with an inability to recall because the memory is repressed. Stephen F. Eisenman, *Abu Ghraib Effect* (London: Reakton Books, 2007).

81. Alfred McCoy, *A Question of Torture: CIA Interrogation from the Cold War to the War on Terror* (New York: Metropolitan Books, 2006).

82. Ibid., 8. Of course that did not mean that physical methods were not used, particularly in countries where many of these CIA methods were exported: Latin and Central America and Vietnam. McCoy writes that psychological methods of torture were accompanied by and led to brutal interrogations. Ibid.

83. Ibid., 185.

84. The United States has included protections against mental torture in the Federal Torture Statute though it has limited the scope of the definition to "prolonged mental harm." See chapter 2.

85. For Secretary of Defense from William Haynes, "Counter Resistance Techniques" (November 27, 2002) (Signed by Secretary Rumsfeld, December 2002), in Danner, ed., *Torture and Truth*, 181-82.

86. Mark Tran, "Cheney Endorses Simulated Drowning," *Guardian Unlimited*, October 27, 2006. http://www.guardian.co.uk/usa/story/0,,1933315,00.html (last visited July 4, 2007).

87. Press Briefing by Tony Snow, White House Conference Center Briefing Room, October 27, 2006. http://www.whitehouse.gov/news/releases/2006/10/20061027-1.html.

88. Ibid.

89. Ibid.

90. During the primaries of the 2008 presidential campaign, Rudy Giuliani stated that waterboarding is not necessarily torture: "It depends on how it's done. It depends on the circumstances. It depends on who does it." Michael Cooper, "Giuliani Questioned on Torture," *New York Times*, October 25, 2007.

91. The former attorney general, Michael Mukasey, refused to term waterboarding as torture during his confirmation hearings. "Mukasey Weighs Waterboarding, Sept. 11 Charges," *Newshour with Jim Lehrer*, February 11, 2008. http://www.pbs.org/newshour/bb/law/jan-june08/mukasey_02-11.html (last visited March 15, 2008). Current attorney general Eric Holder has clearly stated that waterboarding is torture.

92. "Cheney Roars Back: The *Nightline* Interview during His Trip to Iraq; Amid Criticism of White House Methods, Cheney Worries 'People Have Lost Their Sense of Urgency.'" December 18, 2005. www.abc.com.

93. *CCR Report*, 17-18.

94. Ibid., 17.

95. Ibid., 15.

96. Ibid., 24-28.

97. *UN Report*, 29.

98. Ibid., 27-30. The United States consistently denied that the soldiers abused the Quran, but withholding of religious items was authorized for a particular period, and even the *Schmidt Report* mentioned that this took place at least once, 19.

99. John Parry, "'Just for Fun': Understanding Torture and Understanding Abu Ghraib," *Journal of National Security Law and Policy* 1 (2005): 253-84, 255.

100. Ibid.

101. There was a range of memos that emerged during this period that elaborated on the techniques used on high-value detainees. See discussion of the specific techniques in Memorandum for John A. Rizzo, May 10, 2005.

102. Memorandum for John Rizzo, Acting General Counsel of the Central Intelligence Agency, from Department of Justice, Office of the Assistant Attorney General, Jay S. Bybee, August 2002. http://luxmedia.com.edgesuite.net/aclu/olc_08012002_bybee.pdf (last visited January 23, 2011).

103. Ibid., 6.

104. Central Intelligence Agency, Inspector General, Office of Inspector General, "Counterterrorism Detention and Interrogation Activities," September 2001–October 2003, May 7, 2004. http://luxmedia.com.edgesuite.net/aclu/IG_Report.pdf (last visited January 23, 2011).

105. Ibid., see footnote 14 on 14.

106. Ibid., see footnote 26 on 21-22.

107. Ibid., 37.

108. Memorandum for John A. Rizzo, May 10, 2005, see footnote 18 on 13-14.

109. Memorandum for John A. Rizzo, May 30, 2005.

110. Ibid., 3.

111. Scarry, *Body in Pain*, 40.

CHAPTER 4

1. Gandhi, "Young India," June 1, 1921, quoted by Justice Iyer in *Satpathy v. Dani* (1978) 2 SCC 424, 431.

2. *National Human Rights Commission: Annual Report* (New Delhi; NHRC, 2006-2007).

3. The NHRC requires all state governments and union territories to ask the district magistrates and the superintendents of police to send to its office a report of any custodial death or rape within twenty-four hours of its occurrence. The NHRC can ask for information on any case, send its own investigative teams to look into the cases, or rely on other investigative agencies to do so. Concerned with the lack of a proper postmortem to inquire into the cause of death, the commission has also asked for videotapes and detailed reports of the postmortems. In the context of compensation, the commission has requested that the states extract a part of the compensation amount from the errant police persons. Ibid.

4. *National Human Rights Commission: Annual Report* (New Delhi: NHRC, 2003-2004); *National Human Rights Commission: Annual Report* (New Delhi: NHRC, 2001-2002); *National Human Rights Commission: Annual Report* (New Delhi: NHRC, 2000-2001); *National Human Rights Commission: Annual Report* (New Delhi: NHRC, 1999-2000); *National Human Rights Commission: Annual Report* (New Delhi: NHRC, 1998-1999); *National Human Rights Commission: Annual Report* (New Delhi: NHRC, 1997-1998); *National Human Rights Commission: Annual Report* (New Delhi: NHRC, 1996-1997); *National Human Rights Commission: Annual Report* (New Delhi: NHRC, 1995-1996); *National Human Rights Commission: Annual Report* (New Delhi: NHRC, 1994-1995); *Custodial Deaths in Delhi, 2003* (Delhi: People's Union for Democratic Rights, 2004); *Dead Men's Tales: Deaths in Police Custody* (Delhi: People's Union for Democratic Rights, 2000); *Capital Crimes: Deaths in Police Custody, 1980-1997* (Delhi: People's Union for Democratic Rights, 1998); P. A. Sebastian, "The State and the Police," *Economic and Political Weekly* 23 (1988): 2210-11; *Torture in India: A State of Denial* (Delhi: Asian Center for Human Rights, June 2008).

5. *Prevention and Punishment of Torture Bill, 2009: Report of the National Conference on the Prevention of Torture Bill, 2008, as Drafted by the Government of India*, edited by Suhas Chakma (Delhi: Asian Center for Human Rights, July 2009), 1.

6. *Torture in India: A State of Denial*, 3.

7. *National Human Rights Commission: Annual Report*, 2003-2004.

8. India has also signed the International Covenant on Civil and Political Rights (ICCPR) and the UN Declaration on Torture, which prohibit the use of torture. *One Hundred and Fifty Second Report on Custodial Crimes* (Delhi: Law Commission of India, 1994), 16-17.

9. Tarunabh Khaitan, "A Bill Designed to Fail," *Hindu.com*, May 19, 2010. http://www.thehindu.com/2010/05/19/stories/2010051957251300.htm (last visited June 11, 2010). In April 2010, the bill was passed in the Lok Sabha—the lower house of Parliament but the process is stalled due to concerns posed by human rights groups.

10. For instance, the Maneka Gandhi case stated that "the ambit of personal liberty protected by Art. 21 is wide and comprehensive. It embraces both substantive rights to personal liberty and the procedure provided for their deprivation." *Maneka Gandhi v. Union of India* (1978). http://judis.nic.in/supremecourt/qrydisp.asp?tfnm=5154 (last visited July 11, 2005).

11. In addition, Article 22 (1) and 22 (2) are meant to ensure safeguards against arbitrary arrest and detention. Article 22 (1) requires a detained person to be told the charges against him or her as soon as possible and also to be informed of a right to counsel. Article 22 (2) determines that the person detained should be produced in front of a magistrate within twenty-four hours and not be detained beyond that period without an authorization from the magistrate. Even though these articles focus on arrest and detention, these become important safeguards against torture since many cases of torture occur in the context of initial arrest and investigations.

12. For example, in Section 330 of the Indian Penal Code, there are specific provisions that apply in cases of wrongful restraint, confinement, voluntarily causing hurt or grievous hurt to get confessions, and rape and other sexual offenses.

13. The Code of Criminal Procedure is not applicable in certain parts of the country, such as Kashmir and parts of the North East. See R. V. Kelkar, *Lectures on Criminal Procedure* (Lucknow: Eastern Book Company, 2003), 2.

14. Here I focus on the police although it should be noted that many forms of custodial violence are committed by paramilitary forces, the army, and, now, even private squads such as Salwa Judum (militia sponsored by the state of Chhatisgarh). Fact-finding reports on Salwa Judum can be obtained from the website for the Campaign for Peace and Justice in Chhattisgarh, http://cpjc.wordpress.com/reports-by-fact-finding-teams-on-salwajudum/ (last visited January 10, 2010).

15. In their annual reports, the NHRC continually reiterates the need to combat custodial violence, and in particular to demand a change in the law of evidence regarding the burden of proof under section 114 (B) and the removal of sanctions under section 197 of the CrPc that require prior permission to file a case against a state official. The NHRC also demands that each custodial death should be looked into by a sessions judge. *National Human Rights Commission: Annual Report*, 2001-2002; see also *National Human Rights Commission: Annual Report*, 2000-2001; *National Human Rights Commission: Annual Report*, 1999-2000; *National Human Rights Commission: Annual Report*, 1998-1999; *National Human Rights Commission: Annual Report*, 1997-1998; *National Human*

Rights Commission: Annual Report, 1996-1997; *National Human Rights Commission: Annual Report*, 1995-1996; *National Human Rights Commission: Annual Report*, 1994-1995. In 2005, section 176 of the CrPc has been amended so that any custodial death (or rape or disappearance) has to be looked into by a judicial or metropolitan magistrate instead of an executive magistrate (section 176 (1a)).

16. Nirman Arora, "Custodial Torture in Police Stations in India: A Radical Assessment," *Journal of the Indian Law Institute* 41 (1999): 513-29; R. C. Dikshit, "Police and Human Rights Issues," *CBI Bulletin* (December 1994): 3-8; N. S. Kamboj, "Police Custodial Death: A Growing Abuse to Human Rights in India," *Journal of the Indian Law Institute* 36 (1994): 372-77. For a different perspective on the media, see G. S. Bhargava, "Torture as a Human Rights Issue," *Mainstream* 37 (1999): 31-32.

17. Ibid.

18. S. Venugopal Rao, "The Anatomy of Police Violence," in *Police and Emerging Challenges*, edited by S. K. Chaturvedi, 97-101 (Delhi: B.R. Publishing, 1988); Arora, "Custodial Torture."

19. Arora, "Custodial Torture."

20. S. Venugopal Rao, "The Anatomy of Police Violence."

21. In this study using descriptive survey methodology, 269 randomly chosen respondents were interviewed. The list included senior police officials, civil service officers, judicial officers, forensic experts, academics, students, journalists, and members of the general public. Sankar Sen, P. S. V. Prasad, and A. K. Saxena, *Custodial Deaths in India: A Research Study* (Hyderabad: S.V.P. National Police Academy, 1994).

22. Ibid.

23. I thank legal scholar Usha Ramanathan for pointing me to this important observation. However, it is important to note that scholars such as Upendra Baxi also point out that the negative aspect of the police is focused more than their other roles although the crucial difference between the cop scholars and Baxi is that the latter points to the difficulties faced by the police even while acknowledging the high levels of torture that they engage in.

24. I thank feminist and human rights scholar and activist Uma Chakravarti for pointing this out to me.

25. K. G. Kannabiran, *The Wages of Impunity: Power, Justice, and Human Rights* (New Delhi: Orient Longman, 2003); *Sunil Batra etc. v. Delhi Administration and Ors etc.* (1978), http://judis.nic.in/supremecourt/qrydisp.asp?tfnm=5022.

26. Arora, "Custodial Torture." Other scholars who note the significance of colonial continuities include B. Hydervall, "Compensation to Victims of Lock-up Deaths: A Juridical Study," *Criminal Law Journal* (1994): 135-40; Ravi Armugam, "Custodial Violence and Deaths: Problems and Prevention," *CBI Bulletin* (December 1994): 9-20; Justice Gulab Gupta, "Custodial Violence and Human Rights Commissions," *Central India Law Quarterly* 12 (1999): 285-302. Sumanta Bannerjee points out that torture has been both a product of indigenous traditions and reinforced by the British system. Sumanta Bannerjee, "Torture in Custody: Method in Sadistic Madness," *Economic and Political Weekly* 36 (2001): 723-24, 724.

27. See John Langbein, *Torture and the Law of Proof: Europe and England in the Ancien Regime* (Chicago: University of Chicago Press, 1997).

28. Ranajit Guha, "Dominance without Hegemony and Its Historiography," in *Subaltern Studies VI: Writings on South Asian History and Society*, edited by Ranajit Guha, 210-309 (Delhi: Oxford University Press, 1989), 277.

29. B. Hydervall, "Law and Lock-up Deaths in India," *Supreme Court Journal* 1 (1990): 61-67, 62.

30. "Raj" refers to "regime/rule."

31. K. Ravindran, "Custodial Violence and Measures to Curb," *PRP Journal of Human Rights* (January–March 2002): 7-8, 7.

32. Rao, "The Anatomy of Police Violence," 97-98.

33. Upendra Baxi, *The Crisis of the Indian Legal System* (New Delhi: Vikas Publishing House, 1982), 85.

34. Ibid.

35. Ibid., 86.

36. Dikshit, "Police and Human Rights Issues"; Armugam, "Custodial Violence and Deaths: Problems and Prevention"; Sen et al., *Custodial Deaths in India.*; R. S. Saini, "Custodial Torture in Law and Practice with Reference to India," *Journal of the Indian Law Institute* 36 (2): 166-92; Arora, "Custodial Torture"; Subash C. Raina, "Custodial Torture in Police Stations: Causes and Areas of Improvement," *National Capital Law Journal* 5 (2000): 1-20; Archana Sinha, "Torture Is a Challenge to the Administration of Justice," *PRP Journal of Human Rights* 5 (2001): 34-43; Joginder Singh, "Third Degree Violates Human Rights," *Civil and Military Law Journal* 39 (2003): 143-45; Sudesh Kumar Sharma, "Human Rights, Police, and Custodial Violence: A Perspective," *M.D.U. Law Journal* 5 (2000): 40-44. S. Akhilesh, "Brief Study of Custodial Deaths," *CBI Bulletin* 9 (2001): 22-25.

37. See Baxi, *The Crisis of the Indian Legal System*, 130-35.

38. See list of initiatives in the context of police reform. http://www.humanrightsinitiative.org/programs/aj/police/india/initiatives/writ_petition.htm and http://www.humanrightsinitiative.org/publications/police/police_reform_debates_in_india.pdf.

39. In 2005, the Soli Sorabjee Committee also came up with a Model Police Act that, along with the Supreme Court decision, will possibly culminate in serious reforms in the coming years. *Prakash Singh & Ors. v. Union of India and Ors* (2006). http://www.alrc.net/doc/pdf/PrakashSingh.pdf (last visited January 29, 2007).

40. Puran Batria, "Treatment of Women at the Police Station," *Indian Police Journal* (July-September 1982): 41-44; Armugam, "Custodial Violence and Deaths: Problems and Prevention"; Dr. S. Subramanian, "Human Rights and Internal Security Operations," *CBI Bulletin* (December 1994): 1-2; Saini, "Custodial Torture in Law and Practice with Reference to India"; Sen et al., *Custodial Deaths in India*; Wasim Ali Mohd, "Human Rights and Custodial Violence," *Civil and Military Law Journal* 31 (1995): 42-46; Arora, "Custodial Torture"; Justice Markandey Katju, "Torture as a Challenge to Civil Society and the Administration of Justice," *Supreme Court Cases Journal* 2 (2000): 39-43. Sharma, "Human Rights, Police, and Custodial Violence: A Perspective"; Gurpreet K. Pannu. "Police and Custodial Violence," *Journal of Legal Studies* 33 (2003): 40-44; Kaustav Sen, "Custodial Torture: A Preventive Framework," *Central India Law Quarterly* 12 (1999): 334-43.

41. Michelle Brown, "'Setting the Conditions' for Abu Ghraib: The Prison Nation Abroad," *American Quarterly* 57 (2005): 973-98.

42. See Baxi on how torture is not just restricted to the state actors but is also a part of other hierarchical relations that exist in society. Baxi, *The Crisis of the Indian Legal System*, 138-39.

43. Ibid.

44. See exclusive focus on the police and/or reiteration of the Court's initiatives. For example, Suresh Benjamin, "Prevent Torture by the Police and Investigation Agencies," *Criminal Law Journal* 107 (2001): 10-13; A. K. Avasthi, "Police Atrocities, Custodial Violence, Plight of Prisoners, and Human Rights," *Law Review* 21-22 (2001): 15-25; N. Sreeramulu, "Lockup Deaths and Harassment by Police," *Criminal Law Journal* 106 (2000): 149-50; R. S. Verma and I. B. S. Thokchom, "Law Related to Human Rights and Custodial Death," *PRP Journal of Human Rights* 4 (2000): 20-24.

45. M. Deva Prasad, "Law and Torture: Legal Implications from Indian Perspective." http://papers.ssrn.com/sol3/papers.cfm?abstract_id=999862 (last visited October 2008), 3. He does note that there is no clear definition of torture either in the Indian Constitution or in any statute or judicial decision but focuses more on a nonimplementation of the judicial decisions than on tensions within the jurisprudence.

46. *Torture in India: A State of Denial*, 61. See also 61-63.

47. Ibid.

48. As discussed in chapter 5, self-incrimination and custodial violence were linked in the context of an extraordinary law: POTA.

49. *Satpathy v. Dani* (1978) 2 SCC 424.

50. Ibid., 438.

51. The right to silence was claimed under Article 20 (3) and the complementary provision 161 (2) of the CrPc. Section 161 (2) states, "Such persons shall be bound to answer truly all questions relating to such case put to him by such officer, other than questions the answers of which would have a tendency to expose him to a criminal charge or to a penalty or forfeiture." Ibid.; see Ratanlal Ranchhoddas and Dhirajlal K. Thakore, *The Code of Criminal Procedure* (Agra: Wadhwa and Company Law Publishers, 2002).

52. Miranda excluded all incriminating evidence before the safeguards are given but in India it is mainly confession that is excluded by section 26 of the CrPc.

53. *Satpathy v. Dani* (1978) 2 SCC 424, 441.

54. Ibid.

55. Ibid., 454.

56. The Satpathy Court accepted that the only way to effectively combine the right to counsel and the right against self-incrimination was to allow the lawyer to be present during the interrogation to ensure the protection of rights. The Indian Court also realized that ensuring this right was extremely difficult given the lack of widespread legal aid for defendants, so it asked the police to warn the suspect of the right against self-incrimination and to record this. If no lawyer was available, the Court asked for the suspect to be taken to a magistrate, a doctor, or an official/nonofficial to whom the suspect could speak outside of police custody and who in turn could collate a report for the magistrate. This, however, was just a suggestion by the Court, not mandated. *Satpathy v. Dani* (1978) 2 SCC 424.

57. See discussion on Article 21 in Balvinder Kaur, "Torture and Deaths in Police Custody: A Violation of Right to Life," *National Capital Law Journal* 2 (1997): 107-14; A. K. Avasthi, "Police Atrocities, Custodial Violence, Plight of Prisoners, and Human Rights."

58. In fact, section 162 states that while section 161 allows for a statement made during investigation by the police to be put in writing, it cannot be used against the accused. There are certain exceptions. See Ratanlal and Dhirajlal, *Code of Criminal Procedure*, 2002, 229-32.

59. Section 27 allows for a particular admission to be included if it leads to the discovery of a fact even if the person is in the custody of the police and the admission is a confession. This is very controversial since it allows misuse of sections 24-26. See debates on section 27 despite recommendations to strike it down since it is known to be misused by the police. *One Hundred and Fifty Second Report on Custodial Crimes*, Law Commission of India, 41-44; *The State of Bombay v. Kathi Kalu Oghad and Others* (1961). http://judis.nic.in/supremecourt/qrydisp.asp?tfnm=4157 (last visited June 23, 2005).

60. See *One Hundred and Fifty Second Report on Custodial Crimes*, Law Commission of India. Apart from section 164 of the CrPc, the High Court has certain orders to be followed by the magistrate to ensure voluntariness of confessions. The accused are to be told that the recording officer is a magistrate, and asked why they want to confess. They are to be told that they do not have to confess and that anything they do confess will be used as evidence. They are to be asked whether they have been ill-treated or influenced in any way by the police during custody. They are to be assured that they will not be sent to police custody even if they do not confess. They are to be asked to reflect on this outside police influence and then the confession is to be recorded after about twenty-four hours. Once the confession is recorded, it is to be read to the accused and a certificate is to be appended that the statement is true and accurate, and the magistrate must write that he believes that this statement has been voluntarily made. See *Shivappa v. State of Karnataka* (1995) 2 SCC 76.

61. *Sarwan Singh v. State of Punjab* (1957) http://judis.nic.in/supremecourt/qrydisp.asp?tfnm=652 (last visited August 5, 2005).

62. This was a case where three people—Harbans Singh, Gurdial Singh, and Sarwan Singh— were accused of murdering the brother of one of the accused with *kirpan*—a traditional weapon. All three were convicted by the trial court and one was acquitted by the High Court. Ibid.

63. Section 163 of the CrPc disallows the police (or any other authority) from using "inducement, threat, or promise" to get confessions. See *Bram v. United States* (1897), where voluntariness in confessions excluded any "pressure of hope or fear." See chapter 1 for details.

64. Ibid. Ratanlal and Dhirajlal, *The Code of Criminal Procedure*, 229-32. *Sarwan Singh v. State of Punjab* (1957). http://judis.nic.in/supremecourt/qrydisp.asp?tfnm=652 (last visited August 5, 2005).

65. Ibid.

66. Shankaria was accused of killing people—men, women, and children—in the *gurudwara* (Sikh holy place) with a *ghota* (heavy stick) and was also implicated in other murders in that area. In this particular case, the confession suggested that he could only find two rupees as a result of his labors. *Shankaria v. State of Rajasthan* 4 SCC 453 (1978).

67. *Sarwan Singh v. State of Punjab* (1957). http://judis.nic.in/supremecourt/qrydisp.asp?tfnm=652 (last visited August 5, 2005), emphasis added.

68. Ibid.

69. The difference in the way the Sarwan Singh case played out in comparison with the Shankaria case may also be due in part to the difference in the nature of the crime committed by Shankaria, who was a mass murderer. While proportionality of punishment is the basis of most legal systems, Indian jurisprudence on the death penalty has made a distinction between "rarest of rare" cases and other cases that leads to a very careful consideration of whether a particular person deserves the death penalty or not. See *Machhi Singh v. State of Punjab* (1983) 3 SCC 470 after the Bachhan Singh case in 1979.

70. The decision in Shankaria becomes even more curious when we analyze it in relation to another case in the same year about the recording of confessions. In this case, *Chandran v. Tamil Nadu*, the Supreme Court decided that the confession was not acceptable because the magistrate had written that he "hoped" that the confession was voluntary. *Chandran v. State of T.N.* (1978) 4 SCC 90.

71. The Court notes that there were inconsistencies in the doctors' reports, especially in the case of one doctor who initially stated that the injuries could not be the result of the weapon mentioned but later changed his statement (bravely, according to the Court) upon further examination. In addition, the Court accepted that the doctor's note was faulty due to a typographical error. *Shankaria v. State of Rajasthan* (1978) 4 SCC 453.

72. *Shivappa v. State of Karnataka* (1995) 2 SCC 76.

73. In this case, the Supreme Court stated that the confession was not voluntary because the magistrate did not make a "real endeavor" to ensure the voluntariness. Thus, in this case, the truth of the confession was not considered as important as the presence of procedural errors. Ibid. The emphasis on procedure is also accompanied by a debate on who constitutes a police officer. The Supreme Court determined that only those officers who have powers similar to those of police officers, such as excise officers but not customs officers or railway officers, should be considered as being covered by section 162 of CrPc and section 25 of the Indian Evidence Act. *Raja Ram Jaiswal v. State of Bihar* (1963). http://judis.nic.in/supremecourt/qrydisp.asp?tfnm=3552 (last visited August 5, 2005). *Balkishan A. Devidayal etc. v. State of Maharashtra etc.* (1980). http://judis.nic.in/supremecourt/qrydisp.asp?tfnm=4489 (last visited June 23, 2005). *State of Punjab v. Barkat Ram* (1961). http://judis.nic.in/supremecourt/qrydisp.asp?tfnm=4134 (last visited June 23, 2005). The dissenting justice, Subba Rao, in Barkat Ram's case, however, asserts that in essence, safeguards against coerced confessions should apply to any officer to whom the confession is submitted due to similarity of custodial conditions. But the Supreme Court disagreed in *Romesh Chandra Mehta v. State of Bengal* (1968). http://judis.nic.in/supremecourt/qrydisp.asp?tfnm=1937 (last visited July 11, 2005).

74. *State of T.N. v. Kutty* (2001) 6 SCC 550.

75. See chapter 5 for details.

76. In some instances, the Supreme Court would clearly accept a death as custodial, while in others, it would not, without adequately explaining why. For instance, see *Raghbir Singh v. State of Haryana* (1980) where the court accepted the death as custodial. http://judis.nic.in/supremecourt/qrydisp.asp?tfnm=4571 (last visited July 11, 2005). The Court also seemed to be more sympathetic in cases where the victim was an innocent bystander. *Kashmeri Devi v. Delhi Administration and ANR* (1988). http://judis.nic.in/supremecourt/qrydisp.asp?tfnm=8348 (last visited July 11, 2005).

77. *Ram Chander v. State of Haryana* (1983) 3 SCC 335.

78. *Maiku v. State of U.P* (1989) Supp. 1 SCC 25.

79. Ibid., 30.

80. For instance, in cases such as *Haroon Haji Abdulla v. State of Maharashtra* (1967) and *Ashok Kumar v. State (Delhi Administration)* (1977) 2 SCC 233, suspects alleged that they made their statements and confessions under police threat and torture. In *Haroon Haji Abdulla v. State of Maharashtra*, for instance, the Court stated that while it is not illegal to use retracted evidence, it is prudent to have independent corroboration. *Haroon Haji Abdulla v. State of Maharashtra* (1967). http://judis.nic.in/supremecourt/qrydisp.asp?tfnm=2195 (last visited August 5, 2005).

81. *Dagdu v. State of Maharashtra* (1977) 3 SCC 68, 77.

82. Ibid.

83. Ibid., 92.

84. Ibid., 82.

85. This discourse on "worthless witnesses" and class bias is particularly important in the Indian legal discourse. See *State of T.N. v. Kutty* (2001) 6 SCC 550 for discussion of the watchman's role. See also discussion on importance of "educated class" in handcuffing cases. M. L. Upadhya, "Torture in Police Custody and Handcuffing of the Accused," *Central India Law Quarterly* 9 (1996): 458-64.

86. In the Ram Chander case also, the trial court acquitted the police because the court found the witnesses to be of "shady character" and their interests "inimical to the police," and thus the court felt they could not be believed. *Ram Chander v. State of Haryana* (1983) 3 SCC 335.

87. *Capital Crimes*.

88. Ibid.

89. See discussion in Flavia Agnes, "Protecting Women against Violence: Review of a Decade of Legislation, 1980-89," *Economic and Political Weekly* 17 (1992): WS19-WS33. See discussions on custodial rape in *Custody: An Investigation into Five Cases of Sexual Assault* (Delhi: People's Union for Democratic Rights, 2004); *Custodial Rape: A Report on the Aftermath* (Delhi: People's Union for Democratic Rights, 1994); Rakesh Shukla, "Flaw in the Law: Custodial Rape, Inadequate Evidence, and Acquittal," *InfoChange News and Features*, March 2004. http://search.choike.org/cgi-bin/choike.cgi?cs=&q=environment&ch=http:%2F%2Fwww.infochangeindia.org%2Fanalysis19.jsp&fm=off (last visited June 23, 2004).

90. In *Maiku v. State of U.P.* (1989) Supp. 1 SCC 25, there was also alleged sexual torture of Ramdei, who stated that chilies had been thrust into her vagina, but the Court did not believe that due to inconsistencies in the story. Thus, "inconsistency" in a story has often been used as an excuse to avoid addressing "custodial rape" despite changes in some of the laws. Ibid. See also debates in international law on rape as torture. Eveleyn Mary Aswad, "Torture by Means of Rape," *Georgetown Law Journal* 84 (1996): 1913-43. Catharine MacKinnon, "Rape, Genocide, and Women's Human Rights," *Harvard Women's Law Journal* 17 (1994): 5-16.

91. Shukla, "Flaw in the Law."

92. I thank Uma Chakravarti for pointing this out to me.

93. *Satpathy v. Dani* (1978) 2 SCC 424.

94. The Indian Constitution does not have a specific article preventing the use of penal torture (or cruel and unusual punishment, as it is called in the United States). Rather, a combination of articles—Articles 21 (no deprivation of life and liberty except by following a procedure established by law), 14 (right to equality), and 19 (right to freedom)—is used to ensure that there is no use of unfair procedure, arbitrary classification, or unreasonable restrictions in the penal system. The issues that have emerged in the jurisprudence of imprisonment have primarily addressed excesses against persons undergoing trial (termed "undertrials") and convicted prisoners. Acts of illegal state violence have mainly been in the form of solitary confinement or use of fetters, but occasionally there have been extreme forms of physical violence such as blinding of persons undergoing trials. The Indian Supreme Court clearly announced that the prison was not outside the purview of judicial scrutiny and that the prisoners had certain rights, such as the rights to due process, equality, and liberty. *Sunil Batra etc. v. Delhi Administration and Ors etc.* (1978)http://judis.nic.in/supremecourt/qrydisp. asp?tfnm=5022 (last visited August 5, 2005); *Ranbir Singh Sehgal v. State of Punjab* (1962). http://judis.nic.in/supremecourt/qrydisp.asp?tfnm=4079 (last visited April 4, 2005); *Charles Sobraj v. The Suptd., Central Jail, Tihar, New Delhi* (1978); http://judis.nic.in/ supremecourt/qrydisp.asp?tfnm=5021 (last visited August 5, 2005); *Anil Yadav v. State of Bihar* (1982) 2 SCC 195; Arvind Tiwari, "Custodial Torture in Indian Prisons: Overview," *CBI Bulletin* 8 (2000): 9-18; M. L Upadhyay, "Torture in Police Custody and Handcuffing of the Accused," *Central India Law Quarterly* 9 (1996): 458-64.

95. Rakesh Shukla, "Police Torture: Prevention Is Better Than Compensation," *Lawyers Collective* 8 (1993): 9-12.

96. Adriana P. Bartow, quoted in *D. K. Basu v. State of West Bengal*; *Ashok K. Johri v. State of Uttar Pradesh* (1996) http://judis.nic.in/supremecourt/qrydisp.asp?tfnm=14580 (last visited June 23, 2005), emphasis added.

97. Jawahar Lal Nehru, the first prime minister of India, was a great believer in the trickle-down theory of development, so his approach was to focus on big dam projects and on increasing the agricultural productivity of certain regions through the Green Revolution. This is broadly called the Nehru-Mahanalobis model. For an excellent and concise analysis of the postindependent Indian polity, see Nivedita Menon and Aditya Nigam, *Power and Contestation: India since 1989* (London: Zed, 2007).

98. "*Dalit*" refers to self-naming by the formerly termed untouchable castes as representing their power and resistance, and one of the *dalit* community's most important leaders, B. R. Ambedkar, was the chief architect of the Indian Constitution. Ibid.

99. G. Haragopal and K. Balagopal, "Civil Liberties Movement and the State in India," in *People's Rights: Social Movements and the State in the Third World*, edited by Manoranjan Mohanty, Partha Nath Mukherji, and Olle Tornquist, 353-71 (New Delhi: Sage, 1998), 356.

100. "Naxalite movement" refers to the Marxist-Leninist-Maoist-inspired transformative movements in Bengal and Andhra Pradesh that started in the 1960s. See Manoranjan Mohanty, *Revolutionary Violence: A Study of the Maoist Movement in India* (New Delhi: Sterling Publishers, 1977). "Jay Prakash Narayan Movement" refers to a nonviolent movement for "total revolution." See discussion in Baxi, *The Crisis of the Indian Legal System*, 16-21.

101. Haragopal and Balagopal, "Civil Liberties Movement and the State in India," 361.

102. The then Indian prime minister, Indira Gandhi, claiming an internal crisis, declared an internal emergency on June 25, 1975, that lasted till 1977. This led to unprecedented erosion of fundamental rights and institutional processes. See Nivedita Menon and Aditya Nigam, *Power and Contestation*.

103. See discussion in Baxi, *The Crisis of the Indian Legal System*, 16-21.

104. Haragopal and Balagopal, "Civil Liberties Movement and the State in India." Also See Manoranjan Mohanty, Partha Nath Mukherji, and Olle Tornquist, "Introduction," in *People's Rights: Social Movements and the State in the Third World*, edited by Manoranjan Mohanty, Partha Nath Mukherji, and Olle Tornquist (New Delhi: Sage, 1998), 22-24.

105. Haragopal and Balagopal, "Civil Liberties Movement and the State in India," 364.

106. Ajay Gudavarthy, "Human Rights Movement(s) in India: State, Civil Society, and Beyond," in *Human Rights and Peace: Ideas, Laws, Institutions, and Movements*, edited by Ujjwal Singh, 252-75 (New Delhi: Sage, 2009), 255.

107. Haragopal and Balagopal, "Civil Liberties Movement and the State in India"; G. Haragopal, *Political Economy of Human Rights: Emerging Dimensions* (Mumbai: Himalaya, 1997). For a critical engagement on the notion of the "civil rights movement" in India, see Upendra Baxi, "The State and the Human Rights Movements in India," in *People's Rights: Social Movements and the State in the Third World*, edited by Manoranjan Mohanty, Partha Nath Mukherji, and Olle Tornquist, 335-52 (New Delhi: Sage, 1998).

108. Manoranjan Mohanty, "Indian Social Movements' Contribution to the Theory of Rights," Iqbal Narain Memorial Lecture, University of Rajasthan, Jaipur, 7 January 2009 (on file with author).

109. *Report on Torture*, Amnesty International (London: Duckworth, in association with Amnesty International Publications, 1973).

110. A. G. Noorani, "Rule by Torture: Amnesty International Report on Torture," *Economic and Political Weekly* 9 (1974): 477-79, 477.

111. Ibid.

112. *Custodial Deaths in Delhi*; *Dead Men's Tales*; *Capital Crimes*.

113. Usha Ramanathan, *Human Rights in India: A Mapping*, 2001. http://www.ielrc.org/content/w0103.pdf (last visited on January 30, 2006), 2.

114. Ibid.

115. Baxi, "The State and the Human Rights Movement in India," 343.

116. Verma and Thokchom, "Human Rights and Custodial Death."

117. This was reiterated by Justice Frankfurter, who agreed that the due process clause should not be the framework for India. S. P. Sathe, *Judicial Activism in India: Transgressing Borders and Enforcing Limits* (New Delhi: Oxford University Press, 2002), 57.

118. Ibid. Durga Das Basu, *Human Rights in Constitutional Law* (Nagpur: Wadhwa, 2003).

119. *Maneka v. Union of India* (1978) http://judis.nic.in/supremecourt/qrydisp.asp?tfnm=5154 (last visited July 11, 2005).

120. The Law Commission of India also took up the issue of custodial crimes *suo moto* and brought out a detailed report on the issue in 1994. See *One Hundred and Fifty Second Report on Custodial Crimes*.

121. See *Gauri Shankar Sharma v. State of U.P.* (1990). http://judis.nic.in/supremecourt/qrydisp.asp?tfnm=7691 (last visited August 5, 2005). *Bhagwan Singh and Another v. State of Punjab* (1992) 3 SCC 249. After which the Law Commission also recommended the same for custodial death cases. *State of U.P. v. Ram Sagar Yadav*, quoted in *One Hundred and Fifty Second Report on Custodial Crimes*, 41.

122. *Smt. Nilabati Behera v. State of Orissa* (1993). http://judis.nic.in/supremecourt/qry-disp.asp?tfnm=12126 (last visited July 11, 2005).

123. Ibid.

124. One area in which the Supreme Court has consistently taken a stand against offi-cers is when they attempt to defend the use of torture by claiming some kind of immunity due to their authorized powers of investigation. *The State of Andhra Pradesh v. N. Venu-gopal and Others* (1963). http://judis.nic.in/supremecourt/qrydisp.asp?tfnm=3492 (last visited September 6, 2005); *S. P. Vaithianathan v. K. Shanmuganathan* (1994) 4 SCC 569. However, the issue of sanctions under section 197 remains to be resolved and is reiterated by human rights groups.

125. *Smt. Nilabati Behera v. State of Orissa* (1993). http://judis.nic.in/supremecourt/qry-disp.asp?tfnm=12126 (last visited July 11, 2005).

126. In the Kasturilal case, the Supreme Court upheld the right to sovereign immunity, but that was a private tort case. *Kasturilal Ralia Rain Jain v. The State of Uttar Pradesh* (1965). http://judis.nic.in/supremecourt/qrydisp.asp?tfnm=3167 (last visited June 23, 2005).

127. The precedent for the right to compensation was Rudul Sah (1983), which established the right to compensation in cases where there are violation of fundamental rights under Article 226 of the Constitution by the High Court and Article 32 of the Constitution by the Supreme Court. The Court did suggest that ordinarily redressal for violations of fundamen-tal rights should go back to the courts, especially when there is factual controversy, but sub-sequent cases have followed Rudul Sah's suggestions that compensation for violations of fun-damental rights can be awarded in public law cases. This precedent was used in Saheli and Hongray. Saheli, *A Women's Resources Centre and Others v. Commissioner of Police, Delhi Police Headquarters and Others* (1990). http://judis.nic.in/supremecourt/qrydisp.asp?tfnm=7710 (last visited August 5, 2005). *Sebastian M. Hongray v. Union of India and Others* (1984) 1 SCC 339. The state is held responsible for the tortious acts of its employees in these cases and compensation is given. See also *Bhim Singh v. State of J&K* (1985) (4) SCC 677. Compensa-tion for custodial violence came up in a 1989 case, *State of A.P. v. Challa Ramkrishna Reddy* in Usha Ramanathan, "Tort Law," *Annual Survey of Indian Law* 36 (2001): 615-58.

128. Meanwhile the Nilabati Behera case, allowing for compensation for the deprivation of liberty, including custodial torture and death, continued to be used, for instance in *T.C. Pathak v. State of U.P.* (1995) 6 SCC 357.

129. Another case was added to this public interest litigation, the case of the custodial death of Mahesh Bihari in Uttar Pradesh, added by Ashok Johri. *D. K. Basu v. State of West Bengal*; *Ashok K. Johri v. State of Uttar Pradesh* (1996). http://judis.nic.in/supremecourt/qrydisp.asp?tfnm=14580 (last visited June 23, 2005).

130. Ibid., emphasis added.

131. Ibid.

132. Ibid. More specifically, the Court stated that the Indian law excludes both physical torture and mental agony although determining the extent of the trauma prohibited is beyond the "purview of law."

133. Ibid., emphasis added.

134. In Shanti Devi's case in 1997, she was detained without any record for three days and allegedly committed suicide. *Capital Crimes,* 12.

135. *Custodial Deaths in Delhi; Dead Men's Tales; Capital Crimes.*

136. *Capital Crimes,* 12.

137. Ibid., 10.

138. Ibid.

139. *Custodial Deaths in Delhi; Dead Men's Tales; Capital Crimes.*

140. *D. K. Basu v. State of West Bengal; Ashok K. Johri v. State of Uttar Pradesh* (1996). http://judis.nic.in/supremecourt/qrydisp.asp?tfnm=14580 (last visited June 23, 2005), emphasis added.

141. *One Hundred and Fifty Second Report on Custodial Crimes.*

142. Before the D. K. Basu case, the Supreme Court had, in an earlier case—*Joginder Singh v. State of Uttar Pradesh* (1994) 3 J.T. (SC)—suggested the right of the arrested person to inform a concerned person about his or her arrest, and the Court said that he or she should be informed of this right. See *One Hundred and Fifty Second Report on Custodial Crimes.*

143. This information was to be disseminated through the police administrative channels, *doordarshan* (national television), radio, and pamphlets in different languages. The Court declared that these rules had to be followed and that any violation would result in departmental action as well as contempt of court proceedings. *D. K. Basu v. State of West Bengal; Ashok K. Johri v. State of Uttar Pradesh* (1996). http://judis.nic.in/supremecourt/qrydisp.asp?tfnm=14580 (last visited June 23, 2005).

144. The Court also addressed the question of multiple remedies. The criminal prosecutions under Sections 330 and 331 for hurt/grievous hurt for confessions and information are noted by the Court along with section 220, which addresses the issue of confinement with a malicious motive. Ibid.

145. Thus, the Supreme Court came up with a right to compensation despite the absence of a right to compensation in the Indian Constitution. Ibid.

146. Ibid.

147. Ibid.

148. PUDR reports over the years point out that executive magistrates—SDMs—usually exonerate the police and the postmortem report only discusses the cause of death, and if it is preceded by torture or other severe treatment, that is not necessarily mentioned in the report or if it is, it is not given much importance. Thus, the police get away with the torture by calling the death a natural one. Even the First Information Report is not written in many cases, and if there are witnesses, they are threatened by the police. The PUDR reports state that sometimes there is even evidence of collusion among the doctors, the executive magistrate, and the police. Departmental inquiries are used to replace the criminal prosecution process, and if action is taken against the persons involved, they are either exonerated or transferred and then reinstated after a brief period. Prosecution of the guilty is not a priority of the courts. The difficulties of the trial process itself allow very few cases to actually come to the Court due to delays in framing charges, delays in establishing trial dates, lack of witnesses, and lack of resources for the poor defendants. The PUDR has constantly demanded that (1) all cases should be investigated and prosecuted, and compensation should be given; (2) if a police official is indicted by executive inquiry, there should be charges filed: (3) the inquiry report should be made public, as should the postmortem report. See *Custodial Deaths in Delhi; Dead Men's Tales; Capital Crimes.* Often then cases are highlighted only when protests are held and reports brought out by human rights groups.

149. *The Secretary, Hailakandi Bar Association v. State of Assam and Another* (1995) Supp. (3) SCC 736.

150. *The Secretary, Hailakandi Bar Association v. State of Assam and Another* (1996). http://www.judis.nic.in/supremecourt/helddis3.aspx (last visited August 5, 2006). Referring a case to CBI (Central Bureau of Investigation) is often a demand by human rights groups because the CBI is the investigating police agency of India and is not under the control of the police structure, which provides some degree of independence. See *Custodial Deaths in Delhi*; *Dead Men's Tales*; *Capital Crimes*.

151. See the inconsistencies in the jurisprudence in the context of *Lokeman Shah and Another v. State of W.B.* (2001) 5 SCC 235.

152. *Sahadevan v. State* (2003) 1 SCC 534.

153. *Prevention and Punishment of Torture Bill, 2009: Report of the National Conference on the Prevention of Torture Bill, 2008, as drafted by the Government of India*, July 2009, 1.

154. The National Human Rights Commission of India has been monitoring the cases of custodial deaths in the country since its inception in 1993. The NHRC has also consistently, though unsuccessfully, requested each government to ratify the UN Convention against Torture. On the workings of the NHRC, see Thrity D. Patel, "Torture: Human Rights and Accountability of Law Enforcement Agencies," *Central India Law Quarterly* 12 (1999): 539-72; Rajeev Dhavan, Jasleen K. Oberoi, Niharika Bahl, and Dhruv Dhavan, "Step by Step: Fourth Annual Report of National Human Rights Commission, 1996-1997," *Journal of the Indian Law Institute* 41 (1999): 160-200. Usha Ramanathan, *Human Rights in India: A Mapping*.

155. *Capital Crimes.*

156. *Dead Men's Tales.*

157. *Custodial Deaths in Delhi*; *Dead Men's Tales*; *Capital Crimes.*

158. The ACHR filed several complaints with the NHRC and ensured compensation of 5.03 million rupees, and their actions have led to three dismissals of law enforcement officials, the arrest of three others, and departmental action against twenty-nine. *ACHR's Actions against Torture and Other Forms of Human Rights Violations in India*, edited by Suhas Chakma (Delhi: Asian Centre for Human Rights, June 2009).

159. *State of AP v. Upadhyaya*, quoted in *One Hundred and Eighty-Fifth Report on Review of the Indian Evidence Act, 1872* (Delhi: Law Commission of India, March 2003), 137.

160. Deva, "Law and Torture."

161. *Shakila Abdul Gafar Khan v. Vasant Raghunath Dhoble and Anr* (2003). http://judis.nic.in/supremecourt/qrydisp.asp?tfnm=19369 (last visited June 23, 2005).

162. Ibid.

163. Ibid.

164. Ibid., emphasis added.

165. A similar double-edgedness is noted in *Munshi Singh Gautam and Ors. v. State of M.P.* (2004). http://judis.nic.in/supremecourt/qrydisp.asp?tfnm=26587.

166. *Sube Singh v. State of Haryana & Ors.* (2006) http://judis.nic.in/supremecourt/held-dis.aspx (last visited January 11, 2011).

167. Ibid., emphasis added.

168. Ibid., emphasis added.

169. The Prevention of Torture Bill, 2010. http://www.univie.ac.at/bimtor/dateien/india_prevention_of_torture_bill_%202010.pdf.

170. Ibid.

171. Tarunabh Khaitan, "A Bill Designed to Fail."

172. *Prevention and Punishment of Torture Bill, 2009: Report of the National Conference on the Prevention of Torture Bill, 2008, as drafted by the Government of India*, July 2009.

173. Ravi Armugam, "Custodial Violence and Deaths: Problems and Prevention"; Sen et al., *Custodial Deaths in India*; Saini, "Custodial Torture in Law and Practice with Reference to India"; Arora, "Custodial Torture"; Raina, "Custodial Torture"; Sinha, "Torture Is a Challenge to the Administration of Justice."

174. Katju, "Torture as a Challenge to Civil Society and the Administration of Justice," 39.

175. Anand Giridhardas, "India's Novel Use of Brain Scans in Courts Is Debated," *New York Times*, September 14, 2008.

176. See Supreme Court case on narco analysis, lie detection, and brain scanning. *Smt. Selvi & Others v. State of Karnataka* (2010). http://www.indiankanoon.org/doc/338008/ (last visited January 4, 2011).

CHAPTER 5

1. This attack was considered the work of Islamic militant groups such as Jaish-E-Mohammed ostensibly functioning with the help of Pakistan. Almost all attacks of terrorism are initially considered and represented in the media, in popular culture, and by politicians as being the handiwork of Pakistan regardless of facticity. This is similar to the immediate reaction to all attacks in the United States, which are immediately considered as the work of Islamic terrorists.

2. Articles appeared on the antiterrorist actions comparing the United States, India, and Israel. See, for example, Arunabha Bhoumik, "Democratic Responses to Terrorism: A Comparative Study of the United States, Israel, and India," *Denver Journal of International Law and Policy* 33 (2005): 285-345.

3. "India, US, Together in Fighting Terror: Blackwill." *Rediff.com*, December 14, 2001. http://www.rediff.com/news/2001/dec/14parl10.htm.

4. The extraordinary legislations are certainly impacted by the change in political power. Singh rightly focuses attention on the way in which POTA discourses are different than TADA discourses, with the form of the antiterror laws under the BJP being more focused on the nation state as a whole. But what is significant is that there is always either a law that is in place or one that is in the making to combat terrorism. See history of extraordinary laws in Ujjwal Kumar Singh, "Repeal of POTA: What about Other Draconian Acts?" *Economic and Political Weekly* 39 (2004): 3677-80. Also see Ujjwal Kumar Singh, "Democratic Dilemmas: Can Democracy Do without Extraordinary Laws?" *Economic and Political Weekly* 38 (2003): 437-40.

5. Unlawful Activities Prevention Act (UAPA), 2004, is an amended version of an earlier act of the same name passed in 1967. Famous physician and civil liberties activist Binayak Sen was detained under the Chhattisgarh State Public Security Act (CSPSA), 2005, and UAPA, 2004, and sedition laws for two years in Chhatisgarh and now sentenced to life imprisonment. These laws bypass many routine forms of due process through a broad definition of an unlawful activity and acceptance of vague and unreliable evidence. *The Chhattisgarh Special Public Safety Bill, 2005: A Memorandum to the President of India*. Peoples Union for Democratic Rights (PUDR), Delhi, March 2006. http://cpjc.files.word-press.com/2007/07/memo_on_chattisgarh_bill.pdf.

6. Immediately after the Mumbai attacks, an amendment of the Unlawful Activities Prevention Act, 2004, resulting in UAPA, 2008, was passed that has brought back some of the more undemocratic provisions of POTA and TADA, such as prolonged detentions and stringent bail provisions. A. G. Noorani, "The Security State," *Economic & Political Weekly* 44 (2009): 13-15.

7. There are other all-India extraordinary laws, but I am focusing on these two due to their implications for the laws on interrogation and confessions. Some of the other laws introduced in the past are the Preventive Detention Act, 1950 (lapsed due to protest); the MISA, or Maintenance of Internal Security Act, 1971 (repealed in 1978); and the National Security Act, 1980 (closer to the Preventive Detention Act). There are also some state-specific extraordinary laws, such as the Maharashtra Control of Organized Crime Act, 1999, the Madhya Pradesh Special Areas Security Act, 2000, and the CSPSA, mentioned in note 5 above. Another very controversial law is the Armed Forces Special Powers Act (AFSPA), which applies to certain areas of the North East and was applicable to Punjab and Kashmir and gives the army a number of powers in these areas. The army does not have the powers of interrogations. At the same time, it is important to note that this particular act has resulted in a number of extrajudicial killings in these areas since these acts allow for imposing martial law like conditions in these areas. See K. G. Kannabiran, *The Wages of Impunity: Power, Justice, and Human Rights* (New Delhi: Orient Longman, 2003). The Supreme Court upheld the constitutionality of the act in 1997. *Naga People's Movement of Human Rights etc. v. Union of India*, 1997. http://judis.nic.in/supremecourt/qrydisp.asp?tfnm=13628 (last visited September 6, 2005). Prakash Louis and R. Vashum, eds., *Extraordinary Laws in India: A Reader for Understanding Legislations Endangering Civil Liberties* (New Delhi: Indian Social Institute, 2002).

8. Ujjwal Kumar Singh, "State and Emerging Interlocking Legal Systems: Permanence of the Temporary," *Economic and Political Weekly* 39 (2004): 149-54, 149.

9. See discussion on the impact of the UN resolutions on the creation of extraordinary laws in different countries. See ibid. and Kim Lane Scheppele, "Other People's Patriot Acts: Europe's Response to September 11," *Loyola Law Review* 50 (2004): 89-148.

10. Anil Kalhan, Gerald P. Conroy, Mamta Kaushal, Sam Scott Miller, and Jed S. Rakoff, "Colonial Continuities: Human Rights, Terrorism, and Security Laws in India," *Columbia Journal of Asian Law* 20 (2006): 93-234.

11. Ibid.

12. Krishnan, for instance, writes that just as the U.S. PATRIOT Act makes even the most "tangential" association with a "suspicious" organization the basis of punitive action, POTA also defined association with a terrorist group very broadly and put the onus of disproving the link with the terrorist group on the individual. The most contentious issue in both was, of course, the definition of terrorism. Jayanth K. Krishnan. "India's 'Patriot Act': POTA and the Impact on Civil Liberties in the World's Largest Democracy," *Law and Inequality* 22 (2004): 265-300. See also Chris Gagne. "POTA: Lessons Learned from India's Anti-Terror Act," *Boston Third World Law Journal* 25 (2005): 261-99.

13. Mukherji quotes Chomsky's letter to S. A. R. Geelani (the university teacher acquitted of all charges in the Parliament attack case) in this regard: "The atrocities of 9-11 were exploited in a vulgar way by governments all over the world, in some cases by escalating massive crimes on the pretext of 'combating terrorism,' in others by implementing

repressive legislation to discipline . . . terrorist threats." Chomsky quoted in Nirmalangshu Mukherji, "Teachers and War on Terrorism," *Economic and Political Weekly* 38 (2003): 4521-23, 4521.

14. Kalhan et al., "Colonial Continuities."

15. See detailed discussion on colonial laws in Kalhan et al., "Colonial Continuities."

16. Malise Ruthven, *Torture: The Grand Conspiracy* (London: Weidenfeld and Nicholson, 1978).

17. Kannabiran, *The Wages of Impunity*, 23.

18. Kalhan et al., "Colonial Continuities."

19. G. Haragopal and K. Balagopal, "Civil Liberties Movement and the State in India," in *People's Rights: Social Movement and the State in the Third World*, edited by Manoranjan Mohanty, Partha Nath Mukherji, and Olle Tornquist, 353-72 (New Delhi: Sage, 1998).

20. Kalhan et al., "Colonial Continuities."

21. See notes 5 and 7 above.

22. Kannabiran points out that around 258 statutes introduced by the British were operational right up to 1960. Kannabiran, *The Wages of Impunity*, 24.

23. I thank Upendra Baxi for pointing this out to me.

24. Upendra Baxi, *Marx, Law, and Justice: Some Indian Perspectives* (Mumbai: Tripathi, 1993), 85-94.

25. Interestingly, Kannabiran writes that while the Fourty-Fourth Amendment was introduced to ensure that internal disturbance could no longer be used to declare an emergency, as Indira Gandhi did in 1975, it ended up allowing the executive to pass emergency legislations in peacetime. Kannabiran, *The Wages of Impunity*, 74.

26. See the definition of a terrorist act in TADA in Louis and Vashum, eds., *Extraordinary Laws in India*, 163-64.

27. See ibid., 160-78.

28. See in Kalhan how Punjab officials were almost willing to accept that TADA became a preventive detention law. Kalhan et al., "Colonial Continuities."

29. That is increased to sixty, one year, and one year in 1987 and sixty, 180, and 180 days in 1993. Even though the 1993 amendment to the TADA made some changes, it mainly suggested that if the charge sheet is not filed within 180 days, the person can get bail. The judge could still bypass this provision and extend the remand up to one year if the prosecution requests it. Under Section 21 of the act, the presumption of innocence was no longer in favor of the accused in case there is any preliminary evidence that suggests the involvement of the suspect. Louis and Vashum, eds., *Extraordinary Laws in India*; Kannabiran, *The Wages of Impunity*, see chapter 7. The more egregious of the provisions —that confession of a co-accused was to be used against the accused and that confession made to anyone except a police officer would be accepted by the court unless the contrary is proved—were deleted in 1993.

30. He argues this because preventive detention laws cannot detain a person beyond three months without review by a board, but under TADA a person could be detained up to a year. Ibid., 97; K. Balagopal, "In Defence of India: Supreme Court and Terrorism," *Economic and Political Weekly* 29 (1994): 2054-60, 2056.

31. *Kartar Singh v. State of Punjab* (1994) 3 SCC 569, 701.The Supreme Court found this reasonable but K. Balagopal notes that in TADA cases the suspects did not even have the right to appeal to the high courts. Balagopal, "In Defence of India."

32. Louis and Vashum, eds., *Extraordinary Laws in India*, 160.

33. The right to a speedy trial is not a constitutional right per se, but using Article 21, there has been an attempt both legislatively and judicially to define a right to a speedy trial. "Speedy Trial Is a Constitutional Guarantee: Supreme Court," *The Hindu*, October 3, 2006. http://www.hindu.com/2006/10/03/stories/2006100302411100.htm (last visited January 20, 2008). Praveen Dalal, *Right to Speedy Trial*. http://www.naavi.org/praveen_dalal/arbitration_may_21.htm (last visited January 20, 2008).

34. Krishnan, "India's 'Patriot Act,'" 275.

35. Ibid.

36. In Punjab, the insurgency was primarily due to issues of Sikh identity: separate personal code, quotas in military, language, question of water rights and unemployment, and, eventually, a demand for autonomy. In Kashmir, there has been a tension regarding the conflict between the Indian and Pakistani governments on one hand and the aspirations of the people of the state on the other since 1947. The main way in which this conflict has played out is by the use of armed state actions and extraordinary laws. In the process, there has been unprecedented violence in the region and large-scale violation of human rights on the part of the state and the militants as well. *The Crackdown in Kashmir: Torture of Detainees and Assault on the Medical Community* (Boston: Physicians for Human Rights and Asia Watch, 1993); *The Human Rights Crisis in Kashmir: A Pattern of Impunity* (New York: Human Rights Watch, 1993). Jaskaran Kaur, "A Judicial Blackout: Judicial Impunity for Disappearances in Punjab," *Harvard Human Rights Journal* 15 (2002): 269-98. Issues of identity, autonomy, and independence have also been the main concerns for the movements in the North East.

37. Ibid.; Kannabiran, *The Wages of Impunity*; Kalhan et al., "Colonial Continuities."

38. The AFSPA allowed for the bypassing of usual safeguards in arrest, detention, and use of force, providing the right to use lethal force with little accountability. Under AFSPA, once a region is declared a disturbed area, mere warning could allow for the officers to shoot at persons if they do not follow the law prohibiting an assembly of five persons or if they possess firearms. See *Punjab in Crisis: Human Rights in India* (New York: Human Rights Watch, 1991); *Dead Silence: The Legacy of Abuses in Punjab* (New York: Human Rights Watch, 1994).

39. Initially, TADA was introduced for a particular region, but subsequently it became extended to the rest of India.

40. The provisions of TADA were criticized for violating not only national law but also international law, particularly the International Covenant on Civil and Political Rights (ICCPR), since under TADA (and the National Security Act), the protections against arbitrary arrest, detention, and torture were all being bypassed. The National Security Act allowed for detention without charge or trial for up to a year. While there was a review board to ensure that the act was not being misused, the protections were not very effective because of the delay that was allowed under the act and its amended version. See *Punjab in Crisis* and *Dead Silence*.

41. Singh, *The State, Democracy, and Anti-Terror Laws in India*, 67.

42. Ibid.

43. Some of the lawyers in the case were well-known civil rights activists and legal scholars of India, namely, V. M. Tarkunde, Ram Jethmalani, and Rajinder Sachar.

44. The act was introduced multiple times, each time with some changes. Under the Terrorist Affected Areas (Special Courts) Act, Act 61 of 1984, the purpose was to allow for speedy trials of certain offenses. The act allowed for the central government to declare any area a "terrorist-affected area" and set up special courts and judges with a right to appeal to the Supreme Court. This was allowed at the all-India level, with the exception of Jammu and Kashmir. Under the TADA (Prevention) Act, 1985, the act was applicable at the all-India level, including Jammu and Kashmir. This allowed for "[p]revention and coping with terrorist and disruptive activities," as well as "deterrent punishments and designated courts for speedy trials." The context was the terrorist acts in Punjab and Chandigarh but also extended to other parts such as Delhi, Rajasthan, Haryana, and Uttar Pradesh in two years. TADA (Prevention) Act, 1987, was a renewal, and since then TADA was renewed for eight years by extending it again and again until 1995. *Kartar Singh v. State of Punjab* (1994) 3 SCC 569.

45. The question of whether, in a federal system, the Parliament could pass a law on terrorism was posed by the counsels in the Kartar Singh case since the issue of terrorism was an issue concerning "public order" that should be considered under the state list, not the central list. In India, there are three lists distributing the responsibilities of the state and central government: state list, central list, and concurrent list. The Court agreed that terrorism actually affected the integrity and sovereignty of the country and extended beyond the territory of the individual state. Ibid.

46. Ibid., 619.

47. Ibid.

48. Ibid, 620.

49. See discussion in chapter 4 on the nature of the crisis in India in the 1960s.

50. K. Balagopal, "Law Commission's View of Terrorism," *Economic and Political Weekly* 35 (2000): 2114-22; Kannabiran, *The Wages of Impunity*; Haragopal and Balagopal, "Civil Liberties Movement and the State in India"; also see "TADA: Hard Law for Soft State," *Economic and Political Weekly* 35 (2000): 1066-71.

51. Balagopal, "Law Commission's View of Terrorism," 2115.

52. *India: "If They Are Dead, Tell Us"; "Disappearances" in Jammu and Kashmir*, Amnesty International, March 1999, 9. http://www.unhcr.org/refworld/docid/3ae6a9ee4.html (last visited January 11, 2011).

53. See chapter 4.

54. In Andhra Pradesh, for instance, "encounter" killings have been a major cause of concern for human rights groups such as APCLC and Human Rights Forum (HRF). Kannabiran points out that the basis of these encounters has been the operation of the Andhra Pradesh Suppression of Disturbances Act (1967), which was used to designate many of the tribal areas as "disturbed" and allowed the police to shoot at any party of five since a gathering of more than five persons was considered unlawful under the act. *Life, Liberty, and Livelihood: Civil Liberties in Andhra Pradesh*. Vol. 1, *Fact-Finding Committee Reports, 1978-84* (Andhra Pradesh Civil Liberties Committee, 1996); Kannabiran, *The Wages of Impunity*, 9. Amnesty International also points to the high number of disappearances in Kashmir and Punjab. In Kashmir, for instance, they quote certain sources as putting the number of disappearances at two thousand in the 1990s. *India: Torture, Rape, and Deaths in Custody*, Amnesty International. In Punjab, similarly, the number of

disappearances in the 1980s has been focused by human rights groups such as the Human Rights Wing of the Akali Dal and the National Human Rights Commission, which have instituted an inquiry into allegations of thousands of disappearances in recent years. Kaur notes that between 1984 and 1994, human rights groups found more than two thousand illegal cremations in just one district of Punjab. Kaur, "A Judicial Blackout," 272.

55. Singh, *The State, Democracy, and Anti-Terror Laws in India*, 52.

56. Balagopal, "In Defence of India," 2057.

57. Prakash and Vashum, eds., *Extraordinary Laws in India*, 172.

58. Ibid.

59. Rule 15 of TADA allowed the confession to be recorded in the language of the accused and played back to him, and if it is in writing, then it would be signed by the accused and also certified by the police, stating that he recorded it and it was a true account. A memorandum also had to be attached to the confession confirming that the warnings were accorded to the accused and the confession voluntarily made in his presence and recorded by him and confirmed by the accused. The confession in the case of Section 15 was then sent to the chief judicial magistrate or metropolitan magistrate, who sent it to the designated court. *Kartar Singh v. State of Punjab* (1994) 3 SCC 569, 665.

60. Ibid.

61. A very controversial issue in the TADA jurisprudence has been the dilution of safe-guards regarding the misuse of confessions against a co-accused. In Indian jurisprudence, following Anglo-American philosophy, the confession of a co-accused is considered weak evidence, requiring the confession to be taken into account only if all other evidence points toward the co-accused, and even the corroboration of confession of the accused has been suggested by previous courts. After TADA, the confession of a co-accused became a major point of debate and the Court suggested that the confession is evidence and some justices even went to the extent of stating that confession of a co-accused could be used as substantial evidence.

State v. Nalini, 1999. http://judis.nic.in/supremecourt/qrydisp.asp?tfnm=16831 (last visited August 5, 2005); *S. N. Dube v. N. B Bhoir* (2000) 2 SCC 254; *Lal Singh v. State of Gujarat* (2001) 3 SCC 221.

This affected the jurisprudential and statutory safeguards against relying too much on confessions.

62. The state counsel also suggested that whether the confessions would be taken into account by a court would depend on the facts and circumstances of the case. *Kartar Singh v. State of Punjab* (1994) 3 SCC 569.

63. See discussion on the hierarchies between the police in Upendra Baxi, *The Crisis of the Indian Legal System* (New Delhi: Vikas Publishing House, 1982), 88-91.

64. *Kartar Singh v. State of Punjab* (1994) 3 SCC 569.

65. Even while TADA was ostensibly selective, as PUDR documented, it took in its fold people from all walks of life: advocates, judges, students, writers, artists, legislators, strik-ing trade unionists, human rights activists, and even Bollywood actor Sunjay Dutt. *Black Laws and White Lies: A Report on TADA, 1985-1995* (Delhi: People's Union for Democratic Rights, May 1995).

66. Quoted in *Kartar Singh v. State of Punjab* (1994) 3 SCC 569.

67. Ibid.

68. Ibid., 680, emphasis added.

69. These guidelines included the production of the accused in front of a chief metropolitan or chief judicial magistrate, to whom the confession is already sent under TADA. The magistrate was to ask the accused to sign the statement, and if there was any complaint of torture, to ensure that the accused was examined by a medical officer. Also, the Court cautioned that if the person asserted the right to silence during interrogation, that should be respected. The Court also suggested that review committees consisting of government officials be constituted at the central and state levels to monitor the TADA cases. Ibid.

70. Ibid., 734.

71. K. Balagopal, "In Defence of India."

72. Ibid., 2057.

73. Kannabiran, *The Wages of Impunity*, 106.

74. *Gurdeep Singh v. State (Delhi Administration)* (1999). http://judis.nic.in/supremecourt/qrydisp.asp?tfnm=16663 (last visited June 23, 2005).

75. Ibid.

76. Kannabiran, *The Wages of Impunity*, 112.

77. *Wariyam Singh v. State of U.P.* (1995). In *Waryam Singh v. State of U.P.* (1995) the Supreme Court stated that sending the confessional statement of the accused to the chief judicial magistrate was not "mandatory but necessary," determining it to be a procedural irregularity, not a substantive one. *Wariyam Singh v. State of U.P.* (1995). http://judis.nic.in/supremecourt/qrydisp.asp?tfnm=10505 (last visited August 5, 2005).

78. The Court goes to the extent of saying that inducements should be given to the accused in the form of reduced punishment so that the accused agrees to confess due to his or her own desire to repent and speak the truth. *Gurdeep Singh v. State (Delhi Administration)* (1999). http://judis.nic.in/supremecourt/qrydisp.asp?tfnm=16663 (last visited June 23, 2005). Kannabiran writes that this leads to the idea of "effective state" and speedy trials based on confessions. Kannabiran, *The Wages of Impunity*, 111-13.

79. *Lal Singh v. State of Gujarat* (2001) 3 SCC 221.

80. *S. N. Dube v. N. B Bhoir* (2000) 2 SCC 254, 288.

81. Ibid.

82. In *Devendra Pal Singh v. State of NCT of Delhi* (2002) the Court is even willing to acknowledge that apart from the issue of procedural safeguards, the confessions should be believed because they emerge from the highest credible source, namely, the accused person's own "thirst to speak the truth." Singh, *The State, Democracy, and Anti-Terror Laws in India*, 128.

83. This was criticized for being a unilateral decision by the executive, namely, the Indian president. D. Nagasaila and V. Suresh, "Repromulgation of POTO: Is It Legal?" *Economic and Political Weekly* 37 (2002): 371-72.

84. This has been done only thrice in the last fifty years. Krishnan, "India's 'Patriot Act.'"

85. Michael Moore's film *Fahrenheit-9/11* portrays this really starkly in the case of the United States.

86. *People's Union for Civil Liberties and Another v. Union of India* (2004) 9 SCC 580.

87. Ibid.

88. Ibid., 594. The right of the Parliament to introduce this law has been a subject of debate in both the TADA and POTA constitutionality cases. In a federal system such as India's, the workings of the laws also raise questions about whether the extraordinary laws provide more powers to the central government or to the state government. Ujjwal Singh, for instance, writes that the review boards tend to become spaces of contention between the state and the center. The Supreme Court, for its part, tends to uphold the validity of the federal government in the review of POTA cases, pointing to a centralization of power in favor of the federal government. Ujjwal Kumar Singh, "POTA and Federalism," *Economic and Political Weekly* 39 (2004): 1793-97. Also see Ujjwal Kumar Singh, "POTA Review: What Will It Achieve?" *Economic and Political Weekly* 38 (2003): 5155-58.

89. *People's Union for Civil Liberties and Another v. Union of India* (2004) 9 SCC 580, 594.

90. Ibid. and Balagopal, "Law Commission's View of Terrorism."

91. As the Srikrishna Commission pointed out, the killing of Muslims was led by Shiv Sena (Hindu right-wing) leader Bal Thackarey. Praveen Swami, "A Welter of Evidence: How Thackeray & Co. Figure in the Srikrishna Commission Report," *Frontline* 17 (August 5, 2000). http://www.hinduonnet.com/fline/fl1716/17160110.htm.

92. Krishnan, "India's 'Patriot Act,'" 272.

93. See Gautam Navlakha, "POTA: Freedom to Terrorise," *Economic and Political Weekly* 38 (2003): 3038-40.

94. Singh, *The State, Democracy, and Anti-Terror Laws in India*, 63. Each time an attack occurs, a similar rhetoric against the Muslims appears. Consequently, there is also a fear among activists that the new laws will again target Muslims.

95. Singh notes that the focus on these sections reflects the state's perspective that they are not considered to be engaged in democratic activities and thereby should not be considered a part of the "political community." See discussion on 54-55. Singh, *The State, Democracy, and Anti-Terror Laws in India*.

96. *Sarfarosh* (1999), made in the wake of the Kargil conflict between India and Pakistan, was directed by John Matthew Matthan.

97. One of the positive developments of the case was that the Supreme Court agreed with the counsels that POTA did not allow for the confessions of an accused to be used against a co-accused. *People's Union for Civil Liberties and Another v. Union of India* (2004) 9 SCC 580.

98. A. G. Noorani, "Anti-Terrorism Legislation," *Economic and Political Weekly* 38 (2003): 41-42.

99. *People's Union for Civil Liberties and Another v. Union of India* (2004) 9 SCC 580.

100. JKLF, the Jammu Kashmir Liberation Front, is an organization that demands the liberation of Jammu and Kashmir from India and Pakistan. Three others were also charged in the case but were not a part of the trial: Jaish e Momammed, Chief Maulana Masoor Azhar, Ghazi Baba, and Tariq Ahmed.

101. They were charged under CrPc, POTA, and the Explosive Substance Act. The three were sentenced to death under POTA 3 (2) & 302 with 120 B (IPC). *State (N.C.T. of Delhi) v. Navjot Sandhu@ Afsan Guru* (2005). http://judis.nic.in/supremecourt/qrydisp.asp?tfnm=27092 (last visited August 5, 2005).

102. There was a Friends of S. A. R. Geelani Committee set up to point to ways in which an innocent person was falsely implicated in the case and to point to the draconian

aspects of extraordinary laws. See Nandita Haksar and Kumar Sanjay Singh, "December 13," *Seminar* 521 (2002): 120-27; *Trial of Errors: A Critique of the POTA Court Judgment on the 13 December Case* (Delhi: People's Union for Democratic Rights, 2003).

103. See *13 December: A Reader; The Strange Case of the Attack on the Indian Parliament* (New Delhi: Penguin Books, 2006).

104. Ibid.

105. Ibid.

106. *State (N.C.T. of Delhi) v. Navjot Sandhu@ Afsan Guru* (2005), emphasis added.

107. Ibid.

108. Ibid.

109. Ibid., emphasis added.

110. *Satpathy v. Dani* (1978) 2 SCC 424, 454, emphasis added.

111. For instance, judicial custody under Section 32 of POTA after the recording of confessions is not upheld as essential for admissibility of confessions by the Court. The Court writes that while that is an important requirement, at times it may not be possible and judicial remand can be avoided in exceptional instances if the police can convince the magistrate that it is absolutely necessary. *State (N.C.T. of Delhi) v. Navjot Sandhu@ Afsan Guru* (2005). http://judis.nic.in/supremecourt/qrydisp.asp?tfnm=27092 (last visited August 5, 2005).

112. Similarly, the Court concluded that violation of Section 52 of POTA could not be held as a determinant of inadmissibility of confessions. Ibid.

113. See discussion on the recording of confessions in Singh, *The State, Democracy, and Anti-Terror Laws in India*, 129-33.

114. Kannabiran quoted in ibid., 129-30.

115. Advani quoted in Krishnan, "India's 'Patriot Act,'" 271.

116. Karl Marx, "Investigations of Tortures in India," *New York Daily Tribune*, September 17, 1857.

117. Initially, the commission was set up to look into "use of Instruments of Torture by the Native Subordinate Servants of the State for the purpose of realizing the Government revenue." Later it was extended to inquire into cases where torture was being used for police purposes or in criminal cases. The commission received 519 complaints in person (some complainants traveling from three to four hundred miles away) and 1,440 complaints in the form of letters. *Report of the Commission for the Investigation of Alleged Cases of Torture at Madras* (Britain: House of the Commons, July 1855), 1.

118. The methods of torture used during that period included beating, flogging, *kittee*, *anundal*, or standing under the sun with stones on the back, hand, or head, sometimes bent double. Other forms included standing on one leg, or with turban or string tied from neck to knee or toes and insertion of pepper in the vagina of women. Ibid., 15. *Kittee* is a hand press or thumbscrew and *anundal* involves holding stones in different body positions.

119. Marx uses the term "Hindoo officials," suggesting that India was synonymous with "Hindoo," which is obviously not the case.

120. Indian Evidence Act (1872), Indian Penal Code (1860), Criminal Procedure Code (1898), and the Police Act (1861). See discussion of the police reforms and colonial bureaucracy in general in Anuj Bhuwania, "'Very Wicked Children': 'Indian Torture' and the Madras Torture Commission Report of 1855," *SUR International Journal on Human Rights* 10, no. 6 (2009).

121. The report states that though they were constituted to conduct an investigation into all complaints of torture, they considered their charge simply to be to verify the existence or nonexistence of torture, especially since they were not a "criminal tribunal" having powers to punish and redress. *Report of the Commission for the Investigation of Alleged Cases of Torture at Madras.*

122. *"Tehsildar"* refers to a revenue administrative officer.

123. Douglas M. Peers, "Torture, the Police, and the Colonial State in the Madras Presidency, 1816-55," *Criminal Justice History* 12 (1991): 29-56, 38-39.

124. Peers notes that there are more revenue-related tortures, but the Madras Report clarifies that the number of cases is smaller in police-related confessions because there is less reporting. Ibid.

125. Partha Chatterjee, *The Nation and Its Fragments*, in *The Partha Chatterjee Omnibus* (New Delhi: Oxford University Press, 1999), 18.

126. Anupama Rao, "Problems of Violence, States of Terror: Torture in Colonial India," *Economic and Political Weekly* 36 (2001): 4125-33.

127. *Report of the Commission for the Investigation of Alleged Cases of Torture at Madras,* 32.

128. Rao, "Problems of Violence, States of Terror," 4127.

129. There are moments when the report is willing to criticize the British government and the officials for not according adequate importance to the practice of torture in terms of punishment and deterrence. *Report of the Commission for the Investigation of Alleged Cases of Torture at Madras.*

130. Singha talks of this inability to uphold torture as well. Radhika Singha, *A Despotism of Law: Crime and Justice in Early Colonial India* (Delhi: Oxford University Press, 1998), 66-71.

131. Nasser Hussain, *The Jurisprudence of Emergency* (Ann Arbor: University of Michigan Press, 2003), 99-131.

132. The people were protesting against the repressive acts introduced by the British and on that day defied a specific law—the Rowlatt Act—that prohibited any assembly for political purposes. The location of the protest had no exits available. Ibid.

133. Ibid., 128-31.

134. Rao narrates the case of Gunu, who was accused of robbing and drowning his five-year-old niece, was tortured by police officials, and died in custody. There was a judicial inquiry that held the *foujdar* (police official) responsible for torture, but this was represented as an "extraordinary" event. Rao, "Problems of Violence, States of Terror."

135. The immediate response to the Madras Commission on Torture was connected to the Revolt in India in 1857, after which the colonial administration in India came entirely under the control of the British Crown, whereas it had previously been governed primarily by the East India Company.

136. The CRPC and IEA were introduced. Also, the collector-magistrate still had judicial and revenue duties, but the police was reconstituted to eventually form a new colonial police under the charge of Europeans. David Arnold, *Police Power and Colonial Rule, Madras, 1859-1947* (New York: Oxford University Press, 1986).

137. *National Police Commission Report, 1980*, in *Kartar Singh v. State of Punjab* (1994) 3 SCC 569, 678-79.

138. Baxi, *The Crisis of the Indian Legal System*, 135.

139. Kannabiran, *The Wages of Impunity*.

140. *State Gov't of NCT of Delhi v. Sunil and Anr* (2001) 1 SCC 651. http://www.judis.nic.in/supremecourt/helddis.aspx (last visited January 10, 2011).

141. Somini Sengupta, "Extreme Mumbai, without Bollywood's Filtered Lens," *New York Times*, November 11, 2008. http://www.nytimes.com/2008/11/16/movies/16seng.html?scp=4&sq=slum%20dog%20millionaire&st=cse. (last visited January 15, 2009)

142. Navlakha, "POTA: Freedom to Terrorise"; Noorani, "Anti-Terrorism Legislation"; *India: Torture, Rape, and Deaths in Custody*, Amnesty International; C. Raj Kumar, "Human Rights Implications of National Security Laws in India: Combating Terrorism While Preserving Civil Liberties," *Denver Journal of International Law and Policy* 33 (2005): 195-222. See also overview of human rights reports by well-known civil and democratic rights activists. Gobinda Mukhoty, "Torture, Human Rights, Legal Rights," *Economic and Political Weekly* 29 (1994): 1259-63; R. M. Pal, "Torture and Media Awareness," *Mainstream* 37 (1999): 18-19.

143. *D. K. Basu v. State of West Bengal*; *Ashok K. Johri v. State of Uttar Pradesh* (1996) http://judis.nic.in/supremecourt/qrydisp.asp?tfnm=14580 (last visited June 23, 2005).

144. See Balagopal, "Law Commission's View of Terrorism"; Kumar, "Human Rights Implications of National Security Laws in India"; editorial: "POTA: Well-Founded Fears," *Economic and Political Weekly* 38 (2003): 1337. See discussion on dealing with terrorism cases in the pre-9/11 United States in Michael P Scharf, "Defining Terrorism as the Peacetime Equivalent of War Crimes: A Case of Too Much Convergence between International Humanitarian Law and International Criminal Law," *ILSA Journal of International and Comparative Law* 7 (2001): 391-98.

145. The committee worked for about two years and brought out a report in 2003 suggesting changes for the Indian Penal Code, 1860, the Criminal Procedure Code, 1973, and the Indian Evidence Act, 1872. Upendra Baxi, "An Honest Citizen's Guide to Criminal Justice System Reform: A Critique of the Malimath Report," in *The (Malimath) Committee on Reforms of Criminal Justice System*, Amnesty International India, 5-41. http://www.interights.org/doc/AI%20India%20Malimath%20Report.pdf (last visited, March 3, 2006).

146. The debates on the benefits of the inquisitorial versus adversarial become important here. Ibid.

147. The committee recommended that the police powers over the accused should actually be increased by prolonging the time in police custody by thirty days, and the Court's ability to increase the time given to police to produce a charge sheet by ninety more days for certain offenses. Ibid.

148. Ibid.

149. Baxi, "An Honest Citizen's Guide to Criminal Justice System Reform," 5-41.

150. Ujjwal Kumar Singh, "State and Emerging Interlocking Legal Systems: Permanence of the Temporary," *Economic and Political Weekly* 39 (2004): 149-54, 149.

151. This is noted in the Malimath Report, which suggests the introduction of provisions of POTA into ordinary criminal law. Ibid.

152. Singh notes the ways in which the ordinary laws are applied to the TADA and POTA accused and the diluted provisions of the extraordinary laws are utilized to bypass safeguards and ensure enhanced penalties. For example, an accused could be charged with the Explosives Act, while being charged under TADA, which allows the police to use lower standards as evidence for higher penalties. Ibid., 151.

CONCLUSION

1. "Obama's Speech on Afghanistan," December 1, 2009. http://www.cbsnews. com/8301-503544_162-5855894-503544.html (last visited October 26, 2009).

2. Some cases filed against the U.S. government regarding the use of torture are *El-Masri v. Tenet*, 479 F.3d 296 (2007), on extraordinary rendition, and *Ali et al. v. Rumsfeld* (2006), on civil damages for torture.

3. "Italy Issues Fresh CIA Warrants," 25 July, 2005. http://news.bbc.co.uk/2/hi/europe/4716333.stm (last visited July 2, 2007).

4. Lok Sabha Debates on the Prevention of Torture Bill, May 6, 2010. http://www.scribd.com/doc/31599203/Torture-Prev-Bill-LS-Debates-06May2010 (last visited June 4, 2010). Shashi Tharoor is a member of the Indian Parliament.

5. Ibid., 18102-3, emphasis added.

6. Ibid.

7. Ibid., 18115.

8. Ibid., 18102.

9. "Obama's Speech on Afghanistan."

10. Rajeswari Sunder Rajan, *The Scandal of the State: Women, Law, and Citizenship in Postcolonial India* (Durham, NC: Duke University Press, 2003), xii.

11. Another methodological distinction I make is inspired by the work of Kaufman-Osborn, whose writings on the death penalty I read both as a "historically minded political theorist" (as he puts it) and also as an empirically informed political theorist. Kaufman-Osborn, *From Noose to Needle: Capital Punishment and the Late Liberal State* (Ann Arbor: University of Michigan Press, 2002), 3.

12. William Glaberson, "Post-Guantánamo: A New Detention Law?" November 14, 2008. http://www.nytimes.com/2008/11/15/washington/15gitmo.html (last visited December 14, 2008).

13. See chapter 3 for details.

14. Paul Kahn, "Approaches to the Cultural Study of Law: Freedom, Autonomy, and the Cultural Study of Law," *Yale Journal of Law and Humanities* 13 (2001): 141-71, 142.

15. Ibid., 154.

16. Theorists in the law and society or law in society tradition literature have pointed toward a notion of law as a social practice. "Legal discourses are viewed more fundamentally as constitutive of practical interactions among citizens." Michael W. McCann, *Rights at Work: Pay Equity Reform and the Politics of Legal Mobilization* (Chicago: University of Chicago Press, 1994), 6. See also Patricia Ewick and Susan S. Silbey, *The Common Place of Law* (Chicago: University of Chicago Press, 1998). Yet a focus on the official legal discourses continues to be important due to its hegemonic nature.

17. As noted earlier, Foucault's notion of governmentality reigns as the way in which political power is increasingly being understood. Here I draw upon a few influential Foucauldian scholars—Nikolas Rose, Peter Miller, and Mitchell Dean—to explicate this point. Nikolas Rose and Peter Miller, "Political Power beyond the State: Problematics of Government," *British Journal of Sociology* 43 (1992): 173-205. Mitchell Dean, *Governmentality: Power and Rule in Modern Society* (Los Angeles: Sage, 1999).

18. Foucault quoted in Kaufman-Osborn, *From Noose to Needle*, 48-49.

19. Rose and Miller, "Political Power beyond the State," 174.

20. Ibid., 176-77.

21. Kaufman-Osborn, *From Noose to Needle*, 6.

22. Ibid.

23. Ibid., 57-58.

24. Giorgio Agamben also refers to the lack of clarity in Foucault's work on "the point at which voluntary servitude of individuals comes into contact with objective power" and resolves this lack of clarity by designating the "biopolitical body" as the "original activity of sovereign power." *Homo Sacer: Sovereign Power and Bare Life*, translated by Daniel Heller-Roazen (Stanford: Stanford University Press, 1995), 6.

25. Mitchell Dean, *Governmentality: Power and Rule in Modern Society* (Los Angeles: Sage, 1999), 29.

26. Kaufman-Osborn, *From Noose to Needle*, 58.

27. Foucault quoted in Dean, *Governmentality*, 119.

Selected Bibliography

Ackerman, Bruce. *Before the Next Attack: Preserving Civil Liberties in an Age of Terrorism.* New Haven, CT: Yale University Press, 2006.

Agamben, Giorgio. *State of Exception.* Translated by Kevin Attell. Chicago: University of Chicago Press, 2005.

———. *Homo Sacer: Sovereign Power and Bare Life.* Translated by Daniel Heller-Roazen. Stanford, CA: Stanford University Press, 1995.

Agnes, Flavia. "Protecting Women against Violence: Review of a Decade of Legislation, 1980-89." *Economic and Political Weekly* 27 (1992): WS19-WS33.

Akhilesh, S. "Brief Study of Custodial Deaths." *CBI Bulletin* 9 (2001): 22-25.

Amann, Diane Marie. "Abu Ghraib." *University of Pennsylvania Law Review* 153 (2005): 2085-2141.

An-Naim, Abdullahi Ahmed. "Towards a Cross-Cultural Approach to Defining International Standards of Human Rights: The Meaning of Cruel, Inhuman, or Degrading Treatment or Punishment." In *Human Rights in Cross-Cultural Perspectives,* edited by Abdullahi Ahmed An-Naim, 19-43. Philadelphia: University of Pennsylvania Press, 1992.

Arnold, David. *Police Power and Colonial Rule, Madras, 1859-1947.* New York: Oxford University Press, 1986.

Arora, Nirman. "Custodial Torture in Police Stations in India: A Radical Assessment." *Journal of the Indian Law Institute* 41 (1999): 513-29.

Asad, Talal. "On Torture, or Cruel, Inhuman, and Degrading Treatment." In *Social Suffering,* edited by Veena Das, Margaret Lock, and Arthur Kleinman, 285-308. Berkeley: University of California Press, 1997.

Austin, John. *The Province of Jurisprudence Determined and the Uses of the Study of Jurisprudence.* New York: Noonday Press, 1954.

Avasthi, A. K. "Police Atrocities, Custodial Violence, Plight of Prisoners, and Human Rights." *Law Review* 21 and 22 (2001): 15-25.

Baker, Liva. *Miranda: Crime, Law, and Politics.* New York: Atheneum, 1985.

Balagopal, K. "Law Commission's View of Terrorism." *Economic and Political Weekly* 35 (2000): 2114-22.

———. "In Defence of India: Supreme Court and Terrorism." *Economic and Political Weekly* 29 (1994): 2054-60.

Bandes, Susan. "Patterns of Injustice: Police Brutality in the Courts." *Buffalo Law Review* 47 (1999): 1275-1341.

Bannerjee, Sumanta. "Torture in Custody: Method in Sadistic Madness." *Economic and Political Weekly* 36 (2001): 723-24.

Batria, Puran. "Treatment of Women at the Police Station." *Indian Police Journal* (July–September 1982): 41-44.

Baxi, Upendra. "The State and the Human Rights Movements in India." In *People's Rights: Social Movements and the State in the Third World*, edited by Manoranjan Mohanty, Partha Nath Mukherji, and Olle Tornquist, 335-52. New Delhi: Sage, 1998.

———. *The Crisis of the Indian Legal System*. New Delhi: Vikas Publishing House, 1982.

Beard, Jack. "Agora: Military Commissions Act of 2006; The Geneva Boomerang; The Military Commissions Act of 2006 and U.S. Counterterror Operations." *American Journal of International Law* 101 (2007): 56-73.

Beccaria, Cesare. *Of Crime and Punishment and Other Writings*, edited by Richard Bellamy. Cambridge: Cambridge University Press, 1995.

Benjamin, Suresh. "Prevent Torture by the Police and Investigation Agencies." *Criminal Law Journal* 107 (2001): 10-13.

Bhargava, G. S. "Torture as a Human Rights Issue." *Mainstream* 37 (1999): 31-32.

Bloche, M. Gregg, and Jonathan H. Marks. "Doctors and Interrogators at Guantanamo Bay." *New England Journal of Medicine* 353 (2005): 6-8.

Boulesbaa, Ahcene. *The UN Convention on Torture and the Prospects for Enforcement*. The Hague: Martinus Nijhoff, 1999.

Brooks, Peter. *Troubling Confessions: Speaking Guilt in Law and Literature*. Chicago: University of Chicago Press, 2000.

Brown, Michelle. "'Setting the Conditions' for Abu Ghraib: The Prison Nation Abroad." *American Quarterly* 57 (2005): 973-98.

Butler, Judith. *Precarious Life: The Powers of Mourning and Violence*. New York: Verso, 2004.

Caron, David D., and David L. Sloss. "International Decision: Availability of U.S. Courts to Detainees at Guantánamo Bay Naval Base; Reach of Habeas Corpus; Executive Power in War on Terror." *American Journal of International Law* 98 (2004): 788-98.

Chatterjee, Partha. *The Nation and Its Fragments*. In *The Partha Chatterjee Omnibus*. New Delhi: Oxford University Press, 1999.

Chemerinsky, Erwin. "Wartime Security and Constitutional Liberty: Detainees." *Albany Law Review* 68 (2005): 1119-26.

Cohen, Stanley. *States of Denial: Knowing about Atrocities and Suffering*. Cambridge, England: Polity Press, 2001.

Cole, David. "The Priority of Morality: The Emergency Constitution's Blind Spot." *Yale Law Journal* 13 (2004): 1753-1800.

Constable, Marianne. *Just Silences: The Limits and Possibilities of Modern Law*. Princeton, NJ: Princeton University Press, 2005.

Cover, Robert. "Violence and the Word." In *Narrative, Violence, and the Law: The Essays of Robert Cover*, edited by Austin Sarat, Michael Ryan, and Martha Minow, 203-38. Ann Arbor: University of Michigan Press, 1995.

Crocker, Thomas P. "Overcoming Necessity: Torture and the State of Constitutional Culture." *SMU Law Review* 61 (Spring 2008): 221-79.

Danner, Mark. *Torture and Truth: America, Abu Ghraib, and the War on Terror*. New York: New York Review of Books, 2004.

Darmer, M. K. B. "Beyond Bin Laden and Lindh: Confessions Law in an Age of Terrorism." *Cornell Journal of Law and Public Policy* 12 (2003): 319-72.

Das, Veena, Margaret Lock, and Arthur Kleiman, eds. *Social Suffering.* Berkeley: University of California Press, 1997.

Dayan, Joan. "Cruel and Unusual: The End of the Eighth Amendment." *Boston Review.* October/November, 2004. http://bostonreview.net/BR29.5/dayan.html (last visited March 31, 2006).

Dean, Mitchell. *Governmentality: Power and Rule in Modern Society.* Los Angeles: Sage, 1999.

Dershowitz, Alan. "Tortured Reasoning." In *Torture: A Collection*, edited by Sanford Levinson, 257-80. New York: Oxford University Press, 2004.

Dhavan, Rajeev. *The Supreme Court of India: A Socio-Legal Critique of Its Juristic Techniques.* Bombay: Tripathi, 1977.

Dikshit, R. C. "Police and Human Rights Issues." *CBI Bulletin,* December (1994), 3-8.

Dirks, Nicholas B. "The Policing of Tradition: Colonialism and Anthropology in Southern India." *Comparative Studies in Society and History* 39 (1997): 182-212.

Dorfman, Ariel. "The Tyranny of Terror: Is Torture Inevitable in Our Century and Beyond?" In *Torture: A Collection*, edited by Sanford Levinson, 3-18. New York: Oxford University Press, 2004.

Dubois, Page. *Torture and Truth.* New York: Routledge, 1991.

Duner, Bertil, ed. *An End to Torture: Strategies for Its Eradication.* London: Zed, 1998.

Dworkin, Ronald M. "The Model of Rules." *University of Chicago Law Review* 35 (1967): 14-46.

Eisenman, Stephen F. *Abu Ghraib Effect.* London: Reaktion Books, 2007.

Elshtain, Jean. "Reflection of the Problem of 'Dirty Hands.'" In *Torture: A Collection*, edited by Sanford Levinson, 77-92. New York: Oxford University Press, 2004.

Fisher, Louis. *Presidential War Power.* Kansas: University Press of Kansas, 2004.

Fitzpatrick, Peter. "Bare Sovereignty: *Homo Sacer* and the Insistence of Law." *Theory and Event* 5 (2001). http://muse.jhu.edu/journals/theory_&_event.

Forrest, Duncan, ed. *A Glimpse of Hell: Reports on Torture World Wide* (*Amnesty International*). New York: New York University Press, 1998.

Foucault, Michel. "Governmentality." In *The Foucault Effect: Studies in Governmentality*, edited by Graham Burchell, Colin Gordon, and Peter Miller, 87-104. Chicago: University of Chicago Press, 1991.

———. *Discipline and Punish: The Birth of the Prison.* Translated by Alan Sheridan. New York: Vintage Books, 1995.

Gagne, Chris. "POTA: Lessons Learned from India's Anti-Terror Act." *Boston Third World Law Journal* 25 (2005): 261-99.

Garland, David. "Governmentality and the Problem of Crime." In *Governable Places: Readings on Governmentality and Crime Control*, edited by Russell Smandych, 15-43. Aldershot, England: Ashgate/Dartmouth, 1999.

Gathii, James Thuo. "Torture, Extraterritoriality, Terrorism, and International Law." *Albany Law Review* 67 (2003): 335-70.

Glazier, David. "Full and Fair by What Measure: Identifying the International Law Regulating Military Commission Procedure." *Boston University International Law Journal* 24 (2006): 55-122.

Grano, Joseph D. *Confessions, Truth, and the Law.* Ann Arbor: University of Michigan Press, 1996.

Greenberg, Karen J., and Joshua L. Dratel, eds. *The Torture Papers: The Road to Abu Ghraib*. New York: Cambridge University Press, 2005.

Greer, Edward. "'We Don't Torture People in America': Coercive Interrogation in the Global Village." *New Political Science* 26 (2004): 371-87.

Gudavarthy, Ajay. "Human Rights Movement(s) in India: State, Civil Society, and Beyond." In *Human Rights and Peace: Ideas, Laws, Institutions, and Movements*, edited by Ujjwal Singh, 252-75. New Delhi: Sage, 2009.

Guha, Ranajit. "Dominance without Hegemony and Its Historiography." In *Subaltern Studies VI: Writings on South Asian History and Society*, edited by Ranajit Guha, 210-309. Delhi: Oxford University Press, 1989.

Gupta, Justice Gulab. "Custodial Violence and Human Rights Commissions." *Central India Law Quarterly* 12 (1999): 285-302.

Hajjar, Lisa "What's the Matter with Yoo? The Crime of Torture and the Role of Lawyers." Paper presented at the Law and Society Association Annual Meeting, Las Vegas, June 2005.

Haksar, Nandita, and Kumar Sanjay Singh. "December 13." *Seminar* 521 (2002): 120-27.

Haragopal, G., and K. Balagopal. "Civil Liberties Movement and the State in India." In *People's Rights: Social Movements and the State in the Third World*, edited by Manoranjan Mohanty, Partha Nath Mukherji, and Olle Tornquist, 353-71. New Delhi: Sage, 1998.

Hart, H. L. A. "A New Conception of Law." In *Philosophy of Law*, edited by Joel Feinberg and Hyman Gross, 54-68.California: Wadsworth, 1986.

Hobbes, Thomas. *Leviathan*, edited by Richard E. Flathman and David Johnston. New York: Norton, 1997.

Hunt, Lynn. *Inventing Human Rights: A History*. New York: Norton, 2007.

Hussain, Nasser. "Beyond Norm and Exception: Guantanamo." *Critical Inquiry* (Summer 2007): 734-53.

——. *The Jurisprudence of Emergency*. Ann Arbor: University of Michigan Press, 2003.

Hydervall, B. "Compensation to Victims of Lock-up Deaths: A Juridical Study." *Criminal Law Journal* (1994): 135-40.

Johns, Fleur. "Guantanamo Bay and the Annihilation of the Exception." *European Journal of International Law* 16 (2005): 613-35.

Kahn, Paul. *Sacred Violence: Torture, Terror, and Sovereignty*. Ann Arbor: University of Michigan Press, 2008.

Kalhan, Anil, Gerald P. Conroy, Mamta Kaushal, Sam Scott Miller, and Jed S. Rakoff. "Colonial Continuities: Human Rights, Terrorism, and Security Laws in India." *Columbia Journal of Asian Law* 20.1 (2006): 93-234.

Kamboj, N. S. "Police Custodial Death: A Growing Abuse to Human Rights in India." *Journal of the Indian Law Institute* 36 (1994): 372-77.

Kamisar, Yale. "William Pedric Lecture: Miranda Thirty-Five Years Later: A Close Look at the Majority and Dissenting Opinions in Dickerson." *Arizona State Law Journal* 33 (2001): 387-428.

——. "Equal Justice in the Gatehouse and Mansions of American Criminal Procedure: From Powell to Gideon, from Escobedo to . . ." In *The Miranda Debate: Law, Justice, and Policing*, edited by Richard A. Leo and George C. Thomas III, 15-34. Boston: Northeastern University Press, 1998.

Kannabiran, K. G. "Repealing POTA: Some Issues." *Economic and Political Weekly* 39 (2004): 3794-95.

———. *The Wages of Impunity: Power, Justice, and Human Rights*. New Delhi: Orient Longman, 2003.

Katju, Justice Markandey. "Torture as a Challenge to Civil Society and the Administration of Justice." *Supreme Court Cases Journal* 2 (2000): 39-43.

Katyal, Neal Kumar. "Hamdan v. Rumsfeld: The Legal Academy Goes to Practice." *Harvard Law Review* 120 (2006): 65-123.

Kaufman-Osborn, Timothy V. "Gender Trouble at Abu Ghraib?" *Politics and Gender* 1 (2005): 597-619.

———. *From Noose to Needle: Capital Punishment and the Late Liberal State*. Ann Arbor: University of Michigan Press, 2002.

Kaur, Balvinder. "Torture and Deaths in Police Custody: A Violation of Right to Life." *National Capital Law Journal* 2 (1997): 107-14.

Klarman, Michael J. "The Racial Origins of Modern Criminal Procedure." *Michigan Law Review* 99 (2000): 48-97.

Kreimer, Seth F. "'Torture Lite,' 'Full-Bodied' Torture, and the Insulation of Legal Conscience." *Journal of National Security Law & Policy* 1 (2005): 187-229.

Krishnan, Jayanth K. "India's 'Patriot Act': POTA and the Impact on Civil Liberties in the World's Largest Democracy." *Law and Inequality* 22 (2004): 265-300.

Kumar, Balvinder. "Protection against Torture by Police." *PRP Journal of Human Rights* 6 (2002): 12-17.

Langbein, John. *Torture and the Law of Proof: Europe and England in the Ancien Regime*. Chicago: University of Chicago Press, 1997.

Lederman, Marty. "Yes, It's a No-Brainer: Waterboarding *Is* Torture." October 28, 2006. http://balkin.blogspot.com/2006/10/yes-its-no-brainer-waterboarding-is.html (last visited April 21, 2007).

Leo, Richard A. *Police Interrogation and American Justice*. Cambridge, MA: Harvard University Press, 2008.

Leo, Richard A., and George C. Thomas III, eds. *The Miranda Debate: Law, Justice, and Policing*. Boston: Northeastern University Press, 1998.

Levinson, Sanford. "'In Quest of a Common Conscience': Reflections on the Current Debate about Torture." *Journal of National Security Law & Policy* 1 (2005): 231-52.

Lifton, Robert Jay. "Doctors and Torture." *New England Journal of Medicine* 351 (2004): 415-16.

Locke, John. *"The Second Treatise of Civil Government" and "A Letter concerning Toleration."* Oxford: Blackwell, 1966.

Lokaneeta, Jinee. "Revenge and the Spectacular Execution: The Timothy McVeigh Case." In *Studies in Law, Politics, and Society* 33, edited by Austin Sarat and Patricia Ewick, 201-21. Oxford: Elsevier, 2004.

Louis, Prakash, and R. Vashum, eds. *Extraordinary Laws in India: A Reader for Understanding Legislations Endangering Civil Liberties*. New Delhi: Indian Social Institute, 2002.

Luban, David. "Liberalism, Torture, and the Ticking Bomb." In *The Torture Debate in America*, edited by Karen J. Greenberg, 35-83. Cambridge: Cambridge University Press, 2005.

Mackey, Chris, and Greg Miller. *The Interrogators: Task Force 500 and America's Secret War against Al Qaeda*. New York: Little, Brown, 2004.

Margulies, Joseph. *Guantanamo and the Abuse of Presidential Power*. New York: Simon & Schuster, 2006.

Marx, Karl. "Investigations of Tortures in India." *New York Daily Tribune*, September 17, 1857.

Matheson, Duncan. "The Technique of the American Detective." *Annals of the American Academy of Political and Social Science* 146 (1929): 214-18.

Matheson, Michael. "Agora: Military Commissions Act of 2006; The Amendment of the War Crimes Act." *American Journal of International Law* 101 (2007): 48-55.

Mayer, Jane. "Whatever It Takes: The Politics of the Man behind '24.'" *New Yorker*, February 19, 2007.

McCoy, Alfred. *A Question of Torture: CIA Interrogation from the Cold War to the War on Terror*. New York: Metropolitan Books, 2006.

Menon, Nivedita, and Aditya Nigam. *Power and Contestation: India since 1989*. London: Zed, 2007.

Mohanty, Manoranjan, Partha Nath Mukherji, and Olle Tornquist, eds. *People's Rights: Social Movements and the State in the Third World*. New Delhi: Sage, 1998.

Mukherji, Nirmalangshu. "Teachers and War on Terrorism." *Economic and Political Weekly* 38 (2003): 4521-23.

Mukhoty, Gobinda. "Torture, Human Rights, Legal Rights." *Economic and Political Weekly* 29 (1994): 1259-63.

Nagan, Winston P., and Lucie Atkins. "The International Law of Torture: From Universal Prescription to Effective Application and Enforcement." *Harvard Environmental Law Review* 14 (2001): 87-121.

Nagasaila, D., and V. Suresh. "Re-promulgation of POTO: Is It Legal?" *Economic and Political Weekly* 37 (2002): 371-72.

Navlakha, Gautam. "POTA: Freedom to Terrorise." *Economic and Political Weekly* 38 (2003): 3038-40.

Nonet, Phillipe, and Philip Selznick. *Law and Society in Transition: Towards Responsive Law*. New York: Harper and Row, 1978.

Noorani, A. G. "The Security State." *Economic & Political Weekly* 44 (2009): 13-15.

Pal, R. M. "Torture and Media Awareness." *Mainstream* 37 (1999): 18-19.

Pannu, Gurpreet K. "Police and Custodial Violence." *Journal of Legal Studies* 33 (2003): 40-44.

Parry, John T. *Understanding Torture: Law, Violence, and Political Identity*. Ann Arbor: University of Michigan Press, 2010.

———. "'Just for Fun': Understanding Torture and Understanding Abu Ghraib." *Journal of National Security Law and Policy* 1 (2005): 253-84.

Patel, Thrity D. "Torture: Human Rights and Accountability of Law Enforcement Agencies." *Central India Law Quarterly* 12 (1999): 539-72.

Peers, Douglas M. "Torture, the Police, and the Colonial State in the Madras Presidency, 1816-55." *Criminal Justice History* 12 (1991): 29-56.

Peters, Edward. *Torture*. Philadelphia: University of Pennsylvania Press, 1996.

Posner, Eric A., and Adrian Vermeule. *Terror in the Balance: Security, Liberty, and the Courts*. New York: Oxford University Press, 2007.

Posner, Richard A. *Not a Suicide Pact: The Constitution in a Time of National Emergency.* Oxford: Oxford University Press, 2006.

Prasad M., Deva. "Law and Torture: Legal Implications from Indian Perspective." http://papers.ssrn.com/sol3/papers.cfm?abstract_id=999862 (last visited October 2008).

Raina, Subash C. "Custodial Torture in Police Stations: Causes and Areas of Improvement." *National Capital Law Journal* 5 (2000): 1-20.

Ramanathan, Usha. "Tort Law." *Annual Survey of Indian Law* 36 (2001): 615-58.

Rao, Anupama. "Problems of Violence, States of Terror: Torture in Colonial India." *Economic and Political Weekly* 36 (2001): 4125-33.

Rao, S. Venugopal. "The Anatomy of Police Violence." In *Police and Emerging Challenges,* edited by S. K. Chaturvedi, 97-101. Delhi: B.R. Publishing, 1988.

Ratner, Michael, and Ellen Ray. *Guantánamo: What the World Should Know.* White River Junction, VT: Chelsea Green, 2004.

Ravindran, K. "Custodial Violence and Measures to Curb." *PRP Journal of Human Rights* (January–March 2002): 7-8.

Reid, J. E., and Fred Inbau. *Criminal Interrogations and Confessions.* Baltimore, MD: Williams and Wilkins, 1986.

Rejali, Darius. *Torture and Democracy.* Princeton, NJ: Princeton University Press, 2007.

———. *Torture and Modernity: Self, Society, and State in Modern Iran.* Boulder, CO: Westview Press, 1994.

Rodley, Nigel S. *The Treatment of Prisoners under International Law.* New York: Clarendon, 1999.

Rose, Nikolas, and Peter Miller. "Political Power beyond the State: Problematics of Government." *British Journal of Sociology* 43 (1992): 173-205.

Ruthven, Malise. *Torture: The Grand Conspiracy.* London: Weidenfeld and Nicholson, 1978.

Saini, R. S. "Custodial Torture in Law and Practice with Reference to India." *Journal of the Indian Law Institute* 36 (1994): 166-92.

Sarat, Austin. *When the State Kills: Capital Punishment and the American Condition.* Princeton, NJ: Princeton University Press, 2001.

Sarat, Austin, and Thomas R. Kearns. "A Journey through Forgetting: Towards a Jurisprudence of Violence." In *The Fate of Law,* edited by Austin Sarat and Thomas Kearns, 209-73. Ann Arbor: University of Michigan Press, 1991.

Sathe, S. P. *Judicial Activism in India: Transgressing Borders and Enforcing Limits.* New Delhi: Oxford University Press, 2002.

Scarry, Elaine. *Body in Pain: The Making and Unmaking of the World.* New York: Oxford University Press, 1985.

Scheppele, Kim Lane. "Hypothetical Torture in the War on Terrorism." *Journal of National Security Law & Policy* 1 (2005): 285 – 340.

Schmitt, Carl. *Political Theology: Four Chapters on the Concept of Sovereignty.* Translated by George Schwab. Cambridge: MIT Press, 1985.

Scott, George Ryley. *The History of Torture throughout the Ages.* London: Kegan Paul, 2003.

Sebastian, P. A. "The State and the Police." *Economic and Political Weekly* 23 (1988): 2210-11.

Sen, Kaustav. "Custodial Torture: A Preventive Framework." *Central India Law Quarterly* 12 (1999): 334-43.

Sen, Sankar, P. S. V. Prasad, and A. K. Saksena. *Custodial Deaths in India: A Research Study.* Hyderabad: S.V.P. National Police Academy, 1994.

Shapiro, Martin. *Courts: A Comparative and Political Analysis.* Chicago: University of Chicago Press, 1986.

Shapiro, Steven R. "Defending Civil Liberties in the War on Terror: The Role of the Courts in the War against Terrorism; A Preliminary Assessment." *Fletcher Forum of World Affairs Journal* 29 (2005): 103-16.

Sharma, Sudesh Kumar. "Human Rights, Police, and Custodial Violence: A Perspective." *M.D.U. Law Journal* 5 (2000): 40-44.

Shoemaker, Karl. "The Problem of Pain in Punishment: Historical Perspectives." In *Death, Pain, and the Law,* edited by Austin Sarat, 15-42. Ann Arbor: University of Michigan Press, 2001.

Shue, Henry. "Torture in Dreamland: Disposing of the Ticking Bomb." *Journal of International Law, Case Western Reserve* 37 (2006).

———. "Torture." In *Torture: A Collection,* edited by Sanford Levinson, 47-60. New York: Oxford University Press, 2004.

Shukla, Rakesh. "Police Torture: Prevention Is Better Than Compensation." *Lawyers Collective* 8 (1993): 9-12.

Silverman, Lisa. *Tortured Subjects: Pain, Truth, and the Body in Early Modern France.* Chicago: University of Chicago Press, 2001.

Simon, Jonathan. "The Vicissitudes of Law's Violence." In *Law, Violence, and the Possibility of Justice,* edited by Austin Sarat, 17-48. Princeton, NJ: Princeton University Press, 2001.

Singh, Joginder. "Third Degree Violates Human Rights." *Civil and Military Law Journal* 39 (2003): 143-45.

Singh, Ujjwal Kumar. *The State, Democracy, and Anti-Terror Laws in India.* New Delhi: Sage, 2007.

Singha, Radhika. *A Despotism of Law: Crime and Justice in Early Colonial India.* Delhi: Oxford University Press, 1998.

Sinha, Archana. "Torture Is a Challenge to the Administration of Justice." *PRP Journal of Human Rights* 5 (2001): 34-43.

Skolnick, Jerome H. "American Interrogation: From Torture to Trickery." In *Torture: A Collection,* edited by Sanford Levinson, 105-27. New York: Oxford University Press, 2004.

Sreeramulu, N. "Lockup Deaths and Harassment by Police." *Criminal Law Journal* 106 (2000): 149-50.

Stenson, Kevin. "Crime Control, Governmentality, and Sovereignty." In *Governable Places: Readings on Governmentality and Crime Control,* edited by Russell Smandych, 45-73. Aldershot, England: Ashgate/Dartmouth, 1999.

Subramanian, S. "Human Rights and Internal Security Operations." *CBI Bulletin* December (1994): 1-2.

Sunder Rajan, Rajeswari. *The Scandal of the State: Women, Law, and Citizenship in Postcolonial India.* Durham, NC: Duke University Press, 2003.

Sunstein, Cass R. "Recent Decisions of the United States Court of Appeals for the District Court: National Security, Liberty, and the D.C. Circuit." *George Washington Law Review* 73 (2005): 693-709.

Taussig, Michael T. *Defacement: Public Secrecy and the Labor of the Negative.* Stanford: Stanford University Press, 1999.

Thomas III, George C. "The End of the Road for *Miranda v. Arizona*? On the History and Future of Rules for Police Interrogation." *American Criminal Law Review* 37 (2000): 1-39.

Tiwari, Arvind. "Custodial Torture in Indian Prisons: Overview." *CBI Bulletin* 8 (2000): 9-18.

Tushnet, Mark. "Emergencies and the Idea of Constitutionalism." In *The Constitution in Wartime: Beyond Alarmism and Complacency*, edited by Mark Tushnet, 39-54. Durham, NC: Duke University Press, 2005.

Twining, W. L., and P. E. Twining. "Bentham on Torture." *Northern Ireland Legal Quarterly* 24 (1973): 305-56.

Upadhyay, M. L. "Torture in Police Custody and Handcuffing of the Accused." *Central India Law Quarterly* 9 (1996): 458-64.

Verma, R. S., and I. B. S. Thokchom. "Law Related to Human Rights and Custodial Death." *PRP Journal of Human Rights* 4 (2000): 20-24.

Waldron, Jeremy. "Torture and Positive Law: Jurisprudence for the White House." *Columbia Law Review* 105 (2005): 1681-1750.

Walker, Samuel. *The Police in America: An Introduction*. Boston: McGraw Hill College, 1999.

Walzer, Michael. "Political Action: The Problem of Dirty Hands," in *Torture: A Collection*, edited by Sanford Levinson, 61-76 (New York: Oxford University Press, 2004).

Weber, Max. "The Economic System and the Normative Orders." In *Law in Economy and Society*, edited with introduction and annotations by Max Rheinstein, 11-40. Cambridge, MA: Harvard University Press, 1966.

White, Welsh S. *Miranda's Waning Protections: Police Interrogation Practices after Dickerson.* Ann Arbor: University of Michigan Press, 2003.

Žižek, Slavoj. *Welcome to the Desert of the Real*. London: Verso, 2002.

Index

Abu Ghraib prison, 3, 68, 71, 91, 194. *See also* Bybee/Yoo memo

ACHR. *See* Asian Center for Human Rights

Ackerman, Bruce, 22–23, 87

ACLU, 94

Advani, L. K., 188

African Americans, 37

Afzal, Mohammad, 185, 188

Agamben, Giorgio, 25–27, 69–70

Alias (U.S. television show), 115

Alter, Jonathan, 34

Ambedkar, B. R., 149

American Psychological Association (APA), 105

Amnesty International, 28–29, 150–51, 173

Anarchy, law and, 11

Andhra Pradesh Civil Liberties Committee (APCLC), 149–50

APA. *See* American Psychological Association

APCLC. *See* Andhra Pradesh Civil Liberties Committee

APDR. *See* Association of Protection of Democratic Rights

Archetypes, 12

Arora, Nirman, 133, 134

Asad, Talal, 3, 16

Ashcraft v. Tennessee (1944), 38, 51

Asian Center for Human Rights (ACHR), 137, 158–59; on custodial deaths, 130–31

Association of Protection of Democratic Rights (APDR), 149

Association of the Bar of the City of New York, 90–91

AUMF. *See* Authorization of Military Force

Austin, John, 2, 10–11

Authorization of Military Force (AUMF) (2001), 75

Autonomous law, repressive law and responsive law compared to, 12

Balagopal, K., 150, 173, 178, 183

Baxi, Upendra, 13–16, 19, 135, 151, 170, 193, 197

Beccaria, Cesare, 6, 7

Behavioral science consultant teams (BSCTs), 103–4

Bharatiya Janata Party (BJP), 166

BILS. *See* British Indian legal system

BJP. *See* Bharatiya Janata Party

Black, Cofer, 68

Bollywood films, 184

Boumediene v. Bush (2008), 86, 95, 97

Bowden, Mark, 101

Bram model, 35–36

Bram v. United States (1897), 35–36

British colonialism: confession recording and, 192–93; extraordinary law and, 168–69; Jallianwalla Bagh massacre and, 191–92; native police and, 191–92; police brutality and, 133–35, 189–93; police role and, 189–95; rule of colonial difference and, 191

British Indian legal system (BILS), 14–15

British Report on Torture, 167. *See also* Madras Commission Report

Brooks, Peter, 30, 56–57, 139

Brown model, 35, 37

Brown v. Mississippi (1936), 34, 37, 47–48

BSCTs. *See* Behavioral science consultant teams

Bush, George W., 25, 44, 68, 97, 199–200

Butler, Judith, 25, 70

FBI, 8, 17–18, 66–67, 116, 118–20
Federal Torture Statute (1994), 106, 126;
Bybee/Yoo memo and, 73–76; torture
definition and, 81–82
Fifth Amendment, 35, 38–39, 138; in *Chavez
v. Martinez*, 64–65; coercive interroga-
tions and, 36, 139–40; confessions and,
36, 56; in *New York v. Quarles*, 61–62
Finnegan, Patrick, 111
Fitzpatrick, Peter, 27
"Forgetting of violence," 11, 78
Foucault, Michel, 2–3, 9–10, 26, 104, 207;
on eighteenth-century torture, 112–13;
on excess violence, 100–101; on govern-
mentality, 99–100; on political power,
205–6; Weber compared to, 205–6
Fourteenth Amendment (due process
clause), 35, 36–39, 62; in *Chavez v. Martinez*, 64–65
Fourth Amendment, 62
"Frequent Flyer" program, 118–19
Futility, 119–20

Gandhi, Indira, 149, 171–72
Gandhi, Mahatma, 130
Gandhi, Rajiv, 3
Garland, David, 16–17, 100
Gathhii, James Thuo, 88
Geelani, S. A. R., 27, 185–86
Gender-based coercion, 119–20, 125
Geneva Conventions, 75, 84; Common
Article 3 of, 93–94, 96, 126; MCA and,
97; Supreme Court on, 92–93
Ginsburg, Justice, 66
Giuliani, Rudy, 122
Gonzales, Alberto R., 108
Gonzales, Judge, 25, 81
Gordon, Colin, 100
Government: consent for, 4; OGA, 18; state
power and art of, 69
Governmentality: excess violence and,
99–107, 206–8; Foucault on, 99–100; law
related to violence and, 204–8; power
and, 99–100, 204–8
Grano, Joseph, 51, 54
Greer, Edward, 8

Gregg v. Georgia (1976), 39
Griffith, Judge, 47–48
Guantánamo Bay, 2, 72, 84, 104; Church Com-
mittee Report on, 116–18, 121; exceptional
acts and, 25–27, 68–70; hyperlegality and,
70; Obama on, 199; Schmidt Report on, 116,
118–20, 125. *See also* Bybee/Yoo memo
Gudavarthy, Ajay, 150
Guha, Ranajit, 134
*Gurdeep Singh v. State (Delhi Administra-
tion)* (1999), 179–80
Guru, Afsan, 185
Guru, Shaukat Hussain, 185, 188

Habeas corpus, 95–96, 97
Hamdan, Salim, 86, 92–94
Hamdi, Yasser, 87
Haque, Nurul, 157–58
Haragopal, G., 150
Harlan, Justice, 52–53
Hart, H. L. A., 2, 10, 78
Haynes v. Washington (1963), 60
Hobbes, Thomas, 2, 10–11
Human rights, 6, 16; ACHR for, 130–31,
137, 158–59; exceptional acts and, 26–27;
literal denial and, 42; NHRC for, 130,
158, 163; POTA and, 185–86; training in,
police brutality and, 136
Human Rights First, 108–9, 115, 119
Hunt, Lynn, 6
Hussain, Nasser, 70, 191–92
Hydervall, B., 134
Hyperlegality: Bybee/Yoo memo as, 74–78;
suspension of law compared to, 70–71

IACP. *See* International Association of
Chiefs of Police
ICCPR. *See* International Covenant on
Civil and Political Rights
IEA. *See* Indian Evidence Act
Ignatieff, Michael, 4, 5
ILS. *See* Indian legal system
Impermissibility, 8, 199
Implicatory denial, 42
India, 148; civil liberties and democratic
rights groups in, 149–50; denial in,

131–32, 144, 154; emergency in, 149–50; U.S. compared to, 14, 16–17, 31, 202–3

Indian Constitution, 172–73, 181–83; Article 14 in, 175–77; Article 20(3) in, 132, 138, 177; Article 21 in, 131–32, 140, 148, 151–54, 175–78; detention from, 169

Indian Evidence Act (IEA), 132, 159, 176, 197

Indian jurisprudence: Article 20(3) in, 132, 138, 177; Article 21 in, 131–32, 140, 148, 151–54, 175–78; Miranda decision and, 138–40, 202–3; Parliament related to, 174, 176–78; police brutality compared to, 137; on POTA, 170–71, 182–89; statutory safeguard interpretation by, 141–43; structural bias in, 145–46; structural class bias in, 146–47; on TADA, 170–82; torture's description in, 154. *See also* Custody jurisprudence; Extraordinary law; *specific cases*

Indian legal system (ILS): BILS compared to, 14–15; U.S. legal system compared to, 14–16, 202–3

Indian Penal Code (IPC), 132

Indian Supreme Court, 8. *See also specific cases*; *specific laws*

International Association of Chiefs of Police (IACP), 43

International Covenant on Civil and Political Rights (ICCPR), 172

Interpretive denial, 42; legalism in, 43–44

Interrogation, 3, 89–90, 122; gender in, 119–20, 125; religion in, 125–26. *See also* Coercive interrogations

Invention of Human Rights (Hunt), 6

IPC. *See* Indian Penal Code

Iraq, 3, 72

Islam, 125–26, 183–84, 196

Iyer, Justice, 15

Jacoby, Lowell E., declaration, 89–90

Jallianwalla Bagh massacre, 191–92

Jethmalani, Ram, 175

Johns, Fleur, 26, 70

Judiciary: custodial violence responsibility of, 156; third degree and, 42, 46, 48; totality of circumstances test for, 51–52; violence and, 13. *See also specific judges*

Juridico-medical complex, 101–6

"Juristic dependencia," 15

Just Assassins (Camus), 21

Kahn, Paul, 72, 204

Kalhan, Anil, 168

Kamisar, Yale, 51, 54–55

Kannabiran, K. G., 11, 169, 178–80, 188, 193

Kaplan, Amy, 25

Kartar Singh v. State of Punjab, 172, 177–78, 180–82; POTA and, 186–87; TADA and, 174–75

Katju, Justice, 164

Katyal, Neal, 92–93, 98

Kaufman-Osborn, Timothy, 2, 13, 28, 207; on juridico-medical complex, 104–5; on lethal injection, 114–15; on Weber and Foucault, 205–6; on words and deeds, 79

Kearns, Thomas, 11, 28, 29, 78

Kennedy, Justice, 65

Khaitan, Tarunabh, 163

Klarman, Michael, 37

Klein, Naomi, 101

Krishnan, Jayanth, 183

Lal, Surat, 155

Lal Singh v. State of Gujarat (2001), 180–82

Langbein, John, 7

Law: autonomous, 12; community recognition for, 10–11; consent for, 10–11; definition of, 10; fear as basis for, 11; hyperlegality compared to, 70–71; interpretation of, 11; medicine and, 101–6; politics, courts and, 203–4; repressive, 12; responsive, 12; sovereign's command as, 10; violence in relation to, 9–12, 78–80. *See also* Extraordinary law

Law's relationship to violence, 203; context and, 16; denial of, 11–12; Eighth Amendment and, 39–40; excess in, 28, 32–33, 53; governmentality and, 204–8; legitimacy of, 13, 52–53, 79–80; nonstate actors compared to, 13–14, 79; persistence of, 29–30, 32; specific communities compared to, 27–28; tension in, 69, 80–82, 93, 129; in torture debate, 27–30; UN on, 29

Lederman, Marty, 97
Legal Aid Services, 153–54
Legal coercion: constraints against, 5; from state, 4–5
Legal interpretation, physical violence compared to, 13
Legalism, in interpretive denial, 43–44
Legal system: BILS, 14–15; context and, 16; Indian, 14–16, 202–3; U.S., 14–16, 202–3
Legitimacy: for court, 46–48; of law related to violence, 13, 52–53, 79–80
Leo, Richard, 44, 45, 55, 57
Leon v. Wainwright, 62–63
Lethal injection, 40, 79, 104–5, 114–15
Levin memo, 72, 78, 81–83, 127
Liberal democracies: features of, 4; historical development of, 5–6; politics of denial in, 40–46; torture's absence for, 2–4, 34; torture's decline in, 4–5; torture's persistence and, 29–30, 34, 206–8; torture theory in, 30–33
Liberty, security compared to, 23–24
Lindh, John Walker, 86
Locke, John, 4
Luban, David, 77
Lukes, Steven, 4, 19

M., Deva Prasad, 137
Macdonald, Heather, 113, 122
Mackey, Chris, 122
Madras Commission Report (1855), 134; on confession recording, 190, 192–94; consequences of, 192–93; native police in, 189–92; revenue collection in, 190–91
Maiku v. State of U.P. (1989), 145
Malimath Committee, 197
Manchester Manual, 117
Manual for Court Martial, 117–18
Margulies, Joseph, 26, 77
Marshall, Justice, 61–62
Matheson, Michael, 97
Mathews test, 87
Mayer, Jane, 104, 111, 115
MC. *See* Military commissions
MCA. *See* Military Commission Act of 2006

McCoy, Alfred, 101, 102, 123
Media debates, 71; in Indian context, 1, 132–33, 194–95, 200–201; popular imagery in, 1, 17–18, 108–12, 120–21, 184, 194–95
Medical professionals, 6, 103–6
Mental torture, 83–85, 102
Military Commission Act of 2006 (MCA), 3; CIDT and, 96–97; Geneva Conventions and, 97; president's power and, 95
Military commissions (MC), 91–92; Supreme Court against, 94–95
Miller, Geoffrey, 103
Miller, Peter, 205
Miranda decision, 15, 51; confessions and, 54; exceptions to, 54; Indian jurisprudence and, 138–40, 202–3; POTA related to, 187; psychological coercion and, 49–50; support for, 54–55; violence and, 49–53
Miranda model, 35, 38–39
Miranda v. Arizona (1966), 38–39
Miranda warnings, 58–61, 67
Morality: PENS and, 105; pragmatics compared to, 7. *See also* Human rights
Mukasey, Michael, 124
Muslims, 196; POTA and, 183–84; TADA and, 183

Nandini Satpathy v. P. L. Dani, 15, 138–40, 187–89
National Commission on Law Observance and Enforcement, 41
National Democratic Alliance (NDA), 166
National Human Rights Commission (NHRC), 130, 158, 163
National Police Commission, 176
Navlakha, Gautam, 183
Naxalites, 149–51, 184, 196
NDA. *See* National Democratic Alliance
Necessity: for coercive interrogations, 64–67; Miranda warnings compared to, 60–61; physical violence related to, 62–63; in 24, 109–11, 115; of violence, 59–67
New York v. Quarles, 60, 65; Fifth Amendment in, 61–62; public safety exception in, 110–11

NHRC. *See* National Human Rights Commission
Nilabati Behera v. State of Orissa (1993), 152–53, 157
9/11, 18, 202; for exceptional acts, 25, 69–70; extraordinary law and, 167–68, 197; torture debate after, 34. *See also* Guantánamo Bay
Non-citizens, citizens compared to, 85–86
Nonet, Phillippe, 12
Noorani, A. G., 150, 185
Not a Suicide Pact: The Constitution in a Time of National Emergency (Posner, R.), 23–24

Obama, Barack, 2, 199, 201
Odah v. U.S. (2003), 91
Office of Medical Services, 106
Official reports: in India, 130, 134, 154, 159, 167, 176, 189–94, 197; popular imagery in, 117–20; in U.S., 3, 40–46, 105–6, 116–23, 125
OGA. *See* Other Government Agencies
Other Government Agencies (OGA), 18

Padilla, José, 86–89
Pain, 6–7, 9; lethal injection and, 114–15; in punishment, 39–40; self-inflicted, 102, 123; severity of, 76, 77, 80–83; subjective nature of, 117
Parliament, 200; attacks on, POTA and, 166, 185–86; Indian jurisprudence related to, 174, 176–78
Parry, John T., 30, 31–32, 64, 125
PATRIOT Act, U.S., 166, 169; POTA compared to, 182
Peers, Douglas, 190
PENS. *See* Psychological Ethics and National Security
People's Union for Civil Liberties and Another v. Union of India (2004), 182–83
People's Union for Civil Rights (PUCL), 150–51
People's Union for Democratic Rights (PUDR), 147–48, 151, 155–56, 158, 196
Peters, Edward, 7

Physical torture, 82–83; torture conflated with, 40
Physical violence: legal interpretation compared to, 13; necessity related to, 62–63; in *24*, 113–15, 129
PIL. *See* Public interest litigation
Police, 176; on coercion, 44; IACP and, 43; linguistics of, 44; native, British colonial power compared to, 191–92; rank of, in recording confessions, 174, 175, 177; for revenue collection, 190–91; role of, British colonialism and, 189–95; status of, 1–2, 194–95; third degree from, 42
Police brutality, 152, 154, 156–58; British colonialism and, 133–35, 189–93; class distinction in, 175; human rights training and, 136; implicit sanction of, 177–78; Indian jurisprudence compared to, 137; institutional reasons for, 135–37; methods in, 155; reforms for, 136. *See also* Confessions; Custodial deaths
Political power, 205–6
Politics: courts, law and, 203–4; of denial, 40–46; terrorism compared to, 173–74, 184
Popular culture: gender-based coercion in, 120; public opinion and, 71, 121; senior officials' image in, 1–2; third degree and, 43. See also *24*
Popular imagery: in media, 1, 17–18, 108–12, 120–21, 194–95; in official reports, 117–20; of torture, 108–12
Posner, Eric, 23
Posner, Richard, 23–24
POTA. *See* Prevention of Terrorism Act
Power, 69; in governmentality, 99–100, 204–8; political, 205–6; state, 99–101, 204–8; from torture compared to discipline, 9. *See also* President's power
Prakash Singh v. Union of India, 136
President: Congress compared to, 22, 75; Supreme Court against, 86, 92–93, 97–98
President's power: Bybee/Yoo memo for, 74; MCA and, 95; from U.S. Constitution, 74–75; war and, 74–75, 90–91
President's Rule (India), 172

Selznick, Philip, 12
Sengupta, Somini, 1
SERE. *See* Survival, Evasion, Resistance, Escape
Serious abuse, 117–18. *See also* Cruel, inhuman, and degrading treatment; Custodial deaths
Shahzad, Faisal, 60, 66–67, 111
Shakila Abdul Gafar Khan v. Vasant Rughunath Dhoble and Anr. (2003), 159–60
Shankaria v. State of Rajasthan (1978), 142–43
Shapiro, Martin, 46–47
Shivappa v. State of Karnataka (1995), 143
Shoemaker, Karl, 6
Shue, Henry, 19–21
Shukla, Rakesh, 147–48
Shultz, David, 74
Siege (film), 120
Sikhs, 171, 196
Silverman, Lisa, 6, 7
Simon, Jonathan, 27
Singh, Ujjwal, 27, 30, 184, 197, 198
Sixty Minutes, 71
Skolnick, Jerome, 65, 66
Sleep deprivation, 121–23; compared to frequent flyer program, sleep adjustment, 118–19
Slumdog Millionaire, 1, 194–95, 200–201
Snow, Tony, 124
Social action litigation (SAL), 151–52
Sovereign: in exceptional acts, 25–26; in law, 10. *See also* President
Special Rapporteur on Torture, 29
State: legal coercion and, 4–5; power, 99–101, 204–8; reassurance by, 22
States of Denial (Cohen), 42
State (N.C.T. of Delhi) v. Navjot Sandhu (2005), 185–86
Stenson, Kevin, 101
Stevens, Justice, 65, 88–89
Stewart, Justice, 39
Sube Singh v. State of Haryana and Others (2006), 161–62
Sunder Rajan, Rajeswari, 201
Sunstein, Cass, 87, 98–99

Supreme Court (U.S.), 87, 114–15; against military commissions, 94–95; against president, 86, 92–93, 97–98; silence of, 48, 58–59, 69, 85–86, 88, 90, 92–94, 96, 99; totality of circumstances test for, 51–52. *See also specific cases; specific justices*
Surnow, Joel, 109–10
Survival, Evasion, Resistance, Escape (SERE), 104–5, 126; CIDT and, 127–28
Sutherland, Kiefer (Jack Bauer), 17–18, 109, 111–12

TADA. *See* Terrorism and Disruptive Activities (Prevention) Act
Tancredo, Tom, 111, 112
Taussig, Michael, 45–46
Terrorism: definition of, 171; detention and, 22; global, 167–70; local, 167–70; in Mumbai (1993), 183; politics compared to, 173–74, 184. *See also* Prevention of Terrorism Act
Terrorism and Disruptive Activities (Prevention) Act (TADA), 33, 167, 197–98; confession recording and, 171, 174–77, 186–89; confessions and, 174–81, 186; constitutionality of, 172–73, 181; convictions from, 170–71; detention under, 170–71; against distinct groups, 175–76; exceptionality of, 171–74; extension of, 170–71; Indian jurisprudence on, 170–82; *Kartar Singh v. State of Punjab* and, 174–75; lapse of, 172, 181–82; Muslims and, 183; Operation Blue Star and, 171–72; POTA compared to, 185, 186–88; Punjab and, 171–72; safeguards and, 189; "weird jurisprudence of dead act" and, 179
Tharoor, Shashi, 200–201
Third degree, 41, 45; judiciary and, 42, 46, 48; "original meaning" of, 44; from police, 42; popular culture and, 43; torture linguistically compared to, 44
Thomas, George C., III, 55
Thomas, Justice, 64, 87
Ticking bomb scenario, 20–21, 61–62; on *24*, 109–11

Torture: chronology of "progress" against, 35–40; "clean," 102–3; coercive interrogations as, 139–40; compared to discipline, 9; decline of, 4–5, 7, 8; definitions of, 30–31, 75–76, 81–85, 112–15, 117–18, 124, 154, 163; detention compared to, 22–23, 180–81; in eighteenth century, 112–13; "fairy tale" of abolition of, 7; futility and, 119–20; imagery of, 112–14; impermissibility of, 8, 199; institutionalization of, 20–21; liberal ideology of, 77; limitations of the debate on, 7; mental, 83–85, 102; "original meaning" of, 44; physical torture conflated with, 40; popular imagery of, 108–12; psychological, 102, 123, 164; public opinion on, 71, 121; as public spectacle, 9; the room as, 128; routinization of, 123–24; safeguard dilution against, 174–81; sanitization of, 118–20; "specific intent" compared to "general intent" in, 76; theory, 30–33; third degree linguistically compared to, 44; war compared to, 19–20; warrants for, 20; waterboarding, 2, 97, 110, 112, 123–24, 126–28. *See also specific types of torture*
Torture and Democracy (Rejali), 29
Torture Bill (India), 163–64
Torture debate: exceptional act in, 25–27; law related to violence in, 27–30; after 9/11, 34; "should we?" in, 17–25; struggle over, 35
Torture memos, 69, 71; Levin memo, 72, 78, 81–83, 127. *See also* Bybee/Yoo memo
Torture Victim Protection Act, 83
Totality of circumstances test, 63; extraordinary law and, 188; for Supreme Court, 51–52
Troubling Confessions (Brooks), 56
24 (U.S. television show), 17–18, 32, 120–21; Justice Scalia and, 110; necessity in, 109–11, 115; physical violence in, 113–15, 129; ticking bomb scenario on, 109–10; torture definitions on, 112–15, 124

UAPA. *See* Unlawful Activities Prevention Act

UCMJ. *See* Uniform Code of Military Justice
UN. *See* United Nations
UN Convention against Torture and Other Cruel, Inhuman, or Degrading Treatment or Punishment, 30–31, 82; India and, 131
Uniform Code of Military Justice (UCMJ), 92
United Nations (UN), 29–31, 82, 131; extraordinary law and, 168; Resolution 1373, 167–68
United Progressive Alliance (UPA), 166
United States (U.S.): denial in, 3, 72; ILS compared to legal system of, 14–16, 202–3; India compared to, 14, 16–17, 31, 202–3; official reports in, 3, 40–46, 105–6, 116–23, 125; PATRIOT Act, 166, 169, 182. *See also* Constitution, U.S.; Supreme Court, U.S.; *specific legislation*
Universal Declaration of Human Rights, 16
Unlawful Activities Prevention Act (UAPA), 166, 169
UPA. *See* United Progressive Alliance
U.S. *See* United States
U.S. Report on Torture (1999), 3

Vajpayi, Ananya, 27
Vermeule, Adrian, 23
Violence: excess, 28, 32–33, 53, 99–107, 129, 206–8; Jallianwalla Bagh massacre and, 191–92; law compared to, 9–12, 78–80; Miranda decision and, 49–53; necessity of, 59–67; physical, 13, 62–63, 113–15, 129. *See also* Custodial violence; Law's relationship to violence
Voltaire, 6

Waldron, Jeremy, 5, 12, 28, 32, 77
Walker, Samuel, 45–46
Walzer, Michael, 21
War: Cold War, 101; president's power and, 74–75, 90–91; torture compared to, 19–20
War Crimes Act (1996), 93
Warrants, 20

About the Author

JINEE LOKANEETA is an assistant professor of political science at Drew University. She completed her Ph.D. at the University of Southern California–Los Angeles in 2006. Prior to attending USC, she taught political science at Kirori Mal College, Delhi University, India.

www.ingramcontent.com/pod-product-compliance
Lightning Source LLC
Chambersburg PA
CBHW060028030426
42334CB00019B/2229